SOCIAL WELFARE

in Canadian Society

SECOND EDITION

SOCIAL WELFARE

in Canadian Society

ROSALIE CHAPPELL, B.S.W, M.S.W.

Australia • Canada • Mexico • Singapore • Spain • United Kingdom • United States

Social Welfare in Canadian Society, Second Edition

by Rosalie Chappell

Editorial Director and Publisher:
Evelyn Veitch

Executive Editor:
Joanna Cotton

Marketing Manager:
Don Thompson

Developmental Editor:
Toni Chahley

Production Editor:
Bob Kohlmeier

Production Coordinator:
Hedy Sellers

Copy Editor:
Sarah Robertson

Proofreader:
Matthew Kudelka

Art Director:
Angela Cluer

Interior Design:
Joanne Slouenwhite

Cover Design:
Ken Phipps

Cover Image:
Detail from *40 Molière E.*, a collograph by Jacinthe Tétrault

Compositor:
Erich Falkenberg

Printer:
Webcom

Printed and bound in Canada
1 2 3 4 04 03 02 01

For more information contact Nelson Thomson Learning, 1120 Birchmount Road, Scarborough, Ontario, M1K 5G4. Or you can visit our internet site at http://www.nelson.com

Canadian Cataloguing in Publication Data

Chappell, Rosalie, 1955–
Social welfare in Canadian society

2nd ed.
Includes bibliographical references and index.
ISBN 0-17-616833-8

1. Social science – Canada.
2. Public Welfare – Canada.
I. Title.

HV105.C48 2001 361.971
C00-932140-3

This book is dedicated to

the memory of Agnes Wallin,
my brother, Bob Chappell, for his strength and courage, and
my husband, Paul Wallin, for always being there

CONTENTS

ABOUT THE AUTHOR

Rosalie Chappell has practised as a clinical social worker in a wide range of organizations. She has 17 years' experience in the field and has worked as an instructor and practicum supervisor in social service departments in British Columbia and Alberta colleges. As a front-line worker she has had experience in family counselling offices, probation offices, correctional institutions, outpatient alcohol- and drug-counselling agencies, and employment assistance services. She is currently self-employed and specializes in program evaluation and technical writing for the social services.

PREFACE

Canada's social welfare system has undergone tremendous change since the publication of the first edition of this text. Much of that change took place in response to major shifts that occurred in economic, political, and social systems. In many ways, social welfare has arrived at a crossroads where the traditional ways of responding to human need are being challenged by continually shrinking resources and a demand to do more with less. Moreover, social welfare programs are expected to be more accountable and to demonstrate that they are making a positive difference in people's lives. These challenges are not confined to any particular sector: government and nongovernment organizations alike are grappling with many of the same issues and pressures.

Change and challenge are not foreign to social welfare. Most people working in the social welfare system would agree that the only constant in this system *is* change; and it is change that challenges us to find more innovative and effective ways of helping people. This second edition of *Social Welfare in Canadian Society* highlights some of the recent changes in the social welfare system and the ways in which the system is adapting to a new order.

Text Objectives

The objectives of this new edition of the book are similar to those of the first edition:

- to strike a balance between historical and current content
- to explore a wide range of social welfare policies and programs in both the public and private sectors
- to provide real-life examples of social welfare programs from across the country
- to discuss the varied roles of workers in social welfare organizations and programs
- to give examples of how social welfare programs and policies affect a variety of populations in Canada
- to include Canadian content whenever possible and draw from the wisdom of Canadian scholars and researchers
- to present material in a neutral manner, allowing readers to form their own opinions and conclusions

Writing the second edition was every bit as challenging as writing the first. As soon as I completed one section of the manuscript, another section had to be updated. Social welfare would never stand still, I realized, so I had to accept the dynamic nature of the system and choose an arbitrary point at which to stop writing. Given that the social welfare system continues to evolve, this book is intended as a starting point for learning about some of the basic concepts and developments in the field of social welfare. From here readers are encouraged to continue their own journey of discovery of Canada's social welfare system.

A number of excellent sources are available to help readers augment their learnings from *Social Welfare in Canadian Society*. The References section at the end of the book contains a comprehensive list of titles from Canadian literature, the Internet, and other sources that can supplement material in the text. Other good sources for up-to-date information on local and national developments in social welfare are Canadian newspapers, newsmagazines, and radio and television news programs. Another excellent source of information about social welfare is people who work in social welfare agencies. The Instructor's Manual that accompanies this edition suggests innovative ways to tap into local resources and include them in the learning process. For the most current information on social policies, legislation, and programs in Canada, readers are encouraged to visit government and media Web sites; follow site links to the "What's new" or "News releases" pages. Nelson Thomson Learning is pleased to present the *Social Welfare in Canadian Society* Web site. Visit www.SocialWelfare-2nded.nelson.com for links to the most current information on issues related to social welfare, including government links, links to newspapers, and links to the Web sites listed in this book.

Organization

This edition retains the basic three-part structure of the first edition. **Part I** introduces readers to some of the fundamental aspects of Canada's social welfare system, including its aim and philosophical base, historical developments, interdependence with other major systems, and current challenges in a conservative political and economic climate.

Part II is devoted to social welfare's service delivery system. Here readers learn about the various service sectors and the main activities of social agencies. This section also looks at the range of service providers found in social welfare settings and the approaches they use to help people and their environments change.

Part III examines a wide range of social problems and the ways in which Canada addresses these problems through social welfare programs and services. Beginning with a focus on poverty and unemployment, this section goes on to explore some of the issues and programs specific to Canadian families, seniors, Aboriginal people, immigrants and refugees, and people with disabilities.

New to This Edition

To reflect the changes taking place in Canada's social welfare system, certain structural adjustments have been made for this edition and new content has been added. For example, the section on the philosophical foundations of social welfare has been moved into **Chapter 1** to fill out the discussion of the nature of social welfare. This and subsequent chapters place more emphasis on the contributions of various disciplines, such as law enforcement, to the achievement of social goals.

Chapter 2 takes the reader from the colonial era to the end of social welfare's expansion era and recounts many of the historical developments during that period.

Chapter 3, in its discussion of social policy, updates the impact of a new economy, sociodemographic trends, political values, and other factors on Canada's social welfare system.

Readers will find a greater emphasis placed on social welfare in an era of fiscal restraint. A new chapter—**Chapter 4**—looks at some of the ways that social welfare has adjusted to public funding cuts since the mid-1970s. New material is included on intergovernmental relations and the devolution of government responsibilities to other levels of administration.

The chapter on the public, commercial, and voluntary service sectors now appears as the first chapter in **Part II**. This chapter includes new information on the shrinking role of the public sector in the provision of direct services. In turn, the section on the voluntary sector has been rewritten to reflect the challenges facing this sector as a result of government's changing role. Readers will also find that the section on overlapping service sectors has been replaced by a new section, "Sector Collaboration: The Key to Service Delivery in the 21st Century."

Social agencies are the subject of **Chapter 6**. New to this chapter is material about on-line support services and a discussion of direct services in terms of primary, secondary, and tertiary prevention. The section on indirect services has been updated to reflect the trend toward program evaluation and an emphasis on outcomes in social welfare programs. This chapter includes new material on learning organizations and the role of structural social work practice in intraorganizational change.

Chapter 7, in its discussion of service providers, has been updated to include the legislative changes that distinguish social work from social service work. In addition, this chapter has new content on volunteering in Canada.

Chapter 8 has been reorganized for this edition—it contains material merged from various first-edition chapters—and now focuses on the strategies used by social welfare personnel to promote change at the micro and macro levels.

A notable addition to the second edition is **Chapter 9**, which focuses on unemployment, poverty, and the related problems of hunger and homelessness. This chapter takes a careful look at the reforms to employment insurance, social assistance, and other social welfare programs and the way those reforms affect Canada's ability to meet basic human needs.

Chapter 10 looks at the broadening definition of family and includes new information on same-sex legislation and its implications for social welfare benefits. The discussion on family violence has been expanded to include more information about the effects of and responses to spousal and child abuse. To reflect government's identification of children and youth as a national priority, a new section focuses on issues and programs of importance to young Canadians.

Chapter 11 opens with a look at current issues related to an aging population and recent developments under the National Framework on Aging. A new section on aging and health explores the various aspects of healthy aging and related programs. Readers will find that the section on caring for seniors has been expanded to reflect the growing trend toward informal caregiving.

Several revisions have been made to **Chapter 12**, which focuses on Aboriginal Canadians and the social welfare system. New material is included on topics such as Aboriginal–government relations, self-government, healing and wellness in Aboriginal communities, and Aboriginal children and youth.

Readers will also find that **Chapter 13**, on social welfare in a multicultural society, has been revised. These revisions are in response to Canada's new immigration and refugee policies. Information from recent Canadian studies on the immigrant experience has been integrated into this chapter.

Chapter 14, on social welfare and people with disabilities, includes a more comprehensive look at the evolution of disability-related policies and programs, including current government initiatives. New content is found also in the section on voluntary organizations that serve people with disabilities.

The appendixes include three new documents. In response to reviewers' requests, one appendix features a chronology of key events in social welfare and related systems over a 100-year period. This chronology not only notes events that are referred to in the main text but places these events in historical context. The appendixes related to Canada's new social union and Aboriginal action plan provide useful background information for many policies and programs mentioned in the book.

Special Features

This edition retains several special features that were well received in the first edition and aim to enhance the reader's comprehension and enjoyment of the book. These are:

- a list of objectives at the beginning of each chapter to guide the reader through the content
- a variety of charts, tables, graphs, cartoons, and other exhibits to give a visual reference to points made in the text
- definitions of terms in the main text or in text boxes
- profiles and examples of Canadian programs, services, and initiatives
- a section at the end of certain chapters to provide a conceptual link between social welfare and social work practice
- a list of key terms at the end of each chapter to reinforce learning
- a detailed index to help the reader find information quickly and easily

Instructor's Resources

The Instructor's Manual has been updated to help instructors teach their courses more effectively. This manual includes the following components:

- chapter objectives to give context and purpose to each manual section
- ideas for in-class activities to facilitate student learning, to stimulate critical thinking and analysis of the text material, and to help students apply social welfare theory
- suggestions for student assignments to increase students' awareness of social welfare issues, improve research skills, and enhance written and verbal communication
- recommended readings, which can be used as (a) supplementary readings for the course, (b) sources of information for lecture preparation, and (c) resources for student assignments
- a list of Canadian organizations and their contact numbers (including on-line addresses) to facilitate further research on social welfare topics
- a test bank—which includes true-or-false, multiple-choice, and short-answer questions—to assist students and instructors at course review and examination time

I hope this text meets the learning needs of students and is found to be a user-friendly supplement to course assignments and in-class activities. Feedback on this edition of *Social Welfare in Canadian Society* is welcomed; the form on the last page of the book can be used for this purpose.

Rosalie Chappell

ACKNOWLEDGMENTS

Many thanks are due to all the individuals and organizations that supported me in the writing of this book. Special thanks to

- Paul Wallin, my editor-in-residence and research assistant, for his thorough work and creative suggestions;
- my students at University-College of the Fraser Valley, Red Deer College, Malaspina-University College, and Open Learning Agency, who inspired me to write this book;
- the Powell River Public Library staff, who went beyond the call of duty to help me write this book from the "boonies";
- Kelly Creek Community School for introducing me to the world via the Internet;
- the team at Nelson Thomson Learning, and especially my developmental editor, Toni Chahley, who saw me through an intense six months of research and writing;
- those who reviewed the first edition and provided me with invaluable feedback and direction for the second edition: Brian Dwyer, Sheridan College; Luke Fusco, Wilfrid Laurier University; and Paul MacIsaac, Georgian College.
- the many agencies, organizations, and government departments that responded to my requests for information, with particular thanks to Chilliwack Community Services, Prince Edward Island Health and Social Services, the Canadian Association of Social Workers, the Canadian Association of Schools of Social Work, Finance Canada, the Institute for Policy Analysis, Childhood and Youth Division (Health Canada), Status of Women Canada, Citizenship and Immigration Canada, Veterans Affairs Canada, the Caledon Institute of Social Policy, the Council of Canadians, National Council of Welfare, Human Resources Development Canada, and the C.D. Howe Institute.

PART I

SOCIAL WELFARE IN CANADA

An Overview

CHAPTER 1

THE NATURE OF CANADIAN SOCIAL WELFARE

• OBJECTIVES •

I. To explore the concept of "social welfare" and understand its primary functions in Canada.

II. To describe the service delivery function of social welfare, together with its range of income-security programs and personal social services, and to consider different views of and approaches to service delivery.

III. To discuss the interdisciplinary nature of social welfare in terms of service providers, a knowledge base, and the connections between social welfare and other social programs.

IV. To examine some of the political and religious philosophies that influence the focus and activities of Canadian social welfare.

INTRODUCTION

The social welfare system has been a part of Canadian life for only the past 100 years. Nineteenth-century Canadians obtained basic necessities primarily through self-employment (mostly farming), borrowing among neighbours, and trading. Anything resembling a "social problem" was seen as a personal responsibility to be addressed by the individual with assistance from family, friends, neighbours, and other traditional supports. Until the late 1800s, such means of support seemed adequate.

The Industrial Revolution changed people's lives by importing a large segment of the labour force from rural areas and farm-based self-employment into urban centres and a money-based economy. With this change, family roles also shifted. Men took on the responsibility of primary wage earner while women and children became "dependents." If the head of the household became ill, was injured at work, lost his job, or died, the resulting lack of income jeopardized the entire family's financial security. It became clear that the informal helping systems, as well as local charities and churches, were ill-equipped to meet the needs of a modern industrial society. Despite this realization, Canadians were slow in supporting the development of a more formal approach to addressing social and economic problems (Bellemare, 1993).

It took the widespread economic and social disruption of the Great Depression in the 1930s to convince Canadians of the need for government intervention during hard economic times. As Bellemare (1993, 63) notes:

> The Great Depression was an awakening for Canadians—and a rude one at that: the salary system fostered massive problems of economic insecurity and poverty. Unemployment reached proportions never before seen ... Canadians started to gain some clear insight into the magnitude of the problems created by employment shortages. We recognized that unemployment could be involuntary and, more and more, we saw that the unemployed were not responsible for their economic situation ... [C]ollective rather than individual solutions [were] ... immediately required.

The hardships experienced during the Great Depression spurred the general public to demand that government provide a minimum of assistance with respect to income, nutrition, health, housing, and education. Thus, the **social welfare system** developed as a formal mechanism to protect citizens against the economic and social hazards of modern society (Mishra, 1981; Friedlander and Apte, 1980).

Although Canada's social welfare system continues to evolve with respect to its role and function in society, the programs and services it supports, and the influences that shape it, the main features of the system have remained consistent over time; this chapter looks at some of those features.

I. SOCIAL WELFARE: BASIC COMPONENTS

WHAT IS SOCIAL WELFARE?

Although there is no single, exhaustive, or universally agreed upon definition of social welfare, it may be understood in general terms as a system of interconnected and overlapping legislation, policies, procedures, and activities designed to

1) help individuals and groups meet their basic social and economic needs; and
2) prevent and reduce social problems.

To meet these objectives, social welfare activities often focus on preserving the social order. This can involve protecting the most vulnerable members of society (such as children and elderly persons) and controlling, monitoring, or restraining individuals who are assessed to be a danger to themselves or others.

Those responsible for social welfare—such as elected politicians, social policymakers, and program developers—must decide

- *why* new programs and services should be developed and why existing ones should be changed or eliminated (i.e., to better respond to human needs or problems);
- *what* types of programs and services will be implemented (e.g., income-security programs or personal social services);
- *how* social welfare will be governed (e.g., through laws, legislation, and policies) and funded (e.g., through tax revenue);
- *who* will receive the benefits from the available programs and services (e.g., children, seniors, or people with disabilities);
- *when* people will be assisted by social welfare resources (e.g., during periods of unemployment or the retirement years); and
- *where* resources will be located and accessed (e.g., in public or private agencies).

These aspects of social welfare will be explored throughout the book.

It is important to distinguish between social welfare and related concepts and processes. The term *social welfare* is often used interchangeably with other terms such as social security, social services, social policy, social work, and the welfare state. Although these concepts are closely linked, there are differences between them (see Exhibit 1.1).

THE PRIMARY FUNCTIONS OF SOCIAL WELFARE

Meeting Human Needs

A main focus of social welfare activities is to identify and respond to basic human needs. The Social Planning Council of Winnipeg (1987, 1) defines **human need** as "environmental conditions or behaviours which are at odds with what we want them to be. They are statements of human problems, of gaps or discrepancies between what is and what should be." Most of our human needs are met within family, religious, educational, political, economic,

Exhibit 1.1

DEFINITION OF TERMS

Social Security

In Canada, the term *social security* refers to government programs and services that aim to assist people who are limited in their ability to earn income as a result of old age, disability, unemployment, sickness, or other contingencies. Examples include the Old Age Security pension, universal health care, and Employment Insurance.

Social Services

Also known as personal or community social services, *social services* are nonincome programs provided by government or charitable organizations. The primary aim of these services is to enhance social functioning, foster self-sufficiency, and promote health and well-being.

Social Program

Social program is a generic term that usually refers to programs that are developed, implemented, and administered in the areas of social welfare, health care, or postsecondary education.

Social Policy

A *social policy* is a plan or blueprint that guides a government's strategies for helping citizens to meet a wide range of material and social needs.

Social Work

Social work is a profession committed to "helping individuals, families, groups and communities to enhance their individual and collective well-being ... [and to] develop their skills and their ability to use their own resources and those of the community to resolve problems" (CASW, 1997, 1).

Welfare State

The term *welfare state* refers to a country that is committed to correcting the problem of unequal distribution of wealth in a capitalist economy. In addition to implementing social security programs, countries that qualify as welfare states use their powers of taxation to redistribute income from the rich to the poor.

Source: Author.

and other systems. When these systems fail to meet the basic needs of individuals and groups, social welfare programs are often called upon to intervene. The diversity of human beings is such that it is impossible to list all possible needs that arise for people over a lifetime. Social welfare is primarily concerned with those needs related to personal income and employment, human development, interpersonal relationships, community organization, and personal well-being (Zastrow, 1996).

Abraham Maslow's *hierarchy of needs* is one of the most common models used to describe the range of human needs. According to Maslow, a person must meet basic physical or survival needs (e.g., food, water, and air) before trying to meet "higher order" needs related to social interaction, self-esteem, and self-actualization. Exhibit 1.2 illustrates the different levels of human needs as identified by Maslow: basic needs are found at the bottom of the pyramid, with higher-order needs listed successively up the hierarchy.

New human needs are constantly emerging and demanding attention from social welfare resources. For example, it was during the 1980s that most North Americans learned about HIV/AIDS and became aware of the "new" biopsychosocial needs of people who contracted this disease. Since that time, a variety of social welfare programs and services have emerged to support people with HIV/AIDS and their families.

Society's recognition of persistent or emerging needs puts social policymakers in the position of determining which needs should be addressed by social welfare resources and which should be left to the resources of individuals, families, and other informal helping networks. These decisions are mainly influenced by predominant cultural beliefs and attitudes, economic pressures and resources, the political mood of the country, and the agendas of various individuals and groups. Social values play a particularly important role in recognizing unmet human needs and in determining the level of personal and social functioning in society (Johnson, Schwartz, and Tate, 1997; Compton, 1980).

Addressing Social Problems

People are subject to a number of social conditions that strain their ability to meet personal needs. These conditions include social isolation, poverty, racism, unemployment, and crime. Nonetheless, social *conditions* are not synonymous with social *problems*. While a social condition needs only to be objectively measured, a **social problem** must be both objectively measured and subjectively defined as a "problem." In most cases, social problems are social conditions that contradict generally accepted norms or values and create economic or social hardship. Social problems are also conditions that tend to spark some kind of response aimed at correcting the situation (Barker, 1991; Rubington and Weinberg, 1989).

EXHIBIT 1.2

MASLOW'S HIERARCHY OF NEEDS

Source: Adapted from A. Haber and R.P. Runyon, *Fundamentals of Psychology* (McGraw-Hill, 1983), 304. Copyright © 1983. Reproduced with permission of The McGraw-Hill Companies.

The definition of social problems tends to change over time. What is currently perceived as a social problem may have been virtually ignored in the past. A case in point is a statement made by Sainsbury in 1977 (11–12): "Take ... the situation of women who are severely ill-treated by their husbands; this would not at the present time fulfil the conditions of a social problem, and would be approached by the social worker using the criterion of need rather than problem as justification for his intervention." Although this may have been a typical response to spousal abuse in 1977, attitudes toward domestic violence have changed dramatically since that time, as evidenced by the increased number of women's shelters and legislation aimed at preventing and treating family violence. Thus, social welfare policies, programs, and activities tend to reflect what society defines as social problems at any given time.

The social welfare system is primarily concerned with the definition, prevention, and alleviation of social problems that affect both the individual and general society (Sainsbury, 1977). For example, the costs of child abuse are immeasurable for children in terms of human suffering and diminished personal and social functioning. Child abuse is also destructive to society: "It robs all of us of the health, productivity, and contribution of many of its future citizens" (Institute for the Prevention of Child Abuse, 1994, 6). Exhibit 1.3 illustrates the range of monetary costs incurred by violence against women and children. When responding to social problems, those who control social welfare resources must determine whether the focus of intervention should be directed to the individual, to the larger community, or to both.

Unfortunately, the resources needed to address all social problems seem never to be in adequate supply. Social welfare agencies must therefore restrict the scope of social problems to which they will respond. Traditionally, social welfare programs and services have tended to be reserved for the following circumstances:

1) when people are prevented from carrying out important social roles (such as parent or wage earner);
2) when people are unable to obtain sufficient resources for survival and development;
3) when a person's behaviour interferes with the safety or development of others or contradicts social norms;
4) when a significant segment of the population recognizes the situation as a public concern; and/or
5) when a considerable portion of society makes a commitment to address the concerns (Dobelstein, 1978).

Exhibit 1.4 lists the top five social concerns reported by Canadians over a 20-year period. Historically, Canadians have tended to identify the economy as a primary concern. The extent to which the economy and other social concerns are addressed by the system depends largely on the priorities set by Canadians.

EXHIBIT 1.3

EVERYONE PAYS FOR FAMILY VIOLENCE

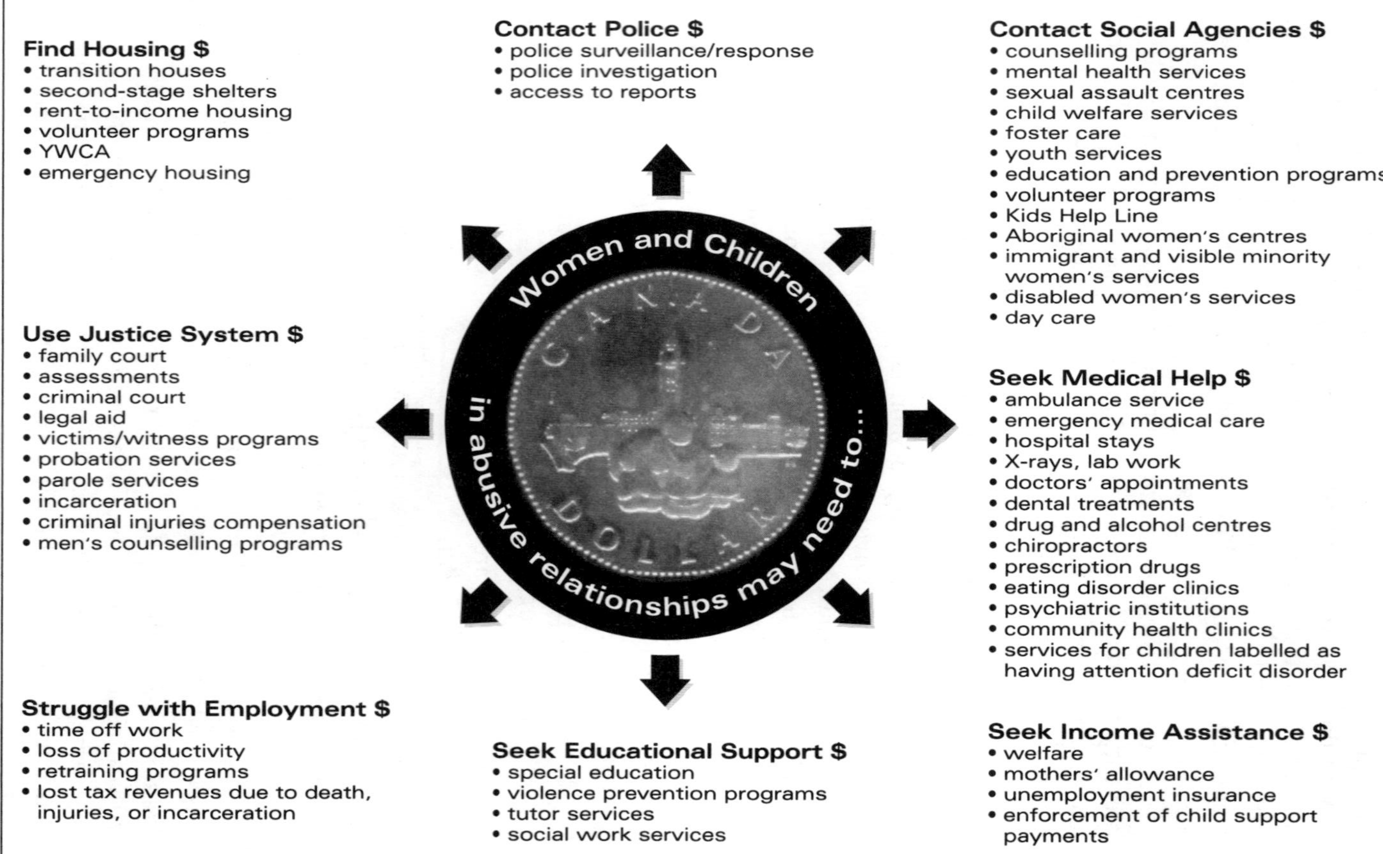

Source: *VIS-A-VIS, 13*(4) (1996, Summer), 12. Reprinted by permission of the Canadian Council on Social Development.

Appendix A highlights some of the major efforts—in the form of legislation, programs, and activities—made during the twentieth century to meet human needs and resolve social problems in Canada.

Exhibit 1.4

TOP FIVE SOCIAL CONCERNS, 1975–1995

1975	1980	1985	1990	1995
Economy	Economy	Unemployment	Economy	National debt
Crime	Crime	Economy	Environment	Unemployment
Violence	Unemployment	Child abuse	Government income	Economy
Unemployment	Violence	Pollution	GST	Crime
Drugs	Drugs	Crime	Child abuse	Government income

Source: Reginald Bibby, *The Bibby Report: Social Trends Canadian-Style* (Toronto: Stoddart, 1995), 95.

II. SOCIAL WELFARE IN ACTION: PROGRAMS AND SERVICES

Social welfare is best understood from a programs and services level. **Social welfare programs** are planned initiatives that provide financial assistance and/or direct services to individuals, families, and groups. The terms *programs* and *services*, as used in this book, encompass both income-security programs and personal social services; taken together, they form a large part of what has come to be known as Canada's **social safety net**.

INCOME-SECURITY PROGRAMS

Income-security benefits are usually tangible basic goods such as money, food, shelter, clothing, and utilities. Social conditions that interrupt income and are beyond the control of the individual (e.g., old age, sickness, disability, and economic recessions) are compensated for through pensions, insurance, grants, and other forms of income benefits. Although the income-security system is often criticized for failing to meet the basic needs of Canadians, it is intended to ensure that all citizens live above a **social minimum** that is defined as a reasonable standard of living. Most income-security programs can be roughly grouped into four categories:

1) **Selective cash transfers** are benefits that are limited to individuals whose income or assets fall below a certain level. Examples include the Guaranteed Income Supplement, social assistance (welfare), and assured income programs for people with severe disabilities.
2) **Social insurance programs** are forced savings plans that require working individuals to contribute to a program that then compensates them when they are not working. Benefits from these programs are claimed as a matter of right and in relation to the claimant's contributions. Employment Insurance and the Canada and Quebec Pension Plans are examples of social insurance programs.
3) **Tax credits** are reductions in the amount of income tax paid by low or moderate income earners. Examples of this type of program are the Canada Child Tax Benefit and the Goods and Services Tax/Harmonized Sales Tax Credit.
4) **Compensation benefits** are awarded to individuals who have suffered a loss as a result of an accident or another person's actions. Workers' compensation and compensation awarded to victims of crime or child sexual abuse fit in this category.

Most income-security programs employ income tests, needs tests, or means tests to determine a person's eligibility for benefits. **Income tests** determine eligibility based on the applicant's income and generally ignore other assets. In the last decade, changes made to Old Age Security and Employment Insurance have required that claimants be income-tested; applicants may be ineligible for benefits if their income is above a certain level.

Needs tests are used to assess an applicant's needs and determine if his or her income is sufficient to meet those needs. Provincial social assistance programs tend to use fairly elaborate needs tests: first, there is an inventory of the applicant's fixed and liquid assets; next, all sources of household income are identified; and, finally the total needs of the household are determined. The applicant is eligible for assistance if the household's needs are greater than its resources (National Council of Welfare, 2000).

Means tests base eligibility on an applicant's income and assets but virtually ignore personal needs. The federal Old Age Pension (which was replaced by Old Age Security in 1951) used means testing to determine eligibility. Means tests are often criticized for being highly intrusive since they require an in-depth inquiry into an applicant's finances, living arrangements, and other personal information and fail to take the specific needs of applicants into account (Block, 1983).

PERSONAL SOCIAL SERVICES

Personal social services are sometimes referred to as "transfers in kind." The aim of these nonincome and intangible benefits is to improve social and economic conditions for individuals and communities. In many cases, these services complement or replace the support and care that one's family and other informal support systems might normally provide.

In Canada, personal social services can be subdivided into four broad categories: (1) socialization programs; (2) personal development programs; (3) therapy and rehabilitation; and (4) information, referral, and advocacy services (Kahn, 1979). There is considerable overlap between the services in each category: for example, a therapy program may provide many benefits related to both socialization and personal development.

Socialization Programs

Socialization can be understood as the act of developing or changing behaviours, attitudes, and values to meet society's cultural norms, goals, and expectations. For the most part, children become socialized through their interaction with family members, neighbours, and other community groups and go on to lead fully functioning and productive lives as adults. In addition to these natural supports, professionals and volunteers in organizations assist in the socialization process by being "role models" or "mentors." These supports are available from a number of programs and services across Canada, including day-care or child development programs and rehabilitation programs for young offenders. Adults also have socialization needs that are met by programs such as anger management groups.

In recent years, various social groups have challenged the definition of "acceptable behaviour" that a person must adopt in order to fit into society. As diversity in culture, sexual orientation, and ethnicity continues to shape society's norms and expectations, we can expect socialization methods and role models to change.

Personal Development Programs

Personal development programs focus on activities that enhance personal qualities and abilities such as self-esteem, communication, and problem-solving. The objective of these programs is to help individuals develop competence and confidence so that they might reach their full potential as contributing members of society. Among the wide variety of personal development programs available are life-skills programs for people with disabilities, skill-building programs for parents, and employment services for women.

Therapy and Rehabilitation

The goal of therapy and rehabilitation programs is to help people restore certain skills or abilities that were diminished as a result of marital breakdown, illness, accident, unemployment, or some other life event. Services in this category include family therapy, child protection services, respite programs for caregivers, occupational therapy, alcohol and drug counselling, and transition homes for abused women and their children. Sometimes these services are "protective" in the sense that they can be used to legally detain people whose violent, sexually inappropriate, suicidal, or otherwise antisocial behaviour poses a threat to themselves or others. In most cases, therapeutic or rehabilitative programs are provided on a short-term basis.

Information, Referral, and Advocacy

Information, referral, and advocacy services help the public learn about and gain access to community programs and assist people with formal complaints about a service they received. These services are usually delivered by paid staff or volunteers of information centres, crisis phone lines, civil rights agencies, human rights commissions, or ombudsman departments. Providers of information, referral, and advocacy services may take on a variety of roles. For example, "social brokers" provide information and help people connect with needed resources in the community, while "advocates" usually act or speak on behalf of those who require assistance in having their rights recognized and met.

A profile of selected personal social services in Canada is provided in Exhibit 1.5.

SELECTIVE AND UNIVERSAL PROGRAMS

In Canada, social welfare programs are delivered either on a selective or a universal basis. **Selective programs** are normally targeted at certain populations (e.g., children or people with disabilities) who meet some predetermined criteria of being "in need." Many selective programs such as social assistance are provided on a short-term or emergency basis, and are restricted to those who can prove their need through income, needs, or means testing.

Universal programs are available to all Canadians as a matter of right regardless of economic status or need. However, applicants for such universal benefits must usually meet basic age or residency criteria. Findlay (1983, 18) observes that because universality ensures that all citizens receive the same quality of service or benefit, it prevents "divisions among those who are entitled and those who are not: it eliminates a two-tier system that results in 'second-class' citizens and 'second-class' services for the less influential." Family allowances, which were introduced in 1945 as Canada's first universal

Exhibit 1.5

EXAMPLES OF PERSONAL SOCIAL SERVICES

Socialization Program

Preschool Program, Child Development Centre, Whitehorse, Yukon

- *What is it?*—a structured classroom program offering small-group experiences
- *What does it do?*—provides opportunities for children to enhance their preacademic and social skills
- *Who is it for?*—preschool-age children with and without special needs

Personal Development Program

"Right For Me" Program, Big Brothers and Sisters of Canada

- *What is it?*—weekly groups led by adult volunteers
- *What does it do?*—addresses difficulties of adolescent development related to peer pressure, body image, alcoholism, problem-solving, career, and other topics
- *Who is it for?*—boys aged 11 to 13

Therapy Program

Manitoba Adolescent Treatment Centre

- *What is it?*—community- and hospital-based mental-health program
- *What does it do?*—provides therapeutic services ranging from brief interventions in crisis situations to intensive longer-term treatment
- *Who is it for?*—children and adolescents who suffer from severe psychiatric and/or emotional disorders

Information and Referral Program

Information Referral Centre, St. John's, Newfoundland

- *What is it?*—one-stop access centre
- *What does it do?*—provides information on, and makes referrals to, a wide range of voluntary sector agencies, organizations, and community-based groups
- *Who is it for?*—the general public

Sources: Child Development Centre, *Child Development Centre*, Whitehorse, YT, 1998; Big Brothers and Sisters of Canada [on-line], available: www.bbsc.ca [2000 February 10]; Manitoba Adolescent Treatment Centre, *Community and Hospital Services Annual Report, 1998–1999*, Winnipeg, MB, 1999; and Community Services Council [on-line], available: www.csc.nf.net/services/res_info.htm [2000 May 5].

program, provided cash benefits to all Canadian families—rich or poor—that had children.

Originally, all Canadian social welfare programs were designed to be selective. During World War II, the notion of universality in social programs was advanced and generally supported by Canadians. As economic problems persisted during the 1970s and 1980s, Canada's universal programs were increasingly criticized for being too expensive and wasteful since they delivered benefits even to individuals who were not "in need" (Block, 1983). In 1989, the Old Age Security pension lost its universal status when high-income pensioners were required to pay back all or part of their pension payments. Similarly, the universal benefits provided under the Family Allowances Act were eliminated in 1993 and replaced by a more selective benefit targeted at low-income families. Today, universal income-security programs are rare in Canada. There remains a variety of universal personal social services such as crisis intervention, family planning, and information, advocacy, and referral services.

III. THE INTERDISCIPLINARY NATURE OF SOCIAL WELFARE

SERVICE PROVIDERS

Within the social welfare system is a broad network of service providers who come from a variety of disciplines but share the common goal of helping others meet their needs. Social workers, who have traditionally held a predominant role in the social welfare field, can be found at various levels in the system. Some provide direct services to clients, while others work at the program design and administration level, and still others serve in program evaluation and policymaking positions.

During the last few decades, many of the approaches and techniques used in social welfare settings have became highly specialized and evolved into new occupations and professions. The generic title of "social worker" has given way to such titles as child and youth care worker, mental-health clinician, addiction counsellor, community support worker, and employment counsellor.

A BROAD KNOWLEDGE BASE

In addition to the many occupational groups that work in social welfare agencies, several academic disciplines study the causes of, and possible solutions to, social problems. These disciplines include the following:

EXHIBIT 1.6

That Awkward Age

"He's at that awkward age … too young for old age security, too old for Opportunities for Youth, too late for family allowance, too conventional for Canada Council or local initiative programs, too poor for tax loopholes, too rich for subsidized housing …"

Source: Len Norris, *That Awkward Age* (1990), p. 127. Reprinted by permission of the Vancouver Sun.

- *sociology*—the study of the development, structure, and functioning of human society;
- *psychology*—the scientific study of the human mind and its functions;
- *psychiatry*—the study and treatment of mental disease;
- *political science*—the study of the state and systems of government;
- *economics*—the social science of the production and distribution of wealth;

- *criminology*—the scientific study of crime; and
- *anthropology*—the study of human beings, especially of their societies and customs (Barber, 1998).

Each of these disciplines has made important contributions to the knowledge base of social welfare.

In recent years, social welfare's knowledge base has grown as frontline workers, researchers, and others search for more effective methods of helping people. One result of this search is the recognition and adoption of certain First Nations and Inuit traditional approaches to wellness. For example, First Nations and Inuit peoples take a holistic approach to healing and emphasize the inclusion of community members, such as elders, spiritual healers, and medicine people, in an individual's or family's healing process. The knowledge and practices derived from First Nations and Inuit cultures are reflected in responses to a number of social problems, including family violence and AIDS.

SOCIAL WELFARE AND OTHER SOCIAL PROGRAMS: CONNECTIONS AND OVERLAPS

Physical and Administrative Overlaps

Because of their different mandates and objectives, social welfare, health, education, and other social programs should in some contexts be considered independently of each other. Social welfare programs, for example, are provided when a person's needs cannot be met by some other means, such as through employment or family relationships; in contrast, health and educational services are provided even though other resources might meet the person's needs just as effectively (Spicker, 1984).

In most cases, however, drawing rigid boundaries around Canada's social programs is impractical since there is considerable overlap among them. One instance of overlap occurs when workers from different fields share the same physical work space; such an arrangement is often found in multiservice centres where health, education, and social welfare services are provided under the same roof. Many social programs are also linked administratively—this is particularly common among health and social welfare services, such as New Brunswick's Department of Health and Community Services.

Multidisciplinary Teams

Professionals from various fields often connect in the context of multidisciplinary or service "teams," which are formed in the community to serve clients who have a variety of needs or concerns or who require assistance from more than one professional or agency. **Multidisciplinary teams** may consist of representatives from a variety of social agencies and academic disciplines. For example, an adolescent who has recently attempted suicide may be served by a team that includes a psychiatrist from a hospital unit, a family therapist in private practice, a suicide prevention worker from a mental-health department, and a volunteer from Big Brothers/Big Sisters. Sometimes the members of a multidisciplinary team will all work for one institution. For instance, a team at an extended-care centre for the elderly may include a resident social worker, a head nurse, a physiotherapist, a recreation therapist, a nutritionist, and an administrator.

Coordinated Efforts

A growing trend in Canada is to coordinate programs provided by federal, provincial, or local levels with those provided by nongovernment social agencies, and to coordinate programs between social welfare, health, education, and other fields. These partnerships are necessary to ensure that both duplication of and gaps in services are kept to a minimum. In addition, coordination is desirable when addressing complex social problems; the various departments or organizations can be managed separately yet each can contribute to the overall operation (Armitage, 1996).

Interprogram coordination is exemplified by the National Crime Prevention Centre and the Canadian Council on Social Development, which have joined forces with local crime prevention groups, police services, and other organizations to prevent and reduce crime in communities across Canada. The National Strategy on Community Safety and Crime Prevention sponsors various programs that provide early-intervention and support services for families and children. One example is YouCAN, a program that helps youth explore the relationship between conflict resolution and violence prevention. Through a series of 20 skill-building workshops, youth learn effective conflict-resolution skills, peer mediation, and other peaceful approaches to resolving differences (Canadian Council on Social Development, 1999a).

IV. PHILOSOPHICAL FOUNDATIONS OF SOCIAL WELFARE

When studying the nature of social welfare, one soon discovers the many, and often conflicting, values, attitudes, and opinions about how society should respond to human needs and the giving of "charity." These belief systems, or philosophies, have the power to shape social welfare, the type of programs and services it endorses, and how these programs are administered.

Since philosophies are subjective, they cannot be proven right or wrong by objective measures; nor is there a consensus as to which philosophy is most favoured by Canadians. Nevertheless, predominant philosophies are reflected in many of the decisions made by social policymakers, who must decide which human needs will be the concern of social welfare and which will be left to the individual. Philosophical differences abound in social welfare and lend themselves to lively debates in social and political arenas across the country.

This section explores some of the political and religious philosophies that have shaped Canada's social welfare system. The political views discussed here should not be confused with the policies of Canadian political parties (such as the Progressive Conservative Party, Liberal Party, and New Democratic Party). Although political parties are influenced by conservative, liberal, and social democratic thought, their platforms rarely reflect any one particular philosophical stance (Bell, 1995).

POLITICAL VIEWS

Conservatism and Laissez-Faire Governments

Conservatism supports the idea of capitalism and its principles of private property, competition in the free market, personal accumulation of wealth, and entrepreneurship. The principle of individualism underlies all conservative thought and emphasizes that the common good will best be served if individuals are left to pursue their personal self-interest with the least interference. For conservatives, therefore, the most desirable government is the one that regulates, controls, or intervenes the least. According to this viewpoint, government intervention in the lives of citizens should be restricted to whatever is necessary to maintain peace and order (Wilensky and Lebeaux, 1965).

Governments that administer according to conservative principles are often referred to as being **laissez-faire** (a French term meaning "to leave alone"). Laissez-faire government policies were strongly influenced by Adam Smith, an 18th-century Scottish economist who urged the state to allow the process of "natural laws," including the law of supply and demand, to take their course without state control, regulation, or intervention in the lives of individuals and industry. The laissez-faire approach was also supported by the notion of social Darwinism. This 19th-century ideology maintained that only the fittest would survive, while the unfit—such as the poor and powerless—should be left alone to compete, struggle for survival, and possibly perish. According to social Darwinists, this process was necessary in order for society to be able to "perfect itself." Conservatism and support for the laissez-faire approach was most popular among Canadians in the late 19th and early

20th centuries (Woodside and McClam, 1994). More recently, the term *neo-conservatism* reflects a renewed interest in laissez-faire principles among Canadian politicians and the general public.

Conservatives generally believe that social welfare programs and services "undermine initiative, weaken moral fiber, and create imbalance in the workings of the marketplace" (Galper, 1975, 3). Thus, conservatives tend to support a **residual approach** to social welfare: that is, social welfare programs should be used conservatively and only as a last resort, when help from one's family, church, banks, and other private sources has been exhausted. Any help that is given by government should be terminated as soon as the individual being helped can once again be self-reliant (Handel, 1982).

Liberalism

In many respects, **liberalism** is similar to conservatism: both philosophies emphasize liberty, individualism, and competitive private enterprise. Liberal values are nevertheless tempered by strong humanistic beliefs and a concern that capitalism and the marketplace are inadequate to fully meet the needs of citizens. According to liberal thought, a capitalist system must be regulated and controlled in order to work effectively (George and Wilding, 1985). Thus, liberals are generally opposed to the laissez-faire philosophy, arguing that

> without state intervention, capitalism cannot solve the problems that it has created for itself, such as great imbalances in income and wealth, cyclical recession, structural unemployment, inflation, and technological development. They see that economic growth in advanced capitalist societies has not abolished poverty; rather, by its very nature, capitalism produces and perpetuates inequality and poverty. (Djao, 1983, 18)

Liberalism generally supports government in the role of "compensator" to address human needs that are not met adequately by the market.

During the late 19th century, the drastic social and economic problems created by the Industrial Revolution and urbanization led many Canadians to question the practicality of social Darwinism and the laissez-faire approach. The prevailing belief that the poor and unemployed were simply lazy was being challenged. Unemployment, poverty, family breakdown, and other problems became viewed as manmade problems resulting from inherent flaws in the capitalist economy. The rise of these more liberal or "enlightened" perspectives on social problems and their causes paved the way for a new approach to social welfare (Frenzel, 1987; Hareven, 1969).

By the end of World War II, there was a growing recognition of government as a potential enforcer of social justice through legislation. A more liberal-minded country grew more supportive of a welfare state that would use its taxing powers to redistribute income, thereby preventing large numbers of people from falling into poverty. Although the welfare state is limited in the extent to which it can protect or help people, it is seen as a useful way to intervene in a capitalist society (Hareven, 1969; Galper, 1975).

Liberals urge governments to accept a reasonable degree of responsibility for meeting people's needs and for protecting people from the risks of modern life such as unemployment, sickness, injury, disability, old age, and poverty. Social welfare programs are expected to help people reach satisfying standards of life, health, relationships, self-development, and well-being. From the liberal viewpoint, social welfare programs are basically good; the major problem with these programs is that there are too few of them, it seems, to meet the demand. As a result of liberal ideals and social action, a broad range of income-security programs and personal social services developed in Canada (Galper, 1975; Wilensky and Lebeaux, 1965).

Socialism

For the most part, **socialism** rejects the competitive values of capitalism, individualism, private enterprise, competition, and the doctrine of laissez-faire. According to socialist thought, major inequalities of resources or economic power in society result in the poor being in bondage to the rich. Thus, to ensure freedom for all citizens, socialists urge governments to take on the role of "stabilizer" by redistributing income more evenly among all citizens. Socialists support collective action by workers (such as the formation of unions) to address unfavourable work conditions, and political action (such as strikes and protests) to influence government policies (George and Wilding, 1985; Boothroyd, 1991).

Since the term *socialism* was coined in the early 19th century, two main camps have evolved: (1) the revolutionary or *communist* camp, which advocates a primarily government owned and operated economy; and (2) the evolutionary or *social democratic* camp, which supports an economy in which a mix of public and private enterprise takes place. Social democracy, which has gained more support in Canada than its communist counterpart, tends to oppose the two extremes of communism and capitalism.

Social democracy maintains that any conditions that threaten personal security—such as unemployment and industrial injury—are the costs of social progress rather than the result of personal shortcomings of the individuals who suffer them. This being the case, social democrats advocate for society to protect and compensate those who fall prey to the risks of social and economic progress. In contrast to the residual approach to social welfare favoured by conservatives, social democrats support an **institutional approach** on the grounds that social welfare programs fulfil a normal and basic function in a modern society and should therefore be universally available to citizens as a matter of right. Universal social programs and the redistribution of wealth from the "haves" to the "have-nots" are the cornerstones of the socio-democratic ideology (George and Wilding, 1985; Wilensky and Lebeaux, 1965).

RELIGIOUS VIEWS

Social welfare's basic commitment to help the poor and needy is rooted in the Old Testament and Judeo-Christian teachings. Philanthropic principles in the Jewish and Christian religions were seen as a reflection of the love of God, not the love of humankind: "The 'theological virtues' were set forth as faith, hope, and charity, the greatest being charity" (Macarov, 1978, 79). Historically, Judeo-Christians believed that charitable works on earth would yield rewards in the afterlife; thus, compassion and relief were given to the poor in compensation for their lack of material possessions. In the New Testament teachings of Christ and his disciples, charitable acts represented a life of selflessness and love of one's neighbour; the giving of charity became as important as personal survival.

With the Protestant Reformation in 16th-century Europe came the belief that success at work, in the form of profits and wealth, was an indication of God's favour. Thus, the Protestant ethic maintained that one must work in this world to be saved in the next. A person's earned prosperity and success were seen as evidence of godly living, virtue, and God's grace. With this new understanding of work and salvation, Protestants began to view poverty as

> an indication of a sinful life and of divine retribution. Therefore such help as was extended to the poor was often accompanied by unsolicited and largely irrelevant advice on how the poor might regain God's grace through the exercise of those human qualities which He apparently admired and rewarded. The poor were urged to appreciate the values of thrift, hard work, self-help, and self-discipline. (Guest, 1980, 16)

In many cases, the giving of charity was discouraged by the Protestant ethic, since helping others on earth was not seen as a way to gain entry into heaven.

Despite its predominantly secular nature, social welfare continues to be shaped by religious doctrine. Richards (1997, 32) notes:

> The two parents of the Canadian welfare state were the traditional left and the church. Under their influence, ordinary Canadians favoured expansion of social programs throughout much of this century. In turn, these preferences led governments of all ideological persuasions toward assigning an ever-larger share of [gross domestic product] to the public sector.

The Roman Catholic Church played a particularly central role in the provision of social services in Quebec until the early 1960s, when the bulk of responsibility for social welfare shifted from the Church to the provincial government. Bellamy (1965, 36) writes that the Roman Catholic Church was well suited to the role of charity provider: "Long experience in ministering to the weak and suffering, backed by a strong administrative organization, dedicated personnel, and wealthy patrons, and its own abundant material resources fitted the Church well for meeting the temporal needs of the people no less than the spiritual needs."

Religious doctrine continues to play an important role in shaping society's perception of social welfare and the giving of charity. Many churches are also actively involved in addressing social issues and promoting social justice. For example, the United Church of Canada recently completed a five-year fundraising campaign to support programs aimed at helping Aboriginal people deal with the effects of residential schools (United Church of Canada, 2000).

Introduction

Canada's social welfare system developed over the past 100 years in response to emerging social problems in a complex industrial society.

Social Welfare: Basic Components

Social welfare may be understood as a system of interconnected and overlapping legislation, policies, procedures, and activities designed to (1) help individuals and groups meet their basic economic and social needs; and (2) prevent and reduce social problems. New human needs constantly emerge and demand attention from the social welfare system; social policymakers must decide which needs should be met by social welfare programs and which should be addressed by personal resources. In contrast to social conditions, social problems must be objectively measured as well as subjectively defined as problems. The social welfare system is primarily concerned with social problems that affect both the individual and general society. Those who control social welfare resources must determine whether interventions should be aimed at meeting individual or community needs.

Social Welfare in Action: Programs and Services

Social welfare programs are planned initiatives that provide financial assistance and/or direct services to individuals, families, and groups. Income-security programs aim to ensure that all citizens live above a social minimum; these programs include selective cash transfers, social insurance programs, tax credits, and compensation benefits. Personal social services are nonincome benefits that are used to improve social and economic conditions for people and communities. These services include socialization programs, personal development programs, therapy and rehabilitation, and information services. Selective programs are provided on the basis of financial or social need, while universal programs are received by all citizens regardless of economic status or need.

The Interdisciplinary Nature of Social Welfare

Social workers and a variety of other occupational groups perform social welfare duties. Several academic disciplines are also concerned with the study and resolution of social problems. There is considerable overlap between social welfare and other social programs such as health and education. In many cases, the combined efforts of several service delivery systems are necessary to ensure comprehensive support.

Philosophical Foundations of Social Welfare

There are many belief systems that influence social welfare programs. Canadian politics has shaped social welfare under the banners of three main philosophies: conservatives believe in capitalism and minimal government intervention; liberals believe that capitalism should be tempered by moderate government intervention to address human needs; and social democrats maintain that government should play a primary role in meeting human needs. Religious influences on Canadian social welfare stem from the charitable acts supported by the Judeo-Christians and the work ethic advocated by the Protestant Reformists. Religions continue to play a role in shaping perceptions of social welfare and addressing social issues.

KEY TERMS

SOCIAL WELFARE SYSTEM 4
HUMAN NEED 5
SOCIAL PROBLEM 7
SOCIAL WELFARE PROGRAMS 11
SOCIAL SAFETY NET 11
INCOME-SECURITY BENEFITS 11
SOCIAL MINIMUM 11
SELECTIVE CASH TRANSFERS 12
SOCIAL INSURANCE PROGRAMS 12
TAX CREDITS 12
COMPENSATION BENEFITS 12
INCOME TESTS 12
NEEDS TESTS 12
MEANS TESTS 12
PERSONAL SOCIAL SERVICES 13
SELECTIVE PROGRAMS 14
UNIVERSAL PROGRAMS 14
MULTIDISCIPLINARY TEAMS 18
CONSERVATISM 20
LAISSEZ-FAIRE 20
RESIDUAL APPROACH 21
LIBERALISM 21
SOCIALISM 22
SOCIAL DEMOCRACY 22
INSTITUTIONAL APPROACH 23

CHAPTER 2

SOCIAL WELFARE DEVELOPMENTS FROM THE COLONIAL ERA TO THE 1970s

• OBJECTIVES •

I. To take a brief look at social welfare in colonial Canada.

II. To examine the reform movements during the late 19th and early 20th centuries and their impact on social legislation.

III. To explore some of the social and economic problems created by the Great Depression and World War II and how they influenced social legislation in the 1940s and 1950s.

IV. To review the major developments in social welfare during the 1960s and the curtailing of social welfare expansion by the mid-1970s.

INTRODUCTION

Although Canada's early inhabitants attended to the social welfare needs in their own communities, a formal social welfare system did not take shape until the middle of the 20th century. It was the social and economic upheavals of the Great Depression and World War II that prompted Canadians to support a welfare state and the role of government as "social manager" (Heclo, 1981).

The 1950s and 1960s were characterized by strong economic growth, high employment, rising government revenues, and a subsequent increase in public spending. Canadians encouraged the government to develop new social programs or reform the existing ones so that a higher standard of living might be realized. The pace of social welfare development quickened during the 1960s with the introduction of major programs such as the Canada Assistance Plan, the Canada/Quebec Pension Plans, and Medicare. Mendelson (1993, 3) comments on the general feeling of optimism among Canadians during this time:

> Perhaps the dominant theme of social policy was an unspoken but common assumption that progress was certain—that with time and some effort, programs would get

> better, the number of poor would decrease, better housing would be generated and ways would be found to "cure diseases" of the body, of the mind and of society as a whole. Progress might be slow for some and fast for others, but progress there would be.

It was in the early 1970s—a period of declining economic growth and falling government revenues—that attitudes toward social welfare began to change. Although governments continued to fund social welfare programs during this time, many Canadians expressed their doubts about the value of the welfare state and its ability to ensure social and economic security (Heclo, 1981). Thus, the mid-1970s marked the end of the expansion era for the welfare state, and the beginning of an extensive restructuring of the social welfare system and of severe cuts in spending on social programs and services.

This chapter provides an overview of the major social welfare policies, programs, and services that were introduced in Canada from colonial times to the mid-1970s.

I. EARLY CONTRIBUTIONS TO SOCIAL WELFARE

THE FRENCH TRADITION

When the Roman Catholic missionaries began colonizing New France in the 17th century, they adopted the French tradition of tending to the sick, the aged, and abandoned or orphaned children. In 1653, Sister Marguerite Bourgeoys (known as Canada's first social worker) founded the Sisters of the Congregation of Notre Dame in Montreal. In addition to carrying out their mission of civilizing the Iroquois "savages" and converting them to Christianity, the Sisters cared for the French settlers and the children who arrived on ships from France. By the late 18th century, French-speaking colonists in Lower Canada were raising funds through voluntary organizations to support the charity functions of the Catholic Church (Bellamy, 1965; Yelaja, 1985).

THE ENGLISH POOR LAWS

When the British settled in newly established Halifax in 1749, they introduced many principles from the **English Poor Laws**, a series of legislative acts that were completed in 1601 by Queen Elizabeth I. Although these laws were promoted as a way to address widespread poverty in England, they were in fact used to stop the commoners from begging and wandering about—activities the ruling class found highly annoying (Zastrow, 1996).

Many aspects of the English Poor Laws influenced the way early British settlers viewed and treated the poor. For example, to ensure that poor people were treated "appropriately," the Poor Laws classified the poor as being either "worthy" or "unworthy" of relief. The **worthy poor** included poor children, who were to be educated and apprenticed, as well as aged, sick, or disabled people, who were to receive relief; in many cases, the worthy poor were herded into large poorhouses, separated only on the basis of gender. The **unworthy poor** were able-bodied unemployed persons, who were often banished to workhouses, where they were expected to learn good work habits and pay for their keep through labour (Guest, 1980; Taylor, 1969; Trattner, 1989).

During Canada's colonial era, the Poor Law legislation assigned the responsibility for managing the poor to local governments (or parishes), which financed relief programs through property tax revenue. Some British settlements were more enthusiastic than others in adopting the Poor Law model and principles. Nova Scotia and New Brunswick, for instance, enacted Poor Law legislation in 1763 and 1786 respectively. Prince Edward Island, limited in the size of its settlements, did not endorse the Poor Laws to any real extent, while Newfoundland preferred its poor to rely on support from family, friends, and charities rather than from legislated relief. In 1792, when Upper Canada adopted many of the English civil laws, the Poor Laws were rejected in favour of voluntary charities, which were set up to tend to the poor and needy (Guest, 1999).

A RESIDUAL APPROACH TO CHARITY

Although government-funded relief was available to the truly destitute in the colonial era, the benefits were meagre and often delivered in a paternalistic, discretionary, and demeaning fashion (Hess, 1993). Asking for charity—even from the churches in French Canada—was discouraged, and recipients of "handouts" were often made to feel like personal failures. Guest (1999, 2201) notes that the reputation of the poorhouses in the larger towns

> was so fearsome that only those facing starvation would seek such help. In New Brunswick some of the smaller communities that could not afford the cost of these institutions auctioned off the care of the poor to local families, an utterly demeaning practice.

For the most part, a highly residual approach to social welfare predominated into the late 19th century. With the passage of the Constitution Act of 1867 (formerly the British North America Act), the bulk of responsibility for social welfare was assigned to the provincial level of government; many of the provinces, in turn, delegated social welfare functions to municipal governments or local charities.

ABORIGINAL PEOPLE AND THE POOR LAWS

The early British settlers in British North America found that many Aboriginal groups relied on family/clan systems to maintain order and provide mutual aid. These systems utilized the expertise of local supports such as spiritual healers, elders, teachers, law keepers, medicine people, and hunters. The British settlers nevertheless viewed Native people as beggars (not unlike European vagabonds) and rejected the Natives' methods on the basis that they were inferior to those valued by European society. Many Poor Law principles and the European values of "discipline, hard manual labour, social stratification, and strong, hierarchical authority structures" were imposed on the Natives in an effort to replace the Native principles of egalitarianism and interdependence (Mawhiney, 1994).

During the 1800s, certain Aboriginal groups in Upper Canada were placed in designated areas called reserves. Foucault (1965, 45) observes: "A parallel can be made between reserves and 'places of confinement' established in Europe during the mid-seventeenth century to isolate and contain the poor, vagabonds, the mentally ill, and delinquents." The "civilizing" and "normalizing" experiments conducted on Native people on reserves in Upper Canada resembled those done on the "undesirables" in Europe. Such experiments served to keep certain categories of people separate from the rest of society and "encouraged Europeans to consider them as having 'something wrong with them'" (Foucault, 1965, 7). Many of these attitudes and practices would persist for another 100 years.

II. THE 1870s TO THE 1920s: AN EXPERIMENT WITH SOCIAL POLICY

During the late 19th and early 20th centuries, a general increase in social consciousness and collective responsibility for one's fellow human beings gave rise to a wave of **social movements**. These movements not only influenced social values and attitudes toward social problems but also played a key role in the decision of governments to take a more active part in the social and economic lives of citizens.

The period from 1870 to the 1920s was a time of experimentation for Canadian governments as they dabbled in social policy and the establishment of a wider range of programs for the poor and needy. Exhibit 2.1 gives some examples of the programs available to the poor during this period. Many early social policymakers tried to move away from the English Poor Law tradition, which was highly discriminating and stigmatizing, toward a more equitable, nonjudgmental, and responsive approach to social welfare. Significant progress was made in social welfare programs during this time. However, there was still considerable debate among Canadians about the value of compulsory government programs, the role of government in social matters, and the boundaries of social policy (Heclo, 1981).

THE LABOUR REFORM MOVEMENT

The roots of labour reform are in the industrialization of Canadian cities. Industrialization created a number of problems for labourers in mining, fishing, construction, and other trades, who were pressured to work long hours for low pay, often in unpleasant or dangerous conditions. Mounting dissatisfaction within the labour force resulted in sporadic protests and the eventual formation of unions. In general, union actions were directed toward raising the standard of living, establishing income-security measures, obtaining higher wages and paid overtime, and gaining recognition from employers as collective bargaining units. By the 1870s, trade unions had become a powerful political force in Canada. Formed in 1873, the Canadian Labour Union addressed several problems related to immigration, child labour, and prison labour; this union also formulated plans for political action, labour organization, and cooperatives. In the mid-1880s, the Trades and Labor Congress of Canada became an influential force in the area of industrial legislation, helping to bring about the eventual passage of seven factory bills (Carniol, 1990; Forsey, 1974).

THE WORKMEN'S COMPENSATION ACT OF 1914

During the early years of industrialization, the use of often primitive and dangerous machines increased the incidence of work-related accidents and injuries. In the late 1800s and early 1900s, workers could sue their employers for injuries that happened on the job. At the same time, employers had the right to dispute such claims by stating, for example, that the injured worker had been negligent. When employers lost, the court made them pay the injured workers. However, if the damage awards were considerable,

EXHIBIT 2.1

SHELTERS FOR HOMELESS MEN IN VANCOUVER, 1910–1920

Name	Clientele	Size	Other Services	Funding
Strathcona Institute for Sailors and Loggers	Transient workers, particularly seamen	40 beds	Letter bureau; baggage room; employment bureau; general social facilities for men visiting city; meals; baths	British and Foreign Sailors Society; fees from those who could afford to pay; donations
Seamen's Institute	Sailors	30 beds	Meals; baths; letter bureau; baggage room; employment bureau	Anglican Church; fees from those who could afford to pay; donations
Canadian Camp Brotherhood	Men from all camps, logging, mining, or railway construction	unknown	Meals; baths; letter bureau; baggage room; employment bureau; doctor; dentist; lawyer	Fees from those who could afford to pay; donations
St. Luke's Home	Homeless men; poor families; aged; convalescent	unknown	Meals; food and clothing for poor families; medical attention	Municipal grant; donations; fees from those who could afford to pay

Source: Adapted from D. Matters (1979), "Public Welfare, Vancouver Style, 1910–1920," *Journal of Canadian Studies, 14*(1), 4.

employers were often forced to declare bankruptcy and shut down their businesses, which hardly benefited the injured workers (McGilly, 1990).

Many trade unions drew public attention to the increasing number of industrial accidents and the shortcomings of the compensation system and pressured governments to take action to improve the situation for workers. In 1914, Canada's first comprehensive and compulsory social insurance plan was established in Ontario. Guest (1980, 44) notes: "The Ontario Workmen's Compensation Act of 1914 was hailed as one of the most advanced pieces of compensation legislation in North America." Under the provisions of the 1914 legislation, all major employers were to contribute to the compensation fund and, instead of directly suing employers, workers and their families were allowed to apply for compensation in the event of a work-related accident. The Ontario act started a workers' compensation movement; by 1920, all provinces except Prince Edward Island had similar legislation (Moscovitch and Drover, 1987).

VETERANS' PENSIONS

World War I was a stark reminder of the vulnerability of the family unit. The considerable loss of human life on the battlefield prompted concerns not only about the increased number of fatherless families but also about the high infant mortality rate, which was seen as affecting the ability of families to replenish "the stock of healthy males" (Moscovitch and Drover, 1987, 24).

The federal government set up a variety of charities to aid Canadian soldiers overseas and to provide relief to soldiers' families at home. A more organized system of relief was established when the government introduced two schemes for veterans' pensions: (1) the Soldier Settlement, which provided unemployed soldiers financial assistance and a parcel of land to farm; and (2) the Employment Service of Canada, an extensive network that helped veterans find jobs across the country. Financial assistance was also available to the families of soldiers who had been lost or killed in combat. The federal government's active involvement in pension programs clearly marked a shift away from the traditional philosophy that families, not government, should be responsible for resolving their own social and economic problems (Struthers, 1983; Guest, 1980).

IMPROVING CONDITIONS FOR WOMEN AND CHILDREN

As the pace of industrialization accelerated, the economic insecurity of families grew. Dependent women and children were vulnerable if a male breadwinner was injured at work, died, or deserted the family; single-parent families increased as divorce became more common; and women who had to work were often forced to leave their children unattended. These concerns coincided with changing attitudes toward women and children and the role of government. Social reformists such as Nellie McClung, John Joseph Kelso, Stephen Leacock, and James Shaver Woodsworth pushed for a more active role by government in family life, particularly in promoting motherhood and protecting children (Strong-Boag, 1979).

The First Wave of the Women's Rights Movement

Women have traditionally supported social action endeavours, particularly as they relate to improved social and economic conditions for women and children. By the late 1800s, the scope of volunteer and organizational work by women had expanded from local to national levels, leading to the formation of organizations such as the Young Women's Christian Association (YWCA), the Woman's Christian Temperance Union, and the National Council of Women. Women also pushed for extended legal and political rights such as the right to vote, to run for and hold political office, to gain access to higher education, and to own certain property. By 1920, the women's rights movement and the lobbying efforts by Emily Murphy, Nellie McClung, and other early feminists had resulted in voting rights for women in all federal elections; women could also be elected to the House of Commons. However, it was not until 1929 that women were finally declared "persons" by the Judicial Committee of the British Privy Council and allowed appointments to the Canadian Senate (Eichler, 1987; Mitchinson, 1987).

Mothers' Pension Movement

By World War I, social and political forces had stimulated the mothers' pension movement, which called for legislated income security for mothers, as well as for abandoned wives and their children. In both Canada and the United States, the traditional practice of institutionalizing abandoned or poor children was giving way to a more enlightened approach of keeping children in the home whenever possible. This change meant that mothers needed additional support to provide the nurturing, care, and attention necessary to raise healthy children. In 1916, Manitoba legislated the first mothers' allowance. This legislation, which provided a small but assured income to all women with dependants, established the government's role as the provider of income security and protector of minimum social standards. Soon after Manitoba took the lead, mothers' allowances were established in Saskatchewan (1917), Alberta (1919), Ontario and British Columbia (1920), Nova Scotia (1930), Quebec (1937), and New Brunswick (1944) (Guest, 1980, 1988).

The Child Welfare Movement

The driving force behind Canada's child welfare movement was John Joseph Kelso, who worked as a reporter for the Toronto *Globe* in the late 1800s. In a series of articles, he stimulated public concern about the neglect and abuse of children in Toronto. Kelso founded the Toronto Humane Society in 1887 and later played an important role in the passage of the 1888 Act for the Protection and Reformation of Neglected Children in Ontario. This act authorized the courts to remove neglected children from their homes and place them in alternative care; it also required trials of juveniles to be separate from trials of adults (Hareven, 1969; Guest, 1980).

In 1893, the Act for the Prevention of Cruelty and Better Protection of Children was passed in Ontario. Considered to be the first comprehensive piece of legislation in North America to protect children, the new act put Canada at the forefront of child welfare legislation. Children's aid societies were promoted by the act, and in 1891 Kelso and his supporters successfully persuaded the government to establish Canada's first children's aid society in Toronto. The act also resulted in the appointment of superintendents to oversee the care of neglected, abused, and dependent children and promoted the placement of dependent children in foster homes rather than institutions (Hareven, 1969; Bellamy, 1965; Guest, 1980).

INCOME SECURITY FOR ELDERLY CANADIANS

During the early 20th century, many Canadians expressed their concern about the ability of the elderly to provide for themselves and for poor families to care for their aging parents. These concerns were reinforced by the fact that a large number of elderly Canadians were applying for public relief. It was not until several provinces started complaining about the mounting cost of relief, however, that a federal old age pension scheme was seriously considered (McGilly, 1990).

The Old Age Pensions Act, enacted in 1927, marked the federal government's commitment to social security on an ongoing basis and established pensions as a right to which all older Canadians were entitled. Despite these inroads, the pension was highly restrictive. To collect pension benefits, Canadians had to be 70 years or older, a remarkably high age requirement compared to that established in other countries with similar old age pension plans. The means test that was used to assess eligibility was also strict and humiliating, "proof that poor-law attitudes still influenced Canadian political leaders in the 1920s" (Guest, 1988, 2033).

III. THE IMPACT OF THE GREAT DEPRESSION AND WORLD WAR II

RISING UNEMPLOYMENT IN THE 'DIRTY THIRTIES'

The Great Depression in Canada was triggered by a combination of factors, including the 1929 stock market crash in the United States and Europe's slow economic recovery after World War I. The severe economic problems in these countries drastically reduced the demand for Canada's primary products. Canada's entire economy, which relied heavily on the selling of raw materials and semiprocessed goods, was hurt as a result (Horn, 1984).

Unemployment rates soared during the Depression years, especially from 1929 to 1933. According to studies done during this period, 19 to 27 percent of Canadians were unemployed in 1933, compared with only 2 to 4 percent in 1929. (The wide range of rates for each of the two years reflects different methods used to measure unemployment.) Some categories of workers, such as unskilled labourers and workers in the export industries, ran a particularly high risk of unemployment (Horn, 1984).

High unemployment created additional social and health problems. For example, by the time the Depression ended in 1939, almost one-third of the Canadian population was too poor to buy adequate amounts of nutritious food. In addition, slum conditions had developed in the larger cities. In 1934, the Lieutenant-Governor's Committee on Housing Conditions in Toronto reported that "there are thousands of families living in houses which are unsanitary, verminous and grossly overcrowded" (Cassidy, 1943, 57–58). Similar concerns were voiced by investigators of housing conditions in Montreal, Vancouver, Winnipeg, and other Canadian cities.

FORMS OF 'RELIEF' DURING THE GREAT DEPRESSION

Although the United States and Britain had a number of social security measures in place, Canada was unprepared to meet the widespread need created by the Great Depression. Since unemployment insurance was nonexistent, those who lost their jobs sought whatever **public relief** was available. The number of Canadians dependent on public relief remained high throughout the 1930s: 1.5 million people, or 15 percent of Canadians, received public relief in 1933; by 1934, the figure had risen to 2 million (Bellamy, 1965; Horn, 1984).

Most provinces provided some form of both direct and indirect relief. *Direct relief* was available in three forms: (1) cash; (2) vouchers for groceries, clothing, or fuel (to ensure that the relief was used for basic necessities); and

(3) relief "in kind" (the provision of actual food, coal, clothing, or other commodities instead of cash or vouchers). *Indirect relief* was provided through government-funded work projects (e.g., road and bridge construction) designed to get the unemployed back to work. These public works projects tended to be poorly planned, uncoordinated, unable to meet the demand, and, despite provincial and federal grants, too expensive for municipal governments to support. Because of their prohibitive cost, most indirect relief programs had been replaced with direct measures by 1932 (Guest, 1980; Bellamy, 1965).

INCREASING DEMANDS FOR REFORM

Not long into the Depression, mass unemployment threatened the social order: "large numbers of unemployed, especially able-bodied unemployed men, began in time to make their discontent and anger unmistakably clear" (McGilly, 1990, 82). To curb the possibility of social anarchy and widespread revolt, the federal government set up work camps in remote regions of the country where single, unemployed men could work in exchange for food, shelter, and other basic necessities. According to some reports, work camp "recruits" were often transient and homeless men who had broken vagrancy laws and were consequently crowded into camps that resembled 19th-century poorhouses. They were put to work building railway lines and clearing forests for 25 cents a day (Yalnizyan, 1994; McGilly, 1990; Guest, 1988).

Despite the government's efforts to curb social unrest, the Great Depression stimulated a number of "imaginative fight-back tactics" among the vast numbers of unemployed (Yalnizyan, 1994, 32). The On to Ottawa Trek of 1935 was perhaps the largest and most well-known protest during the Depression era. Approximately 4000 men from work camps across the country boarded trains and headed to Ottawa to protest unemployment, poor wages, and unacceptable work camp conditions. McGilly (1990) suggests that it was the fear of social anarchy that eventually motivated the federal government to introduce unemployment insurance.

UNEMPLOYMENT INSURANCE ACT OF 1940

During the Depression, private charitable organizations, such as the Federation of Jewish Philanthropies in Montreal and Toronto, and the Canadian Welfare Council, were involved in fundraising campaigns to help people in need. In addition, municipal governments continued to provide relief services. But these avenues of help had little impact on the problem of mass unemployment and widespread need. In fact, many municipal governments found it financially impossible to keep up with the growing costs of welfare (Bellamy, 1965). (See Exhibit 2.2 for a contemporary view.)

Exhibit 2.2

SOCIAL SERVICES TOO COSTLY FOR MUNICIPALITIES

Declaring unemployment and indigency national responsibilities, and education, hospitalization and social service costs beyond the ability of land taxes to meet, seventy-eight British Columbia municipalities presented their case to the Rowell Commission yesterday, in forty-eight minutes, through the Union of British Columbia Municipalities....

Harry J. Sullivan, K.O., spoke for the Union in a succinct, briefly put argument. Municipalities had their responsibilities fixed by the Province with insufficient revenues to meet statutory and fixed requirements as at present. With less than one percent of the area of the Province, they had to provide services for 70 percent of the people, including provincial services under a dozen acts. The main municipal source of revenue was the land tax, producing 85 percent of civic income....

Have No Control

Municipalities, meanwhile, had had no control over provincial legislation, which had gone on adding social service and other costs for cities, towns and villages to pay without any additional revenues....

Relief, hospitalization, social services and education had grown beyond the means of land to finance, Mr. Sullivan continued. The Province, as the higher authority, should assume the care of costs not properly chargeable to land and outside the scope of purely local services. In the past the Province had loaded the municipalities with social services, the civic bill for which in 1935 had been $12,600,000.

By taking care in part of old age pensions, the blind and returned veterans, the Dominion had gone part of the way towards recognizing national charges not referable to land....

In conclusion, the Union submitted that municipalities were an integral part of government closely in touch with the people; that real property had proved an unsatisfactory basis for municipal revenue; that civic duties had been overloaded, without adequate means of meeting them; that provincial grants were not satisfactory as additional means of financing, and that exemption of Crown lands was a heavy imposition under present conditions.

Permanent Commission

The Union submitted, said Mr. Sullivan, that cities should finance strictly local services; that other and national services should be on a wider tax basis; that relief and indigency were national responsibilities, and that education, hospitalization and social services should be financed by other means than a tax on land. The municipalities asked, in conclusion, a permanent commission to review and adjust differences between the three taxation agencies in Canada.

Source: Excerpted from "Social Services Too Costly for Municipalities," *Victoria Daily Colonist*, 22 March 1938, 1–6. Reprinted by kind permission of the Times Colonist, Victoria.

The federal government finally intervened in the unemployment crisis and began sharing the costs of provincial/municipal relief programs. This action was rationalized on the basis that the federal government possessed broader taxation powers, had a greater capacity to borrow, and was in a position to equalize conditions among the provinces, some of which were more severely affected by high unemployment than others. The federal government's involvement, however, was to be temporary since Canada's Constitution made public relief a provincial responsibility. By the time the federal government terminated the cost-sharing program in 1941, it had assumed 40 percent of the total cost of public relief, which amounted to about $1 billion (Bellamy, 1965; Guest, 1980; McGilly, 1990).

Prime Minister Mackenzie King's proposal for a comprehensive unemployment insurance scheme was well received by Canadians, who were beginning to question whether unemployment in fact represented the personal failure of individuals.

> The shiver of universal risk had swept over everyone, and people started demanding protections by pooling that risk across society, and not just at the traditional levels of municipalities and provinces. For the first time, people sought a larger scale of protection, at the highest jurisdictional level, to provide certain minimums. (Yalnizyan, 1994, 31)

Since unemployment was a provincial responsibility, King had to seek a constitutional amendment before the federal government could legislate a national unemployment insurance plan. In July 1940, British Parliament gave the Canadian government this right, and the Unemployment Insurance Act was soon passed. With the exception of veterans' pensions during World War I, Unemployment Insurance was Canada's first large-scale income-security program. Almost 4.6 million Canadians drew unemployment insurance benefits during the plan's first year (Guest, 1980).

THE MARSH REPORT ON SOCIAL SECURITY

Postwar planning of social welfare in Canada reflected a continuing shift of public support from a residual to an institutional approach. In fact, during the 1940s, the foundation for Canada's current social welfare system was laid. A large number of government committees were set up to determine the postwar needs of Canadians, and a series of reports outlining postwar programs were produced. The Marsh Report is perhaps the best-known among the documents concerned with social policy; it was influenced by, and contained many principles from, the famous Beveridge Report that came out of Great Britain in 1942. In March 1943, Leonard Marsh, a prominent social researcher, professor, and author, released his *Report on Social Security* outlining a comprehensive social security plan for Canada. According to Marsh, this plan was long overdue, considering the progress already made in other countries (see Exhibit 2.3).

The Marsh Report called for the implementation of: (1) a national employment program; (2) social insurance and social assistance measures; and (3) children's allowances. A primary objective underlying each social security proposal was that of a social minimum, which Marsh (1950, 35)

Exhibit 2.3

MARSH SAYS CANADA'S SOCIAL SERVICES LAG

Leonard Marsh, of Ottawa, research advisor of the advisory committee on reconstruction, in an interview today named Great Britain, New Zealand and Russia as the countries with the most complete social legislation.

Dr. Marsh, author of the Marsh Report on Social Security, said Russia had the most comprehensive training and educational services of any country today.

"As far as English-speaking countries are concerned, Canada seems to be lagging behind. We lack health insurance, widows' and orphans' pensions, and sickness benefits. Our one redeeming quality is our excellent unemployment insurance."

A delegate to the Canadian Conference on Social Work here, Dr. Marsh emphasized the need for a national health insurance scheme and children's allowances.

Source: "Marsh Says Canada's Social Services Lag," *Victoria Daily Colonist*, 17 May 1944, 7. Reprinted by kind permission of the Times Colonist, Victoria.

defined as "the realization that in a civilized society, there is a certain minimum of conditions without which health, decency, happiness, and a 'chance in life' are impossible." According to Marsh, social security programs were the means by which a social minimum could be established. This minimum, which would have to be set by Canadians, would have as its aim the prevention of poverty.

The Marsh Report was hailed as "the single most important document in the development of the post-war social security system in Canada" (Collins, 1976, 5). However, Marsh's recommendation for a comprehensive and coordinated social security system was virtually ignored by the Canadian government. Marsh's document nevertheless provided the structural plan for Canada's future social security system and paved the way for the development of family allowances (Guest, 1988; Canada, 1994d).

FAMILY ALLOWANCES ACT OF 1944

According to Marsh (1943, 197), the purpose of family allowance legislation was to ensure a minimum income level for Canadian families and, in so doing, "[make a] direct attack on poverty where it is bound up with the strain imposed by a large family on a small income." It was also thought that family allowances would solve the growing problems of poor nutrition and high infant mortality revealed in Depression-era and wartime studies.

Even though its passage required a constitutional amendment, the Family Allowances Act was pushed through Parliament and implemented in 1944. The federally administered program redistributed government revenue to all Canadian mothers who had dependents under age 16. Because the allowance was universal, recipients did not have to prove need or submit to a means test. In its first year of operation, the program cost taxpayers about $250 million, which was until then the most spent on any social security program (Bellamy, 1965; Guest, 1988).

OLD AGE SECURITY ACT OF 1951

The Old Age Pensions Act had been criticized for many years because of its stigmatizing means test and inadequate benefits. In 1951, the act was replaced with two new pension plans: (1) Old Age Security, which provided universal benefits and was fully funded and administered by the federal government; and (2) Old Age Assistance, a means-tested, cost-shared scheme that was paid for by the provincial and federal governments and administered by the provinces. Once again, the federal government had to seek a constitutional amendment before Parliament could legally pass the acts creating these two plans (Guest, 1980; Moscovitch and Drover, 1987; Morgan, 1961).

CANADA'S WELFARE STATE

From the end of World War II to the early 1970s, government departments steadily assumed much of the responsibility for social welfare that private charitable organizations had once enjoyed. This shift represented a movement away from a residual to a more institutional approach to social welfare, creating what is referred to as Canada's **welfare state**. Central to the concept of the welfare state is the recognition that not all opportunities, benefits, and materials in capitalist countries are equally distributed among the general population. Thus, governments have used their power to redistribute income in order to "share the wealth" and prevent large segments of the population from living in poverty (Head, 1984).

The use of redistributive mechanisms was greatly influenced by the British economist John Maynard Keynes, who believed that income-security programs would serve a "pump-priming" function. The inability of low-income families to buy many goods and services, Keynes argued, contributed to a slowing down of the economy. He believed that government-provided cash benefits would encourage low-income earners to spend more money, which would in turn help stimulate the economy. Canada was one of the first countries in the world to adopt the principles of **Keynesian economics**. For almost three decades, these principles were used to justify high levels of government spending with the goal of stabilizing income and consumerism during economic recessions (Bellemare, 1993; Mishra, 1981).

Although income redistribution became a more acceptable practice, Canada never abandoned its capitalist values or practices. Thus, Canada's welfare state has evolved in the context of a mixed capitalist system in which both government and the private market continue to play a role in deciding how resources are produced and distributed (McGilly, 1990).

The original plan for the welfare state in Canada was the establishment "of a set of universal social programs that would protect all citizens from the insecurities inherent in an industrial economy and, more generally, assist them in participating effectively in a modern society" (Banting, 1987a, 148). What in fact developed in Canada was a government system that provided only partial income security to working people and more extensive support to those outside of the labour market, such as seniors and children (Ross, 1987).

IV. FROM PROSPERITY TO DECLINE: SOCIAL WELFARE FROM 1960 TO THE MID-1970S

CANADA/QUEBEC PENSION PLANS

In 1965, the introduction of the Canada Pension Plan (CPP) and its counterpart, the Quebec Pension Plan (QPP), provided a first line of defence for paid workers and their families who suffered a loss of income due to retirement, disability, or death. Although the CPP/QPP was available to 92 percent of the paid labour force when it was first implemented, it was expected to be most beneficial to the many workers who did not have access to employer-sponsored pension plans. Although the CPP and QPP were different in some ways, they had similar eligibility criteria and benefit levels. Both plans were also compulsory social insurance schemes that required persons between the ages of 18 and 70 to make contributions as long as they were in the workforce. Originally, CPP/QPP benefits were available only to those who made more than $600 a year (or $800 a year for the self-employed). Excluded from the plans were housewives, those who had never been employed, and the chronically unemployed (Oderkirk, 1996; Guest, 1980).

Along with the Old Age Security pension plan, the CPP/QPP confirmed the federal government's responsibility for the care and security of elderly Canadians. These plans also took the retirement income system one step closer to ensuring a social minimum for seniors. Although there are many unique features of the CPP/QPP, its historical significance lies in the fact that it was the first income-security program to be fully indexed (i.e., automatically increases as the cost of living rises). Prior to the CPP/QPP, any increases in benefits for income-security programs (such as Old Age Security) had to be authorized by Parliament or provincial legislatures (Guest, 1980; Oderkirk, 1996).

CANADA ASSISTANCE PLAN OF 1966

Prior to the enactment of the Canada Assistance Plan (CAP) in 1966, the provinces were constitutionally responsible for establishing social welfare programs; however, the poorer provinces could not always afford to carry out this obligation. Guest (1980, 7–8) notes: "The impasse that developed because of the incongruity between legislative responsibility and financial capability was one reason for the delay in the establishment of vital programmes of social security in Canada." The introduction of CAP and increased federal aid enabled provinces and territories to expand, integrate, and improve their social welfare programs and "build what would become Canada's social safety net" (Canada, 1994e, 3). A minimum standard of living for low-income groups, regardless of the cause of their need, was thus ensured.

Under CAP, the provinces were required to meet certain standards but were allowed to design and administer social assistance and personal social services, determine their own eligibility rules, set benefit levels, and legislate the development and maintenance of these programs within those standards. In return, the federal government would pay 50 percent of their costs. Social assistance recipients received financial aid to meet basic living needs, including food, clothing, shelter, utilities, and personal needs; in some cases, assistance was also available for transportation, day care, and uninsured health needs such as dental and eye care. Under original CAP provisions, the personal social services were classified as welfare services and were part of an overall strategy to lessen, remove, or prevent the causes and effects of poverty, child neglect, and dependence on social assistance. Welfare services included protection services for children, rehabilitation programs, home support for seniors and people with disabilities, employment programs, community development services, and child care (Canada, 1994e).

THE WAR ON POVERTY

Several events during the early 1960s motivated Prime Minister Lester B. Pearson to introduce a plan to eliminate poverty in Canada. These events included an increasing awareness of poverty, the U.S. government's declaration of war on poverty in that country, and the development of new methods to measure poverty (Johnson, 1987). The prime minister's announcement paved the way for several studies. One, by the Economic Council of Canada (1968, 1), concluded:

> Poverty in Canada is real. Its numbers are not in the thousands, but the millions. There is more of it than our society can tolerate, more than the economy can afford, and far more than existing measures and efforts can cope with. Its persistence, at a time when the bulk of Canadians enjoy one of the highest standards of living in the world, is a disgrace.

Also in 1968, the Senate Committee on Poverty (chaired by Senator David Croll) was appointed to inquire into the problem of poverty in Canada and recommend necessary policy changes. In 1969, the committee reported that one in four Canadians lived below the poverty line. Of particular concern to the committee were the approximately two million Canadians who in

1967 constituted the "working poor"—that is, people whose earnings from employment were not enough to lift them out of poverty. To win the **war on poverty**, the committee suggested that the federal government scrap existing poverty-oriented programs and introduce a federally funded and administered guaranteed annual income (Guest, 1980, 1999).

GUARANTEED ANNUAL INCOME

Based on the ideas of American economists George Stigler and Milton Friedman, a **guaranteed annual income** (GAI) implies that all citizens have the right to a minimum income either as the result of paid work or government subsidies (Canadian Council on Social Development, 1969). According to Djao (1983), a GAI is not a specific income-security program as much as it is a "social goal." If all the provinces adopted a GAI scheme, Canadians would be assured a minimum income based on marital status, number of children, financial resources, age, and geographic location.

Although the Canadian government flirted with the idea of a GAI, a nationwide plan never materialized in Canada. However, several provinces implemented variations of a GAI for seniors who were already receiving the federally funded Old Age Security and Guaranteed Income Supplement. For example, in 1974 Ontario introduced the Guaranteed Annual Income System (GAINS) to ensure a basic income for residents aged 65 and older; the level of benefit depended on how much the recipient needed to live above the poverty line. For beneficiaries of Old Age Security and the Guaranteed Income Supplement, British Columbia introduced the Seniors Supplement to raise their income to the guaranteed level. Similarly, in 1973 Nova Scotia implemented a guaranteed income for seniors through the Special Social Assistance program. Perhaps the most extensive GAI experiment to take place in Canada was MINCOME, a project piloted in Manitoba (see Exhibit 2.4).

SOCIAL MOVEMENTS: SHAKING ESTABLISHED FOUNDATIONS

In the early 1960s, Canada and other Western countries witnessed a flurry of social movements—including the women's movement, the environmental movement, the gay rights movement, and the peace movement—that significantly challenged the status quo. A growing social conscience and sense of collective responsibility for one's fellow human beings found expression in mass demonstrations and protests. Although interested in changing government policies and practices, these social movements were perhaps most intent on changing social values that ultimately oppressed, demoralized, and marginalized people (Smith, 2000; Howlett, 1992).

Exhibit 2.4

MINCOME: MANITOBA'S GUARANTEED INCOME PROJECT

Inspired by American guaranteed income experiments in the late 1960s, the Canadian government offered to pay 75 percent of the costs to any province that would pilot a guaranteed annual income (GAI) program. Only Manitoba was interested in such an undertaking: on June 4, 1974, the federal government and Manitoba signed an agreement and MINCOME (Manitoba Basic Annual Income Experiment) became Canada's "first ever large-scale social experiment in Canada" (Hum, 1985, 38). MINCOME's primary aim was "to evaluate work responses of employable recipients under a guaranteed income" (Canada, 1994d, 32).

With over $17 million of federal money, MINCOME provided an income supplement to over 1000 families from 1975 to 1978 (Hum, 1985). MINCOME benefits were based on a negative income tax method and were reduced ("taxed back") if other income was earned. However, families never received less than the guaranteed annual amount.

Theoretically, a GAI could eliminate poverty yet not reduce the motivation of participants to find and keep work (Hum and Simpson, 1993). However, in reality, analysts found that the "labour market participation did not increase as might have been hoped" (Canada, 1994d, 32).

By 1977, Canada's interest in a GAI had waned and efforts to establish ongoing GAI programs were postponed indefinitely. Nevertheless, the reports on MINCOME provided useful technical and policy data that could be used for future reconsiderations of a national GAI (Djao, 1983).

Among the many social movements of the 1960s, the women's (or feminist) movement was especially effective in influencing social policy. Arguing that "the personal is political," women politicized a variety of issues—for example, family violence—that had been formerly regarded as the exclusive responsibility of individuals and families (Smith, 2000). A primary goal of the women's movement was to eliminate sexism in all areas of human endeavour, including the media, law, education, religion, and science, and to break down established patriarchal power structures that served to oppress and control women (Eichler and Lavigne, 1999; Armitage, 1996). Among the many inroads attributed to the women's movement were changes made to policies and programs related to sexual assault, family violence, employment, income security, and family law (see Exhibit 2.5).

Exhibit 2.5

SELECTED ACHIEVEMENTS OF THE WOMEN'S MOVEMENT, 1969–1995

1969	Women gain legal access to information on birth control and the use of contraceptives.
1971	The Canada Labour Code is amended to give maternity leave to female federal government employees.
1974	Women become eligible for enlistment in the RCMP.
1977	The Canadian Human Rights Act forbids discrimination on the basis of gender and ensures equal pay for equal work.
1979	Women are admitted to Canada's military colleges.
1982	Women's equality rights are entrenched in the Canadian Charter of Rights and Freedoms.
1983	The Canadian Human Rights Act is amended to include provisions on sexual harassment and to ban discrimination on the basis of pregnancy and marital status.
1985	The Spouse's Allowance is extended to widows and widowers aged 60 to 64.
	The Indian Act is amended to restore the status and property rights of Aboriginal women.
1986	The Employment Equity Act, which aims to ensure an equitable participation of women in the workforce, is passed.
1988	The federal government establishes the Women at Risk Program to address the needs of disadvantaged refugee women.
1989	Women are given the right to participate in all trades and occupations in the Canadian forces (except submarine duty).
1993	Stalking becomes a criminal offence.
1995	Intoxication in crimes of violence (including sexual assault) is removed as a basis of legal defence.
	Canada releases its *Federal Plan for Gender Equality*.

Source: Status of Women Canada (1995), *The Royal Commission on the Status of Women: An Overview 25 Years Later*; and *Setting the Stage for the Next Century: The Federal Plan for Gender Equality*, Ottawa, ON.

THE SOCIAL SECURITY REVIEW OF 1973 TO 1976

In January 1973, Prime Minister Trudeau and his Liberal Cabinet called for a federal/provincial review of Canada's social security system. The Social Security Review was launched to design an effective income support and supplement scheme. A secondary objective was "to free personal social services from their residual straight-jacket and move them towards a modern, institutional response to the human problems of urban-industrial society" (Guest, 1980, 187).

Several changes in social welfare programs resulted from the Social Security Review. For example, the review paved the way for Saskatchewan's Family Income Plan (1974), the federal government's Refundable Child Tax Credit (1978), and Manitoba's Income Support Program (1980). In addition, family allowance benefits tripled (from an average of $7.21 to $20.00 a month per child) and were indexed to the consumer price index.

Despite some positive influence on social welfare programs, the Social Security Review was criticized for doing little to correct the problem of low or inconsistent earnings among the working poor and for failing to implement a nationwide GAI. Improvements to Canada's social welfare system were also hindered by a stagnating economy. Moreover, Canadians began questioning the value of social security reforms such as those outlined in the review, given the rising inflation and unemployment rates and a generally unpredictable economy (Guest, 1980; Johnson, 1987).

SHIFTING OF THE TIDE

The first half of the 1970s was characterized by continued growth in social welfare programs; however, this trend had reversed itself by the middle of the decade. Social welfare programs that had once been championed by Canadians were now being questioned on a number of counts. For example, the social welfare system was seen as

> so expensive that costs of social policy were themselves posing a threat to individuals' economic security. It was ineffective, generally in providing high standards of service and particularly in making inroads into the gross inequalities of market-oriented societies. And it was dangerous, threatening to pursue welfare at the expense of individual liberty. (Heclo, 1981, 400)

Keynesian economics was blamed for aggravating rather than stabilizing economic fluctuations; its continued application was further hindered by the problems created by persistent government deficits and a general public dissatisfaction with government spending (Wirick, 1999). In the few years following the Social Security Review, Canada's welfare state entered a new era of dismantlement as neoconservative values, priorities, and policies resulted in the reduction, freezing, or elimination of many social welfare programs (Guest, 1980).

Introduction

A formal social welfare system did not take shape until the middle of the 20th century, when governments were pressured to develop methods of ensuring a higher standard of living for Canadians. The 1960s was a period of rapid expansion of social welfare; by the mid-1970s, this growth had waned considerably.

Early Contributions to Social Welfare

In Canada's colonial era, the French Roman Catholic missionaries tended to needy children and worked to "civilize" Aboriginal people. The British brought to Canada the English Poor Laws, which classified the poor as "worthy" or "unworthy." These laws influenced the government's treatment of Aboriginal people, who were viewed as inferior and placed on reserves. The Constitution Act of 1867 assigned responsibility for social welfare to the provincial governments.

The 1870s to the 1920s: An Experiment with Social Policy

The late 19th and early 20th centuries witnessed a wave of social movements in Canada as governments established a wider range of programs for the poor and needy. Industrialization sparked labour reform, the formation of unions, and the passage of workers' compensation legislation. The introduction of veterans' pensions marked greater government involvement in social welfare. Conditions for women, children, and seniors improved as a result of mothers' allowances, child welfare legislation, and old age pensions.

The Impact of the Great Depression and World War II

Severe economic problems and massive unemployment motivated the federal government to introduce unemployment insurance in 1940. The Marsh Report of 1943 promoted the concepts of a social minimum and family allowances. Income security for seniors strengthened with the passage of the

Old Age Security and Old Age Assistance acts. A more institutional approach to social welfare that emerged in the postwar period led to the creation of Canada's welfare state.

From Prosperity to Decline: Social Welfare from 1960 to the Mid-1970s

Several major pieces of legislation, including the Canada and Quebec Pension Plans and the Canada Assistance Plan, were introduced in the mid-1960s. The war on poverty was accompanied by calls for income-security programs that would provide a minimum income to Canadians. Although the guaranteed annual income scheme failed, it paved the way for a number of GAI-type programs for seniors. The Social Security Review of 1973 led to changes in social welfare programs but did little to help the working poor. By the mid-1970s, Canadians' support for the welfare state was waning as a result of its expense and perceived ineffectiveness.

KEY TERMS

English Poor Laws 28
worthy poor 29
unworthy poor 29
social movements 30
public relief 36
welfare state 42
Keynesian economics 42
war on poverty 45
guaranteed annual income 45

CHAPTER 3

SOCIAL POLICY IN THE CANADIAN CONTEXT

• OBJECTIVES •

I. To explore aspects of Canada's economic and social environment and how they influence social policy and programs.

II. To examine the divisions of power between the federal, provincial, and territorial governments and the attempts the various governments have made to share responsibility for social policy.

III. To describe the policymaking procedure and how policies are amended or repealed.

IV. To consider the various participants in the policymaking process, such as elected officials, government bureaucrats, citizens, and interest groups.

V. To look at the role of values and ideology in social policy and how each is expressed in the political arena.

INTRODUCTION

It is not always evident why a review of the political system is necessary to the study of social welfare. However, as Wharf (1986, 103) points out, "The political system is ... architect, builder, and maintainer of the social welfare system." An important function of the political system is to determine **social policies**—that is, guidelines that are used for deciding which social programs will be available in Canada, to whom social programs and services will be targeted, and how they will be funded and delivered. The primary aim of social policies is to enhance the well-being of society through income-security measures and a variety of personal social services; the Employment Insurance Act, the Canada and Quebec Pension Plans, and the Child Sexual Abuse Initiative are examples of social policies that attempt to meet this aim.

Since World War II, Canadian governments have assumed a greater responsibility for the formation of social policy. In general terms, these responsibilities include the following:

1) *To help the less fortunate members of society meet their basic needs*. This function involves government intervention in the personal and economic lives of all citizens for the sake of the common good. Governments use their power to redistribute income—that is, they use the general tax system to move revenue from middle- and high-income earners to low-income earners.
2) *To assume certain roles that are normally fulfilled by the family and other social institutions when those systems break down*. Certain child welfare legislation, for example, authorizes government representatives to serve as guardians or "pseudo parents" for children who can no longer live with their natural parents.
3) *To define and reinforce widely held beliefs or values that are important to the development and maintenance of society*. These values include safety, economic security, employment, and adequate shelter. Thus, governments are involved in policymaking related to justice, law enforcement, employment benefits and services, housing, and other areas (Richards, 1997; Yelaja, 1987).

There has been a growing dissatisfaction with government involvement in social policy over the last two decades. Critics charge that governmental assumption of many of the traditional roles of family can "subvert family functions, destroy delicate and sustaining family connections, or control the form and style of family life" (Hartman and Laird, 1983, 48). Critics also promote the values of self-sufficiency and independence, challenging the paternalistic role of government. Canadians appear to be divided on the issue of government's role in social policy and of the extent to which government should be involved in people's lives. A poll conducted by Ekos Research Associates found that "close to equal proportions of the population want ... the federal government to do more and to do less" (Pal, 1998, 8). Grady, Howse, and Maxwell (1995, 37), on the other hand, maintain that Canadians generally "believe, down deep, that governments can and should fix things."

Social policies are the product of the following dynamic and interactive components:

1) *Environment*. Social policies are influenced by the local economic, social, and political environment.
2) *Power*. Power plays an important role in social policymaking in terms of who makes the decisions about the distribution and allocation of resources.
3) *Procedures*. Formal procedures govern the adoption of social policy and the passage of social legislation.

4) *Participants*. A broad spectrum of participants influence the policymaking process.
5) *Values and ideology*. People's values and ideology shape the content and direction of social policy.

This chapter explores the role of these five components in the context of social policymaking.

I. SOCIAL POLICY IN A CHANGING ECONOMIC AND SOCIAL ENVIRONMENT

CANADA'S NEW ECONOMY

Much of Canada's labour market has been concentrated in labour-intensive manufacturing for the last 100 years. However, as a result of free trade and other economic changes, Third World producers have expanded their manufacturing base, creating more competition between manufacturers. Canada's inability to compete with other countries on the world market has resulted in the shutdown of many Canadian manufacturing operations and the layoff of thousands of workers. At the same time, dwindling natural resources are causing serious setbacks and job losses in primary industries such as mining, logging, and fishing (Canada, 1994c; Grady Howse, and Maxwell, 1995).

Although there has been growth in the manufacturing of computer and electronic products (a 9.5 percent increase from 1998 to 1999), Canada continues to move from a primarily manufacturing economy to a service economy (Statistics Canada, 1999b). As a result of this shift, the labour force has become more polarized: at one end are unskilled, less-educated workers (often older workers or young adults); at the other end are highly skilled, well-educated persons. Whereas the former group is competing for a diminishing number of jobs, the latter group—most notably in the technology sector—is in great demand (Canada, 1994c, 1994f). This leaves the unskilled workers at highest risk of unemployment and a dependence on income-security programs.

Another trend in the new economy is the shift toward less permanent or part-time jobs that do not offer the security of medical, dental, pension, or other benefits. In 1996, 2.6 million people held part-time positions, compared with only 200,000 people in 1953. Although there has been a steady increase in the percentage of part-time workers employed in managerial and professional positions, most part-time workers are concentrated in low-paying sales and service positions that offer few benefits and little job security (Schellenberg, 1997).

TECHNOLOGICAL CHANGE

Rapid advances in technology have been a key influence on economic and social policy. These advances are largely responsible for reshaping the nature of work in Canada and other industrialized countries. Grady, Howse, and Maxwell (1995, 9–10) note:

> Lasers and remote-sensing equipment do the work of hard-rock miners. Computer-based systems replace the skilled trades in the manufacturing sector. Computer networks displace clerical and secretarial staff and blur the boundary between the plant floor and the front office. This has led to a dramatic shift in skill requirements and in the structure of occupations generally.

Louis Emmerij (1999) acknowledges that the new technologies are enabling workers to produce more with less effort. However, there is a concern that doing less work will mean more unemployment for over one-quarter of the labour force. Menzies (1997) notes that as a result of organizational restructuring and digital communications, more work can be contracted out. The computerization of work, says Menzies (4), is transforming many formerly good jobs "into bad jobs—McJobs—and turning secure full-time employment into insecure part-time and temporary work."

SOCIAL POLICY IN A FREE TRADE ZONE

Over the years, Canada has struck many **free trade agreements** with other countries, including the Canada–U.S. Free Trade Agreement (FTA) in 1988 and the North American Free Trade Agreement (NAFTA) between Canada, the United States, and Mexico in 1994. The result of these agreements is a huge free trade zone of almost 370 million people. Many economists and businesspeople have identified free trade as an essential tool for Canada's economic survival and therefore a way to preserve Canada's social programs. Reid (1992, 9) explains:

> Canada needs foreign markets for its natural resources, since the domestic demand is far too small to sustain current employment levels in this sector. A small country like Canada could never have a large manufacturing base without the ability to export the majority of its production abroad ... This access to foreign markets is the foundation of our prosperity, and without it our governments could not

> even begin to finance the wide variety of universal social programs that Canadians have come to expect.

Although free trade enjoys general support in business circles, some Canadians have voiced concerns about its negative impact on social programs. Two of those concerns (having to do with harmonization and privatization) are summarized below.

Harmonization of Social Programs

Canadian governments have traditionally subsidized many social and regional development programs across the country. Under NAFTA, however, the provision of grants may be considered unfair trade practices. To create a "level playing field" among trading partners, NAFTA requires participating countries to harmonize or otherwise bring their policies and programs in line with those of their trading partners. This means that Canada must reduce government subsidies so that its businesses and regions can compete in similar environments in the United States and Mexico (Spratt, 1992; Drover, 1992). Dillon (1996, 17) notes the changes made to Unemployment Insurance (UI) between 1989 and 1996 as the result of harmonization efforts:

> In 1989, the year the FTA took effect, 87% of the unemployed in Canada qualified for UI, while only about 52% of U.S. workers could collect unemployment benefits.... When the latest round of cuts by the Liberal government is fully implemented, only 40% of unemployed Canadians will qualify for what the Liberals now call "Employment Insurance."

Many social analysts suggest that as a result of free trade agreements, Canada's social programs will gradually look more and more like those in the United States. This trend is illustrated in Exhibit 3.1.

Further Privatization of Social Welfare Programs

Many Canadians fear that free trade will encourage more privatization of social welfare programs and services. The term **privatization** describes a process in which a government withdraws from the regulation, funding, and delivery of services. In the context of social welfare, privatization refers to the shifting of responsibility for meeting human needs to individuals and the private market or to nongovernment organizations that are either nonprofit or profit-making (Social Planning Council of Metropolitan Toronto, 1984). Under NAFTA, the trading partners expect to compete freely in the global market. Thus, "if a U.S. or Mexican company offers equivalent services at

EXHIBIT 3.1

CHANGES TO UNEMPLOYMENT INSURANCE COMPARED TO U.S. PRACTICE

	1989	1993 AFTER TWO CONSERVATIVE BILLS IN '90 & '93	AFTER 1994 LIBERAL BUDGET	AFTER DEC. 1995 LIBERAL POLICY TAKES EFFECT	MOST U.S. STATES
Percent of unemployed covered	87%	64%	49%	40%	1989 – 52% 1993 – 47% 1994 – 33%
Required period of insured employment	10–14 weeks*	14–20 weeks*	12–20 weeks*	420–700 hours (12–20 weeks) 910 hours for new entrants (26 weeks)	24 weeks
Maximum duration of benefits	40–50 weeks*	35–50 weeks*	14–50 weeks*	45 weeks	26 weeks
Benefit levels as percent of previous earnings	60%	57%	55% for most, 60% for low-income families	55% gradually falling to 50% for frequent users	36%

* depending on regional unemployment rate

Source: John Dillon, *Challenging Free Trade in Canada: The Real Story* (Ottawa: Canadian Centre for Policy Alternatives, 1996), 18. Copyright © 1996.

lower costs, it must be allowed to bid against governments (and Canadian firms) to provide these public services" (Clarke, 1992, 13). Wherever there is potential for foreign companies to make a profit—whether it be in nursing homes, day care, or drug and alcohol treatment—Canada is expected to support this private enterprise (Sanger, 1992).

Although trade between Canada and its American and Mexican partners has boomed in the last decade, it is difficult to assess the overall impact of free trade on Canadians. According to NDP trade critic Nelson Riis (Free trade evaluated, 1999), "some of the doomsday scenarios are just now starting to materialize." The implications of this assessment for social welfare remain to be seen.

GOVERNMENT'S RESPONSE TO THE NEW ECONOMY

To deal with the challenges stemming from the dramatic shifts in Canada's economy, social policymakers have in many respects merged social policy and economic policy. The idea of such a merger in Canada is not new. In 1967, the Quebec *Report of the Commission of Inquiry on Health and Social Welfare* recognized that it was "impossible to dissociate the social area of life from the economic area for there is a profound interdependence between these two fields of human activity" (Quebec, 1967, 19).

In its 1994 report, *Improving Social Security in Canada*, the federal government emphasized that "the key to dealing with social insecurity can be summed up in a single phrase: helping people get and keep jobs" (Canada, 1994c, 9). Governments across Canada have introduced initiatives that focus on improving people's economic lives and thereby reducing the need for social security programs. This trend is most evident in provinces where welfare-to-work programs have been implemented. Both Ontario and Alberta, for example, require able-bodied welfare recipients to participate in volunteer or work programs in exchange for welfare benefits. There is every indication that social welfare in the 21st century will emphasize programs that focus on economic growth, the generation of jobs, skill enhancement, and other activities that are work-related and designed to quickly move people from government-sponsored programs to economic independence.

DEMOGRAPHIC TRENDS AND THEIR IMPLICATIONS FOR SOCIAL POLICY

Social welfare policies and programs need to be sensitive to and reflect demographic trends, since these trends alert us to human needs and social problems. Social policies that were designed to meet Canadians' needs in the 1960s will not adequately address Canadians' needs in the 21st century for the simple reason that people and their environments continue to change (Courchene, 1987). Thus, social policies need to continually adjust to social and economic shifts and to reflect the needs created by an aging population and changes in family structure and roles, urbanization, and immigration patterns. The following is a brief discussion of each of these demographic trends and its implications for social policy.

An Aging Population

Canada has a declining birth rate and an **aging population**. There are 3.7 million people over the age of 65, more than double the figure 25 years ago. Exhibit 3.2 illustrates the projected shift in population from 1996 to 2021, at which time seniors are expected to make up 18 percent of the population; by 2041, this figure is expected to rise to 23 percent. As more and more baby boomers enter their senior years, governments will be faced with increased demand for pension benefits, medical and home care, nursing homes, and other social programs for seniors (Finance Canada, 2000a; Statistics Canada, 1999a; Lindsay, 1999).

Changing Family Structure and Roles

The economic and social challenges facing today's families indicate a greater need for appropriate and diverse social welfare programs. Some of the changes related to families, and their implications for social policy, are outlined below:

- *Increase in the number of single-parent families*. Between 1991 and 1996, the number of single-parent (mostly female-led) families increased at four times the rate for two-parent families. In addition to affordable child care, this group requires job training programs and strategies that address the problems of poverty, hunger, homelessness, and social isolation.
- *Changing definitions of "family."* Recent legislation gives same-sex partners rights and obligations similar to those extended to common-law couples. Same-sex legislation will have implications for a number of social policies and programs, including those relating to adoption, pensions, and immigration (Ayed, 2000).
- *Care for the elderly.* As a result of the rising costs of institutional care, more and more family members (mostly adult daughters) are caring for elderly relatives in the home. This trend will increase the need for programs that support caregivers, including adult day care, home support services, and respite services.

EXHIBIT 3.2

CANADA'S AGING POPULATION

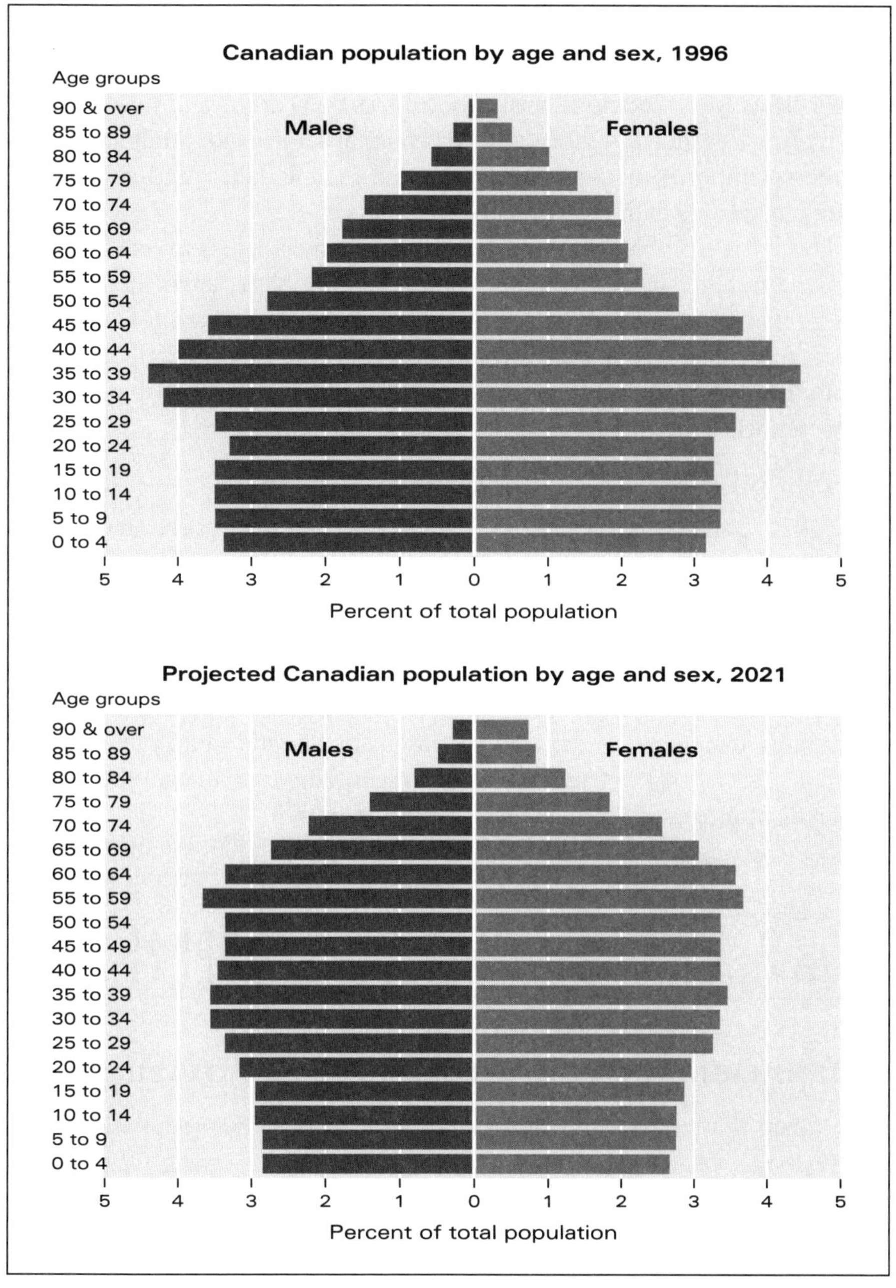

Source: "An Aging Population," from *Canada's Seniors ... At a Glance* poster (Ottawa, 1998), prepared by the Canadian Council on Social Development for the Division of Aging and Seniors, Health Canada. Poster © 1998. Reprinted with permission by Division of Aging and Seniors.

Urbanization

More than 75 percent of Canadians live in urban areas, up from 60 percent at the end of World War II (Zapotochny, 1999). Exhibit 3.3 illustrates the continuation of the increase in **urbanization** in the 1990s. While there are certain economic benefits associated with moving to the city, there is often a social cost as well. Growing social problems such as crime and racial tension may require expanded policing and correctional services for adult and youth offenders, support programs for victims and their families, and counselling services for people with stress-related disorders.

Poverty is a problem in the inner core of many cities. Between 1990 and 1995, the number of poor people living in metropolitan areas increased by 33.8 percent, compared with 18.2 percent in nonmetropolitan areas (Canadian Council on Social Development, 2000a). Progressive social policies are needed to address an increased demand for social housing, shelters for the homeless, and food banks.

Population Shifts and Immigration Patterns

Since 1970, Canada's fertility rate (i.e., the average number of children born to a woman during her lifetime) has been well below the replacement level of 2.1. It is estimated that to offset this low birth rate and loss of population through death and emigration, Canada needs to admit one million immigrants per year (Trempe, Davis, and Kunin, 1997). Immigration influences the type and range of social welfare programs. For example, a growing number of immigrants increases the demand for linguistically and culturally sensitive health and social services, as well as settlement, language, mental-health, and employment programs (Weinfeld and Wilkinson, 1999).

II. DIVISIONS OF POWER: FEDERAL, PROVINCIAL, AND TERRITORIAL RELATIONS

FEDERALISM AND CONSTITUTIONAL PROVISIONS

Federalism is a mechanism that divides political power between national and regional (i.e., provincial and territorial) governments. Irving (1987, 327) describes a federal system as "one that provides for a sense of overall unity while allowing for local or provincial autonomy in certain matters; therefore, in a federal structure, there will be independent central and regional governments each with its own defined areas of jurisdiction." Countries that prefer federalism to other political systems tend to be geographically large and to have a

EXHIBIT 3.3

URBAN AND RURAL CENSUS POPULATION, 1991 and 1996

	Urban population		Rural population		Urban percentage of population		Rural percentage of population	
Province/territory	1991	1996	1991	1996	1991	1996	1991	1996
Newfoundland	304,451	313,819	264,023	237,973	53.6	56.9	46.4	43.1
Prince Edward Island*	51,813	59,460	77,952	75,097	39.9	44.2	60.1	55.8
Nova Scotia	481,508	497,858	418,434	411,424	53.5	54.8	46.5	45.2
New Brunswick*	345,214	360,421	378,686	377,712	47.7	48.8	52.3	51.2
Quebec*	5,351,211	5,597,625	1,544,752	1,541,170	77.6	78.4	22.4	21.6
Ontario*	8,253,842	8,958,741	1,831,043	1,794,832	81.8	83.3	18.2	16.7
Manitoba*	787,175	800,063	304,767	313,835	72.1	71.8	27.9	28.2
Saskatchewan*	623,397	627,178	365,531	363,059	63.0	63.3	37.0	36.7
Alberta*	2,030,893	2,142,815	514,660	554,011	79.8	79.5	20.2	20.5
British Columbia*	2,640,961	3,057,388	641,100	667,112	80.5	82.1	19.5	17.9
Yukon	16,355	18,477	11,462	12,319	58.8	60	41.2	40
Northwest Territories	21,157	27,395	36,492	37,007	36.7	42.5	63.3	57.5
Canada*	**20,907,957**	**22,461,210**	**6,388,902**	**6,385,551**	**76.6**	**77.9**	**23.4**	**22.1**

* excludes some Indian reserves

Source: J. Zapotochny (Ed.), *Scott's Canadian Sourcebook 2000* (Don Mills: Southam Information Products Group, 1999), a Southam publication © 1999, pp. 4–5.

population that is characterized by considerable religious, ethnic, cultural, language, and economic diversity (Khan, McNiven, and MacKown, 1977).

In Canada, federalism originated with the Constitution Act of 1867 (originally the British North America Act). The Constitution divides power between the federal and provincial governments and gives each level its own sources of revenue and the authority to pass certain laws. The responsibilities related to social welfare are outlined in sections 91 and 92 of the Constitution Act: section 91 gives the federal government jurisdiction over unemployment insurance, quarantine and marine hospitals, penitentiaries, Indians, and reservations; section 92 makes the provincial governments responsible for building and managing hospitals and asylums, charities, and public or reformatory prisons. Clearly, the Constitution Act intended for the federal government to play a minor role in social welfare, with the provinces given the bulk of responsibility for delivering and funding social welfare programs (Bellamy, 1965).

SHIFTING RESPONSIBILITIES

Over time, the federal and provincial governments have relinquished many of their separate social welfare responsibilities to each other. Pierre Elliott Trudeau, Canada's prime minister from 1968 to 1985, wrote in 1961 that the two levels of government have assumed or relinquished certain responsibilities in order to achieve social objectives. This exchange reflects

> sometimes subtle, sometimes brazen, and usually tolerated encroachments by one government upon the jurisdiction of the other ... In short, it almost seems as though whenever an important segment of the Canadian population needs something badly enough, it is eventually given to them by one level of government or the other, regardless of the constitution. (382)

The result of this intergovernmental exchange of power and responsibility is what Banting (1987b, 58) refers to as an increasingly "bifurcated welfare state." That is, the original lines separating federal and provincial powers have become blurred, making social welfare a shared responsibility between the two levels of government. Programs for parents and their children provide an example of this shared responsibility: the federal government (specifically Health Canada) sponsors Nobody's Perfect and Community Action Programs for Children, while each province has its own range of programs directed to parents and children, including family support, child protection, and adoption services.

The limited financial ability of the provinces to fund social programs hastened the development of federal–provincial partnerships. When the Constitution Act was drafted in 1867, social welfare matters seemed insignificant and potentially inexpensive since Canada had a relatively small, rural, and self-sufficient population. It seemed that whatever personal difficulties people encountered could be adequately addressed by family, neighbours, churches, charities, or municipal government. It was also the intent of the Fathers of Confederation to delegate the less important and least costly functions to the provinces. However, the problems created by the Industrial Revolution, urbanization, immigration, and other historical events soon made the need for an expanded social welfare system obvious. Social programs rapidly became more important and costly. At the same time, the provinces realized that although they had jurisdiction to provide these programs, they were financially unable to develop them fully. This set the stage for the establishment of cost-sharing arrangements between the federal and regional governments (Guest, 1988; Wallace, 1950; Irving, 1987).

Other reasons the federal government has traditionally sought increased power over social welfare matters, particularly in the area of income security, include the following:

- *Equitable income and services.* In times of widespread need, the federal government is in a better position to redistribute resources from the rich provinces to the poorer provinces. Federal involvement can ensure that social welfare programs are provided in a consistent and equitable manner regardless of the economic state of the province.
- *Sense of national solidarity.* The provision of income-security benefits can contribute to nation-building, to a sense of national unity, and to a general feeling of belonging.
- *Portability of benefits.* To encourage Canadians to move freely across the country, the federal government can ensure that the benefits received in one region are consistent with those available in another region.
- *Economic stability.* The federal government is already responsible for the country's economic policies. Thus, it makes sense that this level of government should also control income-security measures, since they affect the buying and selling of goods and services.
- *Federal visibility.* Actions taken at the federal level—including social welfare provision—can reinforce people's awareness of the federal government and the role it plays in the lives of Canadians (Mishra, 1995; Armitage, 1996).

PROVINCIAL RESISTANCE TO FEDERAL INVOLVEMENT

Canada's federal system has been criticized for inhibiting social policy and the development of social welfare programs and services. Irving (1987, 326) observes: "No other factor, except the nature of capitalism itself, has had such an impact on the evolution of social welfare policy in this country as has the nature of Canadian federalism." The divided power in Canada's system creates what Banting (1985, 49) calls a "form of institutional fragmentation" that limits the government's capacity to introduce new policies. In short, the greater the extent to which political power is dispersed across the country and among different levels of government, the less likely it is that a consensus on policy decisions can be reached.

Traditionally, efforts made by the federal government to develop or revise social policy have been received by the provinces and territories as an unwelcome encroachment in areas that are rightfully (and constitutionally) their domain. One reason behind the regions' reluctance to encourage federal inroads into social welfare is the awareness of the distinct geographical, cultural, linguistic, and social needs of the people in each province and territory. The regional governments maintain that they can best meet these needs by developing their own social welfare programs and services, albeit with continued financial assistance from the federal government (Mishra, 1995; Armitage, 1996).

ATTEMPTS AT CONSTITUTIONAL CHANGE

A large part of Canadian social policy has been shaped by a series of constitutional negotiations. The first of these negotiations culminated in the British North America Act of 1867, an act of the British Parliament. Another significant federal–provincial negotiation took place in 1982 when Canada's Constitution was patriated, giving the Canadian government sole control over constitutional amendments. Quebec nevertheless disagreed with the terms concerning the amending formula and extent of federal powers and refused to sign the document.

Over the years, some provinces have expressed discontent with certain clauses of the Canadian Constitution. The Meech Lake Accord (1987) and the Charlottetown Accord (1992) attempted to amend the Constitution to the satisfaction of Quebec and the rest of Canada. Quebec sought the status of a "distinct society" and the right to develop French-Canadian culture within that province. Since social policy is central to the preservation of the French language and culture, Quebec maintained that social policy should be a provincial rather than federal responsibility. Although both accords failed to fully satisfy Quebec and the other provinces, they had important implications for the direction of social policy. The Charlottetown Accord is particularly noteworthy for the development of the Canadian Unity Agreement, which reinforced the commitment of Canadian governments to preserve major social programs. For example, it was agreed that social welfare programs must "ensure that all individuals resident in Canada have reasonable access to housing, food and other basic necessities" (Canada, 1992b, 3).

CANADA'S SOCIAL UNION

In 1995, the federal government announced that beginning in 1996 a new funding arrangement (the Canada Health and Social Transfer) would replace the Canada Assistance Plan. The federal government invited all provincial and territorial governments "to work together on developing, through mutual consent, a set of shared principles and objectives that could underlie the new transfer" (Canada, 1995a, 13). In 1996, the federal government and a representative from each territory and province (except Quebec) formed the Federal-Provincial-Territorial Council on Social Policy Renewal. While the Province of Quebec supported many of the principles of social policy renewal, Premier Bouchard refused to sign the social union accord since it represented federal intrusion into a provincial jurisdiction (Quebec rejects social union, 1999).

What is termed the **social union** emerged from the work of the Council on Social Policy Renewal. The social union is an umbrella under which Canadian governments at all levels aim to renew and modernize health and social policy. Focusing on the connection between social and economic policies, the social union recognizes that cooperation and collaboration among governments at all levels is critical for the reform and strengthening of Canada's social programs. Under the social union banner, the governments have agreed to engage in joint planning, consultation, and respectful deliberations to improve the social and economic lives of Canadians (Standing Committee on Human Resources, 2000).

On February 4, 1999, Canadian governments signed the Framework to Improve the Social Union for Canadians (see Appendix B), a document that outlines the principles and commitments that will guide future developments in social programming. A full review of the framework is scheduled to take place in 2002, by which time Canadians will have had an opportunity to offer their opinions about the framework, its effects, and how it might be improved.

III. SOCIAL POLICYMAKING PROCEDURES

AGREEMENTS AND LAWS

There are different methods used to create and sanction social policies. For example, social policy can be the result of a mutual agreement between members of government, such as the social union. Social policies can also result from the more complicated process of enacting laws or legislation. At the federal level, social policy proposals are introduced as **bills** to either the House of Commons (most commonly) or the Senate. There are two types of bills: (1) public bills, which are introduced by a Cabinet minister or a member of Parliament; and (2) private bills, which are often in the form of a petition presented by a private citizen or representative from an interest group. All bills are carefully reviewed to ensure that they meet all technical and legal requirements and that they can be supported financially if passed into law. Bills are then given three readings by both the House of Commons and the Senate; if the bill passes in both houses, it is approved by the governor general and becomes a law (also called an "act" or "statute"). (See Exhibit 3.4 for a more detailed illustration of this process.) At the provincial level, bills are reviewed and given three readings by the provincial legislature. If approved, a bill is signed by the lieutenant governor and passed as law (Privy Council Office, 1999a).

THE WAITING GAME: FROM PROPOSAL TO ENACTMENT

It is not uncommon for several months or years to pass between the proposal of a bill and its actual enactment. The bill, which must pass through many stages before it becomes law, may be slowed down as a result of opposition by members of Parliament (Canadian law provides for several "opposition days" to allow the official Opposition to criticize and debate the details of a proposed bill). A bill's enactment might also be delayed so that public and nongovernment lobby groups have adequate time to further debate, deliberate, and negotiate the content and direction of the proposed policy. As a result of these types of delays, the implementation of new social programs may be well overdue by the time social policies are legally sanctioned.

AMENDING AND REPEALING SOCIAL POLICIES

The passage of an act does not always guarantee its permanency; the statute may be amended or repealed altogether. For example, Bill C-21, introduced in 1990, severely amended the Unemployment Insurance Act. Among other

EXHIBIT 3.4

HOW A LAW IS PASSED IN THE HOUSE OF COMMONS AND SENATE

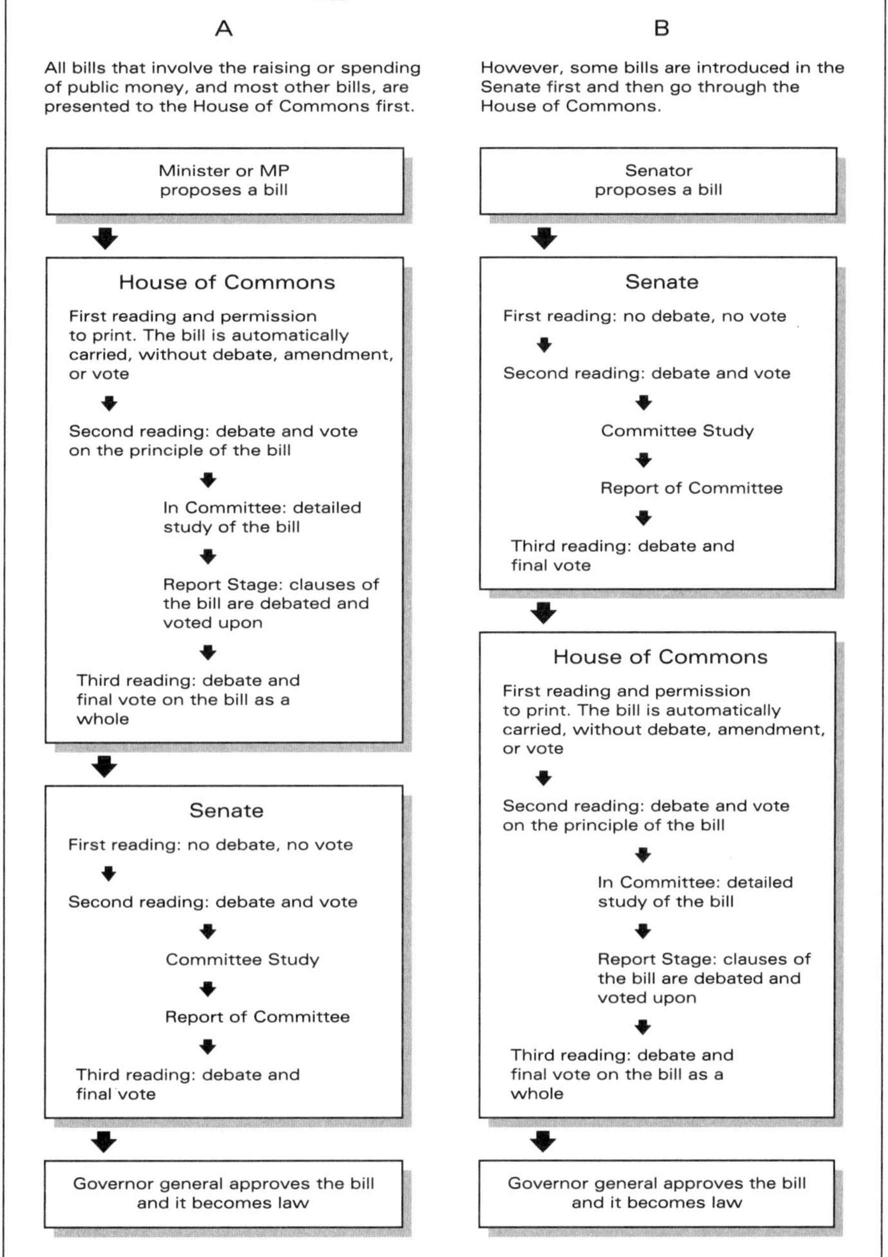

Source: From *The Canadian Citizen*, 1994, p. 18, published by Citizenship & Immigration Canada. Reproduced with the permission of the Minister of Public Works and Government Services Canada, 2000.

things, these amendments paved the way for the federal government to terminate its financial support, introduce more restrictive eligibility criteria, shorten benefit periods, and raise premium rates.

The elimination of the Canada Assistance Plan (CAP) in 1996 is an example of how governments can eliminate an entire piece of legislation. In 1995, the enactment of the Budget Implementation Act gave the federal government the power to repeal CAP and replace it with a new cost-sharing arrangement (the Canada Health and Social Transfer) between the federal and regional governments.

In many cases, the federal government will seek consultation with Canadian individuals, groups, and organizations before implementing major changes to existing social programs. Such was the case in 1994, when the Minister of Human Resources Development proposed a plan to overhaul Canada's social security system. The reform process that took place is outlined in Exhibit 3.5.

IV. PARTICIPANTS IN THE POLICYMAKING PROCESS

THE POLICY COMMUNITY

Pross (1996) describes the interaction of various policymaking groups in terms of a "policy community" that is composed of several concentric rings and overlapping systems (see Exhibit 3.6). At the centre of the action are the federal government bodies (e.g., Cabinet and the Privy Council) that are ultimately responsible for enacting policy. Interest or pressure groups, provincial governments, and Parliament make up the next ring; also included here are federal departments that are not central to social policy but whose actions may greatly influence social policy decisions (e.g., the Department of Foreign Affairs and International Trade Canada). In the outermost ring are foreign governments that influence Canada's economic policies and therefore affect social policy. Each system involved in the policy community continuously interacts with and influences the others. In Canada, no single entity is consistently dominant in the social policymaking process.

THE GOVERNMENT

Elected Officials

The policymaking process—the stages through which policy is developed, implemented, and evaluated—is the primary responsibility of elected officials,

EXHIBIT 3.5

THE SOCIAL POLICY REFORM PROCESS

On January 31, 1994, Lloyd Axworthy, Minister of Human Resources Development, announced a process to reform Canada's social security system. The comprehensive process will involve individual Canadians, parliamentarians, provinces and territories, communities and organizations.

Development of action plan

- The Parliamentary Standing Committee on Human Resources Development has held public hearings on social security and job market concerns and has submitted an interim report.
- Federal/provincial/territorial officials are discussing issues of joint concern.
- Task Force has been advising the Minister on the development of the action plan.

The release of an action plan will give Canadians the information they need to reflect on the issues and discuss proposed solutions and options.

Consultation regarding action plan

- The Parliamentary Standing Committee will hold open hearings to allow individual Canadians as well as affected groups to discuss choices outlined in the action plan.

  The Standing Committee will submit a report to the House of Commons.

Individuals and groups will be given a wide range of opportunities to participate, such as:

- Members of Parliament receive input from constituents
- Interactive and educational television programs
- Workbook presenting the issues and options for reform is completed by individual Canadians
- 1-800 line
- Organized events and conferences

Input from all groups and individuals will be compiled and analyzed. Results will be discussed with provinces and territories so that legislation can be introduced to build the social security system that Canadians want.

Source: *The Process* (Ottawa, 1994), 1. Prepared by Strategic Communications, Human Resources Development Canada.

EXHIBIT 3.6

THE POLICY COMMUNITY

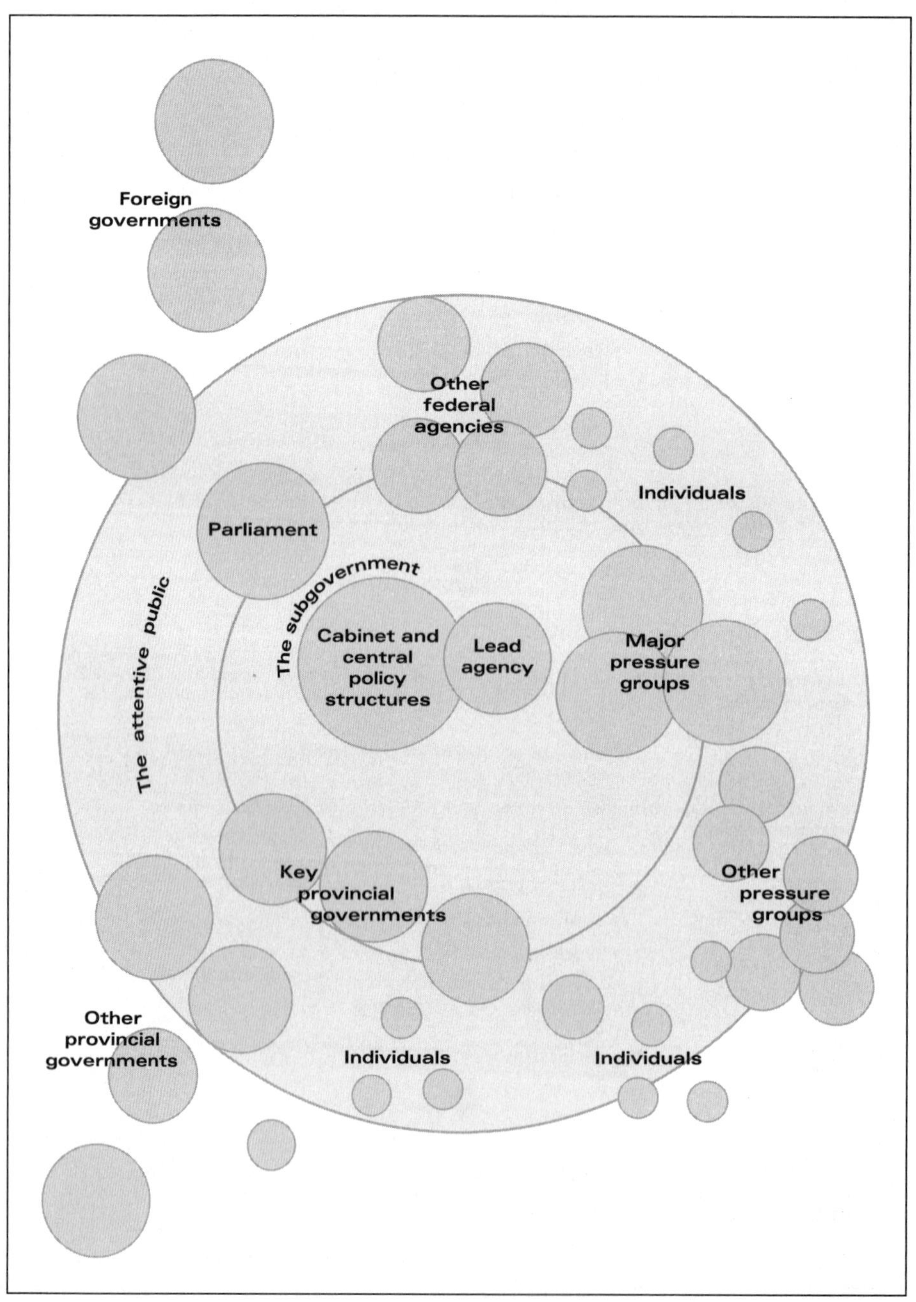

Source: A. Paul Pross, *Groups Politics and Public Policy* (Toronto: Oxford University Press, 1986). Copyright © Oxford University Press Canada 1986.

who are voted into office at the federal, provincial, territorial, and municipal levels. Federally, it is often the minister of a particular department and his or her departmental staff who identify the need for change in policies or laws, consult with others about the proposed solutions, analyze the resources needed to implement the solutions, and ensure that proposals reach the Cabinet for consideration.

Those elected to Parliament play an important role in the formulation stage of social policy. Expected "to represent the public and make decisions for the common good," elected officials must give adequate consideration to all public interests and present fair compromises to Parliament (Chung Yan, 1998, 39). Decisions made by politicians concerning publicly sponsored programs are limited by several political and legal factors. For example, rather than making decisions based on whim or personal bias, elected politicians must adhere to the rule of law. This law establishes the limits of the power that can be legally exercised by government officials and requires that these officials account to the public for how public resources are distributed. The extent of power exercised by government officials is also constrained by constitutional provisions such as the Canadian Charter of Rights and Freedoms, Aboriginal and treaty rights, and language rights for Quebec and Manitoba (Privy Council Office, 1999a).

Government Bureaucrats

Government bureaucrats are hired as public servants and work closely with elected officials. They are important participants in the policymaking process because they

- are often valuable consultants as to which policies may or may not be feasible, and how proposals might best be promoted;
- are typically in contact with both the minister and those who deliver social benefits or services and can therefore facilitate communication between the two levels and give feedback to each;
- can play the role of "reformists" who are able to identify the need for and initiate new policies;
- can pass along their knowledge about how to write policy proposals, draft bills, and prepare other documents that are required for consideration by the Cabinet; and
- play an important role in program design, identifying consumer needs, keeping costs in line with budgets, and otherwise translating policy into concrete programs (Mishra, 1995; Wharf, 1986; Splane, 1987).

Often, government bureaucrats hold their jobs longer than elected officials or appointed ministers, which makes them rich sources of historical information that can be passed along to elected officials.

THE ROLE OF NONGOVERNMENT GROUPS IN POLICYMAKING

Citizen Participation

Since 1968 and Pierre Trudeau's call for "participatory democracy," the Canadian public has developed a greater interest in the design and operation of social welfare programs. One result of this interest has been a trend toward **citizen participation**—a process by which citizens act in response to public concerns, voice their opinions about decisions that affect them, and take responsibility for changes to their community. Citizen participation has played a particularly important role in the development of social policy and programs. In 1969, the Canadian Council on Social Development (1969, 16) wrote:

> Social policies and programs are intended to meet the needs and serve the interests of the individual citizen, living in community with his fellow man. The citizen therefore has a legitimate interest in the objectives, content and effects of these policies and programs; their planning and their adaptation to changing circumstances will benefit from his active involvement. He himself will also benefit.

More recently, Turner (1998a, 8) emphasized the importance of citizen participation in matters concerning the social union: "Canada's success in developing a consensus about its social future depends upon fostering democratic participation and a shared sense of responsibility among its citizens."

There are many different types of citizen participation, including voting in democratic elections, participating in political party activities, making recommendations to government committees or commissions, holding public demonstrations, and lobbying.

Interest Groups

While elected government officials are responsible for moving policy proposals through legislative channels, interest or pressure groups play an important role in influencing social policy decisions. **Interest groups** are organized collectives that try to influence government policies for the benefit of their own members or on behalf of the general public. In Canada, there are five broad categories of interest groups:

1) business associations (e.g., Canadian Manufacturers' Association);
2) labour groups (e.g., Canadian Labour Congress);
3) professional associations (e.g., Canadian Association of Social Workers);
4) research institutes (e.g., Caledon Institute of Social Policy); and
5) advocacy groups and advisory councils (e.g., National Anti-Poverty Organization).

Interest groups generally emerge in support of important causes and compete with one another in the political arena. Although the ideas and opinions of all groups are considered to be equally valued, the degree to which any interest group is able to influence social policy decisions will often depend on how well it can access needed resources, set priorities, devise effective strategies, and form important alliances (Chung Yan, 1998).

Interest groups use a variety of strategies to pressure government to change existing policies, create new policies, or give more support to a specific program or group. Traditional strategies include collective bargaining, polling, disseminating information, meeting directly with policymakers, and publicizing issues and concerns through various media. More radical strategies may involve public rallies, protest fasts or marches, strikes, product or service boycotts, or sit-ins (i.e., the occupation of an adversary's space).

GOVERNMENT AND INTEREST GROUPS: SHIFTING ALLIANCES

For the last 30 years, governments have generally supported interest groups and their role in promoting and facilitating public discussion on a variety of topics. A panel brought together by the Conference Board of Canada in the early 1990s concluded that the efforts of these groups are a key element in a democratic society:

> The only legitimate way for government to develop policy is by accepting, even seeking, information and views from those affected and the public at large. Lobbyists present competing views, supply otherwise unavailable information, propose solutions, provide unique insight and counsel so government can assess the implications of proposed policy. (cited in Overton, 1991, 18)

Starting in the early 1950s, the federal government provided regular funding to many interest groups. Since the late 1980s, however, this funding has been tapering off. Federal funding today is restricted to short-term project grants that are awarded to a limited number of interest groups. Groups that have lost part or all of their funding as a result of fiscal-restraint measures include the National Action Committee on the Status of Women, the Canadian Council on Social Development, the National Anti-Poverty Organization, and the Child Care Advocacy Association. It has been suggested that by cutting funds to interest groups, the federal government may reduce the opposition it receives from these groups when making cuts to social programs. Cardozo (1996, 312) sums up this apparent trend: "If the voices of these critics could be muted, making cuts to the big ticket transfer programs would be easier."

V. THE ROLE OF VALUES AND IDEOLOGY IN SOCIAL POLICY

POLITICAL ELECTIONS: A VALUE-LADEN PROCESS

In a mixed society such as Canada, we can expect that a diverse group of participants will bring equally varied sets of values, beliefs, and expectations to the process of social policymaking. Dobell and Mansbridge (1986, 34) observe:

> Values, over and beyond the objective analysis of issues, play a major role in how governments and non-government groups act and make policy choices. This includes perceptions, intuition, and "visions for the future" as different sectors of society struggle to define the nature of community good.

One arena that highlights values and ideology is the democratic election process at the federal, regional, and municipal levels. Each party that campaigns in an election promotes itself as having a commitment to certain aspects of social welfare and suggests ways to improve social policy or programs. Most political parties in Canada support the *concept* of social welfare; however, the extent to which a party supports the public funding and administration of social welfare is influenced by its particular values, ideology, and political bias. For the most part, a party's platform will reflect conservative, liberal, or socialist principles (for a discussion of these principles, see Chapter 1).

Despite parties' claims of distinctiveness, their social welfare platforms usually overlap. According to Armitage (1996, 141):

> it is not possible to distinguish one political party, federally or provincially, as being exclusively the proponent of social welfare ideals while another is characterized exclusively by opposition. Instead, each party can rightfully claim to have made some contribution to building social welfare in the 1960s and 1970s, while in the 1980s and 1990s each has participated in dismantling and restraining costs.

The blurring of political boundaries has produced what Boothroyd (1991, 121) refers to as "ideological hybrids"; that is, over time it becomes more difficult to identify many real differences between the various political parties with respect to their ideas or values. The general pressure on governments to maintain good fiscal management has made it increasingly difficult to distinguish one party from the next. During the 1997 federal election, for example, all the major parties focused on strategies to reduce deficits and debt so that social programs would be affordable in the future. Mishra (1999, 13–14) observes that "parties of the centre or left can no longer offer social policies which differ substantially from those . . . on the right."

THE RISE OF NEOCONSERVATISM

The 1980s witnessed a dramatic increase in the popularity of **neoconservatism**. Neoconservative governments differ from liberal governments in some important ways. For example, neoconservative governments emphasize a residual approach to social welfare and selective rather than universal programs, while liberal governments tend to support universal social programs and an expansion of social welfare programs. Although liberal and neoconservative governments both recognize the importance of a decent standard of living for all citizens, neoconservatives are reluctant to accept responsibility for maintaining this standard (Prince, 1987; Bracken and Walmsley, 1992). The clash of values between neoconservative and liberal politicians is illustrated in Exhibit 3.7.

Popular support for the neoconservative ideology during the 1980s was evident in the elections of Margaret Thatcher in Britain and Ronald Reagan in the United States. In Canada, support for neoconservatism at the provincial level has been exemplified by the Conservative governments in Alberta (under Ralph Klein) and Ontario (under Mike Harris). At the federal level, the success of neoconservative principles was seen in the election of the Progressive Conservatives (in office from 1984 to 1993), and in the growing popularity of the Canadian Alliance (once known as the Reform Party) since 1993.

Exhibit 3.7

REFORM MP RAISES IRE OF JUSTICE MINISTER

A Reformer's comments opposing same-sex legislation are ugly, irresponsible and demonstrate the party's intolerant ways, says the federal justice minister. Anne McLellan was responding to Garry Breitkreuz, who in a news release Thursday attacked Ottawa's proposed law giving same-sex couples the same rights and obligations as common-law pairs.

"In the 1950s, buggery was a criminal offence," said Breitkreuz's release. "Now, it's a requirement to receive benefits from the federal government. This is a ridiculous rationale for extending government benefits."

McLellan said the comments are unacceptable. "The Reform party can try and change its name, but it can't change its spots," McLellan said in an interview. "This is the same kind of ugly irresponsible commentary that I think unfortunately is all too common for members of the Reform party."

McLellan said the party hasn't changed since former Reformer Bob Ringma told a newspaper in 1996 that if he were a businessman, he'd fire "or move to the back of the shop" a homosexual or a member of an ethnic minority. "This is old-style Reform party politics where they bash people who happen to be a minority who they believe are different than them or somehow lesser than them ... it is ugly."

Breitkreuz, for his part, said he won't back down. In his press release, and in an interview, he said that the same-sex legislation undermines marriage and the family, which in turn hurts children. The Reform party wants marriage, defined as between a man and woman, to be included in the legislation to prevent it from being struck down by the courts. The bill would change more than 60 federal statutes to include same-sex couples.

"Unless the government is willing to protect marriage and the family, I cannot accept this legislation," Breitkreuz said in an interview. "And I'm going to say so loud and clear. (McLellan) could call me all the names in the world that she wants but people are going to see through this whole charade." His reference to buggery is quoted from "her Criminal Code," he said.

McLellan didn't go as far as saying that the party's attempts to amend the legislation are veiled expressions of homophobia. But she did say the comments reflect "a disrespect for the Constitution, for the rights of others, for fundamental Canadian values. For me, it's the bad old Reform party back in Technicolour."

In a crucial vote, the bill made it to a Commons committee for study last week despite the Reform party's opposition to it.

Reformers have objected to the law from the beginning, partly because they want benefits extended to any two people in a relationship of economic independence, such as a son who supports his ailing father.

Breitkreuz called on Canadians to contact their MPs and urge them to vote against the bill.

"I hope that the public are just going to let her know, in no uncertain terms, that this not acceptable."

Source: Nahlah Ayed, "Reform MP Raises Ire of Justice Minister" [on-line], available: http://www.slam.ca/CNEWSPolitics0003/03_reform_CP.html [2000 May 26]. Reprinted with the permission of the Canadian Press.

NEOLIBERALISM

Since the early 1990s, there has been a swing toward what political analysts have labelled **neoliberalism**. Day and Brodsky (1998, 9) characterize the neoliberal approach to government as follows: "The private sphere—the home, the market—is considered worthy of enlargement and sanctification, and the public sphere, including the institution of government itself, is considered dangerous and best kept small." Following its election to power in 1993, the federal Liberal Party clearly demonstrated neoliberal values when it set out to, among other things, downsize government and cut public spending. Whereas previous Liberal governments were made up of *social* liberalists who supported social program spending, many members of Chrétien's Cabinet are *business* liberalists who support pro-market economic policies (Pal, 1998).

The neoliberal trend is not specific to Canada. For example, Tony Blair's Labour government in England and Bill Clinton's Democratic administration in the United States both reflect a less generous and more business-oriented approach to social policy.

Introduction

Social policy in Canada is guided by the political system. Governments are responsible for helping the less fortunate meet basic needs, assuming important roles that families are unable to fulfil, and defining and reinforcing widely held beliefs or values. While some critics charge that government's role in social policymaking is too extensive, others support a further expansion of that role.

Social Policy in a Changing Economic and Social Environment

Canada's new economy is characterized by a shift from a manufacturing economy to a service-based economy, and from full-time jobs to part-time jobs. These changes are largely influenced by globalization, technological innovation, and free trade. While free trade is pushing policies and programs that advance harmonization and privatization, social and economic policy is merging to create an emphasis on getting and keeping jobs. Several social trends are shaping the direction of social policy, including an aging population and changes in family structure, urbanization, and immigration patterns.

Divisions of Power: Federal, Provincial, and Territorial Relations

Although federalism and the Constitution Act give the majority of responsibility for social welfare to the provinces, this responsibility is in reality shared by the federal and regional governments. While the federal government tries to keep social welfare equitable across the country, the provinces want to tailor their policies to their particular culture and needs. Canadian social policy has been shaped by a series of constitutional negotiations, the latest of which is the social union.

Social Policymaking Procedures

Social policy changes can be made through mutual agreement or legislation at both the federal and regional levels. This process can be long and complex, which can result in programs being out of date by the time they are implemented. Social policy is rarely permanent and can be repealed or changed through the legislative process.

Participants in the Policymaking Process

Various groups make up what is known as the policy community. Elected officials and bureaucrats are key players in the social policymaking process. The Canadian public contributes to the development of social policy through citizen participation. Interest groups try to benefit their own members or the general public by influencing government. Federal funding of interest groups has been drastically reduced as a result of fiscal-restraint policy.

The Role of Values and Ideology in Social Policy

Values and ideology play an important role in the social policymaking process. Political elections highlight the values of different parties and their beliefs about social policy. The 1980s were characterized by the electoral success of neoconservative parties; politics in the 1990s has swung toward a neoliberal agenda that supports the downsizing of government and cutbacks in public spending.

KEY TERMS

SOCIAL POLICIES 51
FREE TRADE AGREEMENTS 54
PRIVATIZATION 55
AGING POPULATION 58
URBANIZATION 60
FEDERALISM 60
SOCIAL UNION 65
BILLS 66
CITIZEN PARTICIPATION 72
INTEREST GROUPS 72
NEOCONSERVATISM 75
NEOLIBERALISM 77

CHAPTER 4

SOCIAL WELFARE IN AN AGE OF RESTRAINT

• OBJECTIVES •

I. To review the Progressive Conservative approach to government, the Macdonald Commission, and the strategies used to reduce social spending.

II. To explore neoliberalism and the fiscal-restraint measures introduced by the Liberal government under Jean Chrétien.

III. To examine the changes in funding arrangements between the federal and regional governments, the implications of the new funding arrangements for national standards, and the competition for funds.

IV. To look at various types of strategies that regional governments use to reform social welfare programs.

V. To consider the consequences of fiscal restraint for Canadians, particularly with respect to Canada's economic advances in recent years, the "social deficit," and increasing social problems.

INTRODUCTION

The first half of the 1970s was characterized by continued development in social welfare programs. However, this trend had reversed itself by the middle of the decade. Canada, like other industrial countries, began to experience stagnating economic growth and inflation (**stagflation**) as the rise in wages slowed and government revenues dropped. As a result, governments found it difficult to balance their annual budgets—that is, to collect enough tax and other revenue to cover their expenditures.

Rather than cut costly public programs that Canadians had come to rely on, governments chose to borrow money. Canada continued to spend more than it made in revenue, which resulted in yearly budget **deficits** (i.e., government expenditures exceeding revenues) and a mounting public **debt** (i.e., the total sum of all annual deficits). Canadians remained optimistic that the downturn in the economy was only temporary. By the late 1970s, however, it was obvious that the economy was not improving and that new policies were needed to break the stagflation trend.

Beginning in 1979, several industrial countries began electing more right-wing governments with neoconservative approaches to governance and public spending. According to Grady, Howse, and Maxwell (1995, 19), the role of political leaders was redefined during this time:

> It became conventional wisdom in the 1980s that governments were too large, too inefficient, and too indebted. The job of political leaders was to shrink governments, reduce taxes, and get out of the way of private investors and citizens.

Despite the pressure on governments to spend less, Canada's national debt continued to grow; by 1993, the country had one of the highest debts in the world (Canada, 1994a). Canada had fallen into the classic "debt trap" in which any efforts to reduce the debt were thwarted by the country's slow economic growth and the fact that an increasing amount of revenue was needed to pay the interest on the debt (Mendelson, 1993). Richards (1997, 69) suggests that governments also seemed to be in a state of "debt denial," a condition that made them shy away from considering temporary spending cuts or raising taxes to cover the costs of programs.

By 1995, the national debt stood at $546 billion; $42 billion (or 26 percent of federal spending) was needed annually to pay the interest on the debt. The provincial and territorial governments were saddled with their own respective debts. These accumulated annual deficits, combined with a growing public debt, created Canada's **fiscal crisis** (Canada, 1994c; Swimmer, 1996).

A major problem with annual deficits and growing debt is that, over time, the ability of governments to finance social programs is diminished: money that is needed to fund social programs must instead be used to service a mounting debt. Of particular concern in the mid-1990s was that it was becoming increasingly difficult for governments to fund health care and other services needed for an aging population (Canada, 1999a, 2000a). In the view of the Liberal government, cutbacks in social and other public spending were needed to reduce government deficits (Canada, 1994b).

Some social critics charge that the fiscal crisis of the 1990s was used to rationalize a virtual dismantling of Canada's social welfare system. McQuaig (1995, 9), for example, points out that the deficit became "a key tool for picking away at what many in the elite consider to be our overly generous social welfare system and government policies dedicated to pampering the undeserving, at the expense of the deserving (such as those in the elite)."

EXHIBIT 4.1

THE NATIONAL DEFICIT

Source: Reprinted courtesy of the artist, Bob Bierman.

Despite such criticisms, Canadian governments at all levels have continued to curb public spending, reduce the size of government, and terminate, freeze, or redirect funds from many existing social welfare programs to other priorities and initiatives. In 1991, Prince (1991, 42) predicted that

> social policy and social planning will remain subordinate to the goals of deficit reduction and debt management ... The emphasis in government social policy departments will be on controlling program costs, postponing new programs, engaging in relatively low-cost initiatives, and further rationalizing programs.

What began in the late 1970s as a gradual reduction of social expenditures escalated in the 1990s to a full-fledged overhaul of Canada's social welfare system.

I. THE MULRONEY YEARS: TIGHTENING THE PUBLIC PURSE STRINGS

THE MACDONALD COMMISSION OF 1985

In 1982 the federal government appointed the Royal Commission on the Economic Union and Development Prospects for Canada (commonly known as the Macdonald Commission) to examine the challenges facing Canada's economic and political institutions. The commission was also expected to recommend "appropriate institutional and constitutional arrangements to promote the liberty and well-being of individual Canadians and the maintenance of a strong competitive economy" (Royal Commission on the Economic Union, 1985, 1:xvii). In its investigation of the Canadian social welfare system, the commission concentrated on income-security programs.

The commission's three-volume report, released in 1985, criticized Canada's income-security system for being ineffective, too complex and inequitable, a disincentive to work, and unsustainable in times of unstable economic conditions and changing demographics. The commission's recommendations included the following:

- introduction of a guaranteed annual income scheme to be called the Universal Income Security Program (UISP);
- elimination of the Guaranteed Income Supplement, child tax credits, family allowances, and other programs in order to free up revenue to finance the UISP; and
- an overhaul of the unemployment insurance system (Royal Commission on the Economic Union, 1985).

Although the Mulroney government implemented the Macdonald Commission's recommendation to scrap or reduce funding for several social welfare programs, it failed to act on the recommendation to replace these programs with a guaranteed annual income program. Some of the major changes the Progressive Conservatives made to the Old Age Security pension, unemployment insurance, the Canada Assistance Plan, and family allowances are outlined below.

Clawing Back the Old Age Security Pension

In its 1989 budget speech, the Progressive Conservative government announced that benefits from the Old Age Security (OAS) pension would be "clawed back" from high-income earning seniors. As Rice and Prince (1993, 30) describe it:

the **clawback** means that Canadian seniors repay 15 cents of their OAS pension for every dollar of net income above a threshold ... those with net incomes between $50,000 and $76,332 paid a graduated partial clawback, keeping some of their old age pension; and seniors with net incomes above $76,332 paid the total clawback, losing all of their OAS benefits.

According to the National Council of Welfare (1990, 18), the clawbacks represented "the most significant backward step in Canadian social policy in a generation, because they end the universal nature of the Old Age Security pension." The clawbacks also created a new and complex tax schedule that seniors had to use each year at tax time to calculate the amount of clawback they owed to the government; this particular consequence of the clawbacks contradicted the Progressive Conservatives' stated intention of simplifying the income tax system.

Amending the Unemployment Insurance Act

A number of reports, including the Task Force on Unemployment Insurance (1981), the Macdonald Commission Report (1985), and the Forget Commission Majority Report (1986), emphasized the need to reform the unemployment insurance (UI) program (since renamed employment insurance, or EI). A common criticism of UI was that its benefits provided little incentive for recipients to leave UI and get back to work. In 1990, the passage of Bill C-21 in Parliament severely altered the Unemployment Insurance Act. Most dramatic was the termination of support by the federal government: UI became fully funded by employer and worker contributions. The amendments also resulted in more restrictive eligibility criteria, shortened benefit periods, higher premiums, more severe penalties for persons who quit their jobs without "just cause," and an expansion of active employment programs (Canada, 1994c, 1994g).

The 'Cap' on CAP

Under the Canada Assistance Plan (CAP), the federal government paid half of the expenses incurred by the provinces for social assistance and many personal social services. In early 1991, the passage of Bill C-69 allowed the federal government to reduce its CAP contributions to the three richest provinces (Alberta, Ontario, and British Columbia). This "cap" on CAP meant that any CAP program in those provinces that increased its costs more than 5 percent would have to be funded solely by the province (Canada, 1994a).

In each of the three provinces affected by Bill C-69, welfare rates were either cut or frozen and new social welfare programs were postponed (Canadian Council on Social Development, 1990). Some of the human costs of these drastic cuts in public spending are highlighted in Exhibit 4.2.

EXHIBIT 4.2

CANADA'S SOCIAL PROGRAMS ARE IN TROUBLE

WARNING

Bill C-69 is Hazardous to the Health of Canada's Social Programs

Bill C-69 would cap federal money for the Canada Assistance Plan for two years in Ontario, Alberta and British Columbia ... provinces where half of Canada's poor people live.

Bill C-69 would also freeze federal money for medicare and colleges and universities for two years. If this trend continues, by the year 2004 the federal government would no longer contribute to these programs.

And if the federal government no longer paid the piper, it wouldn't be able to call the tune. Which would mean the end of the national standards which now ensure that all of us, wherever we live, have access to good health care, education and social services. Whether you have access to social programs would depend on which province you live in.

Bill C-69 would take a pair of scissors to Canada's social safety net, cutting some of the strongest ties that bind us together as Canadians.

"Tampering with CAP is tampering with the lives of Canadians whose needs are greatest."

Jean Panet-Raymond,
Vice-President,
Canadian Council on Social Development

"This will only give provincial governments a useful excuse for abandoning poor people to their poverty."

Gabrielle McKenzie-Scott,
President,
National Anti-Poverty Organization

Source: Canada's Social Programs Are in Trouble (Ottawa: Canadian Council on Social Development, 1990), 8. Reprinted by permission of the Canadian Council on Social Development.

Elimination of Family Allowances

The universal family allowance program suffered its first blow in 1989 when benefits were clawed back from high-income earners; the second blow came in early 1993 when the Family Allowance Act was scrapped altogether and replaced with the Child Tax Benefit. Bill C-80 paved the way for the introduction of the new, income-tested Child Tax Benefit, which was targeted at low- and moderate-income families (Human Resources Development Canada, 1994b). The National Council of Welfare (1992) expected most Canadian families—especially those headed by a single parent—to benefit under the new scheme. Opponents of the new Child Tax Benefit, on the other hand, saw the selective Child Tax Benefit as a poor replacement for the universal family allowances and another reminder that universal income benefits in Canada were a thing of the past (Turner, 1995).

THE LEGACY OF THE PROGRESSIVE CONSERVATIVE GOVERNMENT

The fiscally conservative mandate of Brian Mulroney and the Progressive Conservative government identified social spending as an extravagance and a primary target for reduction. From their 1984 election to their defeat in 1993, the Progressive Conservatives adopted an approach to social welfare that was in stark contrast to the welfare state principles Canadians had generally supported since the end of World War II (Rice and Prince, 1993). Gray (1990, 17) uses the phrase "social policy by stealth" to describe the gradual and subtle, yet significant, measures by which the Progressive Conservatives cut social program budgets. Torjman (1995, 1) states: "The social envelope was reduced by many billions of dollars through direct cuts as well as indirect, hidden cuts in the form of clawbacks and the partial indexation of social programs, transfers to the provinces and the income tax system." Because no single cut was easily identifiable, the changes in social program funding were not clearly evident from year to year. Some analysts maintain that the cuts, however subtle their implementation, had consequences that were devastating and felt well after the Progressive Conservatives had left office (Mendelson, 1993).

II. NEOLIBERALISM AND FISCAL RESTRAINT

A NEW LIBERAL DIRECTION

When the Liberals won the federal election in October 1993, they were confronted with two major challenges: (1) to reduce the large national debt (approximately $510 billion); and, (2) to address the structural problems and thorny relationship that existed between the federal and provincial governments (Paquet and Shepherd, 1996). The Liberal Party's Red Book outlined strategies for remedying the country's woes; underlying these strategies was a commitment to "fiscal prudence, modest tax cuts and cautious social spending" (PM favours staying the course, 1999, 5889).

The Liberal Party came into power with a history of generally supporting welfare state principles. Indeed, Liberal governments had been in power when most of the major federal social welfare programs were introduced, including the Old Age Pension Act of 1927, the Unemployment Insurance Act of 1940, and the Canada Assistance Plan of 1966. The Liberals under Jean Chrétien, however, were determined to practise fiscal responsibility and to balance the federal budget by cutting public spending rather than raising taxes (Swimmer, 1996).

TAKING STOCK: A REVIEW OF FEDERAL SYSTEMS

One of the Liberal government's first agenda items after the 1993 election was to complete an extensive review of all federal departments. The government launched its Program Review in 1994 with the goal of finding the most efficient ways to deliver federal programs and services.

With a view to overhauling Canada's out-of-date system of income-support programs and personal social services, Human Resources Development Canada initiated a comprehensive Social Security Review in 1994. This review identified three areas for reform: work (to help Canadians find and keep jobs); learning (to enable workers to get the training needed for employment); and security (to ensure that Canadians in need could enter the labour force and had access to income-security programs). These areas of reform, as well as proposed strategies for change, were outlined in a discussion paper entitled *Improving Social Security in Canada*. Canadians were encouraged to read the document, participate in discussions on social security reform, and make recommendations for improving the social security system.

Having completed its Program Review, the federal government introduced the 1995 budget, "[which] contained some of the most significant program and spending cuts in the history of the country" (Armit and Bourgault, 1996, 1). Included in the budget were plans to drastically downsize most federal departments. The annual operating budget of Human Resources Development Canada was reduced by $1.1 billion, prohibiting any large-scale reform of Canada's social security system (Bakvis, 1997). Torjman (1995, 1) suggests that while "the Social Security Review could have been a milestone in Canadian history," it was sacrificed for what the Liberals saw as a greater cause—that is, getting its fiscal house in order.

1995: A TURNING POINT FOR SOCIAL WELFARE

In its 1995 budget speech, the federal government announced that major cuts would be made in most areas of public spending. The planned cuts, which were expected to save the federal government several billion dollars, included a reduction of $7 billion in transfer payments to the provinces for health, postsecondary education, and social welfare over a two-year period and additional cuts in subsequent years. Later that year, pressure from many of the provinces and territories, coupled with improvements in the economy, led the federal government to reconsider its drastic reduction plan and restore some of the transfer funds (Kroeger, 1996; Canada, 1995a, 2000a).

Although many economists and financial analysts commended the 1995 budget for taking a hard line on government spending, others voiced their concerns about the budget's impact on social programs. Premier Bob Rae of Ontario, for example, stated that the budget "marks the end of Canada as we know it" (Kroeger, 1996, 21). The National Council of Welfare (1995, 1) maintained that the proposed changes

> marked a giant step backward in Canadian social policy. Followed through to its most likely conclusion, it would dismantle a nation-wide system of welfare and social services that took a generation to build. Sadly, the policies of the 1990s would take us back to the 1950s.

Finance Minister Paul Martin defended the budget's position on government spending by insisting that a less drastic budget would negatively affect Canada's economic recovery and ultimately produce higher interest rates, a drop in the value of the dollar, and a loss of confidence in Canada's economy on the part of businesspeople and consumers. Martin also reminded Canadians that the "country simply could not survive the continued build-up of public-sector debt, with an increasing portion of government revenues going to interest payments" (cited in McCarthy, 1995, A10). Martin summed up his position by stating that "there are times in the progress of a people when fundamental challenges must be faced, fundamental choices made—a new course charted. For Canada, this is one of those times" (Canada, 1995a, preface).

III. SHIFTS IN FUNDING PATTERNS AND PRIORITIES

THE CANADA HEALTH AND SOCIAL TRANSFER

A significant feature of the federal government's 1995 budget was the plan to eliminate the Canada Assistance Plan (which funded social welfare programs) and the Established Programs Financing (which funded health and postsecondary education). The federal government announced that beginning in 1996, a new funding arrangement called the Canada Health and Social Transfer (CHST) would govern the transfer of funds from the federal to the provincial and territorial governments.

There are several differences between the CHST and previous funding arrangements. Under CAP, for example, the federal government was obligated to pay half of a province's social welfare program's costs—whatever those costs might be. In contrast, the CHST allows the federal government to provide the provincial and territorial governments with a lump sum or **block fund**. Under the CHST, then, each province and territory receives the same amount of federal dollars on a per capita basis regardless of total program costs. For provinces and territories that have extensive and/or costly programs, the CHST has meant a substantial reduction in federal funding.

Federal transfers to the provinces under the CHST continue to be a combination of cash and tax points. **Tax points** are taxing privileges that the federal government grants to the provinces and territories. A tax point transfer occurs when the federal government reduces its own tax rates to allow provinces to raise their rates by an equivalent amount. This arrangement allows provinces to raise additional revenues without increasing the total tax burden for Canadians (Finance Canada, 2000b). Since 1996, the federal government has steadily reduced the cash portion of the transfer and increased the tax points; it plans to continue the trend until the year 2010, when the cash portion of the transfer will be phased out completely (Steinhauer, 1995). Exhibit 4.3 shows the decrease in cash transfers and increase in tax points over time.

THE EROSION OF NATIONAL STANDARDS

To receive payments under CAP, the provinces and territories had to adhere to certain national standards. For example, CAP ensured that "residency requirements" could not be imposed; that is, an applicant could not be denied welfare benefits on the basis of how long he or she had lived in the province or territory. Other standards required welfare and social services to be

- accessible (financial or other assistance is given to anyone in need);
- adequate (enough aid is given to meet a person's basic needs);
- subject to appeal (decisions made by welfare agencies can be appealed by applicants); and
- available (persons are not required to work in exchange for receiving welfare) (Day and Brodsky, 1998).

Although the residency requirement was carried over from CAP to CHST, the CHST is far less conditional than CAP with respect to the other standards; provinces and territories are free to determine what social programs should exist and what standards should govern the design, funding, and delivery of programs and services.

Exhibit 4.3

CANADA HEALTH AND SOCIAL TRANSFER (CHST), 1993–94 to 2003–04

	CASH[2]	TAX TRANSFERS[3]	TOTAL
		(BILLIONS OF DOLLARS)	
CAP/EPF[1]			
1993–94	18.8	10.2	29.0
1994–95	18.7	10.7	29.4
1995–96	18.5	11.4	29.9
CHST			
1996–97	14.7	12.2	26.9
1997–98	12.5	13.3	25.8
1998–99	12.5	14.2	26.7
1999–00	14.5	14.9	29.4
2000–01	15.5	15.3	30.8
2001–02	15.5	15.8	31.3
2002–03	15.5	16.5	32.0
2003–04	15.5	17.2	32.7

1. CAP—Canada Assistance Plan. EPF—Established Programs Financing.
2. Based on an assumed gradual drawdown of the $2.5-billion cash supplement over four years starting in 2000–01 and of the $3.5-billion supplement over three years starting in 1999–2000.
3. All figures for 2000–01 onward, with the exception of CHST cash, are projections.

Note: Numbers may not add due to rounding.

Source: Department of Finance Canada, *Budget 2000: Improving the Quality of Life of Canadians and Their Children* (Ottawa, 2000), 12. Reproduced with the permission of the Minister of Public Works and Government Services Canada, 2000.

The introduction of the Canada Health and Social Transfer and the establishment of the social union are indicators that the federal government is reducing its central role in setting national standards for social welfare programs and giving the regional governments more discretion in this area. Whitaker (2000, 73–74) sees the federal government's diminished presence in the social welfare arena as

> the end of the era in which the federal government, through the use of the federal spending power, took the lead in policy innovation in a number of key areas. [It is clear] ... that the days of Ottawa as a policy innovator are drawing to a close.

Boadway (1995, 2) points out that although the federal government may be loosening its grip on maintaining national standards, the Canadian Constitution requires it to act in accordance with the following two principles:

1) **Horizontal equity,** "[a] principle that Canadians ought to be treated comparably by the fiscal system regardless of the province in which they live"; and
2) **Vertical equity,** "[a] principle that the federal government should be concerned with national standards to reduce inequalities of income between the wealthiest Canadians and those who are least wealthy, and to enhance equalities of opportunity for those most disadvantaged."

According to Collins (1998), the CHST threatens both horizontal and vertical equity. Horizontal equity may be lost because minimal standards that were available under CAP are not available under the CHST. Because each province and territory is allowed to develop its own standards for social welfare, there may be discrepancies in the programs offered by the various jurisdictions. For example, provinces differ with respect to their eligibility for welfare requirements, which means that a person could be eligible for assistance in one province but not in another. In addition, since the provinces and territories are authorized to create their own standards for social welfare programs, the federal government is no longer able to withhold transfer payments to governments that adopt inferior standards (Ross, 1995).

Vertical equity is jeopardized, since under the CHST the provinces and territories are free to cut funding to welfare and other programs, thereby creating more inequalities between the rich and poor. As Collins (1998, 7) points out: "If one jurisdiction offers more generous assistance, it will attract poor people from other jurisdictions ... For programs which involve entitlements for residents of a particular jurisdiction, there is an incentive to cut entitlements in order to save costs."

THE COMPETITION FOR FUNDS

A unique feature of the CHST is that because federal funding is provided in a block, the provinces and territories have more freedom in how they allocate funds to the separate health, postsecondary education, and social welfare programs. In other words, none of the federal money is earmarked for any particular social program; the block of funding can be divided in any way that the provinces and territories see fit (National Council of Welfare, 1995). By giving the regional governments more freedom in how they use social program funds, the federal government hopes to put an end to the power struggle "that [has] historically plagued federal–provincial negotiations" (Canada, 1995a, 12).

Many Canadians are concerned that without national standards, social welfare will not be an equal contender for funding from the CHST "pie." Whereas health care is governed by the Canada Health Act, there are no legislated standards set for the provision of social welfare. Although postsecondary education is not protected by standards either, it has over the decades fared well as a popular social program. In addition, education lobbyists are likely to be successful at seconding funds for postsecondary education since they tend to be "articulate, cohesive, well financed and well connected to the power structure" (Ross, 1995, 3).

According to Mullaly (1997, 9), social welfare is the least popular program and is likely to "lose out to health and education in any competition for funds." Indeed, in its 2000 budget the federal government granted a $2.5 billion supplement to the provinces and territories to "meet what Canadians have clearly identified as their highest priorities: health and education" (Canada, 2000a, 4). The low priority traditionally given to social welfare is also noticeable at the regional level. For example, when the Ontario government announced in 1999 that more budget cuts could be expected in that province, it was made clear that this move would affect social services but not education and health (Ontario Tories plan more cuts, 1999). These indicators suggest that in the coming years spending on social welfare programs is likely to decline in jurisdictions where social welfare is not a high priority.

IV. SOCIAL WELFARE REFORM AT THE REGIONAL LEVEL

REFORM STRATEGIES

The 1990s proved to be challenging for the provinces and territories in several ways: many were still struggling with their own deficits and rising debt;

others were trying to recover from the impact of the federal government's cap on the Canada Assistance Plan; and all were dealing with the changes to transfer payments under the new CHST. These and other circumstances led many regional governments to re-examine the quality and quantity of their own social programs and to determine how they might deliver programs on smaller budgets (Swimmer, 1996; Gorlick and Brethour, 1999).

In many jurisdictions, social assistance became a prime target for major program reform and funding cuts. Since the CHST put few conditions on how social welfare programs were to be managed and funded, the regional governments were free to set their own standards for welfare provision. The phrase "race to the bottom" has been coined to describe the successive cuts made to welfare benefits across the country: a province would slash its welfare benefits to motivate welfare recipients to leave that province in search of more generous benefits elsewhere; in turn, the more generous provinces would be pressured to cut their own welfare benefits to discourage a large influx of welfare recipients. Besides cutting welfare benefits, many provinces and territories tightened eligibility rules and imposed more stringent conditions on those who were already receiving benefits (Canadian Council on Social Development, 1996).

Besides cutting social welfare funds, governments have adopted other strategies to reform social welfare programs and reduce spending (Albert and Kirwin, 1999). Some of these strategies are described below:

- **Devolution** involves the transfer of responsibility, authority, and conditional funding for programs and services to another level of operation—for example, from a provincial government to a municipal government; from government to the private sector; or from government to individuals, families, and communities.
- **Privatization** is a form of devolution that refers specifically to the shift of responsibility for programs from the public sector to organizations in the private sector.
- **Contracting out** occurs when a government enters into a contract with an agency in the private sector to provide a nonstatutory service not offered by government (e.g., a family service agency provides family support programs, but the government continues to provide child protection services).
- **Purchase-of-service contracts** are a variation of contracting out; these agreements give voluntary agencies full responsibility for providing entire service areas on behalf of government (e.g., Children's Aid Societies provide all child welfare services in Ontario).

The provinces and territories have used these strategies to varying degrees to eliminate their respective deficits and balance their budgets. For example, when Ralph Klein was elected premier of Alberta in 1993, he introduced legislation that aimed to balance the provincial budget in just four years. Alberta was able to eliminate its deficit by raising university tuition fees, privatizing many services, drastically cutting welfare benefits, increasing the pupil–teacher ratio in public schools, and closing hospitals (Steel, 1999).

Alberta's tactics and fiscal achievements did not go unnoticed by the other provinces and territories. Ontario, for instance, followed Alberta's lead and drastically changed the way it funded and delivered social welfare programs. Shortly after becoming premier in 1995, Mike Harris introduced his Common Sense Revolution, a scheme to reduce taxes and the size of the government, create jobs, and reform health, education, and welfare systems. Between 1995 and 1998, Ontario reduced income taxes by 30 percent, "closed hospitals, shifted welfare responsibilities to the local governments, cut education spending, repealed labour laws and began a program of urban amalgamation by forcing together an immense Greater Toronto" (Hillmer, 1999, 1047).

V. FISCAL RESTRAINT: WHAT IT MEANS FOR CANADIANS

BALANCED BUDGETS FOR CANADIAN GOVERNMENTS

In their efforts to improve the country's economic base, Canada's federal, provincial, and territorial governments have made sweeping changes to the social welfare system, especially in terms of cutbacks in social spending. By 2000, seven regional governments had reported balanced budgets. The $10.6 billion deficit that the Harris government inherited when it was elected in 1995 is expected to be eliminated by 2001, and all provinces and territories are expected to have healthy surpluses by 2005 (M. McDonald, 1995; Finance Canada, 2000a). In 1998 the federal government announced that for the first time in nearly two decades, the national budget was balanced. Exhibit 4.4 illustrates federal and provincial surpluses and deficits over a 20-year period.

In his 2000 budget speech, Finance Minister Paul Martin made the following points about how "fiscal prudence" has significantly improved Canada's economic well-being in recent years:

- The [national] deficit is a matter of history.
- Inflation remains in check.

EXHIBIT 4.4

TOTAL FEDERAL AND PROVINCIAL–TERRITORIAL SURPLUS/DEFICIT(–), 1980–81 TO 1998–99

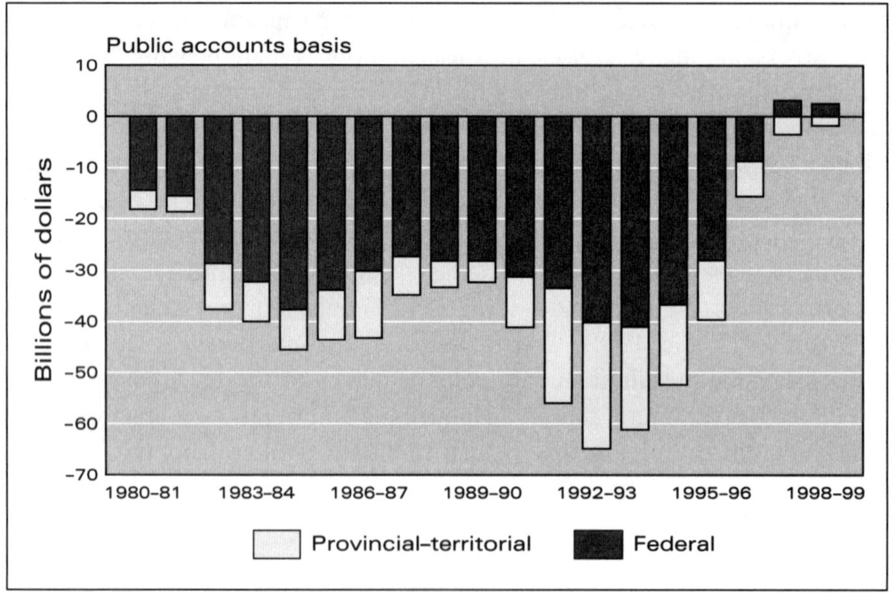

Source: Department of Finance Canada, *The Economic and Fiscal Update: Translating Better Finances into Better Lives* (Ottawa, 1999), 58. Reproduced with the permission of the Minister of Public Works and Government Services Canada, 2000.

- The government debt burden is declining.
- Canada's foreign debt burden is declining.
- Consumer and business confidence are at near-record levels.
- In 1999, more than 425,000 new jobs were created in Canada.
- Our unemployment rate stands at 6.8 percent—its lowest level in nearly a quarter of a century.
- Today, disposable incomes are some 3 percent higher than they were in 1996 (Canada, 2000b, 3–4).

CANADA'S SOCIAL DEFICIT

Despite the economic advances made in recent years, social analysts question the toll that getting Canada's economy in order has taken on the country's social well-being. The term **social deficit** is used to refer to Canada's "unmet human potential," which is attributed largely to major cuts in social expenditures (Stutt and Adelberg, 1998, 5). Concerns about cutbacks and social welfare reform have centred primarily on poverty and family issues.

Poverty

Poverty remains a persistent problem in Canada. The National Council of Welfare (1999a, 1) reports: "A total of 5.1 million people or 17.2 percent of the children, women and men in Canada were poor in 1997. The comparable figures for 1989, the last full year before the last recession, were 3.5 million poor people and a poverty rate of 13.6 percent."

Some social analysts attribute the rise in poverty to continued cuts in welfare rates in many jurisdictions and the lack of standards in place to ensure minimum benefit levels (Ross, 1995). According to Gorey, Hansen, and Chacko (1997, 51), "The single largest clientele affected by welfare reform consists of single parents (typically mothers) and their children"; they go on to describe the negative effects of poverty for this group:

> If one's most basic needs are unmet, it is very likely that progress toward other hierarchical goals, such as the attainment of gainful employment, will be stifled. Conservative policies on social assistance benefits may, in fact, be structural barriers to one of the government's own centrally stated objectives—to move people from welfare to work. (51)

A number of social problems—problems that are expected to be exacerbated if welfare rates are lowered even further—are associated with the incidence of poverty. A rise in the incidence of hunger is one such problem. In 1994, 1.2 percent or 57,000 children went hungry. The use of food banks has more than doubled in the last decade, and close to 40 percent (over 300,000) of users are children (Turner, 1998b; Food bank use on rise, 1999).

Substandard housing and a decline in living conditions is another problem associated with poverty. Substandard homes often have poor indoor air quality, contaminants such as asbestos and mould, and other conditions that can put residents at risk of developing health problems. Substandard housing can also interfere with a child's emotional and social development. Roughly 35 percent of children in poor families live in substandard housing (Ross, 1999; Rethinking child poverty, 1999).

Family Issues

Child protection, family counselling, and support services for working parents have helped families cope with a wide range of stresses. Funding for these and other family services is provided through the CHST. Cutbacks in this funding could give rise to a variety of problems, including the following:

- *Increase in child neglect.* As stress, isolation, and limited resources become more problematic for parents, so too does the potential for child neglect (Wachtel, 1994).

- *Lack of support for victims of child abuse or neglect.* Shrinking funds, increased caseloads, and reduced funding for foster homes will make it more difficult for child protection workers to take appropriate action in cases of child abuse or neglect (e.g., taking children into care for their own protection, or providing supervision services or emotional support services for at-risk families).
- *Increase in domestic violence.* Shelters for abused women and their children report that more women are returning to abusive partners because it is becoming increasingly difficult to feed and clothe their children on reduced welfare benefits (Little, 1999). MacLeod and Kinnon (1996, 36) point out that "there is a very real danger that reductions in funding support will lead to a reduction in concern, understanding and programs to protect and support victims/survivors and to prevent violence."
- *Longer waiting lists.* Reduced funding is likely to result in fewer services and a longer waiting time for the services that do exist. People who need help may give up waiting or not seek help at all if adequate services are unavailable.
- *Diminished access to quality child care.* As government subsidies to child care are reduced, many working parents may be unable to afford the costs of child care. Steinhauer (1995) notes that reduced funding for child care may limit the opportunities for parents to get off welfare and into the labour force or training.
- *Restricted choices for women.* As government subsidies are cut, it is likely that women will become more responsible for the care of children, the elderly, and the sick in the home. Many of these women will be required to give up paid employment to take on unpaid caregiving responsibilities. Little (1999, 66) points out that "it is poor women who cannot afford to pay for a home caregiver that are hardest hit by these cuts ... As women's paid work is reduced this naturally increases their economic dependency on the family."

Cutbacks and social welfare reforms impact not only people who use services but also those who provide services. According to the National Union of Public and General Employees (1996), social service workers are paying a price for reform: "On-the-job stress is reaching epidemic proportions as workers try to cope with larger caseloads, increased demands from clients as other services are gutted, and the ongoing fear of job loss." Exhibit 4.5 addresses the connection between Ontario's social deficit and quality of life in that province.

Exhibit 4.5

QUALITY OF LIFE IN ONTARIO—A WAKE-UP CALL

First, the good news: the quality of life in Ontario, as measured by the Quality of Life Index, is improving and has almost recovered to 1990 levels (100)–reaching 96.9 in the Fall of 1999. The bad news is that the lagging social indicators—the "social deficit"—will undermine progress in other sectors to make this pathway unsustainable.

This is the message of the latest report—The Quality of Life in Ontario Fall 1999—coming from the Ontario Social Development Council and Social Planning Network of Ontario. The report is the fifth in the series on The Quality of Life in Ontario, the last report of the 1990s. It provides a look at progress we have made over the past ten years, the setbacks we have endured, and a set of benchmarks for the beginning of the 21st century.

The Quality of Life Index (QLI) is a tool to measure and monitor changes in living conditions which affect the quality of life in communities. There are twenty community partners across Ontario involved in the QLI project, using the Quality of Life Index to measure changes in their local communities. Their results are reported here along with the provincial QLI.

"This report really should be a wake-up call to the people of Ontario and our governments at all levels," says Malcolm Shookner, Executive Director of the Ontario Social Development Council and author of the report. "We see growing evidence that persistent social problems will undermine economic prosperity and environmental sustainability in the long term. Increasing poverty and inequality will lead to a lower quality of life for all of us."

Social indicators in the QLI are lagging behind the environmental, economic and health indicators, having declined by 29% since 1990. This social deficit is being carried by the poor—mainly women and children—and elderly. It exerts a downward effect on the QLI, even while the environmental and economic indicators are pulling it up. This is not a sustainable pattern.

The economic indicators are showing a steady recovery since 1997, with the economic "boom" in 1999 bringing the QLI value for the economic indicators back to where it was in 1990. This reflects the overall sense of economic recovery reported by a number of sources in the media. But the social deficit is a drag on economic growth. Reports of growing poverty, income disparities, hunger and homelessness indicate a polarization of society that will undermine this economic growth and make it unsustainable.

Source: Canadian Social Planning Network (1999), "Quality of Life in Ontario—A Wake-Up Call" [on-line], available: http://www.ccsd.ca/cspn/qlims.htm [2000 June 7]. Reprinted by permission of the Canadian Council on Social Development.

BUDGET SURPLUSES AND REINVESTMENTS

In its 2000 budget, the federal government noted that "Canada is now in an era of **budget surpluses**" (Canada, 2000c, 3). These surpluses, which are the product of reduced spending and money saved, are held in the federal government's contingency reserve "to protect against unforeseen events" (Canada, 2000b, 7). It is unlikely that the surpluses will be earmarked for social programs. The chief economists of Canada's banks and forecasting firms have recommended that the federal government apply its annual surpluses to bringing down the national debt; according to government reports, that is what the federal government intends to do.

Some of the provinces have announced plans to reinvest their surpluses in programs that suffered cuts in the last few years. For example, in June 1999 Premier Klein reported that Alberta is preparing to "free ... up dollars to reinvest or to invest in priority areas such as health and education" (Alberta eliminates net debt, 1999, 5889). The extent to which social assistance and the personal social services will be priorities for reinvestment remains to be seen.

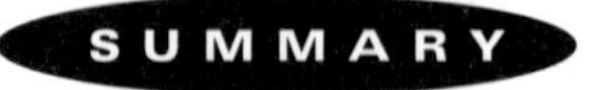

Introduction

A burgeoning public debt and annual deficits during the 1970s made neoconservative policies more attractive to Canadians. The election of more right-wing governments, and an emphasis on Canada's fiscal crisis, was followed by a gradual erosion of Canada's social programs.

The Mulroney Years: Tightening the Public Purse Strings

The Macdonald Commission of 1985 recommended that Canada restructure its social welfare system, institute a guaranteed annual income, and overhaul its unemployment insurance system. In response to these recommendations, the Progressive Conservative government of the early 1990s clawed back the Old Age Security pension, restricted the use of unemployment insurance, capped the Canada Assistance Plan, eliminated family allowances, and cut many other social program budgets.

Neoliberalism and Fiscal Restraint

In the mid- and late-1990s, the Liberal government changed its traditional stance on social spending by introducing its own type of fiscal restraint. In

1994, Human Resources Development Canada initiated a review of Canada's social security system; the changes it recommended were not implemented because the 1994 Program Review indicated a need to downsize the federal government. In the 1995 budget, the Liberals announced major cuts in spending to reduce the federal deficit.

Shifts in Funding Patterns and Priorities

In 1996, the CAP replaced the CHST, which altered the way the federal government supported social programs. The CHST did not demand the same type of standards in Canada's social welfare programs as those demanded by CAP. The federal government appears to be reducing its central role in setting national standards, even though the Canadian Constitution requires it to act in accordance with the principles of horizontal and vertical equity. Because the CHST is provided as a block fund, many Canadians are concerned that social welfare will lose out in the competition for diminished funds.

Social Welfare at the Regional Level

In response to funding cuts under the CHST, many regional governments have cut welfare benefits, decreased social services, and embraced devolution, privatization, contracting out, and purchase-of-service contracts as strategies for reducing program costs.

Fiscal Restraint: What It Means for Canadians

The federal government balanced its budget in 1998, and most of the provincial and territorial governments had achieved balanced budgets by 2000. Although Canada's economy seems to be improving, the cuts in social welfare spending have left the country with a social deficit. Problems associated with poverty and cutbacks in family services are particular concerns. Although some provinces with budget surpluses have promised to reinvest in health and education, little has been said about restoring funds to social welfare programs.

KEY TERMS

STAGFLATION 81
DEFICITS 81
DEBT 81
FISCAL CRISIS 82
CLAWBACK 85
BLOCK FUND 90
TAX POINTS 90
HORIZONTAL EQUITY 92
VERTICAL EQUITY 92
DEVOLUTION 94
PRIVATIZATION 94
CONTRACTING OUT 94
PURCHASE-OF-SERVICE CONTRACTS 94
SOCIAL DEFICIT 96
BUDGET SURPLUSES 100

PART II

THE SERVICE DELIVERY SYSTEM

CHAPTER 5

SERVICE SECTORS: PUBLIC, COMMERCIAL, AND VOLUNTARY DOMAINS

• OBJECTIVES •

I. To review how public-sector social welfare programs are delivered, legitimated, and funded and to consider the strengths and limitations of government service delivery.

II. To explore commercial social welfare programs and services, their legitimacy in Canadian society, funding patterns, and potential strengths and limitations.

III. To examine the types and range of social welfare programs provided by voluntary agencies, how they are legitimated and funded, and their perceived strengths and weaknesses.

IV. To look at collaborative efforts between service sectors and the implications of these efforts for service delivery.

INTRODUCTION

Since Canada's social welfare programs have developed at different times, under different administrations, and in response to different needs across the country, there is no single administrative or funding body for all social welfare services. Rather, there is a mix of service delivery systems, funding sources, and methods for managing programs. The social welfare system comprises two broad service sectors: the public sector and the private sector. The **private sector** can be further broken down into the commercial and voluntary sectors. Thus, there are three general service sectors:

1) The **public sector** includes all programs and agencies that are funded fully by tax revenue, administered by government departments, and delivered by government employees.

2) The **commercial sector**, or proprietary sector, is made up of private profit-making agencies that operate in the competitive business or market arena.

3) The **voluntary sector** is also called the charitable, independent, or third sector. It includes those nongovernment, self-governing, and nonprofit social welfare programs that do not fit neatly into public or commercial categories.

Although these sectors tend to be viewed as discrete entities, there is considerable overlap between them.

Some critics argue that the mix of public- and private-sector service delivery systems has resulted in a social welfare system that is fragmented and poorly coordinated. Wharf (1992, 43), for example, suggests that the social welfare system "is an array of poorly connected programs that confuses professionals and frustrates consumers." Armitage (1996, 118–119) acknowledges the shortcomings of Canada's fragmented social welfare system. However, he also calls attention to its merits:

> The separate identities have provided clients with some choice of service; the client who did not like the services received from the child welfare agency might do better with the services received from a family service or mental health agency, and so on. The separate services have provided independent foci for growth and political support; hence the resources they have in total may be greater than could have been obtained by a unified approach.

In recent years, representatives of many public- and private-sector agencies have formed partnerships to improve the coordination of the service delivery system. Joint efforts between the sectors have attempted to fill service gaps, reduce the duplication of services, and improve access to services. Other shifts are taking place as well. As governments restructure their operations and drastically cut budgets, they are relying more on voluntary and commercial agencies to provide social welfare services. Whether these changes will improve (or worsen) the fragmented quality of the social welfare system remains to be seen.

I. SOCIAL WELFARE IN THE PUBLIC SECTOR

NATURE OF SERVICES

Federal Government

Most of the federal government's contributions to social welfare have been in the area of income-security such as employment insurance, veterans' pensions, the Old Age Security pension, and the Canada/Quebec Pension Plans. The federal government has also helped shape many of Canada's personal social services such as those related to family violence, job search, child care, and programs for women. Over the last two decades, the federal government has transferred many social welfare responsibilities to other levels of government and to the private sector, thus reducing its role as a direct service provider. Despite this diminished role, the federal government remains actively involved in the funding and development of social welfare policies. In recent years, initiatives undertaken at the federal level have tended to be collaborative efforts between the federal government and the provincial or territorial governments, organizations in the private sector, or Aboriginal self-governments. This trend toward the formation of partnerships is reflected in the nearly 300 joint initiatives between various federal departments and voluntary sector organizations (Privy Council Office, 1999c).

Regional Governments

The **regional governments** include the provinces and territories. Each provincial and territorial government is responsible for providing a wide range of social welfare programs such as those related to mental health, child protection, foster care, and social assistance. There are three tiers of responsibility at the regional level: (1) the central government ministry in each provincial capital, which has ultimate responsibility for programs; (2) district and branch offices, which are set up across each province or territory to supervise the services provided in these areas; and (3) local government offices that deliver the services to the community.

Municipal Governments

In Canada, there has never been an established pattern for the delivery of social welfare services at the municipal level. However, this level of government played a prominent role early in Canada's history, when the English Poor Laws required that "the management of the poor, the ailing or the indigent [fall] first to local governments and to property tax for their financing" (Melchers, 1999, 36). In more recent years, **municipal governments** have assumed a greater responsibility for the delivery of social welfare services. This shift has been largely the result of devolution efforts—that is, the transference of control of certain programs from the federal government to regional governments, and from the regional to municipal governments.

Besides assuming a more prominent role in the delivery of social welfare services, some municipal governments have been expected to pay a larger portion of the service costs. For example, in the late 1990s a series of legislated changes allowed the Ontario government to devolve its responsibility for many health, housing, welfare, and social services to the municipalities; in turn, these municipalities were expected to pay up to 50 percent of the program costs out of local property taxes and user fees (protest from the municipal and local taxpayers caused the Ontario government to cut the municipal share back to 20 percent). The Social Planning Council of Metropolitan Toronto (1997) doubts that municipalities will be able to raise sufficient funds through property taxes or user fees to support needed social welfare programs. If municipalities are unable to pay for social welfare and other services, they may have little choice but to contract out the more costly programs to the lowest bidders in commercial operations (Melchers, 1999).

LEGITIMATION AND AUTHORITY

The authority of governments to establish and deliver social welfare programs is rooted in the many policies, legislative acts, and other legal documents that guide the design and implementation of these programs. Public social agencies are legitimated by the Constitution and the rule of law, and monitored by various regulatory bodies at the federal, provincial, and municipal levels. Much of the government's service provision is also legitimated by (1) professionals and others in the community who refer clients to specific public programs; and (2) citizens who seek help directly from government agencies.

FUNDING SOURCES

As noted in Chapter 3, the Canadian Constitution gives the provinces and territories the primary responsibility for social welfare. To help regional governments cover the costs of social welfare programs, the federal government has negotiated various funding arrangements. Federal subsidies for social welfare are often in the form of **transfers**, which are paid to the province or territory on an annual basis. In the fiscal year 2000–01, the federal government will transfer over $40 billion to the provincial and territorial governments (Canada, 2000a).

Three primary systems are used to transfer funds for social welfare to the provinces and territories:

1) *Canada Health and Social Transfer (CHST).* The CHST is a block fund used to finance health care, postsecondary education, social assistance, and personal social services. In 2000–01, payments provided under this program totalled over $30 billion.

2) *Equalization Program.* With additional funding from the federal government, the less prosperous provinces are able to implement social programs (without having to raise taxes to unreasonable levels) that

are of similar quality to those in richer provinces. Equalization payments are unconditional—that is, the provinces that receive them can spend them as they see fit. In 2000–01, payments provided under this program amounted to almost $10 billion.

3) *Territorial Formula Financing (TFF).* This transfer to territorial governments recognizes the higher costs of providing public services in the North. In 2000–01, payments provided under this program totalled nearly $1.5 billion (Canada, 2000a).

Exhibit 5.1 shows the total federal transfers for each funding program over a 10-year period.

Exhibit 5.1

TOTAL FEDERAL TRANSFERS TO THE PROVINCES AND TERRITORIES, 1993–94 TO 2003–04

	CHST[1]	EQUALIZATION	TERRITORIAL FORMULA FINANCING	TOTAL TRANSFERS[2]
		(BILLIONS OF DOLLARS)		
1993–94	29.0	8.1	1.2	37.4
1994–95	29.4	8.6	1.2	38.3
1995–96	29.9	8.8	1.2	39.0
1996–97	26.9	9.0	1.2	36.1
1997–98	25.8	9.7	1.2	35.7
1998–99	26.7	9.6	1.2	36.5
1999–00	29.4	9.8	1.4	39.4
2000–01[3]	30.8	9.5[4]	1.4	40.6
2001–02	31.3	10.0	1.4	41.6
2002–03	32.0	10.3	1.5	42.6
2003–04	32.7	10.7	1.5	43.7

1. Cash plus tax transfers.
2. Equalization associated with CHST tax transfers appears in both Equalization and CHST entitlements. The total has been adjusted to avoid double counting.
3. All figures for 2000–01 onward are projections.
4. First official Equalization estimate for 2000–01. Experience shows that first estimates generally tend to understate Equalization and are subsequently revised upward.

Note: Numbers may not add due to rounding.

Source: Department of Finance Canada, *Budget 2000: Improving the Quality of Life of Canadians and Their Children* (Ottawa, 2000), 13. Reproduced with the permission of the Minister of Public Works and Government Services Canada, 2000.

STRENGTHS AND LIMITATIONS

Following the Great Depression, many Canadians welcomed greater government control and regulation in their lives. The public demand for broader protection from government in times of need marked a shift from the individualistic laissez-faire approach of earlier years to a new "citizenship of entitlement" (Browne, 1996, 13). Government intervention in the form of income security and the personal social services became more accessible. Through these programs, citizens could seek protection from the potential risks of modern industrial society such as poverty, unemployment, old age, and illness.

Until recently, government departments that had social welfare mandates tended to evolve into large bureaucratic systems. These departments are often criticized for making decisions without regard to the public's wishes and for being concerned less with meeting the needs of clients than with preserving the image and authority of department ministers (Grady, Howse, and Maxwell, 1995; Rosell, 1999). Wharf (1992, 41) poses the rhetorical question: "Don't these organizations become bureaucratically rigid, impersonal and remote from those they are meant to serve—the very opposite of the attributes required to provide effective social services?"

In the last decade, the federal and many provincial, and territorial governments have responded to the criticisms of big government by taking drastic steps to downsize their bureaucratic systems, reduce staff numbers, and devolve formerly public programs to the private sector. In the 1995 federal budget speech, Finance Minister Paul Martin encouraged government "to do what only government can do best—and leave the rest for those who can do better—whether business, labour, or the voluntary sector" (Canada, 1995b, 8). By the late 1990s, it had become clear that governments were smaller and doing less (Hikel, 1997).

Is there still a role for government in the social welfare arena? As Browne (1996) points out, there is little consensus in Canada on this issue: neoconservatives favour less government involvement in social welfare; welfare pluralists would like to see government pull out of service delivery but keep funding programs and making policy decisions; and social activists advocate for a non-government grassroots approach to social welfare that emphasizes self-help, collaboration, and voluntarism. Other groups believe that the federal government performs a valuable service in setting and monitoring national standards for social welfare programs and promoting social justice through income redistribution.

Hikel (1997) expects that the role of the federal government as social policymaker will diminish as government shrinks. Smaller governments may

EXHIBIT 5.2

GOVERNMENT ASSISTANCE

Source: Reprinted courtesy of the estate of the artist, Denny Pritchard.

bring about more efficient operations, but analysts worry that policy decisions may not be made in the public's best interests if the federal government is no longer there to "oversee" the social policymaking process.

II. SOCIAL WELFARE IN THE COMMERCIAL SECTOR

NATURE OF SERVICES

Since the 1980s the commercialization of social welfare services has become more common in Canada. Provinces where neoconservative governments have been elected tend to support commercialized operations and to emphasize deregulation, minimal government funding, and reduced service delivery. This trend has created gaps in the delivery of social welfare services, which are being filled by profit-making agencies.

Typically, commercial agencies deliver services that are profitable and that neither government nor voluntary groups want full responsibility for. These services include home care services in Manitoba, group homes for young offenders in Alberta, and services for people with disabilities in Ontario; commercial nursing homes are also common across Canada (National Union of Public and General Employees, 1996). Since commercial enterprises are driven by profit and target their services to a clientele with the ability to pay, they are not considered to be part of the welfare state (Carniol, 1995; Ismael, 1988).

Many entrepreneurial groups choose to provide social welfare services on a profit-making basis. For example, many social workers have opened their own private practices and charge a fee for providing individual or family counselling, workshop facilitation, consultation services, and program evaluation.

Employee Assistance Programs (EAPs) are another example of commercialized social welfare services. Prevalent in government departments, EAPs are also offered by many large corporations and thus have been described as "corporate welfare" schemes. In general, EAP counsellors provide employees with information, referrals, and counselling (particularly as it relates to substance abuse). Although EAPs can benefit the employee in terms of improved health and well-being, their primary purpose is to benefit the employer: helping employees resolve their personal difficulties is one way to ensure their continuing productivity, which in turn improves the company's profitability (Royal Canadian Mounted Police, 1991).

LEGITIMATION AND AUTHORITY

There are several ways in which commercial programs are gaining legitimacy in Canada. For example, the expansion of fee-for-service programs is supported by government privatization policies aimed at reducing public spending; an increasing number of government-issued licences permit commercial enterprises to sell services to the general public. Commercial social welfare services are also legitimated by a growing number of people who question the expense of government-sponsored programs. The many trade agreements struck between Canada and its international neighbours have served as another means of legitimation. NAFTA, for example, supports private enterprise and minimal government involvement in the production of goods and provision of services (see Chapter 3 for a discussion of social policy in a "free trade zone").

FUNDING SOURCES

Commercial groups obtain funds from a variety of sources. Many entrepreneurs charge the consumer a flat rate for services rendered. Some commercial groups utilize a **sliding fee scale**, in which the fee is adjusted according to the client's financial means. Clients who receive services from a commercial agency may be reimbursed for service costs if they are covered under an extended health insurance program or other compensatory program such as workers' compensation.

The government is a growing source of funds for commercial organizations. As governments reduce their involvement in the direct provision of social welfare services, they enter into purchase-of-service contracts with commercial operations. While the commercial agency administers and delivers the service, the government covers the costs of the program. This type of arrangement is becoming increasingly common among nursing homes, day-care programs for children, and homemaking services.

STRENGTHS AND LIMITATIONS

Several advantages of commercialized social welfare programs have been identified. According to Kramer (1981, 169), profit-making agencies "introduce choice into an area long characterized by scarcity and voluntary agency monopoly." Watson (1983, 19) adds: "The historical absence of the profit motive in social services has contributed to shoddy agency management, poor accountability procedures, and service of questionable or uneven quality." The drive to succeed in business is seen as an incentive for commercial agencies to reduce costs, provide effective services, and operate efficiently (Social Planning Council of Metropolitan Toronto, 1984). Other theorists suggest that competition between commercial agencies will tend to result in a higher standard of service; such may be the case when governments purchase services from profit-making organizations and then threaten to cut funds if the required standards are not met (McCready, 1986).

Although commercialization has its advantages, critics question the values upon which the commercial sector is founded. Traditionally, social services have been associated with the welfare state and values that centre on "the alleviation of human suffering rather than the achievement of personal fiscal gain" (Sauber, 1983, 26); the profit motives of commercialized agencies run counter to these basic values. Commercial enterprises are also seen as lacking in social conscience and commitment:

> In order to turn a profit, private enterprise must also satisfy its customers' needs. However, capital invested in the private sector ... has very weak social commitments. It remains loyal as long as it yields a satisfactory rate of return. When a greater return is possible from other investments, the owners will shift their loyalties. (Quarter, 1992, 3)

There is also a fear that commercial services that may be easily purchased by middle- and upper-income groups will not be accessible to low-income groups. Carniol (1995, 86) states: "In a twist of irony, the very social services that were supposed to modify the inequalities produced by the system in the first place end up by being sold to those most able to afford them." This problem was addressed at the World Summit for Social Development (2000): governments that allowed the commercialization of social services were urged to (1) develop effective strategies for regulating the quality of commercial services; and (2) "ensure the equitable provisions of such services."

III. SOCIAL WELFARE IN THE VOLUNTARY SECTOR

NATURE OF SERVICES

There exists such a wide spectrum of voluntary organizations with varying structures and functions that it is difficult to categorize them. However, most voluntary agencies can be classified according to three types: (1) community service agencies that have a bureaucratic organizational structure and a volunteer board of directors (e.g., family service agencies); (2) quasi-public agencies, which are privately incorporated yet depend on total or partial government funding (e.g., Children's Aid Societies); and (3) self-help groups, which are formed by private citizens who share a common interest or concern (e.g., Alcoholics Anonymous) (Armitage, 1996). Voluntary agencies frequently refer to themselves as charitable organizations, nongovernment organizations, or nonprofit organizations. Although the voluntary sector in Canada relies heavily on volunteers (over 1.6 million in 1997), it employs over 1.3 million workers (Picard, 1997).

Browne (1996, 7) points out that as the roles and responsibilities of government evolve, "the voluntary sector changes too and their mutual boundaries shift." The devolution of responsibilities from the public to the voluntary sector has left the latter sector with a greater role in social policy, decision-making, distribution of money and power, and other political and financial matters. A wide range of social welfare programs are now provided by voluntary agencies, including crisis intervention, employment counselling, child and family services, community development, advocacy, information and referral, and the training of volunteers and professionals.

Voluntary social welfare agencies can be divided into two categories: **sectarian** (religious) and **secular** (nonreligious). In early Canada, help of a personal nature was normally the responsibility of sectarian organizations. The traditional leader in the field of social service was the Roman Catholic Church, which, in addition to teaching school and performing religious duties, provided relief to the poor. Although social welfare has largely been controlled by secular administrations in the last few decades, sectarian organizations continue to play an important role in developing and delivering social welfare services at the national and international levels. A 1997 study found that 40 percent of the 75,000 registered charities in Canada were places of worship (only 16 percent were welfare organizations) (Picard, 1997).

LEGITIMATION AND AUTHORITY

Voluntary agency operations are usually governed by a voluntary **board of directors** (or board of trustees). Boards tend to comprise a mix of representatives from the community and often include individuals who have been former recipients of the agency's services. According to Cyril Houlde (United Way of Canada, 2000), the five main responsibilities of a board of directors are

1) to establish the organization's vision and direction;
2) to ensure the financial health of the organization;
3) to ensure the organization has sufficient and appropriate human resources;
4) to direct organizational operations; and
5) to ensure effective community relations.

In general, governments have little control over board activities or decisions. However, a board must be accountable to its funders, members, and stakeholders for its activities and expenditures. The board must also ensure that the agency follows its constitution and operates according to local bylaws and relevant government regulations. As Jaco (1995, 403) notes: "The board of directors legitimates the activities of the agency in the eyes of the community in the same way that politicians and civil servants legitimate government agencies through their accountability to the public."

As it is increasingly called on to meet the needs traditionally met by government, the voluntary sector is likely to gain more legitimacy. There is evidence that Canadians already regard the voluntary sector as a competent service provider. A study conducted by Ekos Research Associates, for example, found that "89 percent of Canadians have a moderate to high confidence in non-profit and voluntary organizations, compared with 76 percent in companies and 57 percent in governments" (Privy Council Office, 1999b). Ultimately, the legitimation of the voluntary sector will depend on how successful the sector is in defining itself and the work that it does. At present, the voluntary sector operates in "a regulatory and legislative vacuum" and is undeveloped in many ways (Picard, 1997, 54).

FUNDING SOURCES

Although voluntary agencies are independent of government, almost two-thirds of their revenue comes from government. Various types of funding arrangements may be struck between voluntary agencies and the government. For example, purchase-of-service contracts are arrangements whereby the government provides the funds for programs, which the agency then administers and delivers. Government grants are also available for program development, demonstration projects, research, and other time-limited projects. Some voluntary agencies rely totally on government to provide a program's core funding; other agencies seek funding from a mix of sources, which may or may not include government. Exhibit 5.3 illustrates the diversity of funding sources found in one British Columbian voluntary agency. Private sources of funding include the United Way of Canada, foundations, churches, business, and unions. Voluntary agencies may also generate revenue from client user fees, fundraising campaigns, and membership dues (Picard, 1997).

Because most voluntary agencies rely so heavily on public funds, the government's drastic cuts in social spending have created a fiscal crisis in the voluntary sector. Almost overnight, entire programs have disappeared as a result of governments' more prudent spending practices. In an effort to fill the gaps left by government, many voluntary agencies have had to "transform ... themselves into fundraisers ..., all competing for scarce dollars" (Picard, 1997, 37). This situation has put considerable strain on private fundraising organizations; the Toronto United Way, for example, reported raising \$51 million in 1996, only about half the amount needed to keep many programs operating.

The competition for funding has forced charities to become more business-oriented; for example, some voluntary agencies are hiring professional fundraisers or are generating revenue through moneymaking activities such as

Exhibit 5.3

DIVERSE FUNDING SOURCES: HOW CHILLIWACK COMMUNITY SERVICES IS FUNDED

PERCENT	
54.0	B.C. Children and Families
12.0	B.C. Health
9.0	Bingo, fee for service, and memberships
5.9	Individual donors
3.0	Canada Immigration
3.0	Canada Health
3.0	B.C. Attorney General
3.0	B.C. Human Resources
2.0	Canada Employment
2.0	B.C. Multiculturalism
2.0	District of Chilliwack
.6	Corporate
.4	Service clubs
.1	Employee groups
100.0%	

Source: Chilliwack Community Services, Revenue, April 1, 1998, to March 31, 1999. Reproduced courtesy of Chilliwack Community Services, BC.

selling products, sponsoring marathons, and running gambling operations. Nonprofit organizations rely heavily on donations made by corporations; in 1998 alone, social service charities received about $145 million from corporate donors. Between 1994 and 1997, the federal government revised its tax system to encourage businesses and individuals to make charitable donations; measures were also introduced to allow charitable organizations to keep more of the revenue they received in donations (Picard, 1997; Privy Council Office, 1999c; Canada, 1999d; Canadian Council on Social Development, 1996).

STRENGTHS AND LIMITATIONS

In 1985 the Macdonald Commission recommended that the voluntary sector assume a greater role in the provision of personal social services in Canada. This suggestion was based on the commission's conclusion that "voluntary organizations are more effective in dealing with social problems than are either market or government organizations" (Royal Commission on the Economic Union, 1985, 811). More recently, the federal government has recognized that

> Canada's voluntary sector plays an increasingly critical and complex role in helping to achieve the goals important to Canadians and ensure a high quality of life. It has become a vital third pillar in Canadian society, working alongside the public and private sectors to make Canada a more humane, caring and prosperous nation. (Privy Council Office, 1999b, 1)

The voluntary sector is recognized for having numerous strengths. Patrick Johnson, an adviser to the federal government on social security reform, describes the sector as an important contributor to Canada's development and identity, and a force that is responsive to emerging human needs (Coalition of National Voluntary Organizations (1994). Judith Maxwell adds: "The voluntary sector is the glue that holds everything together. Charities are the only institutions in society that have as their specific mission to do good" (cited in Picard, 1997, 3). The voluntary sector also "creates and reinforces citizenship through participation, and gives people opportunities to improve the lives of others and to help build and shape their communities" (Privy Council Office, 1999b, 2). More specifically, the voluntary sector contributes to Canada's economic well-being by providing paid employment for 9 percent of working Canadians.

Despite its many positive attributes, the voluntary sector has been criticized for adopting bureaucratic and overly complicated systems of accounting and programming—not unlike those associated with big government; this development may be a function of governments requiring contracted agencies to follow certain "approved" practices (Picard, 1997). Voluntary agencies have also been accused of being "cutthroat" or "profit-oriented" as they compete with other agencies for the shrinking pool of funds (Browne, 1996).

Picard (1997, 55) identifies another problem with voluntary agencies:

> Right now, too many funders clamour to pour money into the sexy project of the hour (say child poverty) and many groups fudge their mandate to cater to that narrow-mindedness. The result is that really good programs struggle because they're not in vogue.

By tailoring programs to meet the government requirements necessary to secure funding, voluntary agencies may be compromising their goals and losing touch with the needs of the communities they serve.

IV. SECTOR COLLABORATION: THE KEY TO SERVICE DELIVERY IN THE 21ST CENTURY

THE BLURRING OF SECTOR BOUNDARIES

The interconnectedness of Canada's public, commercial, and voluntary sectors creates considerable blurring of boundaries between the sectors. This blurring seems to result from two related factors. First, government and private-sector activities are often blended, as in the case of joint projects or shared-cost arrangements. Second, the activities, functions, and roles of private and public social agencies are often similar. The lack of distinction between the sectors is not a new phenomenon; throughout Canada's history, the government has continually shifted its degree of involvement in service delivery, making sector boundaries more or less clear (Rainey et al., 1976).

As Thomas and Wilkins (1997, 110) point out, the 1990s witnessed "the emergence of a bewildering array of new types of public organizations, some of which straddle[d] whatever boundary line remain[ed] between the public and private sectors." These semiautonomous service delivery systems include:

- several types of Crown corporations;
- mixed enterprises involving public and private participation;
- government-owned/contractor-operated organizations (GOCOs); and
- different forms of public-private partnerships, contracting out, and privatization.

Exhibit 5.4 illustrates how these service delivery systems might be arranged on a continuum: at one extreme is the traditional government line department; at the other is the fully commercial operation. The diversity of service delivery systems has served as an impetus for government and the private sector to develop "more meaningful and integrated relationships" (Ford and Zussman, 1997, 278). One such relationship is being established between the public and voluntary sectors.

THE VOLUNTARY SECTOR ROUNDTABLE

An expanded role in the delivery of social services is not the only challenge voluntary organizations are facing: "Changing government roles, increasingly diverse populations and new social economic realities require the sector to broaden, deepen and adapt its approaches—and to do all of these things at once" (Principal recommendations, 1999, 9). Picard (1997, 53) charges that the federal government offloaded major responsibilities onto the voluntary

EXHIBIT 5.4

CONTINUUM OF SERVICE DELIVERY OPTIONS

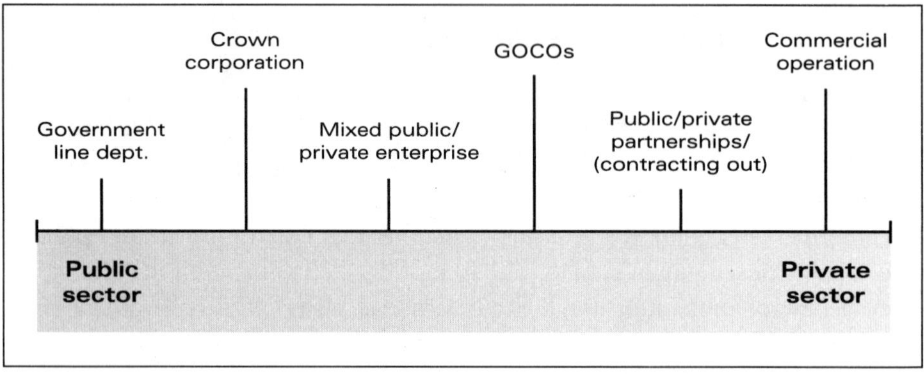

Source: Adapted from Paul Thomas and John Wilkins, "Special operating agencies: A culture change in the Manitoba government," in R. Ford and D. Zussman (Eds.), *Alternative Service Delivery: Sharing Governance in Canada* (Toronto: Institute of Public Administration of Canada, 1997), pp. 109–122.

sector without first developing a plan for maintaining services on reduced budgets; as a result, the voluntary sector "[is] being asked to patch and reweave the social safety net."

In 1995, members of the voluntary sector formed a coalition called the Voluntary Sector Roundtable (VSR) to address the many challenges they are facing as a result of government's fiscal-restraint measures (Voluntary sector pulls together, 1996). Joint tables composed of government and voluntary sector representatives were established to explore and prioritize issues, identify areas requiring further research, and present policy recommendations to government ministers and voluntary sector leaders. In 1999, VSR members released their final report, *Working Together*, which outlines their recommendations for improving the working relationship between the federal government and the voluntary sector; these recommendations were subsequently presented to Cabinet. The Voluntary Sector Roundtable (2000, 1) has described the work of the joint tables as

> the beginning of an ongoing collaborative undertaking to serve Canadians better and enhance their quality of life. Now, after decades of working together in a fruitful but mostly ad hoc basis, and of pursuing common objectives from sometimes divergent or even opposing positions, an historic step has been taken toward working together to achieve mutual goals.

Under the implementation plan outlined in *Working Together*, the partnership between the federal government and voluntary sector will move through three phases:

1) *Commitment.* In the fall of 1999, the voluntary sector and the federal government expressed their commitment to developing a joint accord; the voluntary sector agreed to coordinate the diverse voices within the sector, while the federal government agreed to introduce a national volunteerism initiative.
2) *Construction.* In this phase, an implementation group composed of government and voluntary sector representatives will monitor the research and consultative process taking place between the two sectors. A series of task forces will investigate and make recommendations on such issues as funding, liability, and regulation.
3) *Consolidation.* The consolidation phase, which is expected to be ongoing, will focus on the details of how the public and voluntary sectors will work together. Activities during this phase will include ratifying an accord, establishing a relationship with Parliament, devising an annual reporting process, creating a dispute-resolution process, formulating government-wide principles, and determining how voluntary agency operations will be monitored and funded (Voluntary Sector Roundtable, 2000).

EMERGING AND CONTINUING TRENDS

As government and the private sector work to clarify their various partnerships, Canadians can expect that roles and responsibilities in basic governance will continue to shift. Paquet (1997) suggests that these shifts can be observed at three levels: (1) the macro or national level; (2) the mezzo level, where delivery sectors overlap; and (3) the micro level, where services are delivered. His predictions concerning each of these levels are outlined below.

At the **macro level**, Paquet forecasts, we can expect to see a steady expansion of the role of commercial and voluntary sectors, and a rise in the number of partnerships between government and the private sector. Public confidence in the federal government will increase, reducing the need for the government to devolve service delivery responsibilities to other levels of operation.

At the **mezzo level**, Paquet speculates, the stakeholders in the public, commercial, and voluntary sectors will engage in much more consultation and negotiation as they become more conscious of both their vulnerability and their power. An erosion of boundaries between the sectors and new power-sharing arrangements can be expected as well. Various types of accountability rules will be imposed on each sector, and the courts may become more active in interpreting their respective roles and responsibilities. An increase in the number of public forums will provide opportunities for Canadians to become more involved in the definition of public programs.

At the **micro level**, Paquet predicts, there will be a redefinition of service delivery systems that will reduce the capacity of government to influence program development. A new form of "policing" will be required to ensure that each sector is accountable for its operations. Downsizing in the public sector will have a dramatic effect on unions and significantly reduce their bargaining power.

In the early stages of redefining roles and responsibilities, an overemphasis on performance indicators and rules is likely to characterize the contracts between government and the private sector. As private-sector agencies redesign their operations to meet government expectations, they may start to look more like public agencies than private agencies. Of the boundaries between the sectors, Paquet (1997, 49) notes that "one may expect a growing degree of fuzziness to become the norm."

Introduction

The three main service sectors in Canada's social welfare system are public, commercial, and voluntary; although these sectors are often viewed as separate entities, there is substantial overlap between them. The dispersal of programs and services across three sectors tends to make the social welfare system fragmented and uncoordinated. However, this arrangement offers choice to people seeking help.

Social Welfare in the Public Sector

Many social welfare programs are collaborative efforts between the federal, regional, and municipal governments. Funds for social welfare are transferred from the federal to regional governments through the Canada Health and Social Transfer, Equalization Program, and Territorial Formula Financing arrangements. Although government is criticized for being a bureaucratic and impersonal service provider, it is also seen as having an important role to play in policymaking and funding. Government systems are being downsized, and many programs are being devolved from the public sector to the private sector.

Social Welfare in the Commercial Sector

As the government shrinks its role in social welfare, commercial enterprises step in to deliver services on a profit-making basis. Social welfare programs that tend to be run by the commercial sector include nursing homes, residential homes for children, homemaker services, and day-care centres. Commercial social welfare services are quickly gaining legitimacy through free trade agreements and other schemes that support free enterprise. As a result of competition, the commercial sector has the incentive to deliver services efficiently; however, commercial services may not be accessible to low-income clients.

Social Welfare in the Voluntary Sector

Most voluntary agencies can be classified as community service agencies, quasi-public agencies, or self-help groups. Voluntary agencies are usually governed by a board of directors and may receive funds from government and/or private sources. The service delivery role of the voluntary sector is expanding in response to government downsizing. Voluntary agencies may be compromising their goals as they compete with other agencies for funding.

Sector Collaboration: The Key to Service Delivery in the 21st Century

Cost-sharing arrangements and similar activities have blurred the boundaries between Canada's public, commercial, and voluntary sectors. The new partnership between the voluntary and public sectors will evolve over three phases: commitment, construction, and consolidation. The 21st century is expected to bring further changes—at the macro, mezzo, and micro levels—to the roles and responsibilities of Canada's public, commercial, and voluntary sectors.

KEY TERMS

PRIVATE SECTOR 105
PUBLIC SECTOR 105
COMMERCIAL SECTOR 105
VOLUNTARY SECTOR 106
REGIONAL GOVERNMENTS 107
MUNICIPAL GOVERNMENTS 107
TRANSFERS 108
SLIDING FEE SCALE 113
SECTARIAN 115
SECULAR 115
BOARD OF DIRECTORS 115
MACRO LEVEL 121
MEZZO LEVEL 121
MICRO LEVEL 122

CHAPTER 6

SOCIAL AGENCIES

• OBJECTIVES •

I. To describe the various types of residential and nonresidential social agencies.

II. To review social agency activities and accountability practices.

III. To consider how admission criteria, availability of services, and the problem of stigma may discourage the use of services.

IV. To examine the bureaucratic, collectivist-democratic, and learning-based approaches that may be adopted by social agencies as models of organization.

V. To introduce the concept of intraorganizational change and consider the role that structural social workers may play in this type of change.

INTRODUCTION

Once social policies are developed, organizations are needed to translate those policies into social programs and services. Organizations that have this function are commonly called social agencies. Jaco (1995, 393–394) defines a **social agency** as "a formally structured bureaucratic unit, sanctioned by society, whose goals and activities focus on meeting human need." Examples of social agencies include family service agencies, welfare offices, child protection units, and crisis centres.

Although each social agency has its own unique tasks, administration, organizational structure, goals, and mandate, most social agencies share a number of basic functions and activities. These include the following:

1) securing funding, setting and adhering to budgets, and distributing funding to agency programs and services;
2) assessing client needs and providing service and/or material resources for clients who meet the eligibility criteria;

3) ensuring the quality of services and regularly evaluating the effectiveness of programs;
4) recognizing and reducing gaps in service, and revising or introducing services to meet consumer needs;
5) being accountable to clients, governing boards, funders, and the community for service delivery and use of resources;
6) guiding agency activities by developing and revising policies, procedures, and ethical standards;
7) recruiting, managing, and supervising staff and volunteers and ensuring that personnel performance meets agency and legal standards; and
8) fostering and maintaining positive relationships with the community, helping clients connect with other community resources, and working with other systems to resolve social problems.

Many social agencies organize their programs and services around certain populations such as children and families, seniors, women, or people with disabilities. In addition, programs and services are usually designed and implemented to satisfy a specific purpose or intended outcome; for example, to prevent child abuse a parent support program might coach parents on using nonviolent disciplining techniques. An agency's mix of services will depend on the specific needs of the community and the agency's efforts and ability to tailor programs to meet those needs.

I. TYPES OF SOCIAL AGENCIES AND THEIR SERVICE ENVIRONMENTS

THE SHIFT FROM INSTITUTIONAL TO COMMUNITY-BASED SERVICES

Since the 1960s, formerly institutionalized people have been returning to their communities. The trend toward deinstitutionalization coincided with the election of neoconservative governments that set out to address the high cost of institutionalization. As a result of government cutbacks to institutions and the redirection of funds from institutional to noninstitutional or **community-based services**, there has been a dramatic decline in the number of Canadians living in institutions. According to the 1996 census, approximately 338,000 Canadians resided in institutional settings in that year; almost three-quarters of those individuals were seniors (Lindsay, 1999). With the shift from institutional to community-based services, the range of service delivery models has expanded considerably.

RESIDENTIAL AND NONRESIDENTIAL CENTRES

Residential centres usually provide living quarters, meals, and a comprehensive set of services for people who require round-the-clock care. The type of residential facility that exists in a given community is determined by the needs of its residents. Some common types include the following:

- long-term care facilities or nursing homes for seniors;
- halfway houses for persons recently released from correctional institutions;
- assessment or treatment centres for children or youth with emotional or behavioural disorders;
- community-based group homes for adults with developmental delays;
- in-patient treatment centres for people with alcohol/drug addictions; and
- shelters and transition houses for abused women and their children (Strike, 1989).

There are noticeable trends in the use of residential services in Canada. In general, when community- or home-based services are less available, or their cost is prohibitive, the rate of people referred to residential centres tends to rise. Conversely, when nonresidential services (e.g., home services) are plentiful, the number of people in residential settings tends to decrease (Fabiano and Martyn, 1992).

Nonresidential centres normally provide services on a drop-in, appointment, or outreach basis. These services cater to those who can look after many of their own needs and who do not pose a threat to themselves or to the rest of society. Although some nonresidential programs (e.g., child protection agencies) aim to control or restrain socially unacceptable behaviour, institutionalization is generally unnecessary. Some types of nonresidential centres and services are described below.

DROP-IN AND CRISIS CENTRES

Drop-in centres may provide social opportunities, counselling, information services, and a wide range of informal programs such as "mornings out for moms and tots." These centres are usually sponsored by private nonprofit groups or organizations and are staffed by a combination of professional and volunteer workers. Most drop-in centres cater to a particular demographic group, such as Native people, seniors, teens, or women.

Many drop-in centres are also crisis centres that address a variety of emergency situations, including sexual assault, domestic violence, suicide, alcohol and drug abuse, teen pregnancy, and AIDS. Emergency services are available across Canada to intervene in cases of child abuse or neglect, and to assist people in immediate need of money, food, clothing, and/or shelter. In addition to face-to-face service, many crisis centres have trained staff or volunteers who provide 24-hour telephone assistance to people in distress.

FAMILY SERVICE CENTRES

Family service centres (also known as "parent and child centres," "family service bureaus," or "family resource centres") offer a diverse range of voluntary services, including family counselling, marriage-preparation courses, teen mom support groups, parent education, and child development programs. While their mix of services will reflect the needs of their respective communities, all family service centres are concerned with strengthening families, developing parenting skills, and fostering healthy child development. Family services may be delivered by professional staff or volunteers; on a one-to-one or group basis; in an office setting, the client's home, or social institutions such as churches and schools; and on an appointment or drop-in basis. Family service centres are typically nonprofit organizations that are governed by a board of directors who are members of the community.

WORKPLACE PROGRAMS

It is becoming increasingly common for counselling services to be available through one's workplace in the form of Employee Assistance Programs (EAPs). Not all businesses have established EAPs. However, many large companies across Canada provide EAP services free of charge to employed, retired, or disabled employees and their spouses or dependents. Some EAPs focus on assessment, referral, counselling, and follow-up services for alcohol and drug abuse, while others address such issues as work-related stress, marital conflict, and interpersonal problems. EAP services are usually delivered by paid professionals—often social workers or psychologists—in a setting outside the workplace. In addition to the support they receive from EAPs, employees may be provided with services (e.g., peer counselling) by their unions. Exhibit 6.1 illustrates the EAP model used by a company in the Northwest Territories.

EXHIBIT 6.1

EVERGREEN EMPLOYEE ASSISTANCE PROGRAM

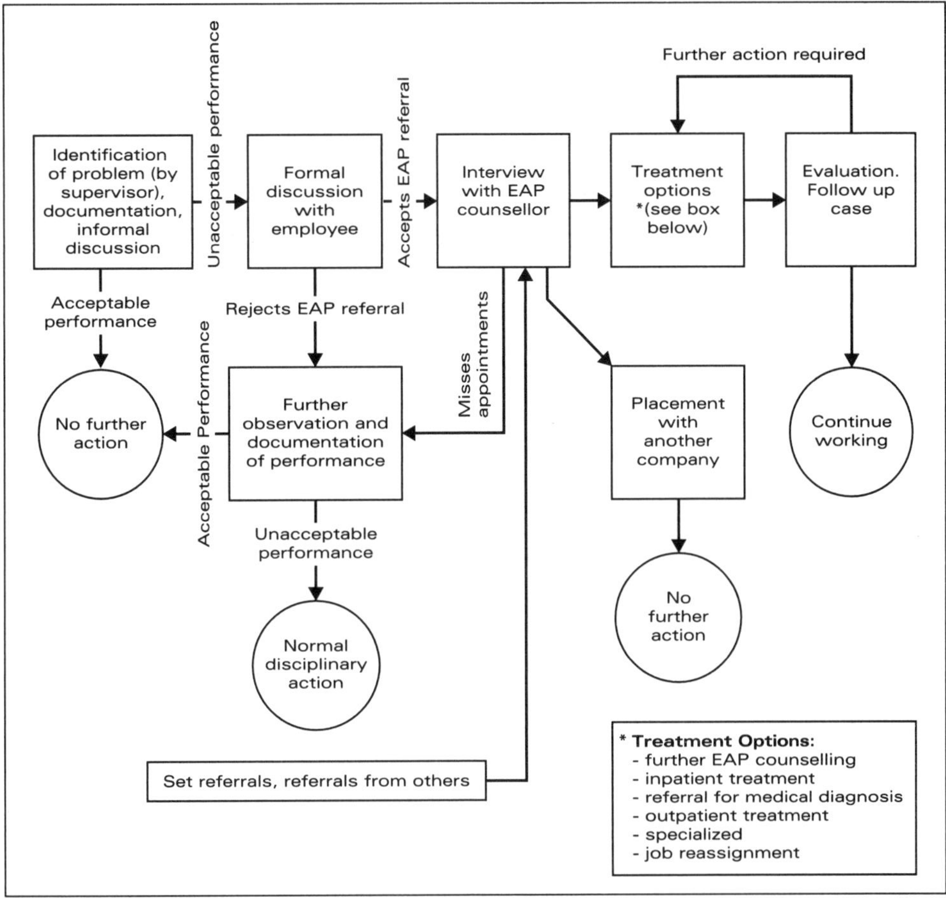

Source: Evergreen Forestry Management Ltd., Employeee Assistance Program, 1996. Prepared by Su-Anne Yeo, Northwest Territories Regional Office, Hay River Dene Band, Hay River Reserve, Northwest Territories. On-line, available: http://www.inac.gc.ca/pubs/fnepi/manage.html [2000 June 1].

ON-LINE SUPPORT

The Internet has become a primary source of information and support for individuals in recent years. More and more social agencies are using the Internet as an alternative to face-to-face service. On-line support has particular benefits for individuals who live in remote locations and cannot easily access social agencies.

Agency Web sites can serve as resource centres, providing visitors with information about the agency's history, the services it offers, coming events and projects, and the like. E-mail, chat rooms, and discussion forums can be used to facilitate services such as information-sharing and counselling. On-line services allow people to deal with sensitive issues—such as sexual assault—anonymously. Social agencies that use the Internet are facing the challenge of finding technologies that will guarantee confidentiality for on-line service users (Shade, 1996). A Toronto-based on-line support network is profiled in Exhibit 6.2.

Exhibit 6.2

ABILITY ONLINE SUPPORT NETWORK

"Putting children and adolescents with specialized needs in touch with the world!"

Ability OnLine is an electronic mail system that connects young people with disabilities or chronic illness to disabled and non-disabled peers and mentors. This easy-to-use network gives "wings" to thousands of children and adolescents by removing the social barriers that can come with having a disability and illness, and by providing opportunities to form friendships, build self-confidence, exchange information, and share hope and encouragement through email messages.

Ability OnLine is also a valuable resource for families and friends anxious to know more about an illness and help manage it. The network provides disabled youngsters and their families with up-to-date information on medical treatments, educational strategies and employment opportunities through peer support. Access to the network is available through the use of a computer, modem and the telephone system, either by dialing directly into the system or via the Internet.

Ability OnLine is entirely funded by private donations from various charitable foundations, corporate sponsors, and private individuals like you.

Source: CanadaAbility OnLine, Toronto [on-line]. Available: http://www.ablelink.org/public/about.htm [2000 June 1]. See the Ability OnLine Web site, at http://www.abilityonline.org.

OUTREACH SERVICES

Outreach services are provided in the client's natural environment, such as the home or a park. The following is an example of how an outreach service might work.

A community support worker is contracted to provide in-home services to a young man living with a physical disability. The worker notices that the young man gets frustrated when trying to remove utensils from a kitchen drawer. In capturing this "teachable moment," the worker is able to help the young man identify the problem and come up with a solution (e.g., arranging for the installation of easy-to-pull drawers). In addition, the worker is in a position to help the young man recognize and deal with his feelings of frustration as they occur.

Many observers believe that the application of helping strategies in "real-life" settings makes outreach services more effective than counselling services that take place in an office or some other "artificial" setting.

Some outreach programs employ "street workers" to seek out and help those who are in high-risk groups, including people living in isolated geographical areas; recent immigrants who do not speak English or French; and persons who are immobile due to age, disability, or some other limiting condition. Also targeted are children and youth living on the street, particularly in urban centres. Street workers can help identify those who may be in immediate or potential need, and assist them in accessing the appropriate services.

MULTISERVICE CENTRES

Many communities offer a variety of programs under one roof. These "one-stop" or multiservice centres provide comprehensive, coordinated, and integrated services for people in need. Services may be aimed at a particular group. For example, a centre may specialize in programs for adolescents and offer such services as a teen drop-in program, mental-health counselling for youth, and tutoring services for young mothers attending high school. Other centres may serve a variety of target groups by providing everything from legal aid services to child development programs.

II. SOCIAL AGENCY ACTIVITIES

Social agency activities that involve face-to-face interactions with clients are called **direct services**; these frontline services aim to prevent or reduce problems experienced by individuals, families, and small groups. **Indirect services** do not usually involve personal contacts with clients but can influence the type and quality of direct services. Examples of indirect services are social administration, program development, and social research.

DIRECT SERVICES: THREE LEVELS OF PREVENTION

All direct services are preventative in the sense that they either try to prevent the emergence of social problems or try to limit the negative effects of a problem that has already arisen. A public health prevention model can be adapted to describe most direct services provided by social agencies. This model suggests that programs and services operate at one of the three levels described below:

1) **Primary prevention** activities aim to prevent the emergence of personal and social problems by educating, providing information, or promoting certain practices. Usually targeted at large segments of the community, primary prevention programs include alcohol and drug education, AIDS-awareness strategies, antiracism campaigns, marriage-preparation courses, family-life programs, and information and referral services.
2) **Secondary prevention** activities are concerned with identifying problems in the early stages of development (i.e., before they become serious or chronic). This level of prevention also involves intervening to control or change the cause of the problem. Examples of social welfare programs and services at the secondary prevention level include victim assistance programs, support services for children and youth, and respite services for family caregivers.
3) **Tertiary prevention** activities aim to reduce the negative effects of problems—such as disability and dependence—that have become chronic or complex. Social welfare programs in this category are commonly referred to as **crisis interventions** and include child protection services, family therapy, residential care for children and youth with severe psychiatric and/or emotional disorders, and in-patient alcohol and drug treatment. Unlike programs in the secondary prevention category, tertiary prevention programs are often mandatory and supported by law (Armitage, 1996). For example, a social worker who has removed a child from an abusive home may make it mandatory for the child's parents to attend alcohol and drug treatment before the child is returned to the home.

Traditionally, tertiary prevention has been the main focus of direct services. In recent years, however, social programmers have shown a greater interest in primary prevention. The gradual shift from tertiary prevention to primary prevention is being driven by a variety of factors, including the following:

- The cost of treating long-term problems is often prohibitive.
- The direct benefits of treating chronic problems are not easily identified or measured.

- Long-term treatment is not an option under many programs.
- A growing number of studies point to the effectiveness of primary prevention programs.
- Governments are showing more interest in building healthy communities through large-scale prevention programs than in treating individuals.
- It is generally agreed that it is easier, less expensive, and more humane to improve the lives of people before rather than after problems develop.

Themes other than the shift to early prevention are emerging in direct services. First, greater emphasis is being placed on strengthening the natural support systems (e.g., friends and extended family) of individuals and reducing dependence on professional systems. Second, the philosophy underlying direct services is becoming more systems-oriented (i.e., problems in living are attributed more to flaws in the social-political-economic environment than to individual failure). Third, there is greater emphasis on helping people develop—through such methods as coaching and information-sharing—the problem-solving skills they need to make informed decisions.

INDIRECT SERVICES

Social Administration

Usually the responsibility of senior employees or a board of directors, **social administration** involves developing or translating policies and procedures, planning and managing direct service activities, and ensuring that the agency meets its goals and objectives. Talcott Parsons (1960), a major contributor to organizational theory, suggests that social administration is carried out at three different levels in social agencies: the institutional level, the managerial level, and the technical level. Although the activities found at each level may overlap, each level is distinct in the types of knowledge and skills that are required.

At the *institutional level*, the values and goals of society are translated into concrete programs and services. Decisions must be made at this level as to the type of social problem that will be addressed and who will be the recipient of the agency's programs and services. The administration must also carve out a niche for the agency in the community, develop a positive public image, and ensure that the agency is accountable to the community for its activities.

Activities at the *managerial level* involve obtaining and allocating resources, designing programs, and recruiting staff and coordinating their duties. An essential task for administrators at this level is to discover effective means for achieving the agency's goals and mandates. This often involves providing appropriate training and professional development opportunities to staff so that they can continue to meet client needs.

The *technical level* is concerned with the direct provision of materials, services, and programs to service users. Important activities at this level include selecting, implementing, and refining interventions that are likely to help clients achieve their goals. Increasingly, social service administrators are responsible for monitoring the effectiveness of programs and ensuring that programs are responsive to the changing needs of the community.

Program Development

Social agencies are mandated to fulfil a number of societal functions and uphold essential cultural values, beliefs, and knowledge. Thus, when developing individual programs, social agencies must ensure that program goals, objectives, and intended outcomes are compatible with the broader community goals (Sarri, 1977). Having decided what type of program is required, the agency formulates goals and objectives. As defined by Health Canada (1996a, 15), *goals* are abstract and "general statements of what a project is trying to do"; *objectives*, on the other hand, "are specific, measurable statements of the desired change(s) that a project intends to accomplish by a given time."

The next step is to figure out how the formulated goals and objectives will be achieved. Developers of a program that seeks to eliminate poverty, for example, may focus on increasing access to training and job opportunities, implementing job search services, or using wage subsidy programs to help welfare recipients enter the workforce. A wide array of strategies can be applied to any given problem, so it is important that program developers examine and compare all the possibilities before choosing a strategy that is most likely to produce the desired outcome (Moroney and Grub, 1981).

Some social agencies implement new programs on a "pilot" basis; the trial period allows an agency to assess the viability of a program before making a long-term investment in it. Whether implemented on a pilot or regular basis, the program—and its activities, processes, and expenditures—must be monitored. The monitoring stage involves observing program activities and determining whether the program is achieving its goals and objectives. During this stage, underperforming features of the program can be identified and modified. Exhibit 6.3 illustrates a 10-step approach to program planning and development.

EXHIBIT 6.3

THE 10-STEP PLANNING MODEL

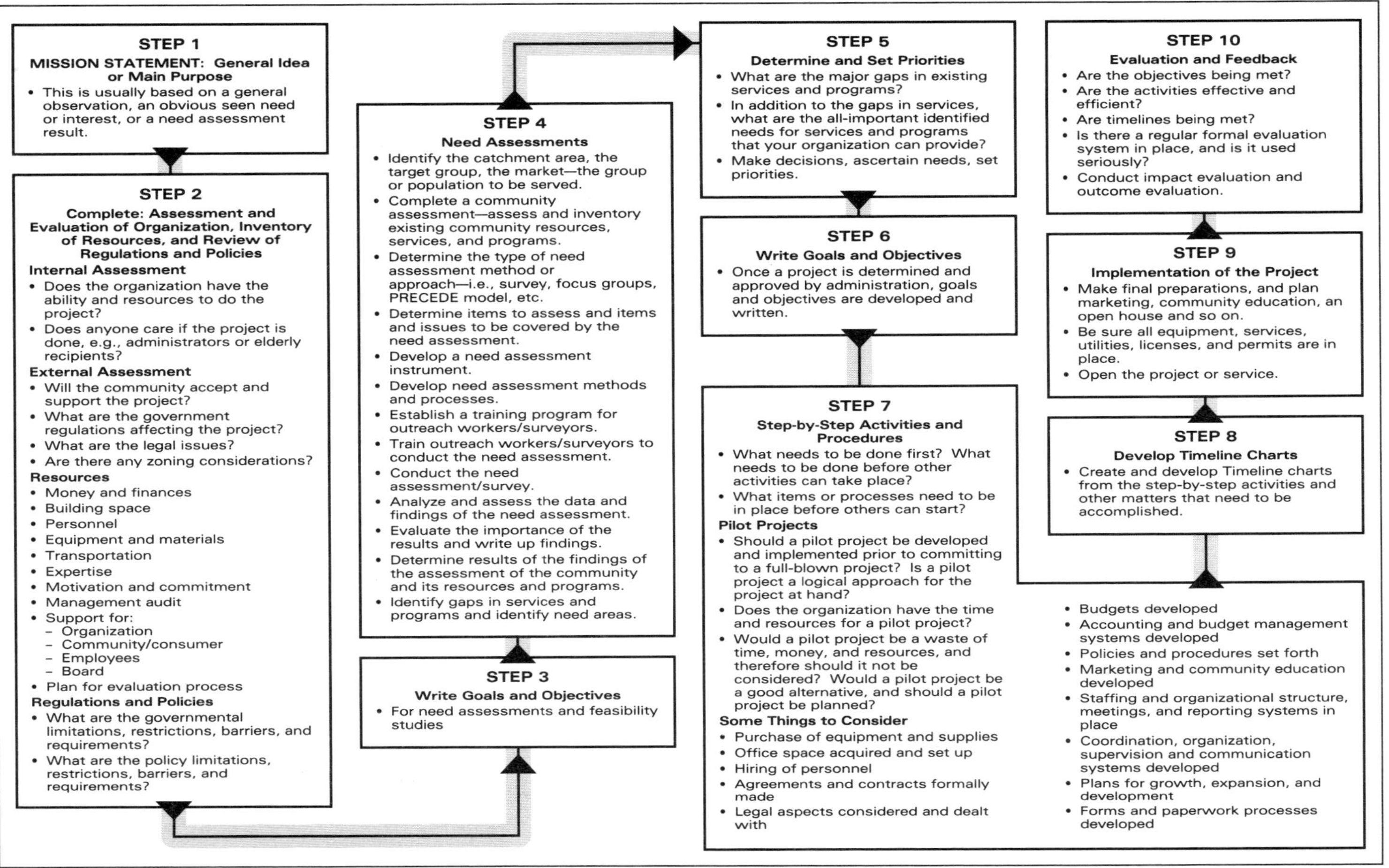

Source: Thomas C. Timmereck, *Planning, Program Development and Evaluation: A Handbook for Health Promotion, Aging and Health Services* (Boston: Jones and Bartlett, 1995), xxiv–xxv.

Social Research

Social research is "applied research"—that is, the information and knowledge obtained through the research is applied to solving problems at the policy, program, or service delivery levels (Grinnell, Rothery, and Thomlison, 1995). Research that is conducted in social agencies is usually in the form of either program or practice evaluation.

Program evaluation may be understood "as the process by which services and programs are systematically examined to determine whether they are needed and used, how well they are run, and whether they meet their stated objective, and whether they are worth the cost" (G. McDonald, 1995, 544). The demand for program evaluation has increased over the last few decades as a result of the rising cost of social programs and the subsequent pressure on government-funded social agencies to prove that their programs are cost-effective. The consumer movement has placed additional pressure on social agencies to demonstrate that their programs are improving clients' lives. There are three main types of program evaluation: (1) process evaluation, which examines how program activities are carried out; (2) cost-benefit evaluation, which looks at the relationship between a program's results and its costs; and (3) impact or outcome evaluation, which determines whether the program has achieved the desired outcomes or results.

Practice evaluation is carried out by individual service providers to determine how effective an intervention is in helping a client. The increasing popularity of this type of research in the social work field is largely attributable to growing professionalism and the need for practitioners to demonstrate their competence. A particularly useful tool for evaluating practice is the *single system research design,* which emerged in the 1970s. Focusing on the individual or family (i.e., the "single system"), this evaluation method is applied during the period in which the client is receiving services. Questionnaires and other measuring devices may be used to track the client's progress. For example, a client working on improving self-esteem could be asked to complete a "self-esteem questionnaire" at each session. A comparison of the scores from the completed questionnaires would reveal whether the intervention's effect on the client's level of self-esteem was positive, negative, or neutral; an intervention not producing the desired results could be modified or replaced with another type of intervention.

A NEW AGE OF ACCOUNTABILITY

The criteria by which social agencies are held accountable have been changing in recent years. In the past, a social agency was deemed accountable if it could provide sufficient information about how funds were spent, who received services, the types of activities offered, how many people completed the program, and the like. External auditors were often hired to assess an agency's degree of **accountability**. Licences, service contracts, and agency documents were also reviewed to determine if the agency was following the required procedures and managing resources appropriately. If the agency met all the requirements, it usually received the auditor's stamp of approval (Minnesota Department of Human Services, 1996; Shipman, 1971).

Since the 1980s, there has been a shift in accountability practices from a *bureaucratic* or *service* focus to an *outcome* focus. An outcome-oriented approach places less emphasis on expenditures and types of program activities and greater emphasis on how resources are used, the purpose of programs, and the effects of program activities on clients. The Minnesota model of service management is among the various outcome-oriented models being adopted by Canadian social agencies. According to this model, the shift to an outcome-oriented approach

> involves fundamental change in how we think about interventions, how programs are managed, how practitioners interact with clients, and how providers are held accountable. On the other side, government will have to shift how it funds, manages and oversees programs. (Minnesota Department of Human Services, 1996, 2)

Exhibit 6.4 presents a comparison of the bureaucratic and outcome-oriented approaches.

III. BARRIERS TO SERVICES

A major concern of social agencies is ensuring that programs and services reach those who need them. Many people are able to identify a need for professional help, locate the appropriate agency, use the services provided, and resolve the issue that prompted them to seek help in the first place. Other people are unable to get the help they need because one or more barriers prevent access to, progress toward, or completion of a social service. This section looks at how social agencies may intentionally or unintentionally discourage the use of services.

Exhibit 6.4

TWO APPROACHES TO SERVICE MANAGEMENT

BUREAUCRATIC APPROACH	OUTCOMES-ORIENTED APPROACH
1. Services-oriented	1. Results-oriented
2. Rules and regulations drive actions—focus is on compliance	2. Desired client changes drive actions—focus is on accomplishments
3. Top-down decision-making	3. Collaborative decision-making
4. Standardized programs/uniform models	4. Individualized programs/diverse models
5. Rigidity in implementation (deliver services in the prescribed way)	5. Flexibility in attaining outcomes (agree on goals but use discretion in achieving them)
6. Management by controlling inputs	6. Management by attaining results
7. Accountability by monitoring delivery processes and reporting on inputs, activities, and numbers served	7. Accountability by monitoring outcomes and reporting actual accomplishments compared with desired results
8. Risk-taking discouraged	8. Incentives to take risks
9. Focus on administration	9. Focus on management/leadership
10. Perceived as self-serving	10. Perceived as serving clients

Source: Adapted from *Focus on Client Outcomes: A Guidebook for Results-Oriented Human Services* (St. Paul: Minnesota Department of Human Services, Community Services Division, March, 1996). Reprinted with permission from the Minnesota Department of Human Services.

ACCESSIBILITY OF SERVICES

Accessibility in the social welfare system relates to how easily people can reach and use programs and services. People requesting social welfare services must usually meet predetermined eligibility criteria before a service is rendered. Each social agency has its own screening devices to ensure that services are limited to people whose concerns are compatible with the goals or mandate of the agency.

Access to programs often depends on the judgment of various "gatekeepers" in an agency. Receptionists and intake workers, for example, are often charged with quickly determining client eligibility, directing applicants to appropriate programs, or referring an applicant to another program in the community. In some cases, applicants can gain access to programs only if they are referred by a designated professional. For instance, some residential alcohol/drug treatment programs admit only those people who have been screened and referred by a physician, addiction counsellor, or EAP counsellor.

A client's immediate access to programs may be hindered by an overly complex referral system. This is often the case when client applications must pass through several agency departments in order to be approved.

Although federal and provincial legislation requires public facilities to be barrier-free and physically accessible, social agencies may discourage access in other ways. For example, frontline workers, receptionists, and other staff who do not speak the same language as their clientele, or respect their cultural values, may inadvertently discourage service usage. Similarly, agencies that fail to create an atmosphere of privacy, comfort, friendliness, and acceptance may discourage potential clients (Jaco, 1995). Services may also be inaccessible if people do not know about them, if they are too expensive (in the case of commercial agencies), or if they are available only during inconvenient times (Johnson, Schwartz, and Tate, 1997).

A growing body of literature on the topic of accessibility (largely spurred by the disability rights movement) and increased levels of program evaluation have helped social agency personnel become more aware of the difficulties people have in accessing services. To better understand their community's access needs, agencies use a variety of strategies such as client satisfaction questionnaires, focus groups involving a cross-section of the community, the inclusion of community members on program planning committees, and regular interagency meetings.

AVAILABILITY OF SERVICES

Availability relates to the existence, number, and coordination of programs in a community. People who have to compete for an insufficient number of services may not always be successful in obtaining the help they need. Services that are poorly distributed across urban and rural areas may also pose a problem for people who cannot afford the time or cost of travelling to the place where resources are located (Johnson, Schwartz, and Tate, 1997).

Community programs that are coordinated are linked together in such a way that people are able to move smoothly from one program to another without experiencing unnecessary delays, gaps in service, or other obstacles. A lack of coordination among social agencies can frustrate clients and prevent them from finding the help they need. For instance, poor communication among community agencies may result in clients receiving inaccurate, confusing, or contradictory information about other community resources.

Services in a community may be too fragmented if clients need to be referred to several different agencies or workers. Poor interagency coordination is also indicated when clients find too many agencies that provide the same service.

Ironically, cutbacks in funding have motivated social agencies to improve interagency relations and coordination. MacLeod and Kinnon (1996, 36) note that in periods of restraint, "it is more important than ever to share information, to share experience, to avoid duplication and to stimulate courage for change." To facilitate interagency coordination, some communities have established social planning councils, advisory committees, multidisciplinary teams, and interagency management committees.

THE PROBLEM OF STIGMA

The value placed on self-sufficiency, independence, and resourcefulness in North America has influenced the social meaning ascribed to "asking for help." To admit that one needs help from "outsiders" is sometimes viewed as a sign of personal inadequacy or failure. This attitude can discourage a person from actively seeking the help he or she needs.

Social assistance is a particularly stigmatizing social welfare program. Handel (1982, 4) observes that people who rely on welfare "are often regarded by others not merely as poor but as different in other ways as well from 'regular people'." According to Torjman (1997, 5), "[welfare] ranks lowest in terms of adequacy and highest on the scale of intrusiveness and humiliation." The stigma attached to welfare can be traced to the English Poor Laws, which made distinctions between the "worthy" poor and the "unworthy" poor. Exhibit 6.5 illustrates the persistence of stereotypes about the poor.

Service providers who are sensitive to the problem of stigma face the ongoing challenge of screening programs and services for potentially stigmatizing effects. One positive development has been changes to the way in which service users are addressed. Since the 1970s, many service providers have rejected the term "patient" (because of its association with sickness and disease) and replaced it with the more neutral term *client*. "Service user," "customer," and "consumer" are other designations that suggest the strengths, rights, and capabilities of the individual.

IV. MODELS OF ORGANIZATION

All social agencies are formal systems in that they operate according to set rules, roles, and procedures. Social agencies nevertheless differ in the model

Exhibit 6.5

CHRÉTIEN SAYS HE'S SORRY FOR REMARKS

Under criticism for "poor-bashing," Prime Minister Jean Chrétien apologized Thursday for suggesting people who collect unemployment insurance or welfare sit at home drinking beer.

"Perhaps, I used a word I should not have used," Chrétien said in the Commons, under persistent questioning by Bloc Québécois Leader Lucien Bouchard. "I could have used another expression. If this offended some people, I do apologize."

But Chrétien's retraction failed to satisfy political opponents and advocates for the poor. They said the prime minister blamed the jobless for their problems—an attitude they fear reflects the government's approach to its current review of social programs such as welfare and unemployment insurance.

Alberta Beaver Creek Reform MP Deborah Grey called Chrétien's remarks arrogant intellectualism, unfortunate and crazy. "There is no dignity in being unemployed in this country and being accused by the prime minister of sitting at home and drinking beer," said Grey.

Bouchard said: "When the prime minister says unemployed people are at home drinking beer, [...] we have to break that mentality, it's very disquieting, especially on the eve of a major reform of social programs."

Added NDP Leader Audrey McLaughlin: "It reflects an attitude that I see reflected in the social programs review, and that is we can punish the victims and somehow solve some kind of problem in Canada." A major thrust of the program review is to funnel money now spent on welfare and UI into job training. Chrétien made his original comments in a speech in Toronto on Wednesday night, declaring that the government has to break the mentality of people who work 10 weeks to qualify for 42 weeks of unemployment insurance.

Source: "Chrétien Says He's Sorry for Remarks," *Calgary Herald* (1994, April 22), A13. Reprinted by permission of the Canadian Press.

of organization they adopt: some agencies prefer a bureaucratic approach; others lean toward more collectivist-democratic models; and still others have shown an interest in adopting learning-based approaches to organization.

For the most part, social agencies search for models of organization that can adapt to a dynamic social-political-economic environment and the evolving needs of service users and providers, funders, and governing bodies. Rarely do social agencies reflect pure forms of any particular organizational model; rather, they tend to borrow principles and methods from a mix of organizational approaches.

SOCIAL AGENCIES AS BUREAUCRACIES

One of the most prominent characteristics of a bureaucracy is its hierarchical organizational structure. At the top of the hierarchy is an individual or a board of directors that oversees and sets policies for the general operation of the agency. Below this unit are the managers who are responsible for the different divisions of the agency (e.g., a division for seniors, a division for children and youth, and so forth). At the next level are various offices or programs, each with its own department head who supervises staff and oversees the office's day-to-day operations. At the lowest level of the hierarchy are the frontline workers and support staff who carry out the program activities, tasks, and services. Agencies with "tall" hierarchies—such as those usually found in government—have multiple vertical layers that tend to increase the potential for bureaucratic red tape, rigidity, and resistance to change.

Under a bureaucracy's hierarchically arranged authority structure, managers in the upper levels of the hierarchy generally have the most say in how programs will change, how resources will be distributed, and who will be hired, fired, or promoted. If workers feel left out of the agency's decision-making process, it may be "difficult for [them] to remain committed to the organization, to adhere to regulations, and to bear with constraints" (Jaco, 1995, 409). Consumers of social welfare services may also feel a lack of control over the decisions that affect the services they receive.

The **bureaucratic model** was popular in the days of "big government." At that time bureaucracies were praised by sociologists for being efficient, reliable, and predictable. As government functions and staff expanded, however, there was a greater need to create smaller and more manageable units, each with its own manager. Today bureaucracies are often criticized for being inflexible, overly complicated, unresponsive, and ultimately inefficient.

COLLECTIVIST-DEMOCRATIC APPROACHES

The popularity of the bureaucratic model began to decline in the late 1970s with the emergence of other organizational models. One such model is the **collectivist-democratic organizational model**, which is characterized by an emphasis on power-sharing and group consensus/negotiation in decision-making. This approach also encourages the inclusion of workers and clients in different aspects of the agency's operations. For example, staff may be invited to join the agency's planning or advisory committee, while former clients may serve on the board of directors.

Collectivist-democratic approaches seek to reduce the inequalities inherent in bureaucratic systems, to empower workers and the people who use services, and to promote an environment of inclusion and cooperation. Although these goals are admirable, the model is not without its weaknesses. For instance, using a democratic consensus-seeking negotiation process to make decisions can be time-consuming. In addition, the emotional openness that such an environment encourages may be a source of discomfort for staff who prefer to work with colleagues on a more objective level.

SOCIAL AGENCIES AS LEARNING ORGANIZATIONS

Over the last 20 years, the rapid and dramatic changes taking place in the economic, political, and technological arenas have created many challenges for social agencies in both the private and the public sector. With its inflexible structure and resistance to change, the bureaucratic model is clearly insufficient to meet the challenges posed by a rapidly changing environment. As Paquet (1997, 35) notes:

> as the pace of change accelerated and the issues grew more complex, organizations (private, public and social) came to be confronted more and more with "wicked problems." And to deal with them, a new way of thinking about governance was required.

To adapt to these changes, a growing number of social agencies are embracing the **learning organization model**. Used in the business sector since the late 1980s, the term "learning organization" (or "organizational learning") has only recently emerged in the nonprofit sector. Senge (1990, 3) describes learning organizations as

> organizations where people continually expand their capacity to create the results they truly desire, where new and expansive patterns of thinking are nurtured, where collective aspiration is set free, and where people are continually learning how to learn together.

The learning organization model is based on the assumption that change is ongoing and that organizations must learn to develop new goals and ways of reaching them continuously, not just at the beginning or planning stages. All stakeholders must be involved in the process and be motivated to devise creative ways of handling issues and problems that arise. As Paquet (1997, 35) states, "For the organization to learn fast, everyone must take part in the conversation." This philosophy is opposed to the top-down approach, in which an elite few at the top of a hierarchy monopolize the governing of the organization. Exhibit 6.6 highlights the unique features of a learning organization.

Exhibit 6.6

WHAT WILL BE DIFFERENT IN THE LEARNING ORGANIZATION?

FROM	TO
Individual	*Individual*
Learning that is canned, sporadic, and faddish	Learning that is continuous, strategically tied to future organizational needs
Learning that is not coherently integrated or sequential	Learning that is developmental
Learned helplessness	Personal mastery, learning to challenge assumptions and to inquire
Team	*Team*
Learning that is focused on task accomplishment with no attention to process	Learning that is focused on group development and on building collaborative skills
Rewards for individuals, not teams	Rewards for teams, whole divisions
Compartmentalization	Cross-functional, self-directed work teams
Organizational	*Organizational*
Learning that is superficial and unconnected to previous skills; truncated learning	Learning that builds over time on previous skill attainment
Learning through structural reorganizations without regard to learning barriers created; structural rigidity	Creation of flexible structures to enhance learning for everyone
Societal	*Societal*
Unawareness of impact on society of policies, tunnel vision	Acknowledgment of interdependence and work to improve society generally
Attempts to control societal influence	Constant scanning and projecting of future trends while working to build a desirable future

Source: K.E. Watkins and V.J. Marsick, *Sculpting the Learning Organization* (San Francisco: Jossey-Bass, 1993), 259. Reprinted by permission of Jossey-Bass, Inc., a subsidiary of John Wiley & Sons.

As they adopt the principles of learning-based approaches, social agencies will have to be continuously learning how to adapt to the effects of globalization, the emergence of new communication technologies, shifts in political power, and other environmental changes. Social agencies will also be challenged to increase their learning capacity by recruiting staff who support learning-based principles and/or helping existing staff develop skills that are conducive to the learning approach (Rosell, 1999).

V. SOCIAL WORKERS AND SOCIAL AGENCIES: CHANGING ORGANIZATIONS FROM WITHIN

Despite their potential to help people, social agencies may intentionally or unintentionally interfere with effective service delivery through defective policies, procedures, or programs. Agency employees are becoming increasingly vocal about the need to change those aspects of the organization that have a negative effect on client service. The effort made by staff to change policies or procedures within their own workplace is called **intraorganizational change**.

Structural social work is gaining popularity in social work training programs as a means by which social workers can change social welfare systems while working within those systems. This model is based on the premise that social agencies have contradictory functions: on the one hand, they provide services that aim to improve the client's quality of life; on the other hand, they provide services only to those whose behaviours conform to the values and institutions supported by the status quo. According to the structural school of thought, it is precisely those values and institutions that may have created the problems for which the service user is seeking help. In such cases, structural social workers work to change the activities that are believed not to be in the best interests of service users or providers (Mullaly, 1997).

Mullaly (1997) maintains that to change a social agency from within, the structural social worker must "radicalize and democratize" the agency. *Radicalizing* an agency involves emphasizing its service function and de-emphasizing its social control function. This means taking every opportunity—such as during staff meetings and supervisory sessions—to describe client problems not as personal dysfunction but as the product of a dysfunctional society. Radicalizing also involves confronting agency policies and procedures (e.g., intrusive screening procedures) that negatively affect service users and working to ensure that clients can access the full range of services that are available.

Democratizing the agency involves taking steps to make the organization less bureaucratic and hierarchical and more democratic and inclusive. This process may include helping service users become more involved in the agency's decision-making process (e.g., encouraging them to serve on the board of directors); replacing boss–subordinate relationships with relationships that are more equal (e.g., "consulting with" rather than "reporting to" supervisors); promoting more democratic ways of decision-making; and sharing responsibilities and information.

Like all forms of social work practice, the structural model recognizes that a social worker's primary responsibility is to the service user, not the social agency. In its *Social Work Code of Ethics*, the Canadian Association of Social Workers (CASW, 1994b, 22) states that in the event of a conflict between the needs of service users and those of agencies, "the professional obligations outweigh any obligations to a workplace." Social workers face the ongoing challenge of meeting their responsibilities to service users without alienating themselves from their agency colleagues.

Introduction

Social agencies have a number of functions in common, such as securing funding, assessing client needs, and ensuring the quality of services. The mix of services an agency offers will reflect the community's needs.

Types of Social Agencies and Their Service Environments

Since the 1960s, many people who at one time received social welfare services in institutional settings are now being supported by community-based services. Residential centres provide round-the-clock care, while nonresidential centres provide services on a drop-in, appointment, or outreach basis. Nonresidential centres include drop-in centres, family service centres, workplace programs, on-line support, outreach services, and multiservice centres.

Social Agency Activities

Direct services are social agency activities that involve face-to-face interactions with clients. Not usually involving personal contact with clients are indirect services, which include social administration, program development, and social research. The accountability practices of social agencies have shifted from a bureaucratic or service focus to an outcome focus.

Barriers to Services

There are a number of barriers that can prevent people from using social welfare services. Factors affecting accessibility relate to an agency's screening procedures, referral system, and environment; factors affecting availability include the number, distribution, and coordination of services in a community. The fear of being stigmatized may discourage people from seeking help.

Models of Organization

Bureaucracies are hierarchal organizational structures with several vertical levels of management and power. Collectivist-democratic models emphasize power-sharing and the use of group consensus and negotiation in decision-making. Learning organizations emphasize principles and skills that will help staff adapt to a rapidly changing environment.

Social Workers and Social Agencies: Changing Organizations from Within

Intraorganizational change occurs when staff alter agency policies or procedures that have a negative effect on service. Structural social workers achieve organizational change by radicalizing or democratizing an agency.

KEY TERMS

SOCIAL AGENCY 125
COMMUNITY-BASED SERVICES 126
RESIDENTIAL CENTRES 127
NONRESIDENTIAL CENTRES 127
OUTREACH SERVICES 130
DIRECT SERVICES 131
INDIRECT SERVICES 131
PRIMARY PREVENTION 132
SECONDARY PREVENTION 132
TERTIARY PREVENTION 132
CRISIS INTERVENTIONS 132
SOCIAL ADMINISTRATION 133
SOCIAL RESEARCH 136
ACCOUNTABILITY 137
ACCESSIBILITY 138
AVAILABILITY 139
BUREAUCRATIC MODEL 142
COLLECTIVIST-DEMOCRATIC ORGANIZATIONAL MODEL 142
LEARNING ORGANIZATION MODEL 143
INTRAORGANIZATIONAL CHANGE 145
STRUCTURAL SOCIAL WORK 145

CHAPTER 7

SERVICE PROVIDERS: A RICH BLEND OF FORMAL AND NATURAL HELP

• OBJECTIVES •

I. To study those aspects of the social work profession related to social work values, ethics, knowledge, practice, accountability, education, and employment.

II. To explore the nature of social service work and legislation that seeks to improve standards in social work and social service work.

III. To consider the nature of self-help groups, the role of self-help groups in social welfare, and the possibility of a partnership between self-help and professional groups.

IV. To look at volunteers in the social welfare context, the various ways in which volunteers help others, and how volunteers are recognized in Canada.

INTRODUCTION

The types of help provided in the social welfare field can be classified as either formal or informal. **Informal help** is provided by "volunteer" or "natural" helpers. This type of help includes unpaid care and support given through structured social service organizations and provided to family, friends, and co-workers. **Formal help** can be divided into professional and self-help:

- **Professional help** is given by paid individuals who bring a recognized knowledge base, formal training, and relevant experience to their practice. In many cases, this type of help is guided by a code of ethics that is specific to the worker's profession. Professionals include social workers, social service workers, clergy, and physicians.
- **Self-help** is a form of mutual aid that is provided in formally organized yet nonprofessional groups. Although run by members

> rather than professionals, self-help groups are regarded as formal collectives because (1) they usually have an organized structure for conducting meetings; and (2) they are often affiliated with national organizations that have appointed leaders (e.g., Alcoholics Anonymous) (Pape, 1990).

During the 20th century, the social welfare system assumed many of the supportive roles once fulfilled by family. The rapid growth of this system in the 1950s and 1960s created strong demand for the services of professionally trained helpers such as social workers. Starting in the mid-1970s, however, changes in socioeconomic conditions prompted Canadian governments to reduce spending on public programs, including social welfare. Although professional helpers are still in demand, people in need are increasingly seeking help from self-help groups and informal helpers, who work outside the professional community. This trend appears to be linked to the ongoing shrinking of government-funded social welfare services, unacceptably long waiting lists for existing programs, increasing dissatisfaction with bureaucratic social welfare institutions, and evidence suggesting that the care provided by self-help groups and informal helpers is likely to be at least as good as that delivered by formally trained professionals.

This chapter examines the professional helpers (specifically, social workers and social service workers), self-help groups, and informal helpers (specifically, volunteers) that, together with other groups, make up the broad spectrum of helpers within the social welfare system.

I. SOCIAL WORK AND THE ROLE OF SOCIAL WORKERS

SOCIAL WORK AS A PROFESSION

Social work is similar to other helping professions (such as nursing, policing, and psychology) in that (1) it possesses a code of ethics; (2) it has the means to regulate and enforce set standards of behaviour among its members; and (3) it has developed a theoretical body of knowledge that guides practice (Cross, 1985). Like other professions, social work also requires its members to reach a certain level of educational preparedness—in terms of knowledge, competencies, and ethics—in order to practice.

One of the characteristics that distinguishes social work from other helping professions is its longstanding association with the social welfare system, which has guided the development and delivery of many of its programs. This association dates back to the late 19th century, when many religion-based charitable organizations were replaced by government-sponsored social agencies, which in turn hired social workers to perform a variety of tasks.

Another distinguishing feature of social work is its multilevel approach to practice. At the *micro* level, **social workers** aim to help individuals, families, and small groups improve their problem-solving skills. At the *mezzo* level, social workers seek to improve conditions in and among social welfare organizations, while at the *macro* level they address broader issues such as social problems. Exhibit 7.1 outlines some distinctions been social work and two other helping professions.

SOCIAL WORK VALUES AND ETHICS

Social work practice is based on a philosophy of humanitarian and egalitarian ideals that shape social work goals and interventions. Underlying this philosophy is a set of values or beliefs about how the world should be, rather than how the world really is. Important social work values include acceptance of and respect for others and the right to self-determination. Social work values reflect the diverse and often opposing beliefs of a pluralistic society and are strongly influenced by culture, relationships, personal experience, individual perceptions, and other factors (Johnson, 1998; Compton and Galaway, 1994).

The extent to which social work values are adhered to in practice is limited. For example, it is important that social workers keep client information confidential. This is because without the assurance that personal information will be kept private, clients will be reluctant to disclose much information about themselves to a worker. Circumstances nevertheless arise that warrant a social worker's disclosure of client information without client authorization. For instance, social workers can breach confidentiality to prevent a crime; to prevent clients from doing harm to themselves or to others; when ordered by a court of law; when child abuse or neglect is suspected; or when supervisors, support staff, agency volunteers, or others have an identified "need to know" (CASW, 1994b).

It is not always easy for social workers to know when to adhere to and when to deviate from established social work values. In 1938 the Canadian Association of Social Workers (CASW) developed a social work **code of ethics** to help social workers make this kind of decision. The primary purpose of a code of ethics "is to provide a practical guide for professional behavior and the maintenance of a reasonable standard of practice within a given cultural context" (CASW, 1983, 2). The CASW code was updated in 1983 and 1994.

Exhibit 7.1

A COMPARISON OF THREE HELPING PROFESSIONS

	Social Work	Psychology	Psychiatry
Focus of attention	Dual focus on individual and environment and interaction between the two	Individual behaviour, which includes internal thoughts, feelings, and emotional responses	Mental illness; wide range of disturbed behaviour and emotional reactions
Assessment/ diagnostic tools	Social history; client interviews; observation	Diagnostic tests (I.Q., personality, etc.); interviews; observation	Medical exam; use of International Classification of Disease; interviews; observation; tests
Intervention methods	Casework; family and/ or group therapy; education/information; referral to community resources	Behaviour modification; psychotherapy; environmental modification	Prescribe psychotropic medication; psychotherapy; biological treatments
Aim of intervention	To help individuals, families, and communities understand and solve personal and social problems	To solve or prevent behavioural, cognitive, and affective problems	To reduce symptoms, change behaviour, or promote personality growth
Specializations	Counselling, group work, social administration, research and evaluation, community organization, teaching	Clinical, experimental, neurological, developmental, social, counselling, educational, industrial, personality	Child, geriatric, forensic, liaison, behaviour, family, sexual, psychoanalysis, research
Education	B.S.W., M.S.W., D.S.W., Ph.D.	B.A. or B.Sc., M.A., Ph.D.	Medical doctor and at least 5 years' psychiatric training
Professional association (national)	Canadian Association of Social Workers	Canadian Psychological Association	Canadian Psychiatric Association

Source: Author.

SOCIAL WORK KNOWLEDGE

While values focus on what is preferred, desired, or good, knowledge is concerned with what is true or false. Social work knowledge derives both from inside the social work profession and from other disciplines. Knowledge that is produced indigenously by social workers is based on the shared experience of workers, individual professional experiences, and applied research. Much of the knowledge that is "borrowed" is from other helping disciplines such as psychology, psychiatry, education, and public health; social work knowledge has also drawn extensively from the academic fields of sociology, philosophy, political science, anthropology, economics, history, and law. It is this "cross-pollination" of various types of knowledge that makes social work a highly **interdisciplinary** field (Johnson, 1998).

Social work's **person-in-environment** focus requires social workers to gain knowledge about the client system, the client's environment, and the client in interaction with his or her environment. At one level, social workers must learn about certain aspects of the client system—for example, work with individual clients requires an understanding of the person's psychological, social, physical, spiritual, and other dimensions. It is also important that social workers learn about the client's environment and how culture, the general economy, the political climate, and other external systems may affect his or her ability to function. Finally, social workers need to be aware of the factors that can influence the interactions between the client and his or her environment (McMahon, 1994).

SOCIAL WORK PRACTICE

The Planned Change Process

Social work involves the transformation of knowledge into practice. The aim of social work practice is to help people become more empowered so that they are able to function more effectively. To achieve this aim, social workers apply a generic, formal, systematic, and scientific set of procedures. This problem-solving process is commonly referred to as the **planned change process**. The planned change process consists of five phases:

1) intake;
2) assessment;
3) planning and contracting;
4) intervention; and
5) evaluation and termination.

The *intake* phase is concerned with screening applicants who apply to social welfare programs. Client needs must be considered in view of the agency's eligibility criteria and resources: that is, can the agency meet the client's needs or must a referral be made to a more appropriate resource? In the *assessment* phase, information about the client's concerns or needs is accumulated and then organized to form an overall picture of the client's situation. In the *planning and contracting* phase, the worker and client decide together what needs to be changed (perhaps a behaviour, emotion, thought pattern, or environmental condition) and then establish a contract that outlines the goals and objectives of the needed change and the types of strategies that will be used to effect the change. The *intervention* phase involves putting the plan into action, monitoring its effectiveness, and modifying strategies as needed to achieve the goal. Toward the end of the contract, the intervention is *evaluated* to determine its effectiveness, and the client–worker relationship is eventually *terminated*. The planned change process does not always evolve in a linear fashion; as new client needs or goals arise, certain phases may be repeated or deferred.

SOCIAL WORK SKILLS

Generalist social workers are trained to apply a wide range of practice skills in their work with individuals, families, groups, organizations, and communities. Three generic skill areas are essential for generalist social work practice:

1) *Interpersonal skills* include communication and active listening skills, the ability to build a working relationship with clients, and interviewing and counselling skills.
2) *Process skills* enable the worker to identify and assess client needs, plan and implement appropriate interventions, make referrals, and develop more effective methods for serving clients.
3) *Evaluation and accountability skills* demonstrate competency in evaluating interventions and holding oneself accountable for one's practice and behaviour (Johnson, Schwartz, and Tate, 1997).

Social work skills can also be thought of in terms of the various roles the worker adopts. Generalist social workers typically assume a wide range of roles. The role of *broker* involves helping individuals and groups connect with needed programs and services in the community. An *advocate* speaks or acts on behalf of a client who is having difficulty exercising his or her rights or accessing needed services. A *mediator* helps people in conflict reach mutually satisfying agreements, while a *consultant* assists organizations in improving service effectiveness and efficiency. A social worker who assumes the role of *mediator* identifies areas of need in the community and establishes new social programs and services for target groups.

The skills and roles mentioned above are generic in that they can be applied to interventions with any size of client system, including individuals, families, and small groups. The illustration of the generalist social work perspective in Exhibit 7.2 reflects the person-in-environment perspective and shows the range of approaches and knowledge used in the helping process.

MULTISKILLING

In recent years, a new approach to social work practice has emerged in the form of **multiskilling**. The Canadian Association of Social Workers (CASW, 1998, 1) defines multiskilling as "an approach to care and/or a concept in which staff are cross trained but not professionally educated in two or more tasks or functions associated with at least two disciplines." Although social workers are still required to obtain accredited education in social work, they are able through multiskilling to receive additional training in tasks that are associated with other occupations. For example, a social worker may be trained to conduct physical mobility assessments, an activity traditionally associated with physical therapy or other health-related functions.

Multiskilling offers advantages that have made it an increasingly popular approach. Some organizations see multiskilling as a way to break up rigid divisions of labour and make professionals more flexible in the tasks they perform. There are potential economic benefits as well: staff numbers can be reduced since more people are prepared to perform a wider range of duties.

Multiskilling is not without its critics, however. According to the CASW (1998, 3):

> Social workers believe that specialized practitioners are needed to assist in meeting the varied needs of people. Neutralizing or diminishing the roles of professions and specialists reduces options for clients and increases the potential for harm.

At its worst, multiskilling may give staff unrealistic expectations about their ability to perform tasks that are complex and thus better left to specialists.

PROFESSIONAL ACCOUNTABILITY

The Canadian Association of Social Workers was established in 1926 as a national federation of provincial and territorial social work associations. At

EXHIBIT 7.2

THE GENERALIST PERSPECTIVE

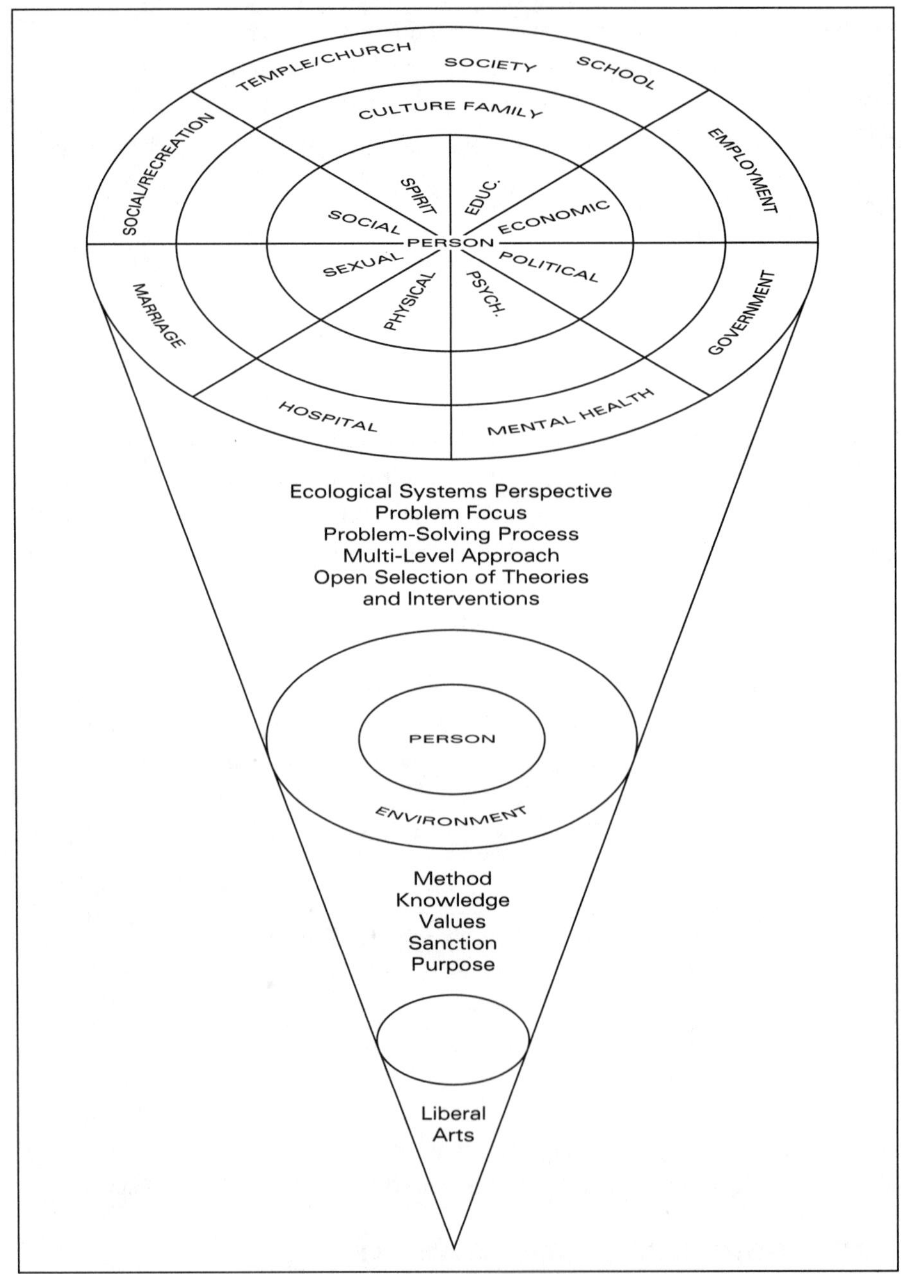

Source: Maria O'Neil McMahon, *A General Method of Social Work Practice: A Generalist Perspective*, 3rd ed. (Needham Heights: Allyn & Bacon, 1996), 24. Copyright © 1996 by Allyn & Bacon. Reprinted/adapted by permission.

present, about 15,500 social workers are registered with a provincial or territorial association (CASW, 2000).

According to its mission statement, the CASW (1994a, 2) "seeks to develop, promote, support and maintain national professional standards of practice of the highest quality." To meet this end, the CASW sets certain standards and guidelines for social work practice in Canada and participates in the development of social work regulation and legislation. The promotion of standards and control is intended not only to protect clients and the general public from incompetent or fraudulent practice, but also to legitimate the profession and its practice. Social workers are expected to practise in accordance with the philosophy, purpose, and standards set by their profession and to be accountable to their clients, their profession, and society.

SOCIAL WORK EDUCATION

Since 1967, the Canadian Association of Schools of Social Work (CASSW) has been the accreditation body for schools offering professional training in social work at the undergraduate, graduate, and postgraduate levels. These three levels of social work education are briefly reviewed here.

Undergraduate Degree

Findings from a 1966 Canadian study, *Manpower Needs in the Field of Social Welfare*, emphasized the need for a Bachelor of Social Work (B.S.W.) to be established in Canada. Thus, Canada's first B.S.W. degree was introduced in 1966. To enter a B.S.W. program, students are required by most universities to complete two years of undergraduate courses, preferably in the liberal arts. The third and fourth years of study (the B.S.W. program) emphasize a strong grounding in social work theory and generalist practice methods.

Graduate Degree

Until 1966, a Master of Social Work (M.S.W.) was the only social work degree available in Canada. An M.S.W. program usually requires one or more years of study following the completion of an undergraduate degree. Students can specialize in specific fields of practice, such as clinical practice, social work administration, or community development.

Postgraduate Degree

The first doctorate program in social work was offered by the University of Toronto in 1951; there are now five such programs across Canada. A Doctor of Social Work (D.S.W.) degree prepares students for work off the frontline, such as teaching in university social work programs, working in upper administration, or conducting research.

As governments devolve many of their service delivery functions to the private sector, many social workers are turning to private practice as a more viable employment option. Canadian schools of social work will need to address the specialized training required for social workers entering private practice—an area that has to date been virtually ignored (CS/RESORS, 1998).

EMPLOYMENT FOR SOCIAL WORKERS

Social workers are employed in a wide range of settings, including school boards, hospitals, voluntary agencies, religious organizations, correctional institutions, Native band councils, and for-profit agencies. In 1994 the federal government identified social workers as one of the occupational groups in demand as a result of Canada's growing "knowledge- and service-based economy" (Human Resources Development Canada, 1994a, 1). According to the Canadian Occupational Projection System, the number of employed social workers rose from approximately 31,000 in 1991 to over 37,000 in 1998. Employment for social workers is expected to rise to about 42,000 by 2005; the accuracy of this forecast will depend on such factors as the health of the economy and ongoing shifts in employment patterns (CS/RESORS, 1998).

There are indications of an ongoing shift in the types of organizations that employ social workers. In 1996, 51 percent of all social workers worked in social service and health service agencies (excluding hospitals), while 29 percent were employed in government or other administrative positions. With annual cuts to hospital, government, and education budgets during the 1990s, the number of social workers employed in the public sector declined. However, the demand for social workers in the voluntary sector, community-based health care, and social administration is expected to increase (Canada, 1996). Employment opportunities for social workers in the commercial sector are also expanding (CASW, 1997).

II. SOCIAL SERVICE WORKERS, GOVERNMENT REGULATION, AND FUTURE DIRECTIONS

SOCIAL SERVICE WORKERS

In the face of ongoing funding cuts and shrinking government programs, many social agencies are hiring social service workers to provide clients with a wide range of direct services. The National Occupational Classification defines **social service workers** as an occupational group that helps clients to cope with and resolve personal and social difficulties. Social service workers are employed by both public and private social agencies, including group homes for youth or people with disabilities, halfway houses for recently released offenders, shelters and transition homes for abused women and their children, crisis centres, and family service bureaus (CS/RESORS, 1998).

Over 40 community colleges and university-colleges across Canada offer one- or two-year programs in social work or social services. Although these educational programs have not developed uniformly across Canada, most combine classroom work with practical experience, focus on a generalist approach to practice, and gear their curricula to the needs of the job market (Lecomte, 1995). By the time they graduate, social service workers have been trained to perform a variety of duties, including: (1) helping clients connect with needed resources in the community; (2) assessing client needs; (3) counselling and giving emotional support to individuals, families, and small groups; and (4) advising clients about their rights and advocating on behalf of clients. Although social service workers and social workers perform similar tasks, the former tend to have fewer responsibilities and less discretionary power. It is not uncommon for a social service worker to serve as a caseworker under the supervision of a social worker.

ONTARIO'S SOCIAL WORK AND SOCIAL SERVICE WORK ACT OF 1998

In the early 1980s, professional social work groups began to raise concerns about the generic use of the title "social worker" by those who do not meet the required educational or competency standards. Since that time, all the provinces have passed legislation that limits the use of the social worker designation to those who meet certain standards and competencies.

In December 1998 the Ontario government passed the Social Work and Social Service Work Act in an effort to recognize the social work profession and improve standards in social work and social services. Under the legislation, a new provincial body called the College of Social Workers and Social Service Workers will have the authority to

1) certify practitioners who meet the required social work/social service work credentials;
2) set and enforce professional and ethical standards;
3) establish complaints and discipline processes in response to public complaints about incompetent or unprofessional social workers and social service workers;
4) foster ongoing professional development of its members; and

5) establish a register of college members, and make that register available to the public (Ontario College of Certified Social Workers, 2000).

Membership in the college is required for practitioners—including those who already have a social work degree or a diploma in social service work—who wish to use the designations "social worker" or "social service worker" in Ontario. Practitioners seeking membership must apply to the college for a qualifications review that will determine their eligibility.

Although Ontario was the last province to legislate social work, it set a precedent in Canada by including in the legislation not only social workers but social service workers. The inclusion of both occupational groups in the legislation reflects their distinct roles in the human services field and is an important first step in the development of high ethical and practice standards for these two groups in Ontario (Ontario College of Certified Social Workers, 2000).

HUMAN RESOURCES STRATEGIC ANALYSIS OF SOCIAL WORK IN CANADA

In 1998 a consortium of professional social work associations began work on a sector study called the Human Resources Strategic Analysis of Social Work in Canada. The study aims to develop a body of knowledge that can be used to identify the challenges facing social workers and social service workers, and to develop strategies for addressing those challenges. It is limited to "the 'social work sector'... [which] includes social workers trained at the university level and social service workers trained at the college level, but not other professionals who work within the social services like psychologists or family therapists" (CASSW, 2000, 2).

A driving force behind the sector study is the extensive changes that are taking place in Canada's socioeconomic environment and their impact on social policies, funding patterns, service delivery, employment for social workers, and social work education and practice. The study is expected to provide much-needed direction to social work and social service training, and a clarification of occupational standards for workers in these fields. Representatives from the Canadian Association of Schools of Social Work, Canadian Association of Social Workers, Canadian Committee of Deans and Directors of Schools of Social Work, Regroupment des unités de formation universitaire en travail social (RUFUTS), and other professional groups initiated the sector study, which is facilitated and co-funded by Human Resources Development Canada. This group's final report is scheduled to be released in the fall of 2000.

III. SELF-HELP GROUPS AND THE PROSPECTS FOR COLLABORATION

CHARACTERISTICS OF SELF-HELP GROUPS

There are an estimated 500,000 self-help groups in North America (Self-help groups, 1999). Different types of self-help groups exist in Canada, but in general they focus on problem-solving (e.g., Overeater's Anonymous), self-development (e.g., Widows Helping Widows), or consciousness-raising (e.g., Senior Power of Regina). Some innovative self-help groups in Canada are profiled in Exhibit 7.3.

Exhibit 7.3

PROFILING SELF-HELP GROUPS IN CANADA

Did you know ...?

- There is a self-help group just for women new to Toronto. NEWTO is for women who have made the move alone and may be feeling isolated and a little overwhelmed. Because it's the only group of its kind, its membership is growing quickly.
- There is an on-line self-help group for caregivers all over Canada who can't get to a meeting but want to talk to others in the same situation. Sponsored by Sympatico's Healthy Way, the group is a source of support for men and women from 22 to 73. Members are people who are taking care of someone they love and are coping with the challenges that responsibility brings.
- There is a self-help organization founded by parents who have lost a child. Bereaved Families of Ontario trains parents to help parents deal with their loss and begin the healing process.

Source: Adapted from Self-Help Resource Centre of Greater Toronto, "Self-Help Facts and Definitions" [on-line], available: http://www.selfhelp.on.ca [2000 April 13]. Reprinted courtesy of the Self-Help Resource Centre of Greater Toronto.

There are a wide range of characteristics that distinguish self-help groups from professional helping networks, including the following:

- *Resonance*. According to Romeder (1990, 28), self-help groups are characterized by resonance, or "the experiencing of reciprocal feelings by two people." Resonance is enhanced through the mutual sharing of feelings and personal experience, and often increases the members' ability to identify with one another. The common denominator in all self-help groups is suffering—a condition with which all group members can identify and which they seek to reduce or eliminate (Pape, 1990).

- *Nonprofessional*. Powell (1995) observes that members of self-help groups consider problems from a subjective perspective: they are concerned with how the problem "feels" and understand the problem because they've "been there." Professionals, on the other hand, tend to look at problems from an objective, neutral, and external perspective, applying theory and analysis to an understanding of the experience.
- *Available and free*. Self-help is usually less structured and more available than professional help. Membership in self-help groups is voluntary and any help given is free of charge. Self-help is also available 24 hours a day and over a period of time that suits the member. Professional help, in contrast, is usually provided on an appointment basis and for a limited period of time that is often determined by the helper. Some professionals, such as those in private practice, work on a fee-for-service basis (Pape, 1990).
- *Egalitarian relationships*. Professional relationships tend to make clear distinctions between the giver of help and the receiver of help, whereas self-help groups emphasize egalitarian relationships and encourage members to simultaneously help and be helped. Responsibility for running groups tends to be divided equally among members of self-help groups; in contrast, most professionally run groups are hierarchical in that they employ leaders who are credentialed "experts" (Romeder, 1990; Pape, 1990).

BENEFITS OF SELF-HELP GROUPS

People join self-help (or mutual aid) groups for a wide variety of reasons. For example, they may believe that "their concerns should not be addressed solely in medical or social service terms" or that their "needs do not fall exclusively under the domain of any one profession or organization"; they may also believe that "traditional services pay insufficient attention to psychosocial considerations or consider them irrelevant or unimportant" (Self-help groups, 1999, 2).

In addition, there is growing evidence linking social support (such as that derived from membership in self-help groups) to improvements in physical health. Social support is believed to increase a person's ability to ward off disease, maintain good health, recover from illness, and cope with serious injury. Other evidence suggests a link between social support, mental health, and general well-being. People who play an active role in self-help groups frequently report improvements in their problem-solving or coping abilities, a greater sense of control over their environment, increased feelings of hope and optimism, and decreased feelings of isolation or loneliness (Self-help groups, 1999).

Another potential benefit of self-help groups is identified in the **helper therapy principle**, developed by self-help expert Frank Riessman:

> By being the helper as well as the receiver of help, a self-help group participant acquires the enhanced self-esteem and feeling of worth that comes with being important to others. The experiential knowledge, gained from coping with a common problem, is valued, just as credentials and technical expertise are valued in a professional helping situation. (Pape, 1990, 5)

Improvements in self-esteem can, in turn, have a positive effect on physical and mental health.

In his study of the self-help movement in Canada, Balthazar (1991) suggests some of the reasons why self-help groups have become so popular in this country. One reason is that our rapidly changing society has contributed to a breakdown of the family and other natural social support systems; self-help groups perform a valuable service in providing alternative social support. In addition, reductions in social welfare programs, the privatization of many helping services, and the promotion of a do-it-yourself attitude have created an environment that is highly compatible with the self-help approach.

SELF-HELP CLEARINGHOUSES

The self-help movement in Canada has grown to the point where self-help clearinghouses have been established. According to the Prince Edward Island Self-Help Clearinghouse (2000), clearinghouses are the "nerve centres for the self-help community," since they play such a central role in the self-help process. Clearinghouses provide information and education about self-help groups, help people find groups that will meet their needs, and publish directories or newsletters that deal with self-help groups and issues. In addition, clearinghouses help people start new groups and provide training to groups at various stages of their development.

SELF-HELP AND PROFESSIONAL GROUPS: A JOINING OF FORCES?

Traditionally, efforts to have professionals and self-helpers join forces have met with considerable resistance. Many self-helpers worry that if professionals are included in self-help groups, a professional rather than self-help framework will dominate the process. As Pape (1990, 6) observes, some self-helpers are concerned that

> with the participation of professionals, the lay helper ideology is at risk ... Even for most well-meaning professionals, it is difficult to take a back seat at a self-help group. There is an accepted norm in today's society that professionals are the only experts who have the skills to solve our problems. As a result, group members are apt to defer to any professionals who are present.

In short, opening up self-help groups to professionals may undermine the entire self-help process, resulting in a loss of the very qualities that make self-help so beneficial.

Some professionals have concerns of their own. In criticizing the self-help group approach, they have expressed the following positions:

1) The planned change process in professional approaches is a more effective agent of change than is experiential learning in self-help.
2) Self-help produces only temporary change because it ignores the underlying causes of problems.
3) The subjective involvement of some self-help members seems fanatical and is likely to lead to overdependence.

Professionals may also feel threatened by the growing support for self-help groups, as well as by the possibility that governments, in their zeal to cut social services and funding, may fasten on self-help programs as a more cost-effective alternative to professional services (Pape, 1990).

Notwithstanding the differences between the two helping groups, Pape (1990) believes there is much potential for collaboration. By working together in the best interests of people in need, professionals and self-helpers can share their expertise while maintaining their unique qualities and strengths. Professionals may find that strong self-help groups complement rather than compete with traditional services; they may also discover that self-help groups are more effective than other types of intervention in helping clients reach their goals. In turn, self-helpers may come to see professionals, "with their training, power and legitimacy," as a valuable resource for groups. Pape (1990, 7) elaborates:

> [Professionals] can educate their clients about the existence and usefulness of mutual aid, can refer their clients to groups, and can play a number of other roles to support new or existing groups. Collaboration ... can be a boon to the mutual aid movement, and to the many people who might take advantage of this resource.

Many self-help groups—particularly those for seniors—already invite professionals to participate in meetings; such an arrangement offers obvious benefits when the issues raised during the meeting are complex and require the response of someone with expertise in medical, social, legal, or other areas (Self-help groups, 1999).

IV. VOLUNTEERS: CANADA'S NATURAL RESOURCE

Volunteers or "natural helpers" complement the professional services provided by social welfare organizations in a variety of ways. These include working with youth (e.g., Big Brothers and Big Sisters); counselling people in distress (e.g., crisis phone lines); visiting the sick or infirm (e.g., candy-stripe programs); supporting women in distress (e.g., women's shelters or drop-in centres); and assisting new Canadians (e.g., host programs for immigrants). According to the 1997 National Survey of Giving, Volunteering and Participating, approximately 7.5 million Canadians (31.4 percent of the population over age 15) volunteer for groups and organizations, and over one-fifth of volunteers devote time to social service organizations. This survey found that the main reason people volunteer for an organization is their belief in the organization's cause. Among volunteers who work outside organizations, 66 percent help relatives not living with them, while 71 percent help people other than relatives. This natural help given to and by relatives, friends, and neighbours is often such a part of everyday life that it is sometimes overlooked (Hall et al., 1998). Examples of natural help are given in Exhibit 7.4.

VOLUNTEER SKILLS AND THEIR BENEFITS

Volunteers acquire **natural helping skills** through informal personal interactions. In a study by Patterson et al. (1992), respondents reported that the natural helping skills they found most helpful were humour, physical

EXHIBIT 7.4

TYPES OF NATURAL HELP PROVIDED BY CANADIANS (15+)

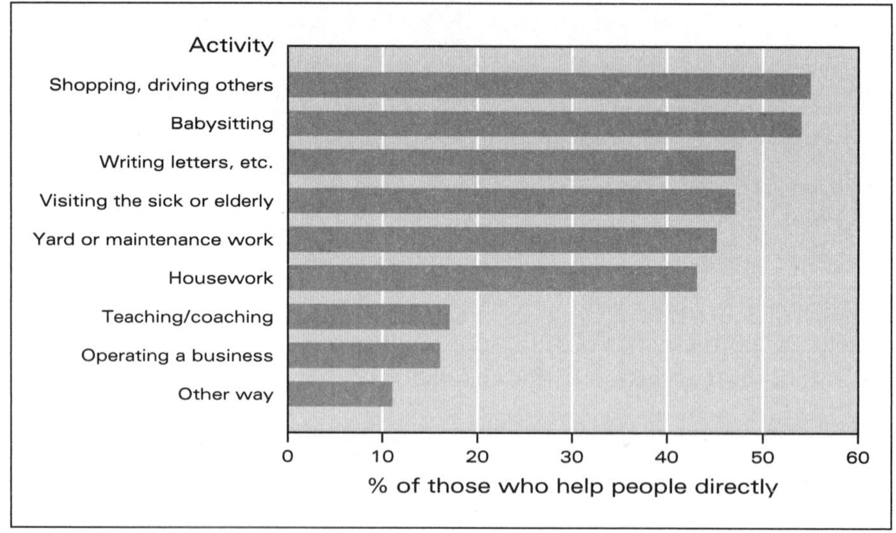

Source: M. Hall et al., *Caring Canadians, Involved Canadians: Highlights from the 1997 National Survey of Giving, Volunteering and Participating*, Cat. No. 71-542-XPE (Ottawa: Statistics Canada, Ministry of Industry, Science and Technology, 1998), 36.

touching, exchange of personal experiences, provision of material resources, reaching out to others, and follow-up contact after the problem was resolved. Emotional support—expressed through listening, encouraging, empathizing, showing concern, and the like—is another important function of natural helping (Gottlieb, 1983). Helping people solve problems by providing suggestions and information and clarifying needs is also central to the natural helping process. According to Romeder (1990), helping skills are most beneficial if the person being helped feels understood and accepted, not judged.

PROFESSIONAL AND GOVERNMENT RESPONSES TO VOLUNTEERISM AND SELF-HELP

In the past, professional groups were reluctant to include informal helpers and self-help groups in the helping process. More recently, professionals have acknowledged that the support given by volunteers and self-helpers is often a viable alternative to professional care. A continuum of care provided by formal and informal helpers can improve the quality of service delivery and give people in need a greater range of services to choose from. For example, a person dealing with depression may benefit from talking through childhood issues with a psychologist; seeing a physician for medical intervention and monitoring; attending a self-help group for mutual support; and enjoying the friendship of a volunteer. Exhibit 7.5 illustrates possible linkages between formal and informal helping systems.

EXHIBIT 7.5

LINKS AMONG VARIOUS FORMAL AND INFORMAL HELPING SYSTEMS

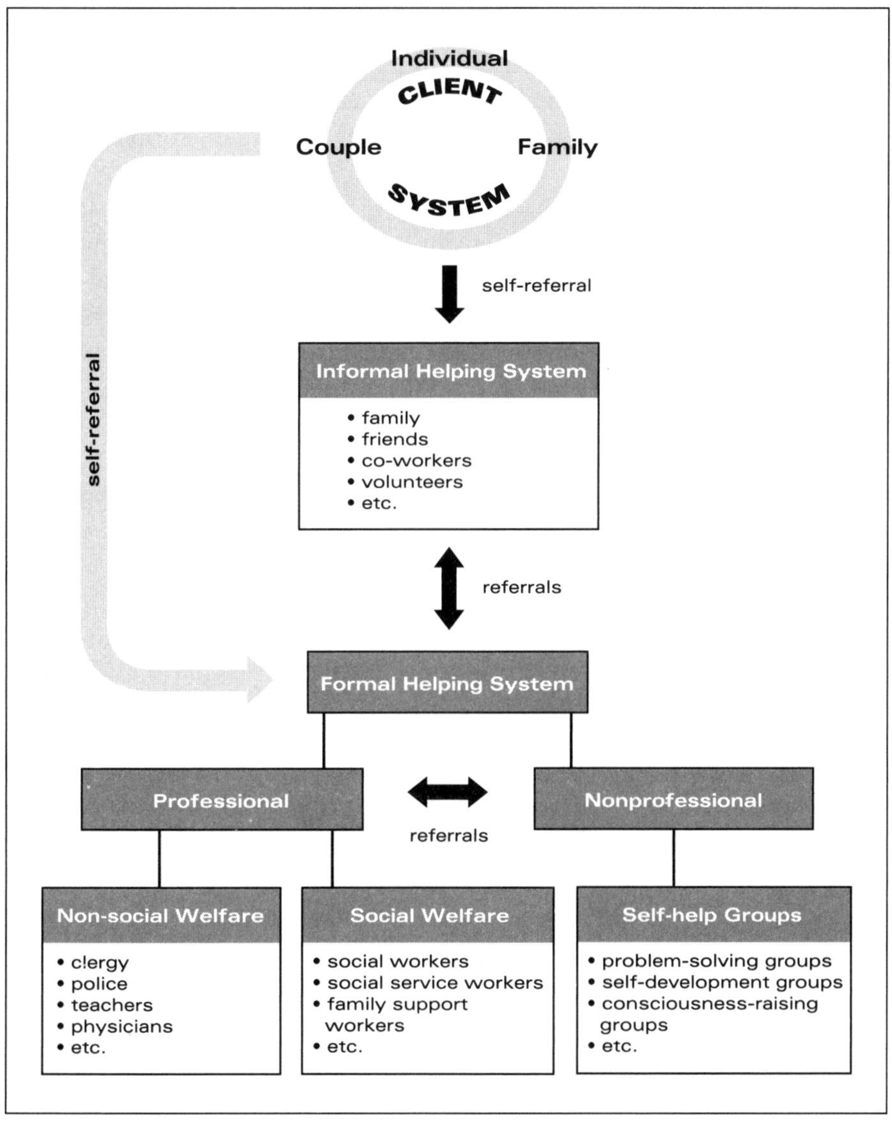

Source: Adapted from Donald Warren, *Helping Networks: How People Cope with Problems in the Urban Community* (Notre Dame: University of Notre Dame Press, 1981), 148. Copyright © 1981 by University of Notre Dame Press. Reprinted with permission.

Economic and political factors have motivated a greater acceptance of nonprofessional help; during periods of fiscal restraint, government downsizing, and budget cuts, self-help groups and volunteers may provide much of the support people need when professional help is unavailable or unaffordable.

Certain practice models emphasize the inclusion of natural support systems in people's lives. For example, the life model of social work practice developed by Germain and Gitterman (1980) has inspired many social workers to focus on helping clients form "real-life" ties, find new supports, re-establish old connections, and generally develop their natural resources. Natural helping networks such as family, friends, and neighbours are viewed as bona fide helpers rather than mere supplements to professional help.

Canadian governments have recently increased their support for self-help and volunteer efforts. For example, the federal government sponsored the 1992 International Conference on Self-Help and Mutual Aid in Ottawa. The United Nations' proclamation of 2001 as the International Year of Volunteers has prompted Canadian governments to recognize the efforts of volunteers and promote further volunteerism. British Columbia, for example, is planning a province-wide volunteer recognition and recruitment campaign that may include "success stories" about volunteers in local newspapers; the distribution of volunteer recognition pins and bumper stickers; and local volunteer recognition ceremonies. This support is no doubt partly motivated by a recognition of the economic value of volunteerism: it is estimated that the amount of work performed by Canadian volunteers is the equivalent of 578,000 full-time year-round jobs. Canadians can expect that more tax dollars will be devoted to efforts to increase this voluntary productivity (British Columbia, 1999a).

SUMMARY

Introduction

Service providers in the social welfare system include professional helpers, self-help groups, and informal helpers. Each group brings to the helping process a unique set of skills and approaches, thereby creating a diverse range of supports for people in need.

Social Work and the Role of Social Workers

Social work has a historical connection to Canada's social welfare system. The social work philosophy is based on humanitarian and egalitarian ideals and is guided by a code of ethics. Basing practice on a person-in-environment framework, social workers use a planned change process to help clients meet their goals. Generalist social workers use interpersonal, process, and evaluation skills. An increasingly popular form of social work practice is multi-skilling. The CASW sets and maintains standards for social work practice, while the CASSW oversees social work schools and educational programs. Employment opportunities for social workers are expected to expand in the coming years.

Social Service Workers, Government Regulation, and Future Directions

Cutbacks in funding and government programs are increasing the demand for social service workers. College programs in social work or social services are offered across Canada; those who graduate to become social service workers often work under the supervision of a social worker. Ontario has passed legislation that has many implications for the practice and regulation of social work and social service work in that province. Professional groups have initiated a study on the social work sector that seeks to identify challenges and develop strategies for the future.

Self-Help Groups and the Prospects for Collaboration

Self-help groups promote the mutual exchange of ideas and feelings, allowing people with common problems to support one another. These groups are characterized by resonance, a lack of professional involvement, availability, and egalitarian relationships, and can provide both physical and mental-health benefits. Self-help clearinghouses help people connect with self-help groups. The inclusion of professionals in self-help group meetings is one example of how professionals and self-helpers might collaborate in helping clients.

Volunteers: Canada's Natural Resource

Canadians volunteer in both social service organizations and natural settings. Natural helping skills are recognized as a vital component of the helping process. In recent years, there has been increasing professional acceptance of, and government support for, the efforts of volunteers and self-help groups.

KEY TERMS

INFORMAL HELP 149
FORMAL HELP 149
PROFESSIONAL HELP 149
SELF-HELP 149
SOCIAL WORK 150
SOCIAL WORKERS 151
CODE OF ETHICS 151
INTERDISCIPLINARY 153
PERSON-IN-ENVIRONMENT 153
PLANNED CHANGE PROCESS 153
GENERALIST SOCIAL WORKERS 154
MULTISKILLING 155
SOCIAL SERVICE WORKERS 158
HELPER THERAPY PRINCIPLE 163
VOLUNTEERS 165
NATURAL HELPING SKILLS 165

CHAPTER 8

SOCIAL WELFARE: PROMOTING CHANGE AT THE MICRO AND MACRO LEVELS

• OBJECTIVES •

I. To explore various aspects of micro-level change and review programs and services that promote change in individuals, families, and small social groups.

II. To define "community" and introduce the basic steps in community needs assessment.

III. To examine macro-level change and community organization in terms of community change, social planning, and social action.

INTRODUCTION

The primary goal of all social welfare programs is to change conditions that threaten individual and/or social functioning. To achieve this goal, a type of intervention must be applied. In the social welfare context, the term **intervention** refers to strategies, techniques, and methods that are used to help individuals, families, communities, or other social systems change. Interventions vary depending on the nature of the problem and size of the system that needs to be changed. The change process may involve either (1) helping people change or adapt to their environment; or (2) changing the environment so that it is more conducive to meeting human needs. Examples of interventions include supporting an individual through the grieving process, teaching a family to listen to and show respect for its members, and helping a community adjust to a large influx of immigrants.

Many social welfare programs that focus on changing people have their origins in the English Poor Laws. In the early days of social welfare, "change" was primarily in the form of imposed work. Herded into workhouses or "houses of industry," the able-bodied unemployed were put to work in the hope that they would "learn or retain the habits of industry and help to offset the cost of their keep" (Guest, 1980, 10).

Social welfare's interest in changing people's environment can be traced to the social reform movements of the late 1800s and early 1900s. Social activists in the urban reform movement, for example, sought changes in housing and health legislation that would reduce poverty and human suffering for city dwellers. Similarly, supporters of the women's rights movement advocated for changes in the social, political, and economic environment that would improve living conditions for women and their children.

In the post–World War I period, a growing amount of research in the helping professions paved the way for a more professional, systematic, and "scientific" approach to changing people and their environments. It was no longer enough for practitioners to simply "mean well"; instead, those working in social welfare were required to obtain formal training in the social sciences and to draw upon a recognized repertoire of technologies in their practice. Until the 1930s, those technologies were based primarily on Freudian principles and the diagnostic school of social work, including formal interviewing skills, procedures for assessing or "diagnosing" human problems, and psychoanalytic strategies or "treatments." Accompanying the emergence of these and subsequent technologies was a recognition of three distinct levels of change, which are described below:

- **Micro-level change** involves face-to-face interactions with individuals, families, and small groups. The primary goal of micro-level change is to help people obtain the resources and skills they require to become self-sufficient. This type of intervention is often referred to as *direct service* or *clinical practice*.
- **Mezzo-level change** generally occurs at the organizational level of social agencies and involves little direct contact with service users. The focus is on changing systems that directly affect clients, such as social service programs, agency policies and procedures, and the delivery of service.
- **Macro-level change** takes place at the community level and seeks to change social conditions. Collective action is usually required at this level of change, since the systems for which change is sought are typically complex and well-established.

Exhibit 8.1 illustrates the relationship between the three levels and gives examples of interventions for each level.

This chapter examines social welfare programs and services that are designed to promote change at the micro and macro levels. Mezzo-level change was covered in the discussion of intraorganizational change in Chapter 6.

EXHIBIT 8.1

LEVELS OF CHANGE AND RELATED INTERVENTIONS

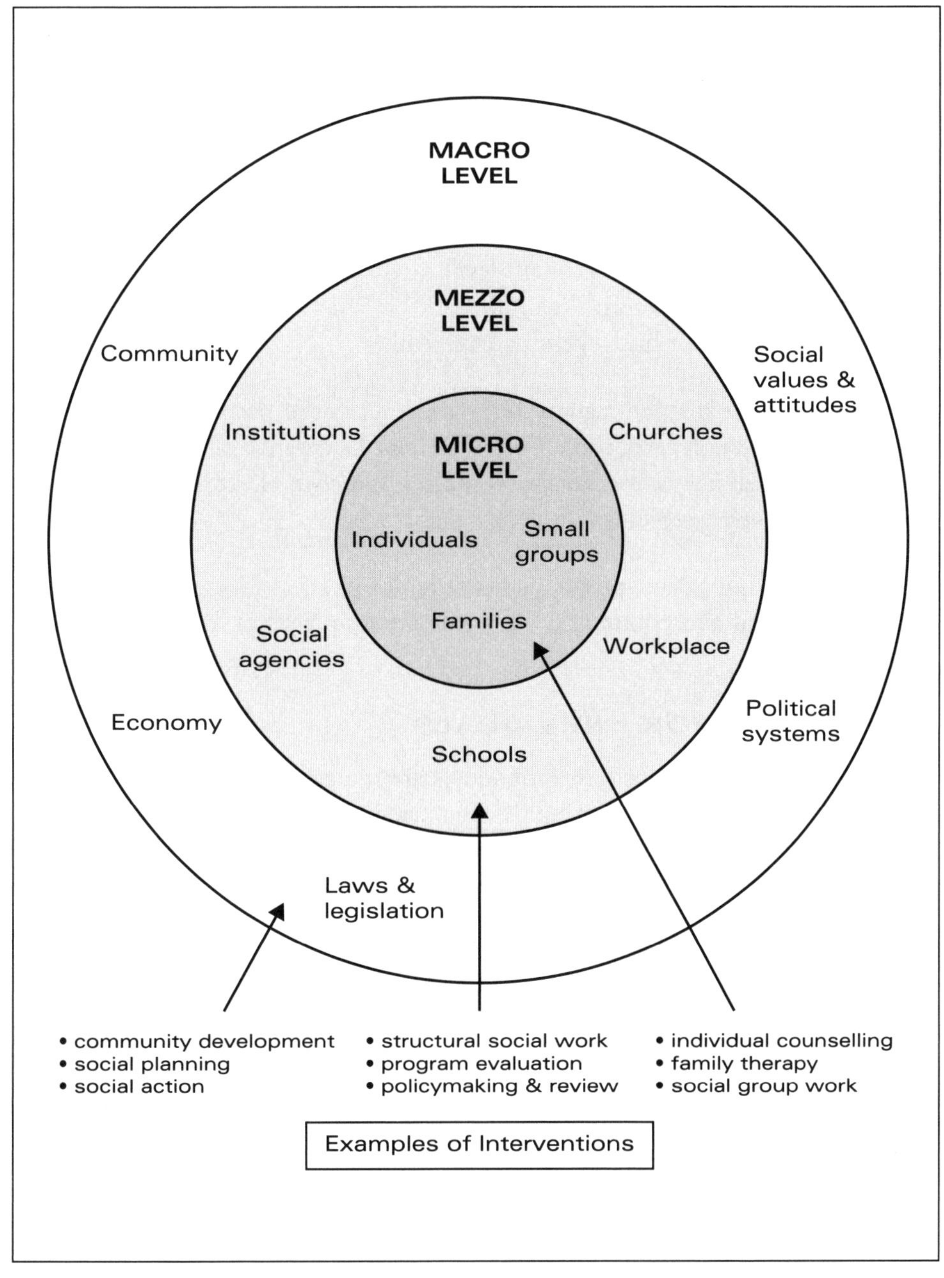

Source: Author.

I. CHANGE AT THE MICRO LEVEL: PROGRAMS AND SERVICES

THE NATURE OF MICRO-LEVEL CHANGE

Social welfare services that focus on micro-level change are aimed at helping individuals, families, and small groups to obtain "the basics they need to survive, subsist, develop, and even flourish within society" (Kahn, 1995, 571). One advantage of such programs is that their limited focus increases the likelihood that needs will be successfully identified and met. One disadvantage is that change at the micro level rarely addresses the root causes of social problems. For example, as Kahn (1995, 571) points out, a food bank that provides food for hungry individuals will

> ensure that, on a given day, a given number of people are fed. But it cannot and does not address the question of why these people are hungry. If the soup kitchen closes, the people it serves will again be hungry.

Despite their limitations, programs that attempt to effect change at the micro level are needed and continue to be a primary emphasis of many social welfare agencies.

PROGRAMS FOR INDIVIDUALS

Programs that are designed for individuals are rooted in the **social casework** approach, which emerged during the organized charity movement in the late 1800s. The casework method prompted a step-by-step approach to counselling and was used by "friendly visitors"—volunteers who visited the poor and provided friendship and support as opposed to financial relief. These visitors were primarily from middle- and upper-class circles and were expected to be role models for the poor (Germain and Gitterman, 1980). Under the influence of the American social worker Mary Richmond, casework eventually became more scientific—as, for example, when it adopted a medical model to explain individual dysfunction. This model required practitioners to conduct a thorough and systematic exploration of an individual's social environment (Johnson, 1998).

Most present-day social agencies that provide direct client services have programs for individuals. Examples include mental-health counselling, alcohol and drug counselling, home-support services for elderly persons, adaptation programs for immigrants, support services for abused women, and victim-assistance programs. Social welfare programs and services designed for individuals are justified on the basis that communities and society in general suffer if individual needs are not sufficiently met. Social workers and other professional helpers also recognize that providing services on a one-to-one basis can be effective in helping people change their behaviour, learn new coping strategies, and either adapt to or change their environment (Fischer, 1978).

Each individual who seeks help from a social agency has a unique set of needs, issues, and concerns. However, most requests for service by individuals relate to one or more of the following areas:

1) *interpersonal conflict*—overt conflict between two or more persons who agree that the problem exists, such as marital conflict, parent–child conflict;
2) *dissatisfaction in social relations*—deficiencies or excesses that the client perceives as problems in interactions with others, such as dissatisfaction in a marriage, with a child or parent, with peers;
3) *problems with formal organizations*—problems occurring between the client and an organization, such as a school, court, welfare department;
4) *difficulties in role performance*—problems in carrying out a particular social role, such as that of spouse, parent, student, employee, patient;
5) *decision problems*—problems of uncertainty, such as what to do in a particular situation;
6) *reactive emotional distress*—conditions in which the client's major concern is with feelings, such as anxiety and depression, rather than with the situation that may have given rise to them;
7) *inadequate resources*—lack of tangible resources, such as money, housing, food, transportation, child care, a job. (Epstein, 1980, 178–179)

Depending on their particular discipline, service providers use a variety of techniques to help individuals deal with these and other issues. Interventions that focus on changing individuals may be based on one or more of a wide range of counselling models, including psychoanalysis, client-centred therapy, gestalt therapy, transactional analysis, behaviour therapy, feminist therapy, rational therapy, and reality therapy.

FAMILY SERVICES

As a primary social unit, the family is responsible for procreating, nurturing, and protecting children, socializing individual members into the larger society, and linking its members to other social institutions. If a family is unable to complete these tasks adequately, its members may seek help from family service agencies.

The origin of family services in Canada can be traced in part to the development of the Canadian Patriotic Fund (CPF) during World War I. To achieve its goal of "maintaining the home life," CPF workers provided support and supervision for large numbers of families who were temporarily without fathers because of the war. Strong-Boag (1979, 25) comments on the likely effect of the CPF: "It seems very probable that the good results that the CPF demonstrated in improved school attendance, better housekeeping, lessened mortality and increased family stability helped further other efforts to shore up the nuclear family as the best guarantor of social order."

In the 1920s and 1930s, **family casework** emerged as a more scientific approach to helping families. In their provision of services, family caseworkers set out "to reinforce and strengthen the endangered family, by drawing in the community's resources, not only in material relief, but in character and spiritual strength as well" (McGill University, 1931).

The needs and problems of families today are diverse and often complex. However, Janzen and Harris (1986, 41–42) suggest that most concerns bringing families to social agencies are related to one or more of the following events:

1) *Addition to the family*. Families seek guidance when the family structure changes, as when a member gets married or remarried, is pregnant, has a new baby, becomes a stepparent, fosters or adopts a child, or takes in an elderly family member.
2) *Separation or loss*. Family support services are often helpful when a family member dies, a marriage breaks down, a family member is institutionalized (e.g., in a hospital, jail, long-term care), a working member loses a job, a child leaves home, or there is a suicide in the family.
3) *Demoralization*. Families may seek help when they feel demoralized or disheartened due to income loss, addiction, infidelity, victimization, delinquency, or family violence.
4) *Change in status or role*. Some families need supportive services to help them get through a member's developmental crisis (e.g., adolescence, midlife crisis, or old age), cope with the loss of the parent role (e.g., when the last child leaves home), or adjust to a change in social status (e.g., a move from "worker" to "retiree").

Exhibit 8.2 lists some of the services that family resource programs in Canada offer families with young children.

Exhibit 8.2

FAMILY RESOURCE PROGRAMS

Did you know that across Canada family resource programs offer:

- support groups for parents
- prenatal programs
- well-baby programs
- drop-in programs
- playgroups
- toy-lending programs
- clothing, toy, and equipment exchanges
- resource library materials
- "warm-lines" (telephone service offering noncrisis support and information)
- referrals and liaison with other community services
- peer counselling and professional counselling
- crisis intervention
- support groups for family violence victims/survivors
- health-related information
- life-skills courses
- employment counselling or training courses
- community kitchen programs
- literacy programs including ESL (English as a Second Language)

Source: Canadian Association of Family Resource Programs (Ottawa, n.d.).

A practitioner who works with family systems may be trained in a variety of disciplines, including social work, psychology, and family therapy. Regardless of their educational background, family service workers generally focus on helping families access resources and fulfil their roles (e.g., as parent, spouse, or provider) more effectively. This focus underlies a broad range of family-oriented programs, such as child protection, family planning, child development, family violence treatment, and family maintenance.

SOCIAL GROUP WORK

A social agency may provide group programs as a more affordable and less time-consuming alternative to individual services. Another advantage of group programs is that they may meet certain client goals—such as the attainment of appropriate social skills—more effectively than one-to-one sessions.

It is common for social workers to use **social group work** to help small groups solve personal or social problems. These groups usually have between three and ten members who share common goals, needs, or lifestyles. Examples of social groups include the following:

- socialization groups (e.g., an anger management group consisting of adolescent boys);
- support groups (e.g., a parent support group that encourages parents to share child-raising experiences and parenting tips);
- educational skill-enhancement groups (e.g., a group that teaches life skills to people with severe disabilities); and
- therapy groups (e.g., a group that helps teenage girls with eating disorders).

Exhibit 8.3 profiles some of the social groups at Catholic Community Services in Montreal.

Social group work originated in the 1800s in settlement houses—large, privately run houses located in city slums. Middle-class facilitators attempted to "use the power of group associations to educate, reform, and organize neighborhoods; to preserve religious and cultural identities; and to give emotional support and assistance to newcomers both from the farm and abroad" (Zastrow, 1996, 590). The techniques used in early social groups were poorly defined; such definition, group leaders claimed, would interfere with the spontaneous nature of the group process.

Grace Coyle, an American settlement house worker, later laid the foundation for modern social group work. Her development of a theoretical framework introduced a strategic or scientific approach to working with small groups; this process emphasized the development of common group goals and democratic decision-making (Tropp, 1977). Coyle (1959) identified three ways by which small groups can meet members' personal and social needs:

- The intimate face-to-face interactions afforded by small groups can facilitate the emotional maturity of members.
- Relationships formed within the group can be effective supplements to outside relationships.

Exhibit 8.3

SOCIAL GROUPS AT MONTREAL'S CATHOLIC COMMUNITY SERVICES

Single Again

A discussion group for separated or divorced women and men that deals with topics like new lifestyle, loneliness, anger, children, and new relationships.

This program will offer you a chance to share concerns with others in similar situations. It will also help you develop insights and learn new ways of coping.

Self-Esteem through Assertiveness

Discover your inner strengths. An 8-week program for men and women offered three times a year.

Join a discussion group to explore:

- New ways of building self-confidence;
- Assertive communication;
- Your view of the world around you and how it affects you;
- The way you think about yourself.

Straight Partners of Gays

For men and women who are presently, or have been, in a mixed sexual-orientation relationship.

- A support group,
- A discussion group,
- A drop-in centre.

An ongoing group for those who have experienced the pain of a partner's "coming out of the closet." Intended to help heal the hurt, channel the anger, and help you cope, this group can give you hope and offer moral support by listening, sharing, and answering some of the most pressing problems that relate to your situation. Questions regarding sexuality, children, health, and other important and relevant issues are addressed. An experienced animator leads the group. Members of the group who understand and can appreciate your dilemma play an important part in the life of the group.

Source: Excerpted from Catholic Community Services (1999), "Support for Adults" [on-line], available: http://www.ccs-montreal.org/adult.html [2000 June 7]. Reproduced courtesy of Catholic Community Services.

- Group experience can help prepare members for more active participation in society as the individual learns to restrain his or her own inappropriate behaviour, the group learns about and discusses social issues, and members receive feedback on how to resolve interpersonal and intrapersonal conflicts.

Small social groups also provide opportunities for members to try out new behaviours and interaction skills in a relatively safe and controlled environment before applying them in the "real world."

II. FIRST STEPS TO MACRO-LEVEL CHANGE: IDENTIFYING COMMUNITY NEEDS

WHAT IS A 'COMMUNITY'?

Although many community developers, social planners, social activists, and social workers concentrate their efforts on changing communities, there is no consensus among these groups as to what **community** actually is. Rothman (1987, 309) explains why defining community can be so difficult:

> Community does not exist as a clear-cut entity in nature in the way that a person or a boulder exists. Communities do not possess inherent or natural boundaries or uniformly agreed-on characteristics. Rather, "community" is a mental construct—a definition imposed on some social aggregation by an observer or analyst—and the construct implies the parameters and phenomena to be considered.

Several theories are available that help us define, conceptualize, and understand community. For example, a community can be understood in terms of (1) its physical or geographical features; (2) the relationships or social bonds that result when people share common activities or interests; or (3) a social system made up of various subsystems (including individuals, families, schools, governments, social agencies, and religious organizations) that continuously interact with and influence one another. Exhibit 8.4 illustrates the flow of resources among families, organizations, and other groups in a community context.

COMMUNITY NEEDS ASSESSMENTS

A **community needs assessment** is used to (1) identify community needs, and (2) determine what actions should be taken in response to those needs.

EXHIBIT 8.4

THE FLOW OF RESOURCES IN A COMMUNITY

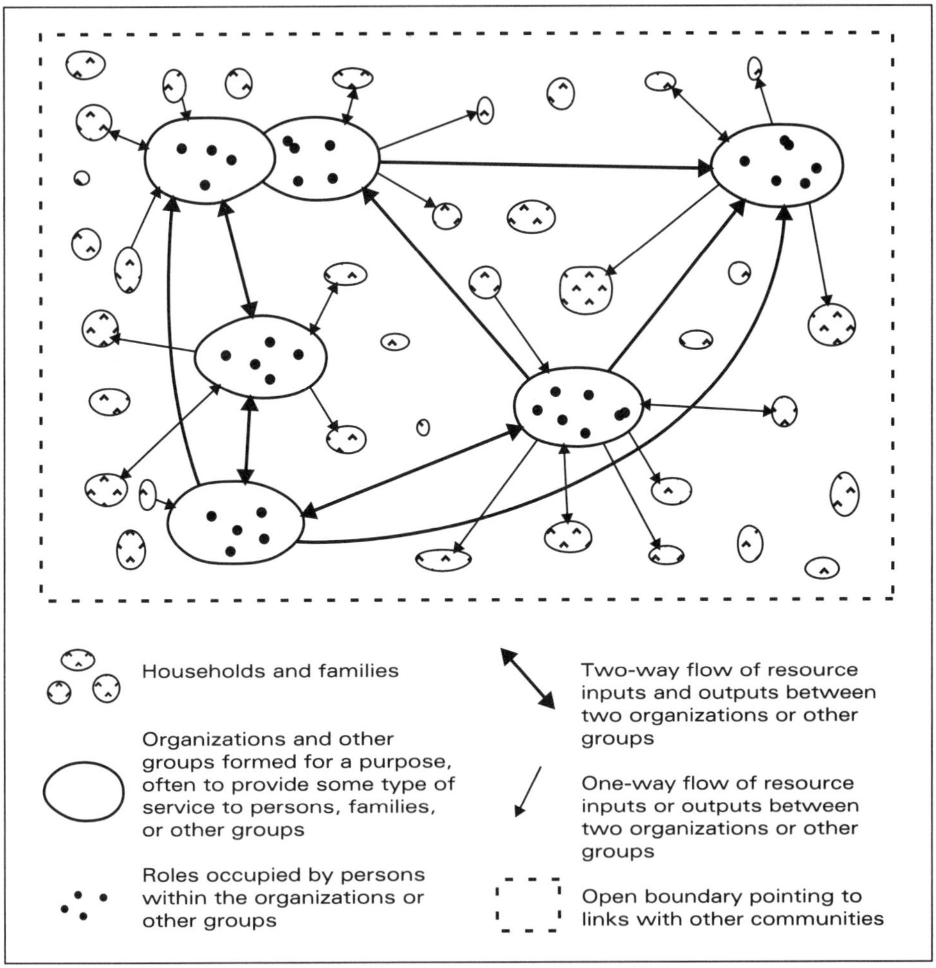

Households and families

Organizations and other groups formed for a purpose, often to provide some type of service to persons, families, or other groups

Roles occupied by persons within the organizations or other groups

Two-way flow of resource inputs and outputs between two organizations or other groups

One-way flow of resource inputs or outputs between two organizations or other groups

Open boundary pointing to links with other communities

Source: Adapted from *Caring Communities: Proceedings of the Symposium on Social Supports*, Cat. No. 89-514 (Ottawa: Statistics Canada, 1991), 19.

Identifying *whose* needs are of immediate concern is usually the first step in the community needs assessment. The selected **target population** may be the community's youth, parent, senior, disabled, Aboriginal, or other identifiable population. The collection of information about the target population will focus on four types of human needs, which are described below:

1) *Felt needs* are those that are perceived by the individual and are thus purely subjective. For example, a person may perceive a personal "need" for a higher income, better housing, less stress, etc.

2) *Expressed needs* are felt needs that are acted on or communicated to others. Individuals who request assistance from social workers or police officers may be said to have expressed needs.
3) *Normative needs* are those perceived by someone—such as a social worker or psychiatrist—observing the person in need. In many cases, normative needs differ widely from felt needs; one person's perception of his or her problem may be entirely different from that of an onlooker. To define a need normatively, statisticians arbitrarily choose some benchmark, standard, or accepted "measuring stick." For example, in measuring poverty Statistics Canada maintains that if a family spends 56.2 percent or more of its household income on basic necessities, that family is living in poverty and therefore "in need" (National Council of Welfare, 1999a).
4) *Comparative needs* become evident when discrepancies are found between two individuals, groups, or other social systems. For instance, a neighbourhood that experiences 10 times as many break-ins as another neighbourhood may have a need for improved safety and security programs such as additional police patrols, a block-watch program, or other protective measures (Zastrow, 1995).

Once examples of each of the four types of human needs have been identified, the community can direct resources to those needs which it has both the will and capacity to address.

Technical Aspects

To identify community needs, community workers must have a good grasp of social research methods. There are two basic technical elements of a community needs assessment:

- The **quantitative approach** tries to establish a cause-and-effect relationship between two or more variables. This approach counts, measures, or otherwise "quantifies" certain conditions or events. Because quantitative data relies on objective measurements such as numbers, rates, percentages, and averages, they are considered to be "hard" data.
- The **qualitative approach** focuses on people's subjective experience of social conditions or events. Information derived from the qualitative approach is considered to be "soft" data, since it is based on people's interpretation of events, conditions, trends, themes, history, or other social phenomena (Health Canada, 1996a).

Each approach uses different methods to collect data. The quantitative approach uses objective information derived from social and health indicators (e.g., statistics or census data) and social surveys. The qualitative approach, in contrast, gathers subjective information through direct observation, focus groups, or interviews. The next two sections describe methods of data collection used by both approaches.

Social Indicators as Quantitative Data

The progress of a country has traditionally been described in economic terms; for example, a country is considered to be in good shape if it experiences growth in its gross domestic product, together with low inflation, high employment, and/or low interest rates. In recent decades, however, **social indicators** have become an important means of measuring a country's general well-being. While economic indicators are unquestionably useful, social indicators provide a more comprehensive picture of people's real-life situation, as well as insight into trends affecting the nation's overall health. Townson (1999) suggests three reasons why the use of social indicators also serves a political purpose:

1) Policy and other decision-makers are interested in "evidence-based" methods to measure how well policies and programs are meeting their objectives.
2) Governments use social indicators as a way to rationalize and account for their spending of public funds.
3) Social and advocacy groups use social indicators to persuade governments to continue funding social welfare programs.

Canada has no single comprehensive system of social indicators. Rather, it uses a variety of indexes and other tracking mechanisms that claim to measure various components of socioeconomic well-being. For instance, the Index of Social Health (ISH), developed by Satya Brink and Allen Zeesman for Human Resources Development Canada, uses 15 different indicators to measure overall population health (see Exhibit 8.5).

The federal and regional governments use population census and surveys to profile the health and well-being of Canadians. For example, information from the 1996 Canada census and the National Longitudinal Survey of Children and Youth is used to monitor the progress of children for the purpose of developing programs for Canadian children and their families. The following two indicators are used to measure a child's well-being:

1) aspects of the child (e.g., injuries and illnesses, behavioural problems, learning successes, and social development); and

EXHIBIT 8.5

SOCIAL INDICATORS: THE INDEX OF SOCIAL HEALTH

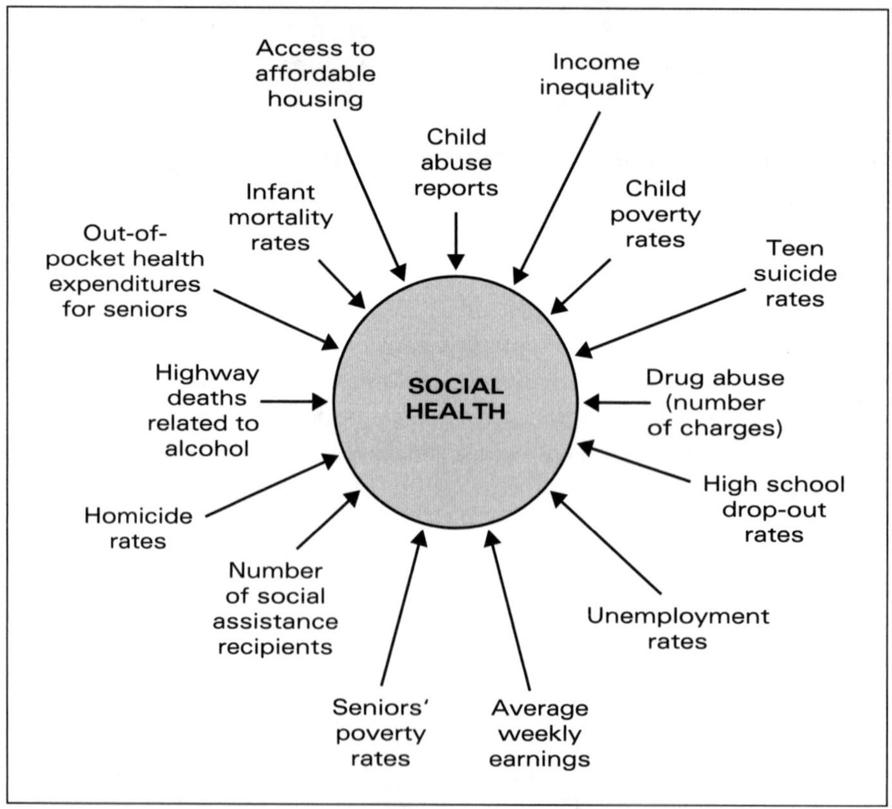

Source: Adapted from S. Brink and A. Zeesman, *Measuring Social Well-Being: An Index of Social Health for Canada* (Hull: Applied Research Branch, Human Resources Development Canada, 1997).

2) aspects of the child's environment (e.g., parenting, family economic security, learning opportunities, quality of housing, and cleanliness of surroundings) (Canada, 1999c).

Townson (1999) criticizes certain social indexes (such as the ISH) for virtually ignoring gender differences and inequalities between men and women. This oversight, she argues, tends to give a misleading picture of the overall population health of a country. Because of this type of limitation, social indicators are only one among many methods used to guide social policy and programming.

Focus Groups and Qualitative Data

A **focus group** is a type of group interview that is often used to collect qualitative data. Typically composed of 10 to 12 participants, a focus group is led by a facilitator who moves the group through a set of predetermined questions. Since they involve gathering information from several people in one sitting, focus groups tend to be less time-consuming than individual interviews. In addition, focus group participants have the opportunity to produce the kind of rich exchange of attitudes, insights, and beliefs that is so central to the qualitative approach. A limitation of focus groups is that sensitive topics (e.g., sexual abuse and addiction) may not be conducive to group discussion; such subjects are best addressed on a one-to-one basis (Barnsley and Ellis, 1992; Health Canada, 1996a).

Mainstream 1992 is an example of a process that relied on focus groups to generate a body of qualitative data. Initiated by the federal and regional governments, Mainstream 1992 provided a forum for representatives from service and advocacy organizations, individuals with disabilities, policy experts, and others to brainstorm ideas related to the integration of people with disabilities into the mainstream of Canadian society. Members of the Roeher Institute organized and facilitated seven focus groups (each consisting of 10 to 15 participants) across the country. The information generated by the focus groups was compiled into a final report and presented to the federal government. Although this initiative's impact on disability-related policies is difficult to discern, the focus group process itself was generally seen as an effective way to enhance citizen participation in the policymaking process (Abele et al., 1998).

III. CHANGE AT THE MACRO LEVEL: COMMUNITY ORGANIZATION

DEFINING COMMUNITY ORGANIZATION

According to Mike Farrell of the National Anti-Poverty Organization, effective change in communities is most often the result not of "large-scale projects or programs" but rather of local initiatives that address the specific needs of individual communities. He goes on to suggest that

> the long-term strategy for Canada must be based on building capacity at the community level. Communities must gain the capacity to address the needs of individual community members and create their own solutions to local problems, especially poverty. (Farrell, 1997, 40)

The term **community organization** refers to strategies used to effect change in communities, neighbourhoods, institutions, and other macro systems. Community organization is especially concerned with enhancing social functioning, reducing social problems, and meeting community needs through social welfare or economic programs. For the most part, change at the community level is the result of planned collective action (Barker, 1991).

According to the classic model of community organization developed by Jack Rothman (1979), community organization involves three main approaches: community (or locality) development, social planning, and social action. These three approaches to community organization are compared in Exhibit 8.6 and briefly explored below.

COMMUNITY DEVELOPMENT

Basic Characteristics

Community development is the process of helping citizens develop their capacity to resolve local problems that directly affect them. The aim of community development is not to challenge and seek reform of established social structures, but rather to work with existing structures to increase the problem-solving capacity of the community.

Citizen participation is an important component of community development. Through citizen participation, a broad cross-section of the community is encouraged to identify and articulate their own goals, design their own methods of change, and pool their resources in the problem-solving process. Citizen participation can be seen in the proliferation of self-help, professional, interest, neighbourhood, block-watch, and other groups that share resources and work together toward a common goal (Harrison, 1995).

Because of its emphasis on including community members, community development is said to have "a grass-roots membership or a 'bottom-up' rather than a professional, bureaucratic, or 'top-down' approach to social problems" (Spergel, 1987, 300). This means that communities typically do not wait for plans and interventions to trickle down from government to the people; rather, local development organizers help communities set priorities and mobilize local knowledge and resources.

It is not uncommon for top-down and bottom-up approaches to converge. This is often the case in isolated communities, which may be the target of both government intervention and self-initiated programs. For example, the Community Futures Program of Human Resources Development Canada provides funds to support local initiatives and entrepreneurship in small Canadian towns. In those same towns, private-sector groups and organizations may form partnerships among themselves to create their own employment opportunities (Loizides, 1994).

One form of community development is a revitalization strategy known as community economic development (CED). CED aims to stimulate local

Exhibit 8.6

THREE MODELS OF COMMUNITY ORGANIZATION

	Community Development	Social Planning	Social Action
1. Goal categories of community action	Self-help; community capacity and integration (process goals)	Problem solving with regard to substantive community problems (task goals)	Shifting of power relationships and resources; basic institutional change (task or process goals)
2. Assumptions concerning community structure and problem conditions	Community eclipsed, anomie; lack of relationships and democratic problem-solving capacities; static traditional community	Substantive social problems; mental and physical health, housing, recreation	Disadvantaged populations, social injustice, deprivation, inequity
3. Basic change strategy	Broad cross-section of people involved in determining and solving their own problems	Fact gathering about problems and decisions on the most rational course of action	Crystallization of issues and organization of people to take action against enemy targets
4. Characteristic change tactics and techniques	Consensus: communication among community groups and interests; group discussion	Consensus or conflict	Conflict or contest: confrontation, direct action, negotiation
5. Salient practitioner roles	Enabler/catalyst, coordinator; teacher of problem-solving skills and ethical values	Fact gatherer and analyst, program implementer, facilitator	Activist/advocate; agitator, broker, negotiator, partisan
6. Medium of change	Manipulation of small, task-oriented groups	Manipulation of formal organizations and of data	Manipulation of mass organizations and political processes
7. Orientation toward power structure(s)	Members of power structure as collaborators in a common venture	Power structure as employers and sponsors	Power structure as external target of action, oppressors to be coerced or overturned
8. Boundary definition of the community client, system, or constituency	Total geographic community	Total community or community segment (including "functional community)	Community segment
9. Assumptions regarding interests of community subparts	Common interests or reconcilable differences	Interests reconcilable or in conflict	Conflicting interests that are not easily reconcilable; scarce resources
10. Conception of the public interest	Rationalist/unitary	Idealist/unitary	Realist/unitary
11. Conception of the client population or constituency	Citizens	Consumers	Victims
12. Conception of client role	Participants in an international problem-solving process	Consumers or recipients	Employers, constituents, members

Source: Adapted from Charles Zastrow, *Introduction to Social Work and Social Welfare*, 6th ed. (Pacific Grove: Brooks/Cole, 1996). Copyright © 1996. Reprinted with permission of Wadsworth, a division of Thomson Learning. Fax 800 730-2215.

business and employment and to improve the social and physical aspects of a community, including education, recreation, transportation, and housing (Perry, 1993). The CED approach emerged in response to the welfare state's failure to ensure full employment, stabilize and stimulate the economy, and provide adequate social and income support for people in need. Many rural communities in particular reject the assistance that is available through the social welfare system. The desire of such communities to devise their own ways of regaining control of their local economy and meeting their own needs is reflected in local initiatives such as housing cooperatives, used-clothing exchanges, community home-care operations, community kitchens, recycling, and job-readiness programs (Boothroyd and Davis, 1991; Loizides, 1994).

Historical Roots

Community development originated in settlement houses such as the one Sarah Libby Carson opened in Toronto in 1899. These houses were established with the "aim of bridging the gulf between rich and poor" (Bruce, 1966, 143). Local residents were given an opportunity to learn from their educated middle-class "peers" about social problems and how to resolve them. Although the type of activities that took place in settlement houses depended on funding and resident needs, most activities—such as vocational training, recreation, and English classes—had an educational focus. In time, settlement house workers became known as social workers (Woodside and McClam, 1994).

SOCIAL PLANNING

Basic Characteristics

Social planning involves a wide range of activities, including the identification and assessment of community problems and needs; the design of programs, services, and facilities to address those needs; and the integration and coordination of programs in the community. The Social Planning Network of Ontario (2000, 1) defines the primary focus of organizations that have a social planning mandate:

> Social planning organizations exist to build and strengthen community. This mission focuses on the social impact on individuals, families and communities of larger social, economic, political, and cultural forces in society. It also encompasses advocating for the development of essential community and social supports as provided through human service systems.

Social planning organizations are committed to social development in a variety of areas, including health, safety, economic security, and education. Examples of social development efforts include urban renewal and the planning of new towns, neighbourhoods, and housing projects. A primary objective of these initiatives is to improve the general functioning of residents by meeting their specific needs. An apartment block for seniors, for instance, may offer special safety and security options as well as facilities for recreation and social events.

Citizens are usually included in social planning decisions and activities. For example, social planners may recruit individuals, help them form working groups, encourage participants to share their ideas and resources, and collectively tackle local problems. Social planners may also assist social agencies and community organizations in forming interagency committees to improve the coordination and delivery of social welfare services.

Historical Roots

In Canada, social planning originated in the organized charity movement and subsequent establishment of Charity Organization Societies (COSs). These societies set out to coordinate the efforts of social agencies and integrate services so that people who were truly in need could access programs more easily. During the Industrial Revolution, COSs focused primarily on urban conditions and the improvement of slum areas, the creation of city parks and recreation sites, the development of health and sanitation legislation, and the enforcement of building codes (Woodside and McClam, 1994).

The social planning movement took off during the 1950s, 1960s, and early 1970s in response to continued economic growth and the rapid expansion of social programs. During this time, most social planning efforts focused on coordinating social programs and services in communities. Due to the increased demand for planning on several levels, three types of social planning councils emerged: (1) councils that worked in government departments or ministries; (2) councils that were part of the United Way administration or operated as separate planning committees; and (3) independent councils that were privately funded and governed by their own boards of directors.

In the past two decades, social planning has taken place in an entirely different context. The withdrawal of government from social policy functions has left many small-town social planning councils struggling to survive with reduced budgets and skeleton staff. Some councils, especially those in large cities, have been able to secure funding sufficient to obtain staff and other resources needed to fulfil social planning functions. Other social planning councils are made up of volunteer committees (Social Planning Council of Metropolitan Toronto, 1997; Ginsler, 1988). Exhibit 8.7 profiles four social planning councils in Canada.

Exhibit 8.7

EXAMPLES OF SOCIAL PLANNING COUNCILS

Council	Mission	Activities
Social Planning and Research Council of British Columbia	To promote the social, economic, and environmental well-being of citizens and communities	• Conducts research and consults with communities, organizations, and governments • Works to reduce hazards, create safety, and increase access for people with disabilities • Supports training and community capacity-building
Edmonton Social Planning Council	To build communities, identify trends and emerging social issues, and create opportunities to debate those trends and issues	• Tracks increases in poverty and accompanying social problems • Advocates for more effective and humane social programs and policies • Assists in the start-up of community social services
Social Planning Council of Winnipeg	To provide action-oriented leadership in social planning and effecting social policy changes	• Identifies and defines social planning issues, needs, and resources in the community • Develops and promotes policy and program options to policymakers • Raises community awareness of social issues and human service needs, social policy options, and service delivery alternatives
Social Planning Council of Ottawa-Carleton	To provide the residents of Ottawa-Carleton with the means to exercise informed leadership on issues affecting their social and economic well-being	• Examines government policies and monitors their impact on citizens • Brings citizens together to address pressing community issues • Communicates alternatives to social issues through the media • Informs decision-makers on key issues

Sources: Excerpted from Social Planning and Research Council of British Columbia [on-line}, available: http://www.sparc.bc.ca/ [2000 April 20]; Edmonton Social Planning Council [on-line}, available: http://www.edmspc.com/Aboutus.htm [2000 April 20]; Social Planning Council of Winnipeg [on-line}, available: http://www.spcw.mb.ca/about.html [2000 April 20]; and Social Planning Council of Ottawa-Carleton [on-line}, available: http://www.spcottawa.on.ca/introe.htm [2000 April 20].

SOCIAL ACTION

Basic Characteristics

Social action refers to collective and coordinated efforts that aim to solve a social problem, correct an injustice, or meet a human need. This approach usually involves attempts to influence those with power (e.g., politicians) to change certain policies, laws, procedures, and institutions that are deemed to be inadequate. In many cases, social activists act on behalf of a segment of the population who are believed to be disadvantaged or oppressed.

A local event in which human rights have been violated is often used as a catalyst for social action. Take as an example a single mother on welfare who is evicted from her apartment because she cannot pay the rent with the social assistance she receives. In this case, social action that arises in response to the eviction would not only address the inadequacy of welfare benefits for the evicted woman and her children but would also call attention to the inadequacy of benefits for *all* welfare recipients. Unlike community development, social action does not require a consensus within the community to indicate a need for change. Indeed, social action may take place even though a majority of the community denies the existence of a problem.

Social activists rely on the collective efforts of "average" citizens to achieve their goals. This **grassroots approach** is evident when members of a community are brought together because of a common concern and go on to establish an organization or group committed to addressing that concern (Burghardt, 1987; Connaway and Gentry, 1988). Mothers Against Drunk Drivers (MADD), for example, was founded by mothers whose children had been killed by impaired drivers. Social action on the part of MADD and similar grassroots organizations involves lobbying various levels of government for changes to impaired driving legislation (MADD Canada, 2000).

To achieve social action goals, social activists use a variety of strategies. Three of these strategies are outlined below:

1) *Collaboration* (or cooperation) strategies—such as education, persuasion, and lobbying—tend to be used when there is general agreement about the social action goal and the means to achieve it.

2) *Campaign* strategies—such as the use of publicity, endorsements by important public figures, and petitions—are often preferred when there is considerable disagreement about the proposed goal and/or the methods to be used.

3) *Contest* strategies—such as demonstrations, protest marches, and sit-ins—are used when there is strong opposition to the proposed goal (Connaway and Gentry, 1988).

While there are countless organizations that aim to enhance the quality of community life, not all organizations engage in social action activities. Social action organizations are independent, community-based operations, with members who advocate on their own or another group's behalf. An example of such an organization is the National Anti-Poverty Organization (NAPO). Since 1971, members of NAPO—many of whom have had personal experience with poverty—have worked with low-income communities to eliminate poverty in Canada. More specifically, NAPO members represent low-income Canadians during national political debates on poverty-related issues; ensure that low-income groups are represented in decision-making and policymaking at the local level; and serve on several committees that address issues concerning the poor, including welfare fraud, reduced employment insurance benefits, housing, homelessness, food banks, and single-parent families living in poverty (NAPO, 2000).

Historical Roots

While the organized charity movement focused on helping people adjust to existing social conditions and services, reformists from the settlement houses fought for changes in social institutions. Since settlement houses were located in the poorest sections of town, settlement workers became clearly aware of the conditions and problems caused by poverty. These early social workers rejected the prevailing laissez-faire philosophy and strove to correct social inequities and injustices for disadvantaged groups (Burghardt, 1987). Until the professionalization of social work in the early 20th century, all social workers were social reformers: "Whether through visits to the poor and homeless, demonstrations in the streets, or surveys to expose shocking conditions, the first social workers were crusaders whose full-time occupation was social action" (Thursz, 1977, 1274).

Social movements that occurred at the turn of the century, and later during the 1960s and 1970s, were headed by social activists. Those reform movements that have had the greatest influence on Canadian social policies and programs have focused on the needs and interests of specific groups, including children, women, labourers, Aboriginal peoples, persons with disabilities, gay men and lesbians, and the poor.

SUMMARY

Introduction

The main goal of all social welfare programs is to change conditions that threaten personal or social functioning. A variety of interventions are used to create change at the micro, mezzo, and macro levels.

Change at the Micro Level: Programs and Services

Micro-level change is directed at individuals, families, and small groups. Social casework uses a variety of techniques to help individuals address needs, issues, and concerns. Family service workers help families access resources and fulfil important roles. Social groups are often used to help people with similar goals and concerns work toward better social functioning.

First Steps to Macro-Level Change: Identifying Community Needs

A community can be broadly defined as a group of people, a place, or a system. Community needs assessments are used to determine what a community needs and what resources are required to meet those needs. These assessments rely on the quantitative approach, which uses objective data such as social indicators; and the qualitative approach, which gathers subjective data from such sources as focus groups.

Change at the Macro Level: Community Organization

There are three basic approaches to community organization that aim to effect change at the macro level. Community development is the process of helping citizens work with established social structures to resolve the problems that affect them. Social planning involves citizens in the planning, development, and coordination of services in a community. Social action refers to lobbying and other collective efforts to correct injustices or meet human needs.

KEY TERMS

INTERVENTION 171
MICRO-LEVEL CHANGE 172
MEZZO-LEVEL CHANGE 172
MACRO-LEVEL CHANGE 172
SOCIAL CASEWORK 174
FAMILY CASEWORK 176
SOCIAL GROUP WORK 178
COMMUNITY 180
COMMUNITY NEEDS ASSESSMENT 180
TARGET POPULATION 181
QUANTITATIVE APPROACH 182
QUALITATIVE APPROACH 182
SOCIAL INDICATORS 183
FOCUS GROUP 184
COMMUNITY ORGANIZATION 185
COMMUNITY DEVELOPMENT 186
SOCIAL PLANNING 188
SOCIAL ACTION 191
GRASSROOTS APPROACH 191

PART III

MEETING THE NEEDS OF CANADIANS THROUGH PROGRAMS AND SERVICES

CHAPTER 9

ADDRESSING UNEMPLOYMENT AND POVERTY IN CANADA

• OBJECTIVES •

I. To provide an overview of unemployment in Canada and recent changes in the unemployment insurance program.

II. To examine poverty in Canada and the poverty-related problems of hunger and homelessness.

III. To review government responses to the problems of poverty, hunger, and homelessness.

IV. To consider welfare workers and the challenges they face.

INTRODUCTION

Despite reports that Canadians are feeling more secure about their economic well-being, families have less disposable income than they did a decade ago (Canadian Council on Social Development, 2000b). In addition, poverty rates are on the rise in Canada and there are growing inequalities of income between rich and poor Canadians. The National Anti-Poverty Organization (NAPO, 1999) describes this **income inequality** in the following way:

> If we take all of the income in Canada and divide it up like a pie ... we find that the richest fifth of Canadians receives 44.3% of all income in Canada and the poorest fifth receive only 4.6% of the income. In other words, the richest fifth receives almost ten times as much money as the poorest fifth.

The widening gap between rich and poor has been attributed to changing demographics, globalization, technological innovation, and cuts to income-security programs (Zyblock, 1996; Battle, 1997). In 1998, the United Nations used its Human Development Index to determine the income gap between the rich and poor in 17 countries; Canada was found to have the tenth-largest gap (Canadian Council on Social Development, 1999b).

To reduce income inequality, Canadian governments have established income-security programs designed to ensure that individuals and families receive a minimum income regardless of how much they make through earnings or how much property they own (Melichercik, 1995). Canada's income-security programs aim to achieve the following objectives:

- The sharing of our resources so as to provide an adequate income in relation to community standards
- The maintenance of an appropriate degree of income security or stability
- The equitable treatment of individuals and families in different situations and with different levels of need
- The provision of an incentive to encourage people to take advantage of their opportunities
- The encouragement of people to take responsibility for their own lives and livelihood when they are able to do so
- Respect for the personal dignity of the beneficiaries (Royal Commission on the Economic Union, 1985, 773)

Examples of income-security programs in Canada include Employment Insurance, Old Age Security, the Canada and Quebec Pension Plans, social assistance, veterans' pensions, the Guaranteed Income Supplement, and the Canada Child Tax Benefit.

In their study of Canada's income-security programs, the Canadian Council on Social Development discovered that the poorest 20 percent of Canadians receive almost 40 percent of all government-sponsored income-security benefits. Within this low-income group, close to half are families headed by a senior; roughly one-third are single unattached people under age 65; and about one-tenth are single-parent families (Lochhead, 1998).

I. UNEMPLOYMENT IN CANADA

THE PREVALENCE AND CONSEQUENCES OF UNEMPLOYMENT

Canada's unemployment rate has steadily declined in recent years: in 2000, the unemployment rate dropped to 6.8 percent, its lowest level in nearly 25 years

EXHIBIT 9.1

UNEMPLOYMENT RATE FOR CANADA, 1946–2000

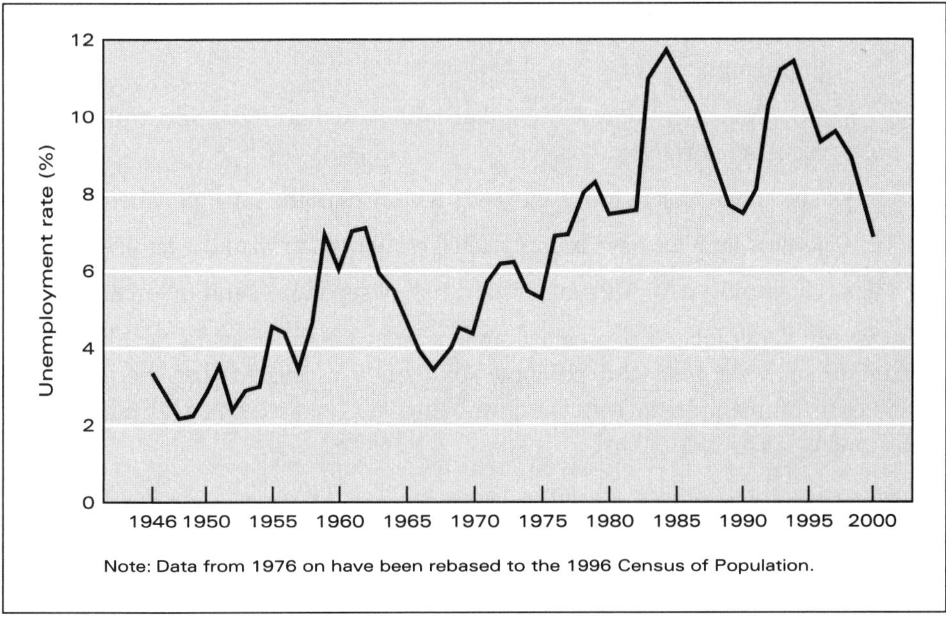

Sources: S. Crompton and M. Vickers (2000, Summer), "One Hundred Years of Labour Force," *Canadian Social Trends* (Ottawa: Statistics Canada, Cat. No. 11-008), No. 57, p. 11; and Canada, *The Budget Speech 2000* (Ottawa: Department of Finance, 2000).

(see Exhibit 9.1) (Canada, 2000b). However, as the following suggests, unemployment continues to be a problem for certain populations:

- The unemployment rate for young people reached 14.5 percent in late 1999 (Statistics Canada, 1999c).
- Aboriginal peoples are about 2.4 times more likely than the general population to be unemployed (Mendelson, 1999).
- Approximately 44 percent of persons with disabilities are unemployed (Fawcett and Shillington, 1996).
- Recent immigrants to Canada have an unemployment rate of about 29 percent (Badets and Howatson-Leo, 1999).

Unemployment has many economic and social costs. Bedard (1996) estimates that in 1994, unemployment cost Canada as much as $77 billion in lost revenue. As for social costs, unemployment has been associated with poor health, family breakdown, depression, suicide, crime, and other social problems. More specifically, studies have indicated the following:

- Unemployed men—especially those who have been unemployed for a year or more—have higher mortality rates than the general population.
- The unemployed tend to experience higher levels of social and psychological stress, and to have higher suicide rates, than the general population.
- Unemployment and white-collar crimes such as fraud and embezzlement are correlated.
- The rate of violent crime increases with rises in the unemployment rate.
- Jobless families have more familial conflict than working families.
- Unemployed families are at high risk of separation and divorce.

Social problems related to unemployment increase the costs of health care, mental-health services, and policing. One study estimated that the health-care costs of unemployment-related problems in Canada totalled $1 billion in just one year (Bedard, 1996).

THE TRANSITION FROM UI TO EI

Canada's unemployment insurance (UI) system was originally designed to "promote the economic and social security of Canadians by supporting workers from the time they leave one job until they get another" (Dingledine, 1981, 7). Since the passage of the Unemployment Insurance Act in 1940, the UI system has undergone several changes, the most dramatic of which occurred in the 1990s. During that period, the federal government stopped funding UI (the program is now funded by joint contributions made by employers and workers), tightened the criteria for determining eligibility, and shortened the period during which workers can draw benefits.

The overhaul of the UI system was prompted by a recognition of the following flaws (some of which were left uncorrected by the changes):

1) UI did not help people who were unemployed for long periods to adjust to changes in the labour market.
2) The program had become a way of life for seasonal workers, who worked for short periods and then drew UI for the rest of the year.
3) UI was easily abused by employers, who organized their hiring, work schedules, and layoffs around the weeks required for workers to qualify for benefits.
4) The continually rising premium rates that were necessary to maintain the system were an increasing burden for employers and workers.
5) Coverage did not extend to a large segment of the workforce.

6) UI did little to encourage individual responsibility for finding and maintaining employment (Canada, 1994c).

The reform was also fuelled by the prohibitive cost of the UI program—which doubled from $8 billion in 1982 to almost $16 billion in 1995—and by public opinion polls indicating that almost three-quarters of Canadians supported an overhaul of the program (Human Resources Development Canada, 1995b).

With the passage of the Employment Insurance Act in 1996, Unemployment Insurance became Employment Insurance (EI). The name change—which was meant to emphasize employment and de-emphasize work disincentives (Richards, 1997)—was minor compared to other revisions. These included

- using number of hours (rather than weeks) worked to determine the amount of benefits received;
- reductions in maximum insurable earnings and benefits for frequent users;
- the clawback of benefits from high-income earners;
- the addition of part-time workers to those eligible for benefits; and
- tightening of the criteria used to determine eligibility for the Family Income Supplement (Human Resources Development Canada, 1995b; Clark, 1995b).

PASSIVE VERSUS ACTIVE PROGRAMS

Since the mid-1980s, there has been a general shift in industrialized countries away from "passive" income-security programs and toward "active" programs. **Passive programs** focus on providing benefits, essentially leaving it up to recipients to find their way into—or back into—the workforce. In contrast, **active programs** play a direct role in helping unemployed people enter or re-enter the workforce; these programs include employment counselling, job search skill development, wage subsidies, earnings supplements, self-employment assistance, job creation partnerships, and skills loans and grants (Human Resources Development Canada, 1995a). While passive programs are often criticized for encouraging dependency, active programs are regarded as a means of fostering autonomy (Melchers, 1999).

According to the OECD (Organization for Economic Co-operation and Development), between 1991 and 1993 over three-quarters of Canada's financial support for the unemployed went to passive measures such as unemployment insurance. Leon Muszynski (1994, 2), a policy associate with the Caledon Institute of Social Policy, has criticized this trend, commenting that "Canada's commitment to active labour market programing, compared to [that of] other countries, is inadequate."

In 1996, the federal government shifted to a more active approach when it agreed to cost-share provincial and territorial employment benefit programs that met the following criteria: demonstration of measurable results (e.g., less dependency on income-security programs); promotion of partnerships among government, employers, and private-sector organizations; reduction in program overlap and duplication; and encouragement of individual responsibility for finding work (Human Resources Development Canada, 1996). Like cost-shared programs, federally sponsored employment programs have become more active in recent years; programs such as the Youth Employment Strategy and the Aboriginal Employment Program both provide opportunities for participants to gain work experience and develop skills in the commercial, voluntary, and public sectors.

THE EI SURPLUS

The percentage of unemployed people receiving EI benefits declined from 83 percent in 1989 to 42 percent in 1997 (see Exhibit 9.2) (Laliberte, 1998). The 1996 changes affected women and youth the most: the number of women receiving EI dropped by 20 percent between 1996 and 1999, while the number of recipients aged 25 and under decreased by 27 percent. The dramatic decline in the number of EI recipients has resulted in significant cost savings: by the fall of 1999, the EI account had a surplus of $21 billion (EI surplus said excessive, 1999).

In 1998, Human Resources Development Canada reported that the number of EI beneficiaries had dropped for two reasons. First, the new EI program introduced more restrictive eligibility rules. (It is estimated that if the eligibility rules from 1989 had been used in 1997, 20 percent more people would have been eligible for benefits.) Second, the composition of the unemployed population has changed. Under EI, only those who have worked in the last 12 months are eligible for benefits, making from 18 to 38 percent of all unemployed persons ineligible for benefits. Other analysts note that many women and youth contribute to EI but are not able to accumulate enough hours to qualify for EI benefits because they work in irregular or part-time positions. Still others attribute the drop in the number of EI beneficiaries to the growing economy and job creation (EI changes evaluated, 1999).

Whatever the reasons for the decline, the fact remains that more working Canadians are contributing to the EI fund and fewer contributors are eligible for benefits once they become unemployed. As time goes by, the

EXHIBIT 9.2

PERCENTAGE OF UNEMPLOYED ELIGIBLE FOR EI BENEFITS, 1982–1997

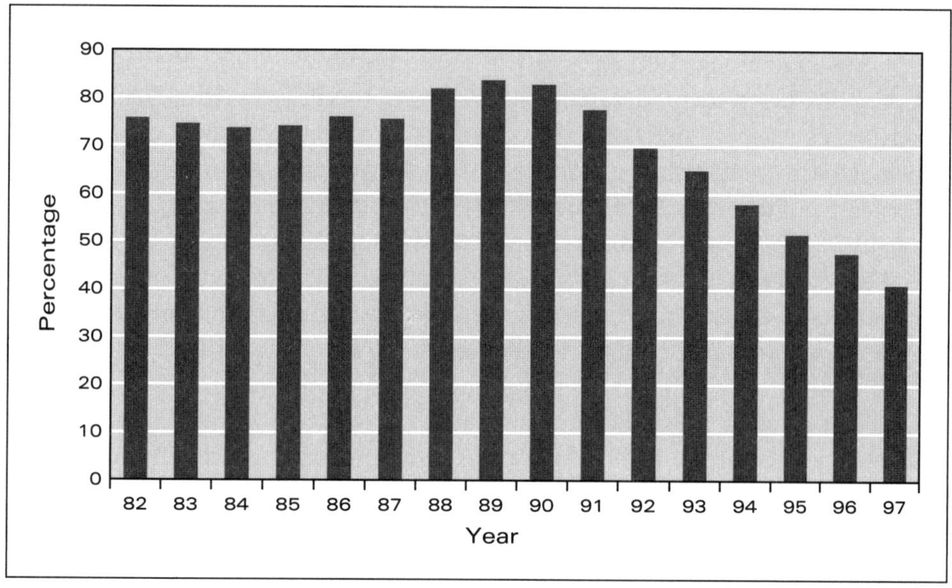

Source: National Anti-Poverty Organization, *The 50th Anniversary of the UN Declaration: A Human Rights Meltdown in Canada* (Ottawa, 1998), 35.

EI system is taking on more and more of the characteristics of a selective income-security program.

II. POVERTY IN CANADA

THE RATE AND DEPTH OF POVERTY

There are various ways to measure poverty. Statistics Canada uses low-income cutoffs to determine the point at which a family crosses into poverty. These cutoffs are based on the number of family members and the size of the community where the family lives. A family is considered to be living in poverty if it spends 56.2 percent or more of its gross income on basic requirements such as food, shelter, and clothing (National Council of Welfare, 1999a).

Poverty rates are on the rise in Canada: in 1997, 17.2 percent of Canadians lived in poverty, compared with 13.6 percent in 1989. Groups that are at a higher risk for poverty include female-led single-parent families,

Aboriginal people, young adults with families, and recent immigrants. For the most part, poverty rates are worsening for these groups. The outlook is more positive for the senior population; the poverty rate for seniors has been falling steadily over the years, reaching an all-time low of 16.9 percent in 1997 (National Council of Welfare, 1999a).

Poverty among children is of particular concern. In 1989, the House of Commons resolved to eliminate child poverty by the year 2000. This goal was never reached: in 1989, 14.5 percent of Canadian children were poor, compared with almost 21 percent in 1996. Child poverty is much higher in female-led single-parent families than in two-parent families (60.4 percent versus 12.7 percent) (National Council of Welfare, 1999c).

The National Council of Welfare distinguishes between the rate of poverty and the severity or **depth of poverty**. By measuring the depth of poverty we are able to discover the extent to which Canadians are living below the poverty line and how much income is needed to bring all Canadians out of poverty (National Council of Welfare, 1999a). Exhibit 9.3 shows the incomes of eight family types as a percentage of the poverty line; unattached men under 65 are living the furthest under the poverty line, while unattached women over 65 are living the closest to the poverty line.

EXHIBIT 9.3

DEPTH OF POVERTY BY FAMILY TYPE, 1997

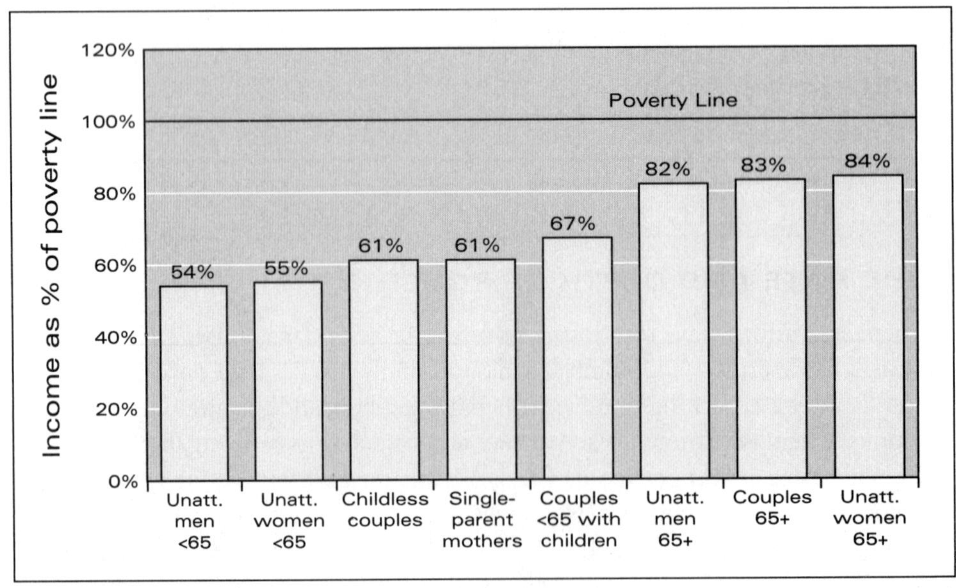

Source: National Council of Welfare, *Poverty Profile 1997* (Ottawa, 1999), 54. Reproduced with the permission of the Minister of Public Works and Government Services Canada, 2000. Cat. No. H67-1/4-1997E.

EFFECTS OF POVERTY

As a result of studies such as the National Longitudinal Survey on Children and Youth (NLSCY) and the National Population Health Survey, we have a better understanding of the effects of poverty. For example, we know that poor people tend to experience more health problems and to be at higher risk for substance abuse and violence (National Advisory Council on Aging, 1996; Taylor, 1991).

Concerns are growing about the impact of poverty on children's development. According to Ross (1999), "Poor families are more likely than others to experience stress in the home, they are less likely than others to live in safe neighbourhoods and are less likely to enjoy access to the cultural and recreational activities that most Canadians take for granted." Other studies indicate that poverty negatively affects children's ability to do well in school; a poor education may, in turn, limit future work opportunities, thereby ensuring a life of disadvantage (Alberta Alcohol and Drug Abuse Commission, 1992).

POVERTY-RELATED PROBLEMS

Hunger

In Canada, the terms "hunger" and "food insecurity" are used to refer to a person's "inability to obtain sufficient, nutritious, personally acceptable food through normal food channels or the uncertainty that one will be able to do so" (Davis and Tarasuk, 1994). Hunger is directly linked to poverty or factors that may lead to poverty, such as rising costs of food, shelter, and other basic necessities; long-term unemployment; and cutbacks in income-security programs. An estimated 2.7 million Canadians have difficulty obtaining sufficient food (Kalina, 1995).

The incidence of child hunger is one of Canada's greatest concerns. The NLSCY reports that

- approximately 57,000 Canadian families with children under 12 experience hunger;
- most hungry families live in large urban centres and are headed by single mothers;
- about one-third of hungry children live in low-income families (i.e., the working poor); and
- Aboriginal families living off-reserve are four times more likely than non-Aboriginal families to experience hunger (cited in McIntyre, Connor, and Warren, 1998).

Data from the NLSCY show a correlation between hunger and several long-term negative effects:

> Nutritionally deprived children experience more health problems than food-secure children including anemia, weight loss, colds, and infections. Additionally, they are more prone to school absences, and may encounter challenges in both concentration and learning. (cited in McIntyre, Connor, and Warren, 1998, 3)

The primary consequence of hunger for adults is poor health. For example, among women who report experiencing hunger, there is a high incidence of chronic health conditions such as back problems and migraines (McIntyre, Connor, and Warren, 1998).

Homelessness

The National Anti-Poverty Organization (NAPO, n.d.) estimates there are at least 200,000 homeless people in Canada, the vast majority of whom live in large urban centres such as Montreal, Toronto, and Vancouver. Homelessness is rarely the consequence of any single factor; rather, it is a complex problem that usually results from an interaction of social, economic, political, and institutional factors.

NAPO divides the homeless population into two groups. The **visible homeless** live on the street, in shelters, or in temporary housing situations. The **hidden homeless** are those who use vehicles or abandoned buildings for shelter, sleep over at other people's homes, trade sex for a place to stay, or (if children) are placed in foster homes. People who are living in physically and/or sexually abusive situations (primarily women) are at a particularly high risk for homelessness. Other high-risk groups include "tenants of single-room occupancy hotels and rooming houses; people living in overcrowded and unsafe housing; and disabled persons living in inaccessible housing" (NAPO, n.d.).

Homelessness is associated with a variety of related problems. For example, unsanitary, damp, and overcrowded living conditions contribute to a wide range of infectious diseases, including HIV/AIDS. Children who are homeless are prone to behavioural problems; tend to be socially, physically, and cognitively delayed in their development; and often experience mood swings, depression, sleeping disturbances, and bed-wetting. The homeless population is also at high risk for mental illness, substance abuse, injury, and physical or sexual assault (Hourston, 2000).

III. CANADA'S RESPONSE TO POVERTY: GOVERNMENT INITIATIVES

SOCIAL ASSISTANCE

Social assistance has been called the "income program of last resort" because it is given only to those who have exhausted all other avenues of support and can prove they are in need. Each province and territory is constitutionally responsible for developing its own social assistance system, including legislation and procedures for determining eligibility, benefit rates, appeal procedures, and the monitoring of welfare provision. As a result, there are 13 different social assistance programs across Canada, including Ontario Works, BC Benefits, and Supports for Independence (Alberta) (National Council of Welfare, 1997).

The decision of the federal government to replace the Canada Assistance Plan with the Canada Health and Social Transfer reduced federal cash transfers by several billion dollars and left the provinces and territories with little choice but to take a hard look at their own social programs and spending practices. Many provinces saw social assistance programs as primary targets for reform. Restructuring efforts have largely focused on freezing welfare rates, cutting special assistance, clamping down on welfare fraud and abuse, and making passive welfare programs more active (National Council of Welfare, 1997). Exhibit 9.4 shows the significant decline in provincial and territorial welfare benefits between 1986 and 1998.

Alberta was the first province to restructure its welfare system; between 1993 and 1997, there was a 63 percent drop in Alberta's welfare rolls. Major reforms were also introduced in Ontario following the 1995 election of the Progressive Conservatives. A central feature of Premier Mike Harris's "Common Sense Revolution" was the complete overhaul of Ontario's welfare system. The passage of the Social Assistance Reform Act in 1997 resulted in the creation of Ontario Works, the province's new social assistance program. The Ontario Social Safety Network (1998) points out the implications of the new legislation:

> Under Bill 142, assistance becomes a virtual loan program with so many criteria to receive it, obligations to remain on it and concessions for future repayment of it through income, assets, etc. that many in real need will be unable to receive the help that would assist them through a time of financial crisis.

The Social Assistance Act also gives the Ontario government the authority to reduce or terminate the benefits of current recipients. In 1997–98

EXHIBIT 9.4

PROVINCIAL AND TERRITORIAL WELFARE BENEFITS IN CONSTANT DOLLARS, 1989 AND 1999

	Single Employables				Single Parent, One Child			
Province	1989	1999	% change 1989–1999	% change 1998–1999	1989	1999	% change 1989–1999	% change 1998–1999
Newfoundland	4,628	1,142	–75.3%	–0.1%	11,782	11,501	–2.4%	–1.1%
Prince Edward Island	8,622	5,316	–38.3%	–1.7%	11,886	9,277	–22.0%	–5.7%
Nova Scotia	7,303	4,374	–40.1%	–2.9%	11,685	10,152	–13.1%	–3.9%
New Brunswick	3,493	3,168	–9.3%	–1.7%	9,469	9,924	+4.8%	–1.7%
Quebec	4,366	6,024	+38.0%	+0.7%	10,607	10,541	–0.6%	–4.2%
Ontario	7,807	6,623	–15.2%	–1.7%	14,011	11,279	–19.5%	–4.9%
Manitoba	7,476	5,352	–28.4%	–1.7%	10,910	8,941	–18.0%	–5.8%
Saskatchewan	6,036	5,540	–8.2%	+3.0%	12,329	9,483	–23.1%	+0.4%
Alberta	5,965	4,824	–19.1%	–1.7%	11,185	9,079	–18.8%	–2.8%
British Columbia	6,727	6,131	–8.9%	–1.7%	12,152	11,231	–7.6%	–4.9%
Yukon	8,795	10,945	+24.5%	–1.7%	14,536	15,770	+8.5%	–4.1%
Northwest Territories	Not available	8,299	Not available	+12.4%	Not available	18,121	Not available	+5.3%

NOTE: "Using the Consumer Price Index, all the dollar figures [in the above table] are expressed in constant 1999 dollars to factor out the effects of inflation and to show the real purchasing power of welfare benefits over time" (30).

Source: Adapted from National Council of Welfare, *Welfare Incomes 1999* (Ottawa, 2000), 33–36. Reproduced with the permission of the Minister of Public Works and Government Services Canada, 2000.

alone, the benefits of some 14,800 welfare recipients were either cut or terminated following the introduction of new welfare fraud and abuse measures (Ontario Ministry, 2000b).

Although most provinces and territories have introduced changes to their welfare systems, Ontario's welfare reforms have been truly revolutionary. The trend of rising welfare benefits (which had continued under the leadership of the New Democratic Party) was reversed following the election of the Conservatives: in 1995, welfare benefits for all recipients (with the exception of seniors and people with disabilities) were cut by 21.6 percent. Cuts to welfare benefits have continued in Ontario (albeit at a more gradual rate), resulting in the removal of 472,090 people from the welfare rolls by 2000 (National Council of Welfare, 1997; Ontario Ministry, 2000a).

WELFARE-TO-WORK PROGRAMS

Welfare-to-work programs, also known as **workfare**, are intended to help welfare recipients make the transition to work and self-sufficiency. These programs provide public benefits in exchange for participation in a work or community service program. Sayeed (1995, 7) adds: "Under the broadest definition, workfare includes both compulsory and voluntary programs aimed at providing welfare recipients with work experience, training and counselling."

Welfare-to-work programs are not a totally new phenomenon in Canada; compulsory work programs were common during the Great Depression, although they were phased out when the economy picked up during World War II. Since the elimination of the Canada Assistance Plan in 1996, the provinces and territories have been free to implement welfare-to-work programs without penalty from the federal government. Among the reasons for implementing workfare programs are (1) to deter able-bodied persons from drawing welfare; and (2) to assist chronically unemployed people in re-entering the workforce.

Today's welfare-to-work programs bear little resemblance to the Depression-era work camps where able-bodied men worked in exchange for their public relief. Rather, workfare programs are likely to redirect welfare recipients to volunteer placements, employment subsidy positions, and other forms of work experience. In situations where wages are lower than the welfare rate, participants may receive a combination of wages and a top-up of welfare benefits. Workfare programs also emphasize the use of action plans or contracts between welfare recipients and governments. These agreements specify the training program, job search plan, or other work-related activity in which the welfare recipient agrees to participate.

Most workfare programs have built-in incentives to encourage welfare recipients to make the transition to paid employment. For example, welfare benefits may be gradually reduced as earnings increase—in keeping with the overall workfare goal of ensuring that "families are better off working" (Torjman, 1998, 2). Able-bodied welfare recipients who do not participate in work-related activities can expect to be penalized; although the penalties vary across jurisdictions, they usually involve a cut in welfare benefits (Gorlick and Brethour, 1999).

Problems with Workfare

There is much controversy about the implementation of welfare-to-work programs in Canada. Supporters of workfare accuse passive welfare programs of destroying the incentive to work, and assert that "any job is a good job" (Canadian Council on Social Development, 1999b, 2). Opponents of workfare question its ability to move people off welfare and into jobs that pay enough to support individuals and their families (National Council of Welfare, 1997). According to Jacobs (1995, 17), workfare "necessarily involves low-skilled, poorly paid work with few long-term prospects." Similarly, Torjman (1997, 5) maintains that workfare programs create little more than "a pool of poorly-paid, marginalized workers who can become a source of cheap labour."

Doubts have also been raised about the cost and effectiveness of workfare programs. According to studies conducted in the United States—where workfare has been a central feature of the welfare system for several years—low-cost workfare programs that offered few supports produced little success in terms of monetary savings, lower poverty rates, or reduced numbers of welfare recipients. When more costly and comprehensive workfare programs were introduced, welfare recipients were more likely to move into the workforce "but at costs that clearly outstripped the financial benefit of doing so" (Clark, 1995a, 5). Preliminary reports of Canada's experience with welfare-to-work programs are similarly discouraging. For example, job creation programs implemented in Alberta from 1993 to 1996 cost $55.7 million—over three times the cost of benefits for single employables (Boessenkool, 1997).

CHILD BENEFITS

One response of federal and regional governments to the problem of child poverty has been the introduction of **child benefits.** Although Canada's child benefit system has evolved over the years, its main objectives remain the same; three of these objectives are articulated below:

1) *Horizontal equity*—to recognize the heavier financial demands that families with children have compared to childless couples and single

people with the same employment incomes; to acknowledge the contribution that all parents make to society in raising future citizens, workers, and taxpayers.

2) *Income equality*—to supplement the incomes of poor and modest-income families with children.
3) *Economic stabilization*—to put cash into the hands of parents and thereby stimulate consumer demand, aiding recovery from recession. (Battle and Mendelson, 1997, 7)

A number of child benefit schemes have been introduced, revised, and scrapped over the years. The most recent of these schemes is the National Child Benefit (NCB) introduced in 1998.

Under the NCB, the federal government provides direct income support through the Canada Child Tax Benefit (CCTB), a tax-free monthly payment made to low-income families with children under 18. Since 1998, the CCTB has consisted of a basic benefit and a supplement or "increase." In 2000, families received a maximum annual CCTB of $2056 for the first child and $1853 for each additional child. In addition to the monthly payments, the federal government provides the provinces (except Quebec, which opted out of the NCB initiative), territories, and First Nation governments with extra funds to expand programs targeted at low-income families with children. These programs vary across jurisdictions but may involve

- providing working parents with cash benefits to offset the costs of employment;
- increasing the number of government-subsidized child-care spaces;
- developing early childhood services for at-risk children; and
- covering the cost of certain health services that are not covered under medical insurance. (Canada, 1999h, 2000f, 2000g)

The NCB plans to reduce child poverty by lowering the **welfare wall** for low-income families with children. The federal government explains:

> In many cases, the policies and programs designed to help low-income families on social assistance have made it difficult for them to work without losing benefits for their children. Some parents may find themselves financially worse off in low-paid jobs as opposed to welfare, and may lose drug, dental and additional health coverage for their children. This "welfare wall" makes it difficult for families to enter and to stay in the labour force. (Canada, 1999i, 1)

EXHIBIT 9.5

HOW THE NATIONAL CHILD BENEFIT WORKS

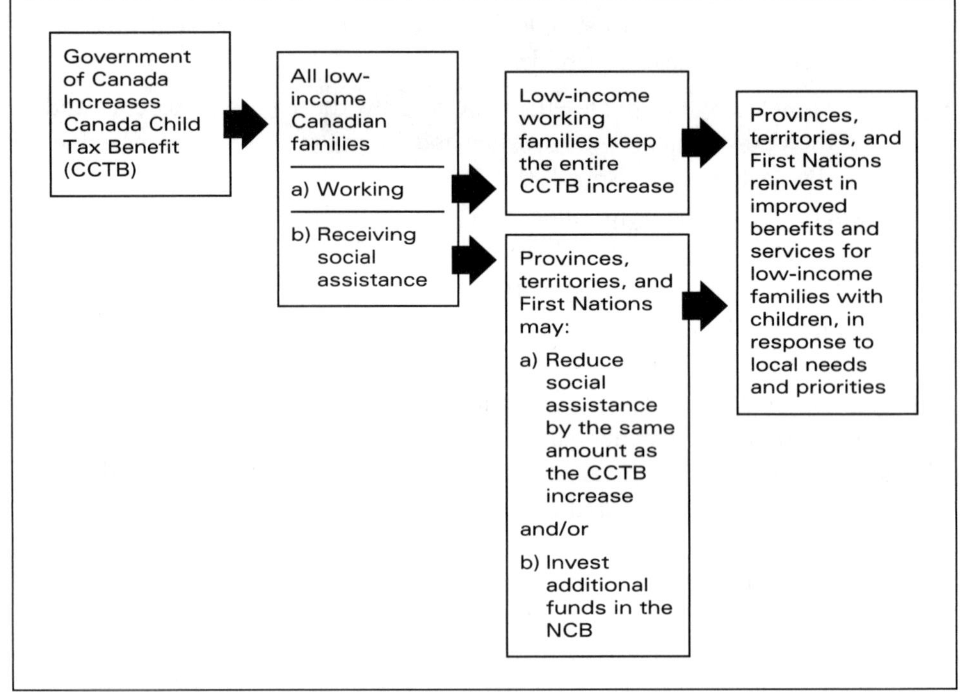

Source: Canada (1999, July), The National Child Benefit: What It Means for Canadian Families [on-line], available: http://socialunion.gc.ca/ncb/ncb_e19.html [2000 June 23].

By providing additional financial support and services to cover child-related expenses, the NCB enables parents to participate in the workforce and at the same time meet their children's needs (Canada, 1999h).

The federal government allows the regional governments to reduce welfare payments for families that receive both the CCTB and social assistance (see Exhibit 9.5). By ensuring that families on welfare do not earn more money than a low wage-earning family, this reduction creates a built-in incentive for families to obtain money through employment rather than welfare. Some social analysts are critical of governments that reduce welfare payments for CCTB recipients. The National Council of Welfare (1998, 8), for example, argues that this practice

> discriminates against families whose main source of income is welfare. Single-parent families are particularly disadvantaged because of the high percentage of these families on welfare. And because 90 percent of poor single-parent fami-

lies are headed by mothers rather than fathers, the Canada Child Tax Benefit winds up discriminating against women.

According to the National Council of Welfare, the federal government is investing billions of new dollars in child benefits that, as a result of the reduction option, will reach only about one-third of poor families with children.

RESPONSES TO HUNGER

Next to seeking assistance from relatives, **food banks** are the most common strategy used by families to deal with hunger. Approximately 800,000 Canadians (300,000 of whom were children) relied on food banks in 1999, more than double the number who used food banks 10 years before (see Exhibit 9.6). Canada's first food bank, which opened in Edmonton in 1981, was conceived as a temporary response to the hardships experienced during Canada's economic recession. However, demand for food banks grew, and by 1999 there were roughly 700 food banks across the country (Wilson, 1999; Food bank use on the rise, 1999). McIntyre, Connor, and Warren (1998) criticize this method of addressing hunger by pointing out that (1) food banks rarely have enough food to meet the demand; (2) the food supply relies on donations, which tend to be inconsistent; and (3) the food itself may be substandard.

EXHIBIT 9.6

CANADIAN FOOD BANK USE, 1989–1999, SELECTED YEARS

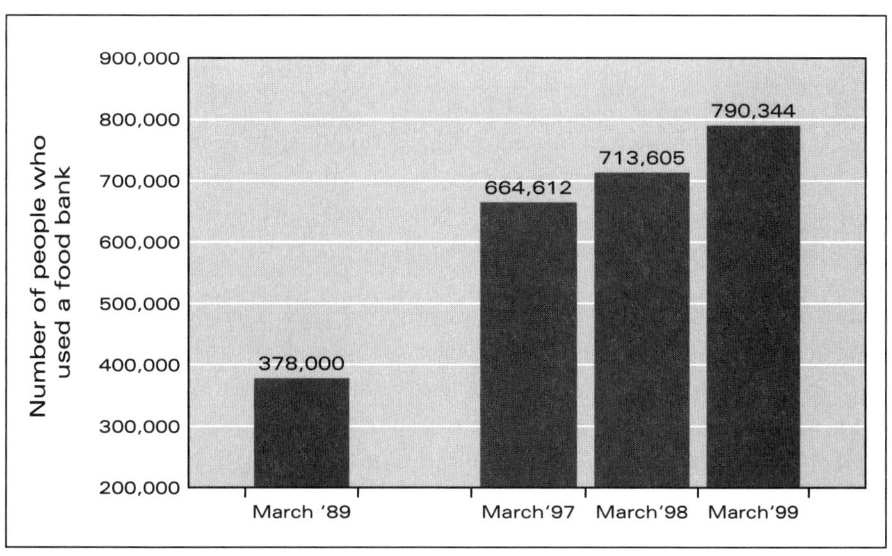

Source: B. Wilson, *HungerCount 1999: A Growing Hunger for Change* (Toronto: Canadian Association of Food Banks, 1999), 3.

The problem of hunger is also being addressed by *community-action food projects*. These grassroots initiatives use a community development approach to reduce hunger in individual communities. An example is the "community kitchen," where "people get together to cook for themselves and their families, sharing the costs and then taking the food home to be used at a later time" (Kalina, 1995, 21). Another initiative is the "community garden," where people can grow their own produce to use or share with others in the community.

A government response to hunger occurred in October 1998, when representatives from Canada and 185 other countries met at the World Food Summit and made the commitment "to reduce the number of undernourished people by half no later than the year 2015" (Agriculture and Agri-Food Canada, 1998, 1). Canada's *Action Plan for Food Security* has been developed as a framework to guide public- and private-sector organizations in their efforts to combat hunger; this national plan will financially support a variety of activities and initiatives that "address the many aspects of food security, including ensuring a safe and nutritious food supply for all, finding ways to increase food production in a way that is both environmentally and economically sustainable, and promoting health and education" (Agriculture and Agri-Food Canada, 1998, 1).

RESPONSES TO HOMELESSNESS

Housing, like food and clothing, is one of the basic necessities of life. As Chisholm (1995, 20) points out:

> Having a secure, affordable home that meets minimum standards of health and safety gives an individual a starting point from which to participate in the community and the economy, as well as a sense of security, an address and an identity. It has a positive effect on an individual's ability to hold down a job, on a child's performance at school and the health of everyone in the household.

Unfortunately, a lack of affordable housing is driving increasing numbers of Canadians into homelessness each year.

To address the problem of affordability, the federal government (through the Canada Mortgage and Housing Corporation) subsidizes various social or **assisted housing projects** specifically designed for low-income Canadians. Assisted housing developments have changed over the years. In the 1960s, low-income families were concentrated in huge, ghettolike complexes that tended not only to isolate but also to stigmatize the poor. Since the early

1970s, assisted housing units have been integrated into mixed-income urban housing developments in which a proportion of a building's units are designated for low-income earners. The main problem with assisted housing projects is that the demand for units exceeds the current supply. Another drawback is that people who apply for assisted housing may be disqualified if they do not meet predetermined "needs" criteria (Pomeroy, 1996).

In December 1999, the federal government allocated $753 million to initiatives that aimed to eliminate and prevent homelessness in Canada. The cornerstone of this effort is the Supporting Communities Partnership Initiative, which calls on all levels of government and private-sector organizations to work together on the common problem of homelessness. According to Human Resources Development Canada (1999d, 2), this collaborative effort will

> put in place the seamless web of services and supports that people need to make a successful transition from the street to a more stable and secure life. It will also help in the development of long-term plans to address the underlying causes of homelessness and to develop a prevention agenda. This approach is rooted in the notion that a continuum of supports at the local level works best.

The Supporting Communities Partnership Initiative will focus attention on populations at greatest risk for homelessness, such as out-of-school youth and Aboriginal people living in urban areas.

IV. WORKING WITH LOW-INCOME GROUPS

Traditionally, social workers have devoted much of their time to helping people cope with the effects of poverty and improve their life circumstances. Social workers have also rallied to many poverty-related causes and advocated on behalf of low-income individuals and groups. With the emergence of new fields of social work, many social workers have turned their attention to working with nonpoor populations. However, a substantial number of social workers continue to help people meet their financial and other basic needs through welfare, employment assistance, housing, and food programs.

INCOME MAINTENANCE WORKERS

Social workers who work in welfare or income maintenance offices are known by such designations as "welfare worker" or "financial assistance worker." These individuals provide direct services to people on social assistance. In recent years, **income maintenance workers** have concentrated less on personal counselling and more on assessing eligibility for benefits, monitoring progress, and helping welfare recipients complete training, find work, or gain work experience through volunteering. As workfare programs are established in some provinces, income maintenance workers are likely to play a greater role in helping people make the transition from welfare to work.

Income maintenance departments in some jurisdictions hire social service workers rather than baccalaureate-level social workers. Social service workers thus hired receive the appropriate training and are generally paid less than a degree-holding social worker. Other jurisdictions prefer to hire social workers because of their advanced skills in dealing with complex problems such as addiction and family violence.

Challenges of Income Maintenance Work

Helping people meet their basic needs, resolve personal issues, and become empowered individuals can be a rewarding experience for welfare workers. However, these workers face a variety of challenges as well. Zastrow (1996, 98) identifies some of the frustrations that welfare workers may encounter in government income maintenance departments:

- the "extensive paperwork" that is usually required;
- trying to meet client needs when existing programs offer inadequate supports;
- having unrealistically large caseloads;
- trying to stay on top of frequent and often complex program and legislative changes;
- dealing with a bureaucratic system that is bogged down with "extensive 'red tape'"; and
- working with clients who lack motivation to change or improve their life situation.

Ultimately, welfare workers may become disillusioned in the face of circumstances outside their control. For example, they may find their helping role at odds with the hard reality that there is little they can do to help people change their life circumstances when welfare benefit rates continue to drop and the cost of living continues to rise. Furthermore, the ongoing tightening of eligibility criteria is putting welfare workers in the unenviable position of having to tell single mothers, for example, that legislative changes require them to find paid work or be cut off welfare.

Another challenge for welfare workers is maintaining an unjaded view of poor or unemployed clients. For a variety a reasons ranging from depression to lack of success in the past, some clients may lack the motivation to find work or participate in a training program. Such clients may demonstrate a lack of interest in the "help" that is offered—for example, by missing appointments or not following through on proposed action plans (Zastrow, 1996). This can leave welfare workers feeling less than enthusiastic about their clients.

Working with people who are dealing with poverty and its related problems requires a particular attitude and approach. Those who work with the poor must take into account "the influence on behaviour, attitudes, and lifestyle of poverty and its associated conditions, such as poor housing, poor schooling, and limited neighborhood childcare and recreational facilities" (Epstein, 1988, 32–33). To accomplish this task, social workers and social service workers require specialized knowledge about poverty and its effects. More generally, workers need to be sensitive, empathetic, and nonjudgmental when dealing with clients. Zastrow (1996) adds that it is important for the worker to recognize and call attention to every sign of progress, as well as to convey a sense of confidence in the client's ability to succeed.

Introduction

Canadian families have less disposable income than in the past, poverty rates are rising, and the income gap between the rich and the poor is widening. To reduce income inequality, Canadian governments have introduced a wide range of income-security programs that are used primarily by seniors, single people, and single-parent families.

Unemployment in Canada

Although overall unemployment is declining in Canada, certain groups of people are underrepresented in the workforce. Unemployment has economic costs and has been associated with social problems ranging from family breakdown to crime. The overhaul of the unemployment insurance system resulted in a dramatic decline in the number of people who are eligible to receive benefits, as well as a greater emphasis on making employment programs more active. The EI fund has accumulated a massive surplus because while more people are contributing to EI, fewer are collecting benefits.

Poverty in Canada

A growing number of Canadians live in poverty; of particular concern is the rising rate of child poverty. Poor adults tend to have more health problems than the general population, while children living in poverty are at high risk of experiencing developmental problems. Hunger and homelessness are two poverty-related problems being experienced by a growing number of Canadians.

Canada's Response to Poverty: Government Initiatives

Provinces have been responding to the reduction in federal cash transfers by restructuring their welfare systems; welfare reform has been especially dramatic in Ontario and Alberta. Welfare-to-work programs are being implemented to move people off welfare, although questions have been raised about their cost and effectiveness. Monthly payments for low-income families with children are provided through the National Child Benefit initiative. The problems of hunger and homelessness are being addressed through food banks, assisted housing projects, and collaborative efforts such as the Supporting Communities Partnership Initiative.

Working with Low-Income Groups

Social workers have traditionally worked with the poor and are often employed by income maintenance offices. Although working with poor and unemployed populations can be rewarding, welfare workers face challenges related to bureaucratic systems, inadequate welfare benefits, and restrictive eligibility rules.

▼ KEY TERMS

INCOME INEQUALITY 197
PASSIVE PROGRAMS 201
ACTIVE PROGRAMS 201
DEPTH OF POVERTY 204
VISIBLE HOMELESS 206
HIDDEN HOMELESS 206
WELFARE-TO-WORK PROGRAMS (WORKFARE) 209
CHILD BENEFITS 210
WELFARE WALL 211
FOOD BANKS 213
ASSISTED HOUSING PROJECTS 214
INCOME MAINTENANCE WORKERS 216

CHAPTER 10

SOCIAL WELFARE AND THE CANADIAN FAMILY

• OBJECTIVES •

I. To look at trends and legislation related to family formation.

II. To examine initiatives and legislation aimed at eradicating family violence in Canada, as well as the problems of spousal violence and child abuse.

III. To explore a variety of issues, concerns, and programs related to Canadian children and youth.

IV. To consider various aspects of social work practice with families.

INTRODUCTION

In proclaiming 1994 the International Year of the Family, the United Nations called attention to the importance of families and their changing needs and responsibilities. In spite of this recognition, there is no single, universally accepted definition of "family." However, for the purpose of collecting data about Canadian families, Statistics Canada defines a **census family** as a married or common-law couple with or without children, or a lone parent with never-married children, living in a private household (Statistics Canada, 1997a). This is a broad definition, encompassing nuclear families (i.e., two parents with children), childless couples, single parents with children, extended families (i.e., several generations living together), retired couples with grown children, common-law couples, and blended or recombined families. Exhibit 10.1 illustrates the breakdown of types among the 7.8 million families living in Canada.

The family may also be defined in terms of its function in society. The Vanier Institute of the Family (1992, 34–35) offers the following functional definition of the family:

EXHIBIT 10.1

CANADIAN FAMILY TYPES, 1996

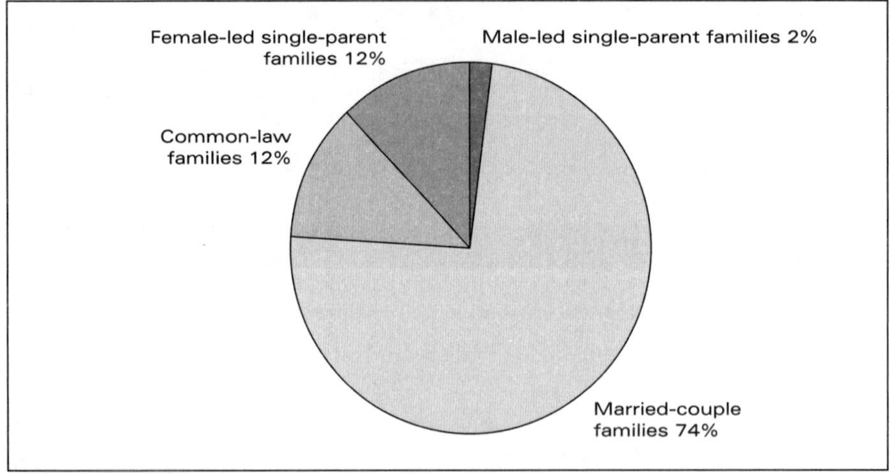

Source: Statistics Canada (1997), "1996 Census: Marital Status, Common-Law Unions and Families," reproduced from Statistics Canada's Web site *The Daily,* http://www.statcan.ca/Daily/English/971014/d971014.htm [2000 June 16].

Any combination of two or more persons who are bound together by ties of mutual consent, birth and/or adoption/placement and which serves the interest of individuals and societies by ensuring the

- physical maintenance and care of its members; and/or
- addition of new societal members through procreation or adoption and their relinquishment when mature; and/or
- socialization of children for adult roles, such as those of spouse, parent, worker, neighbour, voter and community member; and/or
- social control of members (the maintenance or order within the family and groups external to it); and/or
- production and consumption of goods and services needed to support and maintain the family unit; and/or
- maintenance of family morale and motivation to ensure task performance both within the family and the other social groups.

Such an inclusive definition of family emphasizes the diversity of family activities and tasks and is not limited to any particular cultural environment.

The government's role in family affairs has shifted over the years. During the development of the welfare state, the government became directly involved in parent–child relationships, in the social control of dangerous family members, and in the protection of vulnerable children and adults. With the exception of statutory programs like child protection services, regional governments have pulled out of providing the bulk of direct services to families; increasingly, governments are contracting with voluntary and commercial social agencies to provide these services. However, Canadian governments continue to create and support public policies that strengthen the family unit and foster self-sufficiency.

Each province and territory is constitutionally responsible for developing its own family policies and programs. As a result, there is considerable disparity in the type and range of family services across the country. There is also a general lack of coordination among family services within provincial and territorial jurisdictions. Quebec is the only province in Canada that has developed a comprehensive family/child program; launched in 1997, Quebec's Family Policy is a combination of child allowances, early education and child development services, and parental-leave programs (Standing Committee, 2000).

According to Baker (1997), attempts to develop a coordinated system of family services have been frustrated by the lack of agreement among Canadians about what family policy and programs should consist of, or even how "family" should be defined. Politicians and social policymakers, Baker suggests, tend to avoid making family policy decisions if the issues involved are too controversial or not reflective of traditional party agendas. Issues such as abortion, same-sex legislation, and wages for homemakers are examples of sensitive policy issues. That said, Canadian governments have made some progress with regard to policy development in these areas.

I. FAMILY FORMATION

Family formation refers to the founding of the family unit through marriage, cohabitation, procreation, or adoption; the term is also used in reference to the re-formation of the family following marital separation, divorce, or loss of a family member. Through census data, we are able to identify certain trends in family formation.

MARRIAGE AND COHABITATION

Although married-couple families still constitute the majority of Canadian families, this family type is on the decline, having dropped 17.8 percent between 1991 and 1996. During the same period, there was a sharp rise in the number of common-law couple families; by 1996, one in seven couples were in common-law relationships (Statistics Canada, 1997a).

Common-law living arrangements are particularly common among young adults. Children are being raised in an increasing number of common-law families: in 1996, almost half of all common-law families included children (from a current or previous relationship), compared with one-third of families in 1981 (Milan, 2000).

DIVORCE AND SEPARATION

Changes in the Divorce Act and social attitudes have made divorce a more socially acceptable option for people in unhappy marriages. Most divorcees are women, since men tend to remarry more often than women (Statistics Canada, 1997a).

The divorce rate in Canada has been on the decline since 1988 (see Exhibit 10.2). Some social analysts attribute this trend to an increase in the number of couples remaining married; others attribute the falling divorce rate to a rise in the number of unmarried couples and/or married couples who have separated without obtaining a legal divorce (Milan, 2000).

Until recently, studies suggested that children of divorce and separation were at high risk for delinquency, drug abuse, and school dropout. Evidence now suggests that "parental conflict, not parental separation, has the most adverse effect on children" (Canadian Paediatric Society, 2000, 1). The negative effects of marriage breakdown can be reduced if conflict between ex-spouses is kept to a minimum and there is a concerted effort to ensure that the child's relationships with both parents are close and secure. Continued contact with an abusive or addicted parent, however, is usually not in the child's best interest. Social welfare, health, legal, and other services can help to guide parents through the separation process (Canadian Paediatric Society, 2000).

SINGLE PARENTHOOD

Between 1991 and 1996, the number of single-parent families increased at four times the rate of two-parent families, reaching a total of 1.1 million in 1996 (Statistics Canada, 1997a). Divorce is the main reason for single parenthood: "In 1996, divorce was behind the formation of 58% of lone-parent families, compared with less than 24% in 1931" (Milan, 2000, 8).

EXHIBIT 10.2

DIVORCE RATE FOR CANADA, 1921–1997

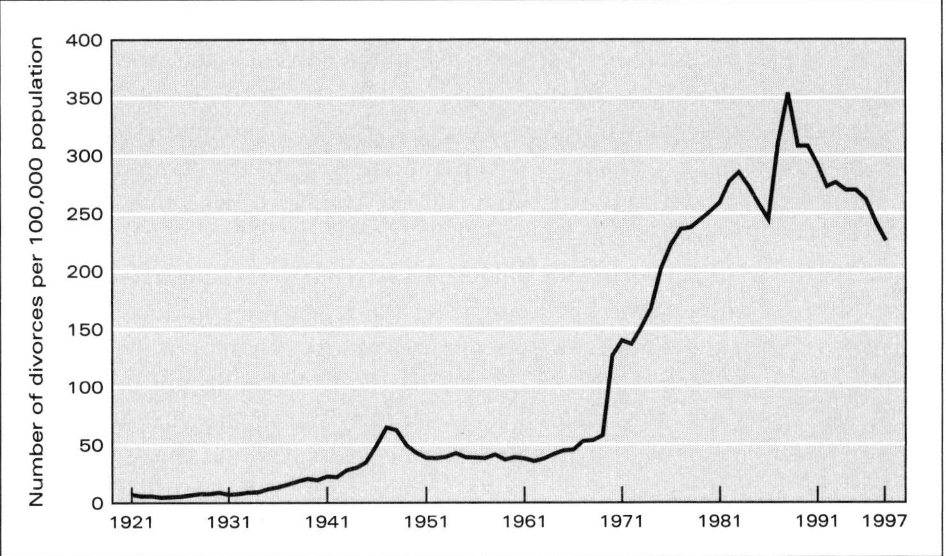

Source: A. Milan, "One Hundred Years of Families," *Canadian Social Trends* (2000, Spring), No. 56, p. 6. Cat. No. 11-008.

The majority of single-parent families are headed by women, a phenomenon that is often attributed to a general increase in women's economic independence and a decrease in the stigma attached to having children outside of marriage. The number of children living in single-parent families has also increased over the years: almost one child in five lived with a single parent in 1996, compared with one in six in 1991 (Statistics Canada, 1997a).

Single-parent families face a variety of economic challenges. For instance, many single mothers are young and have limited education, job skills, and experience, so securing a well-paying job can be difficult. A single wage and a lack of affordable child care make it difficult for many single mothers who *are* employed to earn enough to keep themselves and their families above the poverty line. In addition, few single mothers receive child support payments. These and other factors put female-led single-parent families at a greater risk of living a life of economic disadvantage (Milan, 2000).

LEGITIMATION OF SAME-SEX UNIONS

One of the greatest challenges for the gay rights movement has been in the area of family status and law. Only recently have Canadian governments considered **same-sex unions** in the context of "family," with same-sex partners having the same rights and responsibilities as heterosexual couples. In May 1999, the Supreme Court of Canada ruled that Ontario's Family Law Act was unconstitutional because it restricted the definition of "spouse" to heterosexual couples and therefore discriminated on the basis of sexual orientation. In response to the ruling, Ontario—and later Quebec, British Columbia, and the federal government—amended existing legislation to recognize same-sex unions and extend to same-sex partners the same rights and responsibilities as those enjoyed by heterosexual common-law couples (Gays win landmark ruling, 1999; Ontario passes gay-rights bill, 1999).

The recognition of same-sex unions will have an impact on legislation at both levels of government. For example, at the regional level adoption laws may be expanded to allow same-sex couples to adopt children. At the federal level, 68 statutes will be revised, including the Old Age Security Act, the Canada Pension Plan, the Income Tax Act, and the Immigration Act. Although it is not clear how many couples will be directly affected by the same-sex legislation, one study estimates that 140,000 Canadian couples (1.6 percent of all couples) are gay; the accuracy of this estimate will be tested in 2001 when—for the first time in census history—people will be asked about their sexual orientation (Canada, 2000e; Lawton, 2000; Alberta struggles with gay issues, 1999).

One concern about same-sex legislation is that it will raise the cost of social programs since more people will have access to pensions, tax exemptions, and other spousal benefits. The federal government has responded to this concern by pointing out that while same-sex couples will have greater access to services and benefits under the legislation, they will also have additional financial and social obligations. There has been political opposition to the same-sex legislation. The Canadian Alliance, in particular, has argued that if benefits are to be extended to same-sex couples, they should also be extended to others living in a relationship of economic dependence (e.g., a mother who supports her adult daughter through university) (Same-sex bill passes, 2000; Ayed, 2000). The debate over same-sex legislation—as well as other legislation having to do with redefinitions of "family"—is likely to persist well into the 21st century.

ADOPTION SERVICES

Many families choose to increase their membership by adopting one or more children. **Adoption** is a legal process that transfers the rights and duties of birth parents to adoptive parents. The federal government is responsible for international adoptions, while each province and territory has its own legislation governing the domestic adoption process. In most cases, domestic adoptions take place through provincial and territorial child welfare authorities, children's aid societies, or private licensed adoption agencies.

Social trends are changing some aspects of adoption in Canada. For example, more single women are choosing to keep their babies rather than put them up for adoption; as a result, there are fewer infants available for families wishing to adopt a baby (Adoption Council of Canada, 2000). At the same time, adoption agencies are finding it more difficult to find suitable adoptive homes for "hard to place" children—that is, children who have spent most of their lives in foster care, come from abusive backgrounds, or have developmental, medical, or physical disabilities. As Sobol (Adoption Council of Canada, 2000, 1) notes, "for older children there is more repair work that must be done." To help children settle into the adoptive home, some organizations (including child protection agencies) provide adoptive families with information and support.

Newfoundland and British Columbia are among those provinces that have recently amended or replaced outdated adoption legislation to better reflect modern needs and trends. Although adoption legislation varies across provinces and territories, the general trend is toward

- giving children more say in their adoptions;
- increasing the accessibility of information that can help adult adoptees and birth parents reunite;
- allowing open adoptions so that children can maintain contact with their birth family; and
- expanding eligibility criteria to allow unmarried couples, heterosexual or homosexual individuals, and same-sex couples to adopt.

II. FAMILY VIOLENCE IN CANADA

INITIATIVES AND LEGISLATION

In Canada, the term **family violence** refers to the stalking, physical assault, or killing of a spouse; the physical, psychological, or financial abuse of a person aged 65 or older; or the physical or sexual abuse of a child under the age of 18. Family violence is not a new phenomenon in Canada. However, it has only been in the last 20 years that Canadian governments have been committed to the eradication of family violence (Fitzgerald, 1999).

In 1988, the first phase of Canada's Family Violence Initiative provided the provinces and territories with funding to develop programs such as shelters for abused women and their children, training for professionals and volunteers who work with survivors of abuse, and campaigns to increase public awareness of family violence. Many of the programs initiated during the second phase of the Family Violence Initiative (A Call to Action), which ran from 1991 to 1997, paid special attention to the needs of Canadians living in remote or rural areas, ethnocultural or minority groups, Aboriginal people, and persons with disabilities. The current phase of the Family Violence Initiative, launched in 1997, continues to fund programs as well as integrate many of the separate federal family violence projects into a single strategy; this latter phase is unique in marking "the transition from a *time-limited* to a *long-term* federal commitment to reduce family violence" (Health Canada, 1998c, 12).

A variety of legislated changes have attempted to make systems more responsive to the incidence of family violence. These changes include the following:

1) *Establishment of family violence courts.* Specialized courts in Manitoba and Ontario hear only those cases having to do with spousal, child, and senior abuse. The purpose of such courts is (a) to expedite the processing of cases (thereby reducing the chances of loss of victim and witness information); and (b) to ensure consistency and appropriateness of sentencing across cases.
2) *Expansion of treatment programs for abusers.* By 1998, 42 programs in federal correctional facilities and 32 community-based programs were available for abusers sentenced to prison terms of two or more years.
3) *Expanded family violence legislation.* Family violence legislation recently passed in Prince Edward Island, Manitoba, Saskatchewan, Alberta, and the Yukon provides support for victims of abuse. For example, the legislation gives police the authority to remove an abuser from the family home; it also gives a victim the legal right to remain in the home.
4) *Increased police powers and new protocols.* Changes in criminal law and procedures enable officers to be more responsive to reported incidents of family violence. Since 1983, as a result of changes to the Criminal Code definition of "physical assault," officers have had the authority to arrest an alleged abuser on "reasonable or probable grounds," without witnessing the assault or requiring evidence of actual bodily harm to the victim. Some police departments have also developed protocols for responding more promptly and effectively to women who request emergency assistance (Fitzgerald, 1999; British Columbia, 1996b).

SPOUSAL VIOLENCE

Prevalence and Effects

Spousal violence is a widespread social problem that affects Canadians from all walks of life and all socioeconomic groups. About 17 percent of all victims of violence are victims of spousal violence and the majority (88 percent) of these are women. Women who are young (18–24 years), and who have been in a relationship for less than two years, are most at risk for abuse. Although the majority of reported incidents of spousal abuse are classified as "common assault," a substantial number of incidents result in death; wives are three times more likely than husbands to be killed by their spouse (Fitzgerald, 1999; Health Canada, 1995b).

Certain forms of spousal violence, such as husband abuse and abuse in same-sex relationships, are underrepresented in the literature. According to small-scale descriptive studies of husband abuse, abused men tend to suffer more psychological than physical harm and are likely to reciprocate the violence. Among same-sex couples, male couples tend to report more incidents of abuse than female couples. More research into the various forms of spousal abuse is required before conclusions can be drawn about their extent and severity. The evidence thus far indicates that woman abuse by a male partner is the most prevalent and serious form of spousal abuse (Fitzgerald, 1999; Tutty, 1999).

The effects of spousal violence are well documented. Among women who are abused, 50 percent suffer physical injury and almost 10 percent experience internal injuries or miscarriage (Health Canada, 1995b). The psychological consequences of spousal violence include anxiety, depression, and low self-esteem; about one-quarter of abused women turn to alcohol, drugs, or medication to help them cope. Abused women are likely to have difficulty learning, maintaining a job, and participating fully in social and other activities. There is a correlation between spousal violence and the treatment children receive from their parents; abused parents tend to withhold affection and have more difficulty parenting. Spousal violence has economic costs as well. In Canada, the health and related services (not including hospital admissions) required by abused spouses cost an estimated $1.5 billion each year (Johnston, 1994; MacLeod and Kinnon, 1996).

Responses to Spousal Violence

As a result of the Family Violence Initiatives, governments and voluntary agencies have been able to collaborate on a number of services to meet the needs of abused women and their children. These services include

- residential support (e.g., shelters and transition houses);
- nonresidential support (e.g., information, referral, and support services);
- self-help and facilitator-led groups;
- bioenergetic therapy; and
- integrated and feminist counselling services (MacLeod, 1996).

Over the last 30 years, shelters and transition houses have emerged as primary resources for abused women and their children. According to the 1997–98 Transition Home Survey, there were 470 shelters across Canada in 1998; over 89,000 women and children were admitted to shelters during that year (Fitzgerald, 1999). As a result of the federally funded Shelter Enhancement Program, existing family violence shelters can be upgraded so that they are better able to meet health, safety, and security standards. The Shelter Enhancement Program has also earmarked funds to construct new shelters in First Nations communities and to adapt existing shelters to meet the special needs of children, youth, seniors, and persons with disabilities.

In addition to programs that respond to incidents of spousal violence, there are a wide range of primary prevention strategies that attempt to prevent spousal abuse before it occurs. The National Clearinghouse on Family Violence, in particular, is a major force in health promotion activities committed to increasing public awareness of spousal abuse and other forms of family violence (MacLeod and Kinnon, 1996).

CHILD ABUSE

Prevalence and Effects

The term **child abuse** is used generically to describe the mistreatment or neglect of a child on the part of a parent, guardian, or caregiver that results in "injury, or significant emotional or psychological harm, or serious risk of harm to the child" (Health Canada, 1997a, 1). Thus, child abuse includes physical or sexual abuse, physical neglect, and emotional abuse. Although traditionally social researchers have focused on child abuse within the context of the family, more recently they have turned their attention to child abuse that occurs outside the family; institutional abuse, for example, may occur in schools, child-care and health centres, foster homes, and other community settings (Wachtel, 1997).

Data on the extent of child abuse are sketchy. According to police-reported cases in 1997, 23 percent of the victims of sexual and physical assaults were children under 18; this statistic, however, does not reflect the extent of child abuse (Fitzgerald, 1999). The federal government is in the process of developing a national system that will measure the prevalence of child abuse in Canada.

The effects of abuse on children depend on such factors as the length of time over which the abuse occurs, the child's developmental level, and the relationship between the child and the abuser (Meston, 1993). However, studies on child abuse generally agree on the following:

- Children who are physically and emotionally abused are more aggressive than other children, have delinquent tendencies, and experience difficulties in their relationships with others (Health Canada, 1997a).
- Adults who were sexually abused as children tend to distrust others, suffer from sleep disturbances, and experience low self-esteem, depression, and feelings of self-hatred (Health Canada, 1993, 1997b).
- Infants who are physically neglected are at risk for developmental delays (Health Canada, 1997a).
- Children who are emotionally rejected by their parents are more likely than other children to exhibit hostility, dependency on others, and emotional instability (Health Canada, 1996c).
- Children who witness violence are more likely to have low self-esteem, exhibit high levels of anxiety, and experience behavioural and mental-health problems (boys tend to be aggressive, while girls tend to suffer from depression) (Bala et al., 1998; Health Canada, 1996c).

There is a growing body of research that links child abuse to risk-taking behaviours in adolescence. For example, in their study of 142 Canadian high-school students, Manion and Wilson (1995) found a correlation between physical abuse and alcohol use, and between neglect and running away from home. Adolescents who witnessed spousal abuse were also at a high risk for using illicit drugs and having suicidal thoughts. Exhibit 10.3 illustrates the link between abuse and adolescent risk behaviours.

Responses to Child Abuse

Programs aimed at preventing child abuse or dealing with its effects include the following:

- *Primary prevention programs* focus on raising public awareness about child abuse and neglect, and helping people develop knowledge and skills that can reduce the incidence of maltreatment. These programs include public education campaigns, personal and community safety programs, educational programs, marriage-preparation courses, prenatal classes, parent education, and outreach services.

EXHIBIT 10.3

THE LINK BETWEEN MALTREATMENT AND ADOLESCENT RISK BEHAVIOURS

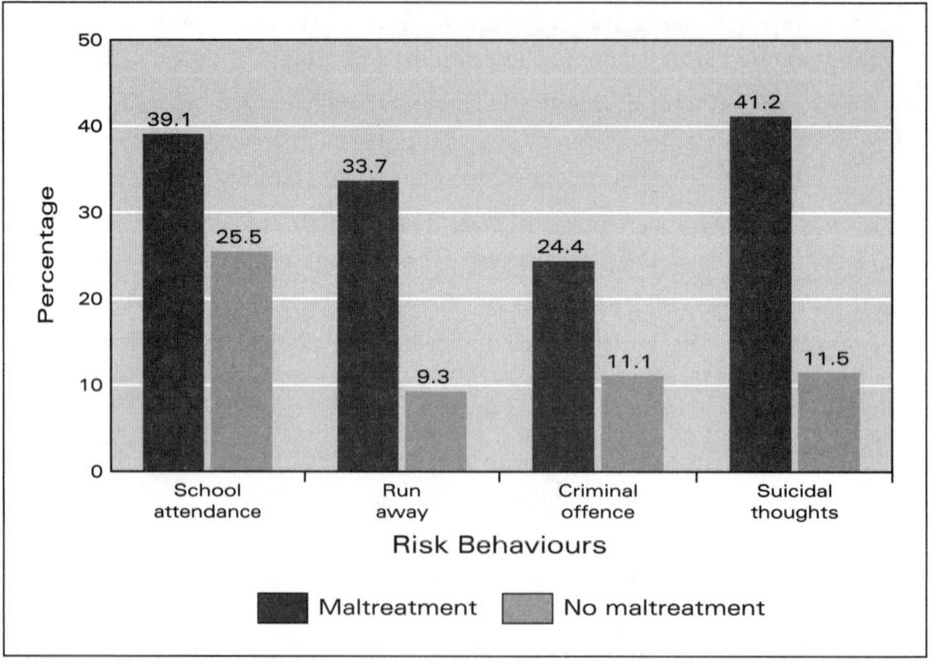

Source: I.G. Manion and S.K. Wilson, *An Examination of the Association Between Histories of Maltreatment and Adolescent Risk Behaviours* (Ottawa: Health Canada, 1995), 26. Copyright © Minister of Public Works and Government Services Canada, 2000.

- *Secondary prevention programs* attempt to interrupt abuse or neglect at the earliest stage possible, and to target high-risk populations. These programs include prenatal nutrition programs, infant development programs, family support services, remedial schooling, crisis lines, and parent support groups.
- *Tertiary prevention programs* provide intervention services as well as support and treatment for both child victims and their abusers. These programs include child protection services, foster care, parenting programs, family preservation projects, and programs for children who witness violence (Wachtel, 1997).

Although primary prevention programs are increasingly being seen as a wise investment in the future of children and society in general, tertiary prevention programs have traditionally received the lion's share of financial and human resources. Many tertiary programs—such as government child protection departments and children's aid societies—have an investigative function. Child protection "teams" operate in accordance with their government's child and family legislation and work closely with the police when responding to cases of child abuse or neglect. At times, child protection authorities have to remove a child from the home and place him or her in temporary foster care. There are various types of foster care in Canada, including private residences, specialized foster homes for children with special needs, and assessment or group homes for older children in care.

III. CHILDREN AND YOUTH: A NATIONAL PRIORITY

CHILDREN'S NEEDS AND HEALTHY DEVELOPMENT

There is a wealth of literature on what children need to develop into healthy, happy, productive human beings. Steinhauer (1996) suggests that children have four basic needs: biological, physical, cognitive, and emotional/social. Exhibit 10.4 illustrates the key influences on a child's development.

Recent studies are helping Canadians better understand the needs of children and the extent to which they are thriving—or not thriving—in Canada. For example, the National Longitudinal Survey of Children and Youth (NLSCY), which began collecting data in 1994, is tracking the progress of 22,500 Canadian children from infancy to adulthood. The purpose of this study is to gain a better understanding of the factors that influence a child's development (Statistics Canada, 1997b). According to the NLSCY, while Canadian children are in the main physically, emotionally, and socially healthy, a substantial number experience problems. Child development experts emphasize the importance of addressing these problems promptly in order to prevent "ill health, inferior school performance, unsatisfactory social relationships and ultimately poor labour-market opportunities down the road" (Ross, Scott, and Kelly, 1996, 8).

THE NATIONAL CHILDREN'S AGENDA

In May 1999 the Federal-Provincial-Territorial Council on Social Policy Renewal unveiled the National Children's Agenda (NCA), a new working agreement between the various levels of government that emphasizes a nation-wide approach to child well-being. Exhibit 10.5 outlines some of the disturbing trends that explain the need for a national approach. The government

EXHIBIT 10.4
KEY INFLUENCES ON CHILD DEVELOPMENT

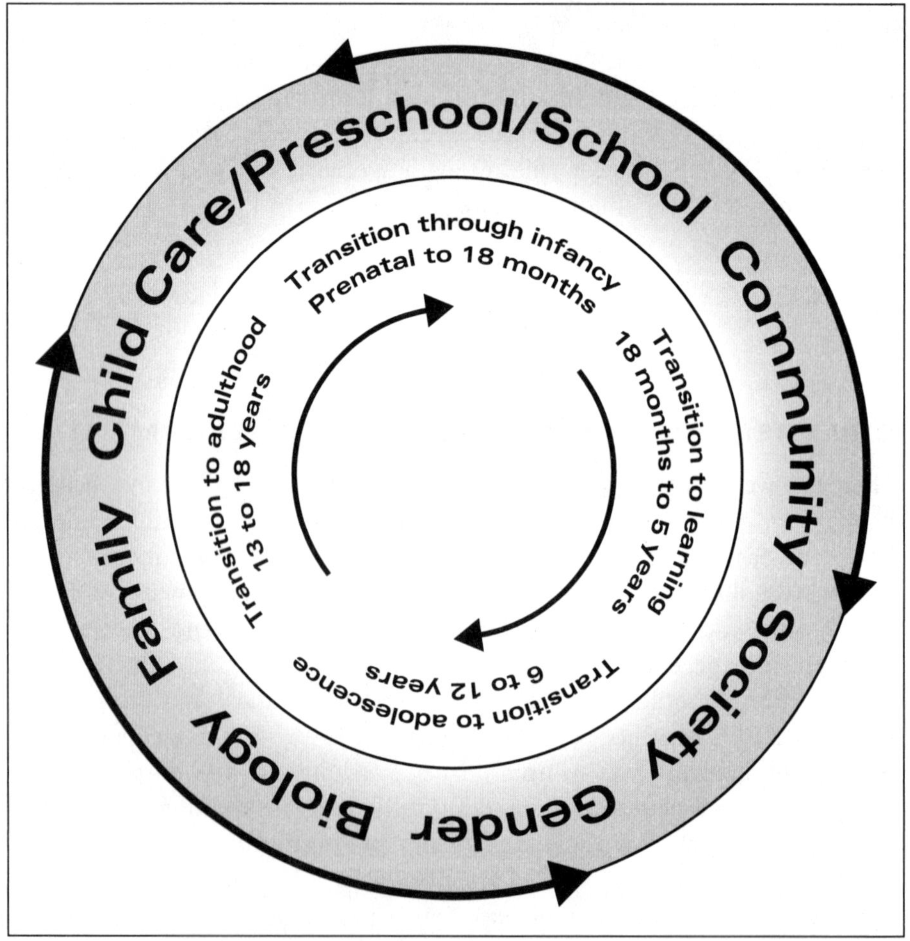

Source: Canada, *A National Children's Agenda: Developing a Shared Vision*, Cat. No. H39-494/1-1999E (Ottawa, 1999), 10.

of Quebec, while agreeing with the principles underlying the NCA, chose not to participate in the multilateral initiative "because it wishe[d] to assume full control over programs aimed at families and children within its territory" (NCA, 1999a).

The NCA (1999b, 6) has articulated its vision for Canada's children:

- Canadians want their country to be one where all children thrive in an atmosphere of love, care and understanding, valued as individuals in childhood and given opportunities to reach their full potential as adults.

Exhibit 10.5

WHY DO WE NEED A NATIONAL CHILDREN'S AGENDA?

NATIONAL CHILDREN'S AGENDA OBJECTIVES	TREND REPORTED IN *THE PROGRESS OF CANADA'S CHILDREN 1999/2000* (CCSD, JANUARY 25, 2000)
1. Supporting parents and strengthening families	• A growing number of families are experiencing work/family tension. • Only 40 percent of parents agree with the statement: "Canada values its young children."
2. Enhancing early childhood development	• The number of child-care spaces has dropped or remained static over the last five years. • There is increasing evidence that quality early childhood care benefits a child's development.
3. Improving economic security for families	• Two-thirds of Canadians report no improvement in their finances over the past two to three years. • Income disparities among families continue to grow. • The child poverty rate is dropping slowly but remains 50 percent higher than it was 10 years ago.
4. Providing early and continuous learning experiences	• Public spending on education has risen in actual dollar terms but fallen as a percentage of GNP. • University tuition fees rose more than 125 percent between 1990 and 1999.
5. Fostering strong adolescent development	• More teens are smoking. • Youth are at high risk for STDs. Sex education resources have been cut back.
6. Creating supportive, safe, and violence-free communities	• 300,000 children under 12 are reported to have witnessed violence at home in 1996. • A growing number of children are under the care of child welfare agencies. • There is growing evidence that environmental pollution threatens children's health.

Source: Canadian Council on Social Development, *Backgrounder: Why Do We Need a National Children's Agenda?* [on-line], available: http://www.ccsd.ca [2000 February 21]. Adapted by permission of the Canadian Council on Social Development.

- Respected and protected from harm, children will grow up to respect and protect the rights of others. Valued, nurtured and loved, they will grow up able to contribute to a society that appreciates diversity, supports the less able and shares its resources.
- Given the opportunity to develop their physical, intellectual, emotional, social and spiritual capacities to their fullest, children will become tomorrow's successful and enthusiastic parents, caregivers, workers and citizens.

Embedded in this vision are four goals: (1) good physical, emotional, and spiritual health; (2) safety and security; (3) success at learning; and (4) social engagement and responsibility.

Collaboration is seen as key to the achievement of the NCA's goals. Future initiatives for children and families are likely to be the result of partnerships between various disciplines (e.g., social services, health, education, and justice), levels of government, and nongovernment organizations and groups. The federal government's commitment of about $7 billion per year (primarily through the National Child Benefit system) enables the provincial, territorial, and First Nation governments to develop new initiatives and enrich existing ones. Programs developed under the NCA umbrella will focus on improving the level of benefits and services to low-income families with children and helping parents make the transition from welfare to gainful employment (NCA, 1999a; Canada, 1999c, 2000a).

EARLY CHILDHOOD DEVELOPMENT PROGRAMS

Early childhood development programs aim to reduce risk factors in the home and thereby increase the chances that children will have a healthy start in life. The first five years of a child's life, in particular, are believed to make a significant difference in how well children do in school, cope with life's challenges, and ward off chronic disease in their adult years (Canada, 1999c).

A variety of programs sponsored by the federal government focus on prevention and early intervention for high-risk children and their families. Health Canada's Community Action Program for Children, for example, funds a number of projects across Canada that target children aged 5 and under who live in poor or teen-parent families; have developmental delays; exhibit social, emotional, or behavioural problems; or have experienced abuse or neglect. Each province and territory has its own early childhood development programs. New Brunswick's Early Childhood Initiatives, for example, is a prevention-focused program for preschool children whose health is at risk (Health Canada, 1999e; Canada, 1999c).

CHILD CARE

An important aspect of the early childhood experience is the quality of care a child receives; indeed, **child care** in the early years is believed to be "the strongest predictor of success when that child enters the school system" (British Columbia, 1999b, 2). There are various types of child-care programs in Canada, including programs that are run by government, commercial profit-making operations, and nonprofit voluntary agencies. The growing demand for quality child care in recent years has been attributed to the increase in the number of single-parent families (mostly led by women) and families with two working parents. Among Canada's 2.3 million children, 40 percent aged 5 and under receive child care outside the home (Juggling the demands of children and work, 1997); Exhibit 10.6 shows the percentage of children needing such care in each province.

Although Canadians generally agree that quality child care is important, the child care system has been criticized for exhibiting the following characteristics:

- *Lack of affordability.* Reduced federal transfers and increased competition for funds are resulting in fewer subsidized child-care spaces. Poor working families are hardest hit by these cuts (University of Toronto, 2000; National Council of Welfare, 1999c).
- *Inaccessibility.* The number of children who need child care is far greater than the number of children who actually use child care (National Council of Welfare, 1999c).
- *Insufficient regulation.* In 1999, just over one-quarter of Canadian children were cared for in regulated child-care programs. Most child-care centres are not required to adhere to minimum standards of health and safety, child-to-caregiver ratio, number of children, size of program, or staff training requirements (National Council of Welfare, 1999c).

Although the federal government committed $720 million to child-care initiatives in 1993, the dispersal of this money has been delayed by the Social Security Review of 1994, the transition from the Canada Assistance Plan to the Canada Health and Social Transfer, and the formation of Canada's social union (Doherty, Friendly, and Oloman, 1998). In its 2000 budget speech, the federal government invited the provinces and territories to agree on an action plan to support early childhood development by the end of the year. At the Annual Premiers' Conference in August 2000, the premiers reconfirmed their commitment to early childhood development and made proposals to the federal government with respect to priorities, principles, and funding requirements; the

EXHIBIT 10.6

THE NEED FOR CHILD CARE BY PROVINCE, 1996

	Birth to 2 years old			3 to 5 years old			6 to 12 years old			Total birth to 12 years old		
	Total children	Children with mothers in paid labour force	% of children needing care	Total children	Children with mothers in paid labour force	% of children needing care	Total children	Children with mothers in paid labour force	% of children needing care	Total children	Children with mothers in paid labour force	% of children needing care
Newfoundland	19,344	10,166	53%	21,781	12,213	56%	56,861	32,969	58%	97,986	55,348	56%
Prince Edward Island	5,309	3,794	71%	5,892	4,106	70%	13,906	9,588	69%	25,107	17,488	70%
Nova Scotia	33,146	18,803	57%	36,933	21,219	57%	86,343	53,055	61%	156,422	93,077	60%
New Brunswick	22,662	14,972	56%	28,949	15,170	52%	70,425	43,224	61%	126,036	73,366	58%
Quebec	275,026	163,666	60%	290,252	160,866	55%	627,028	399,561	64%	1,192,306	724,093	61%
Ontario	439,851	262,157	60%	458,643	276,775	60%	1,024,079	710,770	69%	1,922,573	1,249,702	65%
Manitoba	44,985	24,837	55%	46,939	30,105	64%	106,311	75,944	71%	198,235	130,886	66%
Saskatchewan	40,059	24,750	62%	44,529	29,766	67%	107,127	79,583	74%	191,715	134,099	70%
Alberta	116,518	71,838	62%	124,515	82,343	66%	289,243	211,372	73%	530,276	365,553	69%
British Columbia	141,582	77,844	55%	143,659	84,186	59%	337,797	244,910	73%	623,038	406,940	65%
Total	**1,142,482**	**672,827**	**59%**	**1,202,092**	**716,749**	**60%**	**2,719,120**	**1,860,976**	**68%**	**5,063,694**	**3,250,552**	**64%**

Source: National Council of Welfare, *Preschool Children: Promises to Keep* (Ottawa, 1999), 46. Reproduced with the permission of the Minister of Public Works and Government Services Canada, 2000.

outcome of the premiers' proposals is yet to be determined (Canada, 2000a, 6; Canadian Intergovernmental Conference Secretariat, 2000).

PARENT SUPPORT PROGRAMS

The nature of the interaction between parent and child is a key factor in how a child develops physically, socially, and cognitively. Findings from the NLSCY suggest that although a child's development may be hindered by risk factors such as poverty, parental depression, and prenatal problems, parenting is "a much more significant contributor than risk factors to a child's development" (Statistics Canada, 1997b, 7).

Problems in parenting are closely related to a range of child behaviour problems, but especially to conduct disorders (Statistics Canada, 1997b). According to Stevenson (1999, 3–4), children who exhibit conduct disorders are 36 times more likely to have parents who use "ineffective, aversive, inconsistent or negative disciplining most of the time" than they are to have parents who rarely use these disciplining techniques.

Studies from Canada, the United States, and Britain suggest that children living in female-headed single-parent families are at greater risk for emotional, behavioural, academic, or social problems than are children living in two-parent families (see Exhibit 10.7). For example, according to findings from the NLSCY:

> The likelihood that a child with a lone mother will have one or more behaviour problems was 1.8 times higher than that of a child with two parents, even when controlling for income differences between families. In contrast, the odds of a child from a low-income family having one or more behavioural problems was only 1.2 times that of a child who is not from a low-income family. (Statistics Canada, 1997b, 8)

While single parenthood does not in itself cause behavioural and other problems among children, there is a strong correlation between such problems and factors associated with single parenthood, such as stress, fatigue, and depression (Lipman et al., 1998; Stevenson, 1999).

A wide range of **parent support programs** exist in Canada "[to] give parents the resources and skills they need to raise their children, and give children the potential for a stable and secure family environment" (Canada, 1992a, 10). The Nobody's Perfect Parenting Program, for example, targets parents with young children. Through the provision of information, mutual aid, and parenting skills training, Nobody's Perfect helps parents better understand their

EXHIBIT 10.7

PROBLEMS EXPERIENCED BY CHILDREN IN TWO-PARENT VERSUS LONE-MOTHER FAMILIES

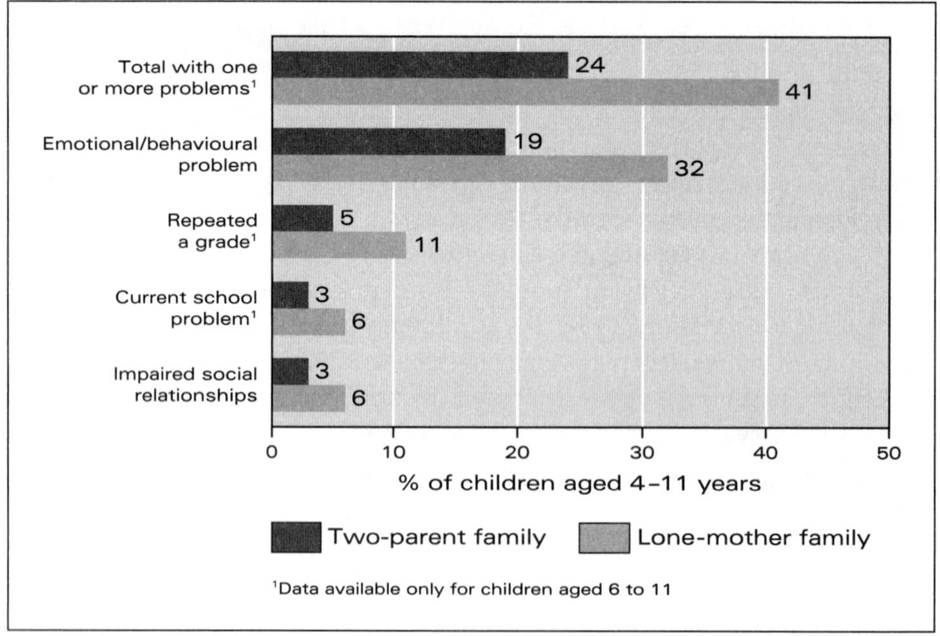

Source: Statistics Canada, "Canadian Children in the 1990s: Selected Findings of the National Longitudinal Survey of Children and Youth," *Canadian Social Trends* (1997, Spring), No. 44, p. 8. Cat. No. 11-008.

children, relate to their children in more positive ways, and enhance self-confidence and coping skills (Thurston and O'Connor, 1996). Other parent support programs are designed for parents who have teenagers. British Columbia's Parents Together Program, for instance, offers weekly self-help groups for parents who are experiencing difficulties with their teenagers; a trained volunteer facilitator helps parents raise and resolve issues, share knowledge about raising teens, and provide mutual support (Vancouver Public Library, 1999).

CHILD AND YOUTH MENTAL HEALTH

The extent to which a person's mental-health needs are met during childhood has a strong influence on one's ability to be an independent, self-controlled, and productive adult. Mental-health problems in young people commonly manifest as behavioural problems such as physical aggression, sexual acting out, poor school performance, property offences, alcohol and drug abuse, running away from home, and suicide attempts. According to a study that was conducted in Ontario, one out of every six children exhibits a behavioural problem (Ross, Scott, and Kelly, 1996). Among the most important factors influencing a child's mental health are quality of relationships with parents and siblings, level of stability in the home environment, and disciplining style used by parents.

Experts in the mental-health field stress the importance of recognizing and treating mental-health problems in children and youth as early as possible (Nova Scotia, 2000). A variety of nonresidential mental-health services for children and youth have been established in Canada. These services include the following:

- *Assessment.* Psychological, speech, and other tests are used to diagnose developmental disorders or delays, learning disabilities, attention deficient disorders, or other difficulties.
- *Individual and family counselling.* A variety of topics may be addressed, such as grief and loss issues, anxiety, depression, eating disorders, and thought and behaviour disorders.
- *Support and educational groups.* Small groups of children or teens meet to discuss and engage in activities related to anger management, self-esteem, parental divorce or separation, and other topics.
- *Creative therapy.* Art, play, dance, and the like are used to help children and youth deal with sexual abuse and other traumatic experiences.
- *Suicide intervention.* Individual counsellors or suicide intervention teams provide crisis intervention services for children, youth, and their families.
- *Distress lines.* Trained counsellors or volunteers provide telephone response and referral services for children and youth in crisis or in need of emotional support.

For children and youth experiencing severe emotional, social, and/or behavioural problems, residential mental-health programs are available. An example is Manitoba's Intensive Treatment Program, a hospital-based program for adolescents that "provides multidisciplinary, multi-faceted and intensive treatment services" (Manitoba Adolescent Treatment Centre, 1999, 7). Other programs offer nontraditional mental-health services for young people; in Nova Scotia, for instance, "adventure-based school and camp activities [are provided] for high-risk youth from the community and youth correctional facilities" (Nova Scotia, 1999a).

YOUTH AND DELINQUENCY

A study on youth and crime by Stevenson et al. (1999, 20) points to family problems and economic disadvantage as the underlying reasons for delinquency among children and youth:

> Children living in low-income households can be affected by low-quality housing and transient, run-down neighbourhoods. Parental frustration may lead to substance abuse and violence in the home, which in turn may place children at risk of becoming involved with a delinquent peer group and potentially criminal activity.

Children growing up in poor single-parent families are at highest risk for criminal activity. A lack of money often limits the extracurricular activities that a child can participate in; "as a result," Stevenson (1999, 5–6) notes, "these children may have more unstructured and unsupervised free time, and thus become more vulnerable to negative influences."

Many social welfare programs are in place to help families resolve issues that contribute to delinquency in youth. For example, child and youth care, teen outreach, child and family services, and other types of youth-oriented programs provide short-term individualized support for youth who are having difficulty coping with family tensions, school-related conflicts, and other stressful situations. Youth counsellors may use a variety of interventions to help youth deal more effectively with anger and aggression, including the teaching of communication skills, anger management, and stress-reduction techniques. Big Brothers and Sisters of Canada (2000) is among the many voluntary organizations across Canada that have a youth focus; in this program, volunteer big brothers and sisters are matched with youth for the purpose of providing guidance, emotional support, and companionship.

IV. SOCIAL WORK WITH FAMILIES

Working with families, an important component of the social welfare system, is becoming the primary focus of many fields of social work. Helping families meet their basic needs, deal with problems such as family violence, and generally reach their goals can be highly rewarding.

There are challenges as well. As the definition of family continues to expand, so too does the need for social workers to broaden their knowledge base. Social workers must continually hone their assessment and intervention skills to help families deal with the effects of globalization, an aging population, and other environmental changes.

Social workers are also being required to help Canadian families cope with the consequences of cuts to social welfare programs and government policies aimed at promoting independence and self-sufficiency. Much of the responsibility that governments once assumed has been devolved to families. This shift is reflected in the growing number of families that are obliged to provide eldercare and child care in their homes because professional services have become unavailable, unaffordable, or unsuitable. Increasingly, social workers must help families discover their own "internal" strategies for meeting needs and resolving problems, as opposed to relying on "external" government-sponsored supports.

The term **empowerment** is often used to describe the goal of many family services. When social workers engage in empowering activities with families, they are essentially helping family members to help themselves and, ultimately, manage their own lives. Empowerment can be observed when a family is able to (1) identify its needs and know where to go to get those needs met; (2) advocate on its own behalf so that needed resources can be accessed; and (3) have input into the programs and policies that directly affect them.

To become empowered, families need to know about the services that are available to them. Social workers can either provide these services directly or connect families with appropriate community resources. Exhibit 10.8 outlines the various service components that are available in most provinces and territories.

Introduction

The Statistics Canada definition of "census family" encompasses a broad range of family types. Since family policies have developed separately within each province and territory, there is considerable disparity in the type and range of family services across Canada. Politicians are sometimes reluctant to address family policy if the issues are too controversial.

Family Formation

Married couples constitute the majority of Canadian families, but there has been a steady rise in the number of common-law couples. Although divorce and separation have become more socially acceptable, they can have negative consequences for children. Changes in women's socioeconomic status, as well

Exhibit 10.8

SOCIAL WORK WITH FAMILIES: TYPES OF SERVICES AND ACTIVITIES

TYPE OF SERVICE	RELATED ACTIVITIES
Prevention	• sharing information about family violence, substance abuse, and mental-health issues • family planning • parent education • early childhood education
Early Identification and Intervention	• respite services • stress management courses • drop-in programs for parents and children • infant development programs • parent support/self-help groups • supportive counselling and feedback for parents
Assessment	• family history • identification of sources of stress • referral to community resources • developmental screening
Intervention	• family therapy • marriage counselling • personal counselling • parenting-skills training • therapy groups for abusers • outpatient alcohol and drug counselling
Residential Programs	• inpatient alcohol and drug treatment • institution-based psychiatric care • extended care for seniors • group home for adolescents

Source: Author.

as in social attitudes, have resulted in an increase in the number of female-headed single-parent families. The Supreme Court of Canada's legitimation of same-sex unions is challenging the traditional definition of "family." Social trends are changing certain aspects of adoption; for instance, there are fewer infants available for adoption because more single women are choosing to keep their babies. Some provinces have changed their adoption legislation to better reflect modern needs and trends.

Family Violence in Canada

Family violence is a social problem that governments have committed to eradicate through legislation, policies, and programs. Seventeen percent of all victims of violence are victims of spousal violence, and the majority of these victims are women. The effects of family violence on its victims include long-term physical, mental, emotional, and financial problems. Shelters and transition houses have been the primary resources for abused women and children. Among programs aimed at preventing child abuse, tertiary prevention programs have traditionally received the lion's share of resources.

Children and Youth: A National Priority

Children need to have certain basic needs met if they are to develop into healthy and productive adults. The National Children's Agenda works with all levels of government to focus on child well-being. Early childhood development programs target children aged 5 and under to give them a good start in life. Demand for quality, affordable, and regulated child-care programs has grown with the rising number of single-parent and two-income families. There is a correlation between parenting style and behavioural problems in children; parent support programs help people deal with the challenges of parenting. Child and youth mental health is most influenced by the relationship between children and their families; a wide range of residential and nonresidential programs have been established to address child and youth mental-health issues. Delinquency among youth has been linked to economic disadvantage; various social welfare programs help youth deal with issues that contribute to delinquency.

Social Work with Families

Working with families is becoming the focus of many fields of social work. Governments are devolving much of family support programming to the family unit. To help families cope with their new responsibilities, social workers engage families in activities that promote "internal" and "empowering" solutions.

KEY TERMS

CENSUS FAMILY 219
FAMILY FORMATION 221
SAME-SEX UNIONS 224
ADOPTION 224
FAMILY VIOLENCE 225
SPOUSAL VIOLENCE 227
CHILD ABUSE 228
CHILD CARE 235
PARENT SUPPORT PROGRAMS 237
EMPOWERMENT 241

CHAPTER 11

SOCIAL WELFARE AND OLDER CANADIANS

• OBJECTIVES •

I. To look at public and voluntary initiatives that have emerged in response to Canada's aging population.

II. To consider methods of meeting the environmental needs of seniors as they relate to living arrangements and housing.

III. To explore the main components of healthy aging.

IV. To examine aspects of institutional and community-based care for seniors and the role of informal caregivers.

V. To consider the nature of social work practice with elderly populations.

INTRODUCTION

As Canada's baby-boom generation enters its senior years, the senior population is expected to grow from 12 percent of the population in 1998 to an unprecedented 23 percent in 2041 (Canada Mortgage and Housing Corporation, 1999). Canada isn't alone in having an **aging population**; all western industrialized countries are witnessing varying degrees of the same phenomenon. This global demographic shift prompted the United Nations to declare 1999 the International Year of Older Persons (IYOP). The primary purpose of the IYOP was to promote an international awareness of aging and to recognize and celebrate seniors' contributions; the IYOP also provided "a good opportunity to gain a more balanced view of what aging involves, both for individuals and for society—rather than relying on stereotypes and one-side accounting" (Celebrating seniors' contributions, 1998, 3).

Those who see the aging trend as a problem for Canadians tend to base their argument on two assumptions: (1) a greater proportion of resources (such as health care, social services, public pensions, and housing) will be consumed by a growing number of retired or "noncontributing" members of society; and (2) people in the workforce will have to support the retired population, a burden that is both unreasonable and unsustainable.

The National Advisory Council on Aging counters such arguments by pointing out that today's seniors continue to contribute to society well after retirement and, on average, are both healthier and more financially secure than previous generations of seniors (Celebrating seniors' contributions, 1998). In addition, while there is little doubt that an aging population will put pressure on existing programs, institutions, and infrastructures, costs in other areas will drop. For example, by the time the baby boomers reach their senior years, the school-age population will be considerably smaller than it was in the 1960s and 1970s; as a result of this demographic shift, governments will be able to redirect the money saved on education to areas such as health care (Hale, 1999).

The following social policy areas have been identified as among those which will be influenced by an aging population:

- *safety and security*—issues related to elder abuse, crime against seniors, and physical injury;
- *technology and aging*—the challenges of using "basic" technologies such as automated teller machines, voice mail, and computerized library systems;
- *supportive housing for seniors*—the need for flexible housing and related supports that can enable seniors to live independently in their own homes;
- *older women*—the need to find ways to improve conditions for senior women, who are generally worse off than their male counterparts when it comes to income, health, and housing;
- *income security*—the need to ensure that retirement income programs are adequate;
- *health concerns*—worry among seniors that government cutbacks, the rising costs of health care, and health-care reform will jeopardize the quality of health care in the future; and
- *aging in place*—the need to adapt homes, transportation, and other systems so that seniors can **age in place** (i.e., live in their homes for as long as possible) (Newfoundland and Labrador, 1999; Hale, 1999; Health Canada, 1998a).

In the discussion that follows, the terms "senior," "older Canadian," and "elderly person" are used interchangeably to refer to a person aged 65 or over.

I. RESPONSES TO CANADA'S AGING POPULATION

NATIONAL INITIATIVES

There are a variety of national initiatives that have been developed to promote "the health, well-being, self-sufficiency and participation of seniors" (MacLeod and Associates, 1997, 1). For example, the Seniors Independence Program, launched in 1988, supports projects aimed at enhancing the quality of life for seniors. In 1993 the new Ventures in Independence encouraged collaboration among seniors, governments, voluntary agencies, and business in its efforts to direct more attention to the needs of vulnerable or at-risk seniors.

In 1995 the Seniors Independence Program and Ventures in Independence merged to form New Horizons: Partners in Aging. Through New Horizons, seniors and various seniors' organizations were able to develop programs that focused on improving "the health, well-being and independence of seniors in situations of risk or prevent situations which put seniors at risk" (Health Canada, 1995a, 3). These programs included recreational activities in seniors' centres, lifelong learning programs, and information and referral services.

NATIONAL FRAMEWORK ON AGING

Many factors determine a person's quality of life in the senior years. Health Canada (1999a, 1–2) suggests that **healthy aging** is the accumulated effect of conditions and choices made throughout one's life. Factors that determine healthy aging include income, social support, health practices, environmental conditions, and coping skills. Since these determinants are not the responsibility of any one sector, the need for a coordinated and collaborative plan becomes apparent. There is also a need to develop policies and programs that will be flexible enough to meet the needs of seniors and the rest of the population throughout the life span (Health Canada, 1999a).

In 1994 the Federal-Provincial-Territorial Ministers Responsible for Seniors approved the development of a National Framework on Aging (NFA) to help them coordinate their efforts and develop policies that meet the needs of an aging society. At the core of the NFA are a shared vision statement and five principles (see Exhibit 11.1). Although it supports the NFA's principles, Quebec intends to address the needs of seniors through its own health and social service programs rather than through the NFA (Health Canada, 1999a, 1999b). Since 1998 the Federal-Provincial-Territorial Ministers Responsible for Seniors have been working on a database of seniors-related information that can be used to develop and improve policies and programs for seniors (Health Canada, 1999b).

EXHIBIT 11.1

THE NATIONAL FRAMEWORK ON AGING

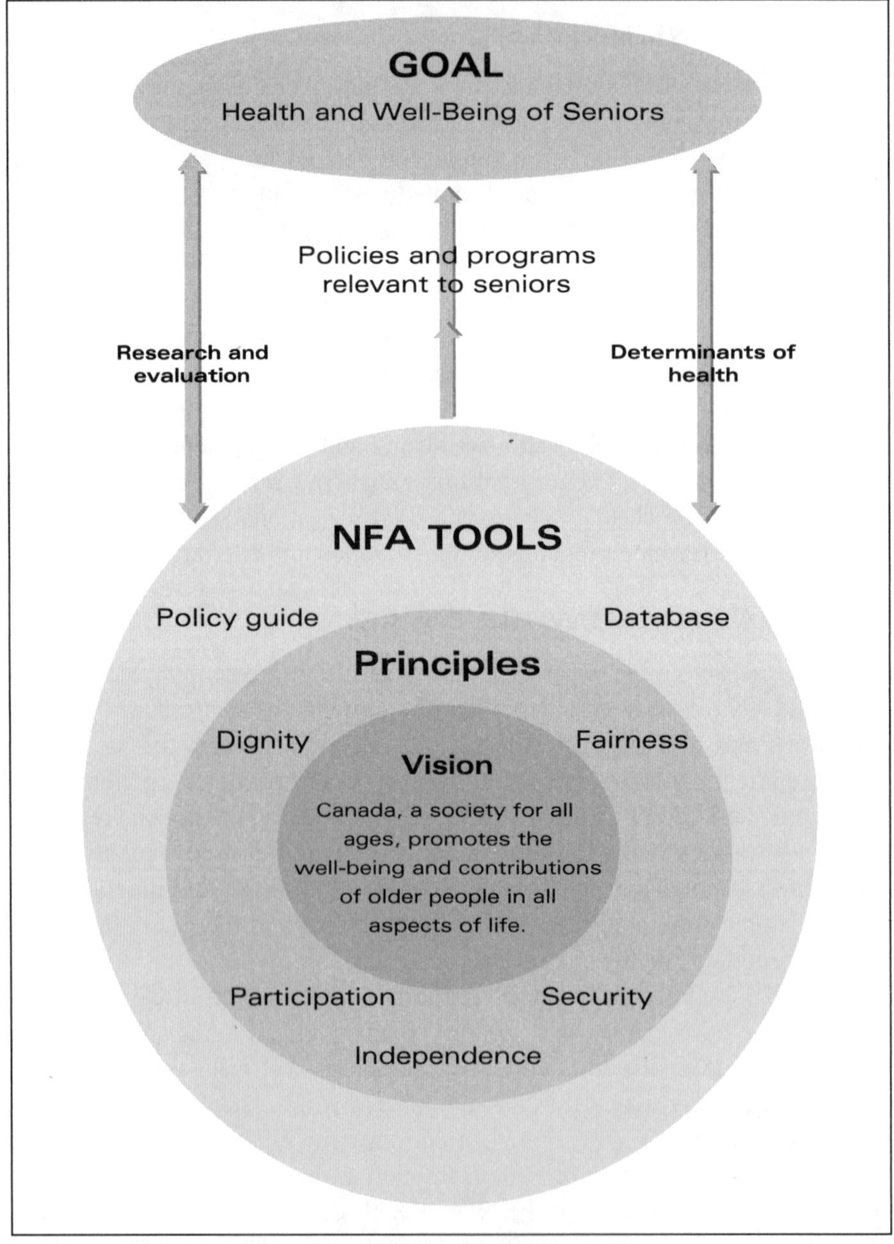

Source: Health Canada, Division of Aging and Seniors (1999), "The National Framework on Aging," from *Introduction: National Framework on Aging* [on-line], available: http://www.hc-sc.gc.ca/seniors-aines/pubs/nfa-cnv/en/nfa3_e.htm [2000 April 29]. Copyright © 2000. Reprinted with permission from the Division of Aging and Seniors, Health Canada.

SENIORS' ORGANIZATIONS IN THE PUBLIC AND VOLUNTARY SECTORS

At the federal level, the National Advisory Council on Aging makes recommendations to the Minister of Health on issues concerning Canada's aging population and seniors' quality of life. Another federal department is the Division of Aging and Seniors, a centre of expertise that works in conjunction with other government departments and seniors-focused organizations in the areas of research, policy and program development, and information-sharing on matters of concern to seniors (Health Canada, 2000a).

At the regional level, advisory councils and secretariats make recommendations to provincial and territorial governments on policies and programs that concern seniors. These bodies typically publish newsletters and directories of services, coordinate policies and programs, and advocate on behalf of older people (Novak, 1997).

A broad spectrum of voluntary organizations, councils, associations, networks, and committees are also seeking to meet the needs of seniors. These groups usually promote an independent lifestyle among seniors—that is, seniors are supported in their efforts to age in place, carry out daily activities within a normal community context, and make decisions about their own lives. Organizations that provide seniors' programs usually focus on a specific aspect of seniors' independence, such as physical or mental health, income, transportation, housing, human rights, or personal safety and security.

II. CREATING SUPPORTIVE ENVIRONMENTS FOR SENIORS

LIVING ARRANGEMENTS

The term **living arrangement** is used to refer to the number of people one lives with and the types of relationships one has with those people. A person's living arrangement usually changes over time and is influenced by such factors as marriage, childbirth, departure of children from the home, and death of a spouse (Changes in living arrangements, 1996).

Most seniors live with a spouse or by themselves. Women over 75 are more likely than their male counterparts to live alone, usually because of the death of a spouse. Over one-third of all Canadians living alone are seniors; among this population, 70 percent are widows (A time to grieve, 1998). For many women, the later senior years are characterized not only by the loss of a spouse, but also by diminished social supports, isolation, depression, and the onset of health problems and physical disabilities. Because of these and other factors, women are more likely than men to be institutionalized (Changes in living arrangements, 1996).

The number of seniors who live with people other than their spouse is decreasing. Improved income-security benefits for seniors over the years is believed to be a main reason that seniors continue to live in their own homes (Priest, 1993). Living arrangements other than living alone or with a spouse include the following:

- *Foster care.* A senior lives in the home of an unrelated family and receives meals and housekeeping services.
- *House/home sharing.* An owner/renter and a tenant share the same living space; the tenant may provide personal care, housekeeping, or perform other duties in exchange for reduced rent.
- *Group home.* A group of unrelated people live in the same house and share the household expenses and maintenance; each person has his or her own bedroom and shares the common areas of the house.
- *Accessory apartment.* Part of a single-family dwelling is converted into a self-contained suite, or an apartment is built onto the existing structure.
- *Granny flat.* A senior lives in a portable, self-contained unit placed on the property of a single-family residence. (Canada/National Advisory Council on Aging, 1992)

The living arrangement a senior chooses usually depends on his or her health, income, and family relationships, as well as gender, ethnic background, marital status, and proximity to support services (Senior Citizens' Secretariat, n.d.). Trends in the living arrangements of seniors are shown in Exhibit 11.2.

HOUSING OPTIONS

Adequate housing is central to everyone's quality of life, but it is particularly important for seniors. In his article on housing patterns and older people, Montgomery (1977, 253) states:

> The quality of the housing environment becomes increasingly significant in the lives of many aged families and individuals. And the quality of this limited world largely determines the extent to which they will retain their independence; the amount of privacy, auditory and visual, they will experience; how often they will visit with friends;

EXHIBIT 11.2

LIVING ARRANGEMENTS OF OLDER SENIORS, 1971–2011, SELECTED YEARS

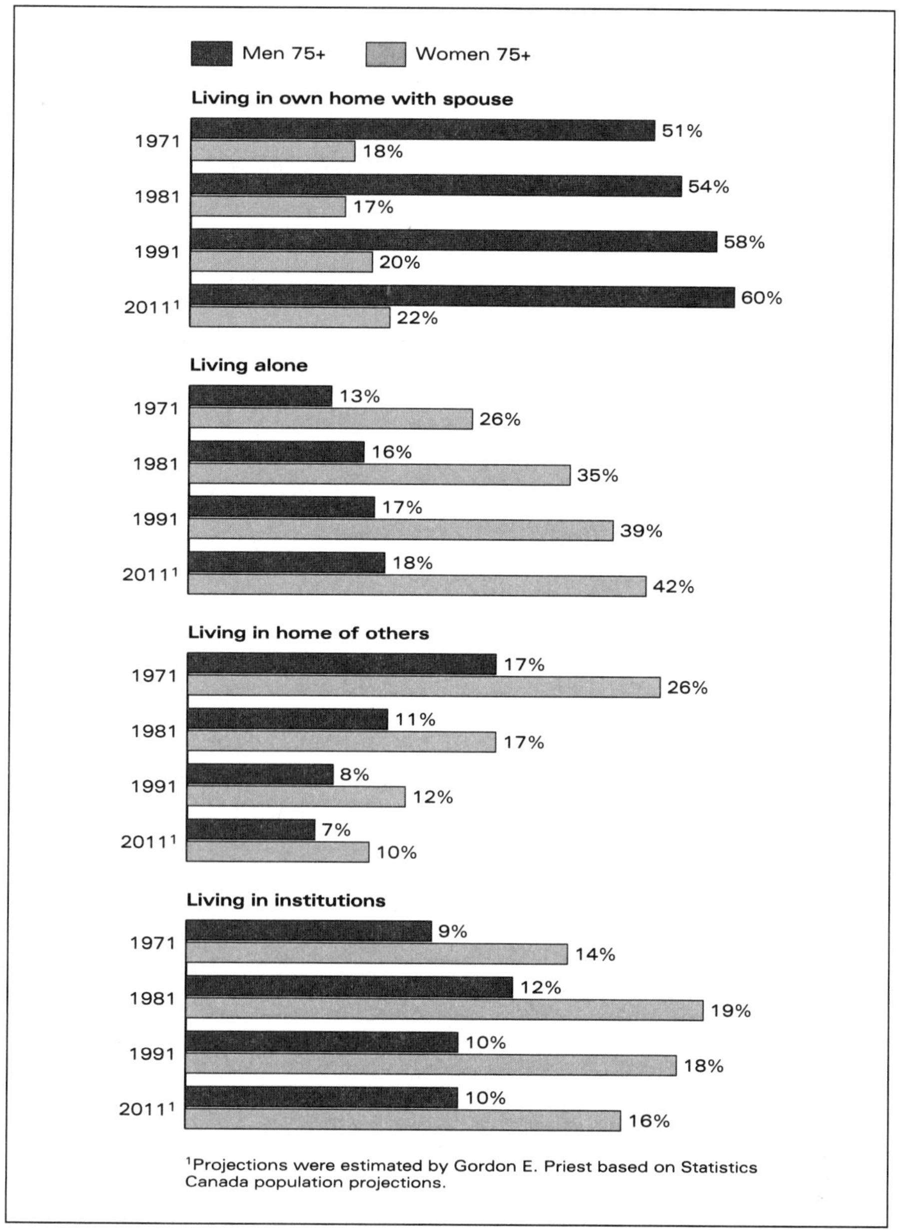

Source: G.E. Priest (1993, Autumn), "Seniors 75+: Living Arrangements and Lifestyles," *Canadian Social Trends* (Ottawa: Statistics Canada, Cat. No. 11-008), No. 30, p. 25.

> their sense of place; and their ability to exercise a measure of control over the immediate environment. Housing often is a major variable, physically, socially and psychologically, in the lives of older persons.

A growing number of seniors are living alone as a result of divorce, single parenthood, or having few or no children. There has also been a shift from institutionalization to community-based care, which includes family members caring for an elderly relative. These and other trends have implications for the types of housing that seniors require (Canada Mortgage and Housing Corporation, 1999).

Among the housing options available to Canadian seniors are single-unit housing (private, detached dwellings) and multiple-unit buildings (e.g., apartments or townhouses). These dwellings may be part of a cooperative housing project, owned within a condominium building, or rented. **Supportive housing** combines housing with a variety of services. For example, retirement homes allow the resident to own or rent a self-contained private apartment and have access to a communal dining room, nursing station, and activity areas; retirement communities provide self-contained living units within a small "village" of shopping, health-care, and other facilities (Ontario Non-Profit Association, 1997).

Most seniors own their homes. In 1996, 84 percent of families headed by a senior, and 50 percent of all unattached seniors, were homeowners (Lindsay, 1999). Several government programs aim to help seniors live independently in their homes for as long as possible. For example, Home Adaptation for Seniors' Independence, a program funded through the Canada Mortgage and Housing Corporation, helps seniors with disabilities modify their homes so that they are better able to perform daily living activities. Home adaptations may include installing a shower seat or grab bars in the bathroom, or building wheelchair ramps or lifts (Health Canada, 2000a).

III. COMPONENTS OF HEALTHY AGING

In recent years, research has focused on minimizing the health problems associated with aging. There is a general consensus among experts that healthy aging is strongly correlated with good physical and mental health, social support, prevention of elder abuse, financial security, and an active involvement with life (Crompton and Kemeny, 1999). In this section, we review those components of healthy aging. Exhibit 11.3 further illustrates the relationship between healthy aging and various aspects of a person's life.

EXHIBIT 11.3

THE COMPONENTS OF HEALTHY AGING

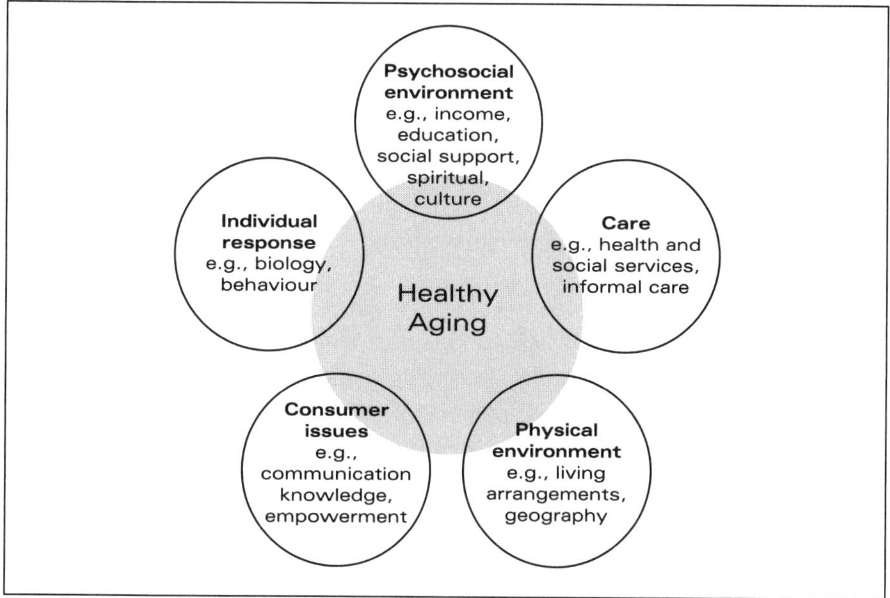

Source: From *Partners for Action: A Canadian Workshop on Seniors and Medication, Alcohol and Other Drugs*, Health Canada, 1995. © Minister of Public Works and Government Services Canada, 2001 [on-line], available: http://www.hc-sc.gc.ca/hppb/alcohol-otherdrugs/pube/partners/rpte.htm [2000 May 26].

PHYSICAL HEALTH

In preindustrial times, only a small segment of the population lived past the age of 65. Today, however, a 65-year-old woman can expect to live to the age of 87, while her male counterpart can expect to live to 82. This increase in **life expectancy** is the result of improvements made in nutrition, pre- and post-natal care, housing, sanitation, health care, disease control, and general lifestyle (Profile of Canada's seniors, 1999).

Although the majority of seniors report that their health is good or excellent, health problems become more likely as the body ages. A longer life expectancy also creates a larger population of the "very old" (80+ years), a group that is more prone to illness and injury than younger seniors. Because they tend to live longer than men, women usually spend more years in poor health (Lindsay, 1999).

Physical Fitness

Physical fitness is an important component of successful aging since it contributes to physical and psychological well-being and therefore enhances an individual's ability to remain independent. Studies show that almost half of seniors walk, garden, or swim on a regular basis. Almost 90 percent of seniors are physically mobile and are able to walk without difficulty or assistance (Gender and need for technical aids, 1999).

Despite these positive reports, the risk of physical limitation due to sensory loss, accidents, illness, or other circumstance increases as one ages, especially among those over the age of 75. It is common for elderly persons to develop multiple disabilities that increase the need for caregivers and technical aids such as walkers, wheelchairs, hearing aids, and electronic controllers for lights, telephones, and home appliances (Seniors and disabilities, n.d.).

Drug Abuse

Although the use of illicit drugs and alcohol tends to decline with age, prescription drug use (which can lead to drug abuse) tends to increase. Seniors consume an estimated 20 to 30 percent of all prescription drugs in Canada. Improper use of prescription drugs can intensify existing health problems or create new ones. Health risks increase when more than one drug is used. Multiple-drug use is highest among seniors who report having stressful lives and a lack of emotional support from family and friends (Bergob, 1994).

Few seniors take advantage of the various treatment options for drug abuse that exist, such as detoxification, residential, and outpatient treatment services. Health and social service caregivers continue to search for innovative ways to tailor programs to the specific treatment needs of seniors. The Seniors Well Aware Program in Vancouver, for example, provides assessment, counselling, life-skills training, and other services specifically for older people who are experiencing problems with alcohol or prescription or over-the-counter medications (Seniors Well Aware Program, 1999).

MENTAL HEALTH

Mental health or well-being may be understood in terms of a person's acceptance of self, purpose in life, perceived autonomy and environmental control, personal growth, and positive social relations (Wigdor and Plouffe, 1991). The 1996–97 National Population Health Survey found that the degree of emotional well-being experienced by seniors is closely linked to the status of their health: "Many seniors in poor health are likely living with chronic pain, which is often associated with increased levels of mental distress" (Crompton and Kemeny, 1999, 22). Above-normal stress levels among seniors have been linked to change and loss associated with aging (e.g., forced retirement, separation from loved ones, death of a spouse, and reduced physical activity) (Prasil, 1993; Healthy lifestyles and aging, n.d.).

Dementia

The number of seniors experiencing mental-health problems is expected to increase. Among older seniors, Alzheimer's disease and related dementias are the most common and debilitating mental-health problems (National Advisory Council on Aging, 1993a). **Dementia** has been defined as "a clinical syndrome characterized by severe losses of cognitive and emotional abilities, [which] interferes with daily functioning and the quality of life" (Burke et al., 1997, 24). The Canadian Study of Health and Aging estimates that 8 percent of Canadians over age 64 suffer from some form of dementia; this figure is expected to triple by the year 2031 (see Exhibit 11.4). For reasons yet to be determined by researchers, women are more likely than men to suffer from Alzheimer's disease (Burke et al., 1997).

EXHIBIT 11.4

TRENDS IN DEMENTIA AMONG SENIORS

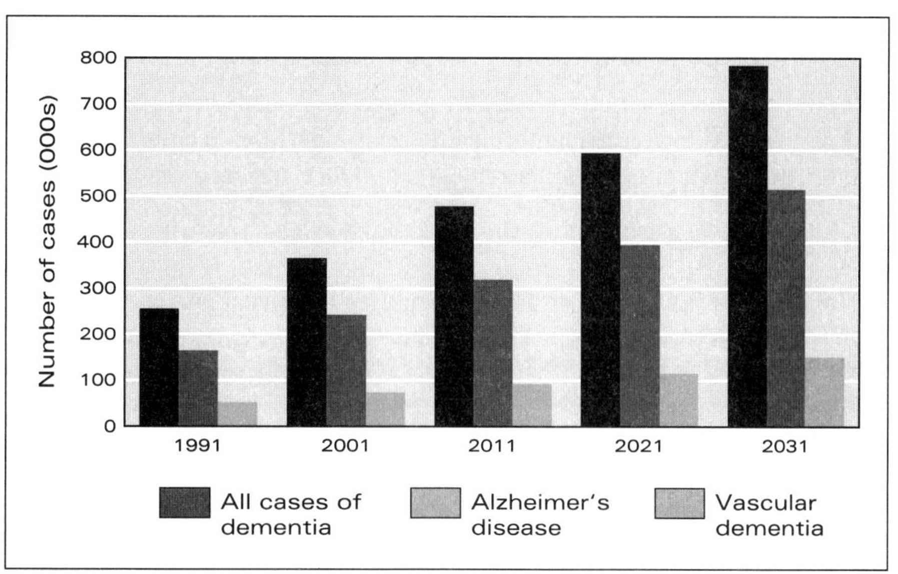

Source: M.A. Burke, J. Lindsay, I. McDowell, and G. Hill (1997, Summer), "Dementia Among Seniors," *Canadian Social Trends* (Ottawa: Statistics Canada, Cat. No. 11-008), No. 45, p. 25.

Depression

Depression is another common mental-health problem among the elderly population. A wide range of factors can contribute to depression, including the death of a loved one, diminished physical or cognitive abilities, decreased activity levels, and declining income. If prolonged, depression can lead to suicide. Health Canada (1994b) reports that "males in the oldest (and fastest-growing) age groups (80+) have the highest suicide rates of any age group."

Mental-Health Services

There are a wide range of community resources across Canada that help seniors deal with mental-health problems. About half of Canada's seniors with dementia are cared for in institutions such as nursing homes and long-term care units; the other half receive care in the community. Nonresidential mental-health services for seniors include the following:

- consultation outreach teams, which provide initial consultation for elderly persons in their homes or in long-term care facilities;
- outpatient geriatric clinics, which provide diagnosis, assessment, and treatment in a nonresidential setting;
- geriatric day programs, including psychiatric day hospital programs and day care for chronically ill patients; and
- psychogeriatric day hospitals, which provide assessment and short-term treatment. (Health and Welfare Canada, 1988)

Also available are a variety of support groups (e.g., bereavement groups for widows and widowers), mental-health programs (e.g., one-to-one counselling), and crisis intervention services (e.g., police and medical response).

SOCIAL SUPPORT

Social support is essential to maintaining good physical and mental health in the senior years. As Crompton and Kemeny (1999, 24) point out:

> Some of the health-related effects of aging are buffered when people have someone they can confide in and can count on, and who can give them advice and make them feel loved. Conversely, lack of such support is a powerful risk factor for poor health, perhaps because people have no one to help shield them from the effects of various stressors.

Although social support can be derived from personal friendships and social or professional affiliations, Canadian studies indicate that spouses and adult children are the main sources of emotional support for seniors (McDaniel, 1993).

Social interaction has mental as well as physical benefits. Socializing with others gives seniors an opportunity to think, reason, solve problems, reminisce, and otherwise exercise their mental capacities. According to Crompton and Kemeny (1999, 25), "seniors who are involved in a variety of activities appear to have strong cognitive capacity, while those with very little social involvement report having trouble concentrating, solving problems and remembering events."

Seniors who lack an adequate support system of their own can participate in programs that facilitate social interaction and connection. For example, **intergenerational programs** match seniors with children or youth and encourage the two groups to interact with and learn from each other. The Volunteer Grandparents Society of Canada and Intercultural Grandmothers Uniting are two examples of intergenerational programs.

In mentoring programs, seniors support and interact with at-risk children in a variety of settings, including the classroom. Mentoring can have a positive impact on a child or youth's self-esteem and confidence and at the same time give the senior an opportunity to share experiences and learn about younger generations. Exhibit 11.5 identifies some of the common traits that make seniors and adolescents such a potentially good match.

Exhibit 11.5

A PERFECT FIT

The late Maggie Kuhn, the outspoken American activist who founded the "Gray Panthers," felt that adolescents and seniors have many common traits. For example:

- Both groups are not taken seriously. The old are told, "We don't do it that way anymore." The young are told, "You don't know what you're talking about."
- Both have limited incomes.
- Both are going through dramatic bodily changes. The young are growing hair; the old are losing hair.
- Both are "confronted" to the drug scene, though faced with different drugs and different "pushers."
- Both can be in varying degrees of conflict with the middle generation.
- Both have difficulty securing employment because age discrimination against the young and old is still rampant.
- Both are free to be agents of social change.

Source: Excerpted from National Advisory Council on Aging (1998, Summer), "A Perfect Fit," from Reconnecting the Generations, *Expression, 11*(4), 3. Copyright © 1998. Reprinted with permission from the Division of Aging and Seniors, Health Canada.

PREVENTION OF ELDER ABUSE

While child abuse and the abuse of women captured the public's attention in the 1960s and 1970s, elder abuse emerged as a recognized social problem in the 1980s. **Elder abuse** has been defined as "any action/inaction which jeopardizes the health or well-being of an older person" (Lukawiecki, 1993, 4). Abuse against an elderly person can take the following forms:

- material abuse such as financial exploitation;
- physical abuse such as pushing, shoving, or physical assault;
- psychological abuse such as chronically threatening, swearing at, or insulting the older person; and
- neglect or failing to provide necessary help such as meal preparation, housework, or personal care. (Canada/Seniors Secretariat, 1992, 1)

A national survey of 2000 Canadian seniors conducted in 1990 showed that about 4 percent of elderly Canadians experienced some form of abuse or neglect; this finding probably underestimates the extent of the problem, given the tendency of abuse victims to underreport (Podnieks et al., 1990). According to the Revised Uniform Crime Reporting Survey, seniors were victims in 2 percent of all violent crimes reported to police in 1997. Roughly one-quarter of abusers are family members (Fitzgerald, 1999).

A number of legislative changes have been introduced to protect elderly members of our society. For example, Newfoundland, Prince Edward Island, Nova Scotia, and New Brunswick have introduced **adult protection legislation**. The remaining provinces and territories have amended their legislation to include the protection of seniors (Fitzgerald, 1999). Some seniors and professional groups reject adult protection legislation on the grounds that "seniors are not children that need to be protected by the State" (National Advisory Council on Aging, 1993b, 5).

There are a variety of programs and services aimed at preventing and treating elder abuse. Prevention is often a focus of seniors' groups, health units, and nursing homes. Many communities have established multidisciplinary teams to detect, assess, and treat elder abuse. Similarly, community committees may have strategies for educating the public about elder abuse; developing elder abuse protocols, policies, programs, and procedures; and strengthening information and support networks for seniors. The extent to which these and other community-based strategies are successful depends greatly on the involvement of seniors and seniors' organizations (Health Canada, 1998a).

FINANCIAL SECURITY

Although some seniors draw income from investments, most depend on Canada's **retirement income system**. This system was established with two goals in mind: "to ensure that elderly people have incomes high enough to allow them to live in dignity no matter what their circumstances were during their working years; [and] to maintain a reasonable relationship between income before and after retirement so that old age does not bring a drastic reduction in a person's standard of living" (National Council of Welfare, 1999a, 1). Canada's retirement income system is made up of three main components:

1) *Federal-provincial-territorial income support programs*. These programs include the Old Age Security pension, the Guaranteed Income Supplement, and the Spouse's Allowance, all of which are funded by general tax revenues. Many provinces and the territories augment these programs by providing cash supplements.
2) *Government pension plans (CPP/QPP)*. Self-supporting social insurance schemes, such as the Canada and Quebec Pension Plans (CPP/QPP), require employed persons and their employers to make regular contributions; a pension can then be drawn after retirement.
3) *Private pension plans*. In preparation for their retirement years, many working Canadians contribute to occupational pension plans and Registered Retirement Savings Plans. (National Council of Welfare, 1999a)

By 1995, the financial implications of an aging population had become clear. It was estimated that "the CPP fund would be depleted by 2015 and contribution rates would have to increase to 14.2 percent by 2030 to cover escalating costs" (Canada, 1998, 13). In 1997 the federal government reformed the CPP by raising the contribution rate and thereby making the plan financially sustainable (Canada, 1999g).

There is little doubt that Canada's income retirement system has raised income levels among seniors and decreased the general poverty rate for people aged 65 and over. The system has nevertheless been criticized for failing to provide benefits high enough to keep many seniors out of poverty. Seniors who have no sources of income other than income-security benefits run the greatest risk of falling below the poverty line.

KEEPING ACTIVE IN THE SENIOR YEARS

Seniors at Work

A 1999 Gallup poll found that 16 percent of Canadians over 65 are in the paid workforce and that 38 percent of Canadians plan to work part-time after they retire. Various explanations for this trend have been offered. For example, pension experts predict that Canadians will be required to work longer because of the strain placed on income-security programs by an aging society (Canadians to work longer, 1995). The National Advisory Council on Aging suggests that many people are prolonging their participation in the workforce because they are physically and mentally capable of working. The fact that many people are either retiring at a younger age or postponing retirement indefinitely is making the transition from work to retirement a much less disruptive experience than it has been in the past (Celebrating seniors' contributions, 1998).

Volunteering

Many retired seniors choose to contribute to society through volunteering. People engage in volunteer work for a variety of reasons. According to the National Advisory Council on Aging (1989), many seniors volunteer in order to give something back to society, work on behalf of a social or political cause, share experiences with other people, fulfil a need for new experiences and learning, or meet and connect with others.

The 1997 National Survey of Giving, Volunteering and Participating found that almost one-quarter of Canadian seniors volunteer their time to organizations and special causes. In addition, many seniors (primarily women) regularly help other seniors and provide unpaid child care outside of formal organizations (Hall et al., 1998). Over the years, the public and voluntary sectors have acknowledged the social and economic contributions of older volunteers. Indeed, the volunteer work done by seniors has an estimated economic value of "between $764 million and $2.3 billion annually"; furthermore, the unpaid caregiving provided to spouses and others by seniors is seen as "a vital force in reducing health care costs" (Canada, 1999e, 3).

Political Activism and Consultation

Senior advocacy groups that address issues of concern to seniors can be found across the country. For example, the Ontario Coalition of Senior Citizens' Organizations, the Manitoba Society of Seniors Inc., and the Saskatchewan Seniors Mechanism represent seniors in their respective provinces; advise local and provincial governments on matters that concern seniors; and work to enhance the image of, and quality of life for, seniors (see Exhibit 11.6).

In 1985, the largest senior protest in Canadian history took place in response to the federal government's proposal to deindex pension payments. The collective action of seniors and others forced the government to scrap the deindexation plan. More recently, seniors from across the country "severely criticized" the federal Minister of Finance's 1996 plan to replace the Old Age Security pension and the Guaranteed Income Supplement with the Seniors

Exhibit 11.6

GREY POWER IN ACTION

- The Manitoba Society of Seniors Inc. was started by a group of older Manitobans in 1979 who felt there was a need for a united voice on issues affecting them ... We inform all levels of government, social service agencies, business and the media about issues affecting older adults today, such as health care, pensions, housing, transportation, utilities, as well as lifestyle and financial issues.
- [The] mission [of the Ontario Coalition of Senior Citizens' Organizations] is to improve the quality of life for Ontario's seniors by encouraging seniors involvement in all aspects of society, by keeping them informed on current issues, and by focusing on programs to benefit an aging population.
- Saskatchewan Seniors Mechanism brings together Saskatchewan Seniors' organizations in order to:
  * promote a united voice
  * research and take action on issues affecting seniors
  * create awareness of and coordinate resources and services for seniors.

Sources: Excerpted from Manitoba Society of Seniors [on-line], available: http://www.msos.mb.ca/ [2000 April 20]; Ontario Coalition of Senior Citizens' Organizations [on-line], available: http://www.web.net/~ocsco/ [2000 April 20]; and Saskatchewan Seniors Mechanism [on-line], available: http//wwww.mbnet.mb.ca/crm/sk/advoc/ssm1.html [2000 June 12].

Benefit (National Council of Welfare, 1999b, 5). In response to these protests, the federal government cancelled the proposed Seniors Benefit in 1998. The political clout of seniors is expected to increase as more and more baby boomers enter their senior years (Canada Mortgage and Housing Corporation, 1999).

Increasingly, seniors are being consulted by government officials about a wide range of issues. In 1999, the federal government established the Canada Coordinating Committee (CCC), a group that consults with seniors across the country about everything from housing and health to the role of seniors in society. According to Yhetta Gold, a member of the CCC, seniors want to have a greater say in decisions that affect not only their own generation but younger generations as well. This interest in broad social issues, Gold believes, reflects a desire on the part of seniors "to make significant and lasting contributions to their communities and to Canadian society" (Canada, 2000d, 3).

IV. CARING FOR SENIORS

INSTITUTIONAL CARE

Although most seniors live independently, some require the supports that only institutional care can provide. Seven percent of Canada's seniors live in nursing homes, and an estimated 35 percent of nursing-home residents have Alzheimer's disease. Elderly women are more likely than elderly men to live in a nursing home and, once placed, tend to stay longer than their male counterparts (1.4 years versus 0.6 years for men).

The care provided in nursing homes normally includes round-the-clock nursing services, the administration of medications, and therapeutic services. Residents may have physical limitations or illnesses that necessitate assistance with personal care functions (e.g., bathing, eating, and dressing) and mobility (e.g., getting in and out of bed and moving around the facility) (Lindsay, 1999; Burke et al., 1997).

The rising cost of institutional care, coupled with the growing number of seniors and dementia cases, is putting increasing pressure on health, social service, housing, and other systems to develop alternative service delivery models for those seniors who require 24-hour support (Burke et al., 1997). Pressure is also coming from seniors themselves. Increasingly, Canadian seniors are voicing their dissatisfaction with bureaucratic and impersonal institutions and are seeking alternative sources of care and support (Health Canada, 1998a).

COMMUNITY-BASED CARE

To reduce health-care expenses yet maintain quality health services, many provinces and territories have shifted from costly institutions to more affordable community- and home-based care for the elderly. With the help of expanded home care services, geriatric day hospitals, adult day care, community-based nursing services, government assistance programs, and care provided by family and friends, many seniors are able to postpone moving to a nursing home or avoid it altogether.

In many cases, a geriatric assessment is used to assess an elderly person's health, psychological, social, and other needs and to determine which services will allow the senior to live independently. There are many noninstitutional services that may be available through outpatient clinics or in the person's home. These services include the following:

- medical interventions (e.g., nutrition programs, psychiatric care, medication, or surgery) to prevent or reduce the effects of organic disease or disability;

- physical rehabilitation (e.g., physiotherapy or massage therapy) to improve or maintain physical functioning;
- assistance measures (e.g., walkers, hearing aides, wheelchairs) to improve or maintain social functioning; and
- professional health-care measures (e.g., in-home nursing or homemaker services) to improve or maintain health and hygiene and to ensure safety in the home (Health and Welfare Canada, 1990).

The Prince Edward Island Home Care Support Program is an example of the many programs across Canada that offer a full range of noninstitutional services for seniors. Among this program's core services are assessment, case coordination, personal care, coordination of community supports, and respite care for in-home caregivers (Prince Edward Island, 1998).

INFORMAL CAREGIVING

A growing trend in community-based services is to shift more of the responsibility for elder care to families. It is estimated that just over 10 percent of Canada's seniors require some form of home care and that 90 percent of this care is provided by family members (Chisholm, 2000). In most cases the spouse is the primary caregiver for an elderly person; many of these caregivers are seniors who have health problems of their own (Health Canada, 1998a). If the spouse is unavailable or unable to provide the necessary care, the responsibility usually shifts to an adult child (usually daughters). About 60 percent of those caring for the elderly are middle-aged women, most of whom are married with children and have jobs outside the home (Frederick and Fast, 1999). Caring for the elderly generally involves helping with instrumental tasks (e.g., cooking and cleaning) and personal care (e.g., bathing and dressing) (Cranswick, 1997).

Recently concerns have been raised about the potential effects of caring for an aging person. Health Canada (1998a, 6) identifies some of these effects:

> **Caregiver burden** is the term used to describe the negative consequences of caring for an older person. These consequences include depression, psychological distress, lowered life satisfaction, interpersonal conflict, social isolation, and stress-related physical health complaints. Another impact is financial. Caregivers who take a leave from work often find themselves out of pocket, as their earnings are deferred and their benefits reduced.

Caregivers who assist people with dementia are at particular risk; Health Canada (1998a) reports that this group is almost twice as likely as other caregivers to experience depression and chronic health problems. In addition, women—the primary caregivers—may be prevented by work, family, and other obligations from providing the intensive care that people with dementia require. Burke et al. (1997, 27) point out the implications of this emerging dilemma: "A drop in the number of women able and willing to provide the intensive informal care required for a growing number of people suffering from dementia will add to the increased demand for high-cost institutional care; at the very same time, pressures to reduce institutionalization may grow." The search for satisfactory methods of caring for people with dementia will intensify as the population ages.

Care for the Informal Caregiver

A greater reliance on informal caregiving has created a need for specialized services to help those caring for elderly persons (see Exhibit 11.7). Caregiver services aim to reduce the stress associated with being a caregiver and to supplement the care provided by informal helpers. For example, the Richmond Caregiver Support Program in British Columbia offers a range of services to help caregivers learn effective self-care strategies, ways to prevent burnout, and methods of dealing with difficult emotions related to caregiving; these services include skill-building courses, drop-in support groups, telephone and personal support, and a resource centre (Richmond Connections, 1999).

In some communities, **respite services** have been set up to give caregivers a break from their caregiving responsibilities. These services include day-care centres for the elderly, temporary placement of the elderly person in a residential setting, and home support workers who help the regular caregiver with housework and meal preparation or provide companionship to the elderly person.

V. SOCIAL WORK PRACTICE WITH ELDERLY POPULATIONS

Social work practice is in many ways the same with elderly clients as with other populations. However, as Watt and Soifer (1996, 44) point out, **gerontological social work** requires highly skilled workers: "In addition to understanding a wide range of theoretical constructs concerning the biological, psychological and social aspects of adulthood and aging, the social worker must understand complex cultural and interpersonal structures that transcend several generations."

EXHIBIT 11.7

POLICY AREAS ASSOCIATED WITH SUPPORTS FOR VOLUNTEER CAREGIVING

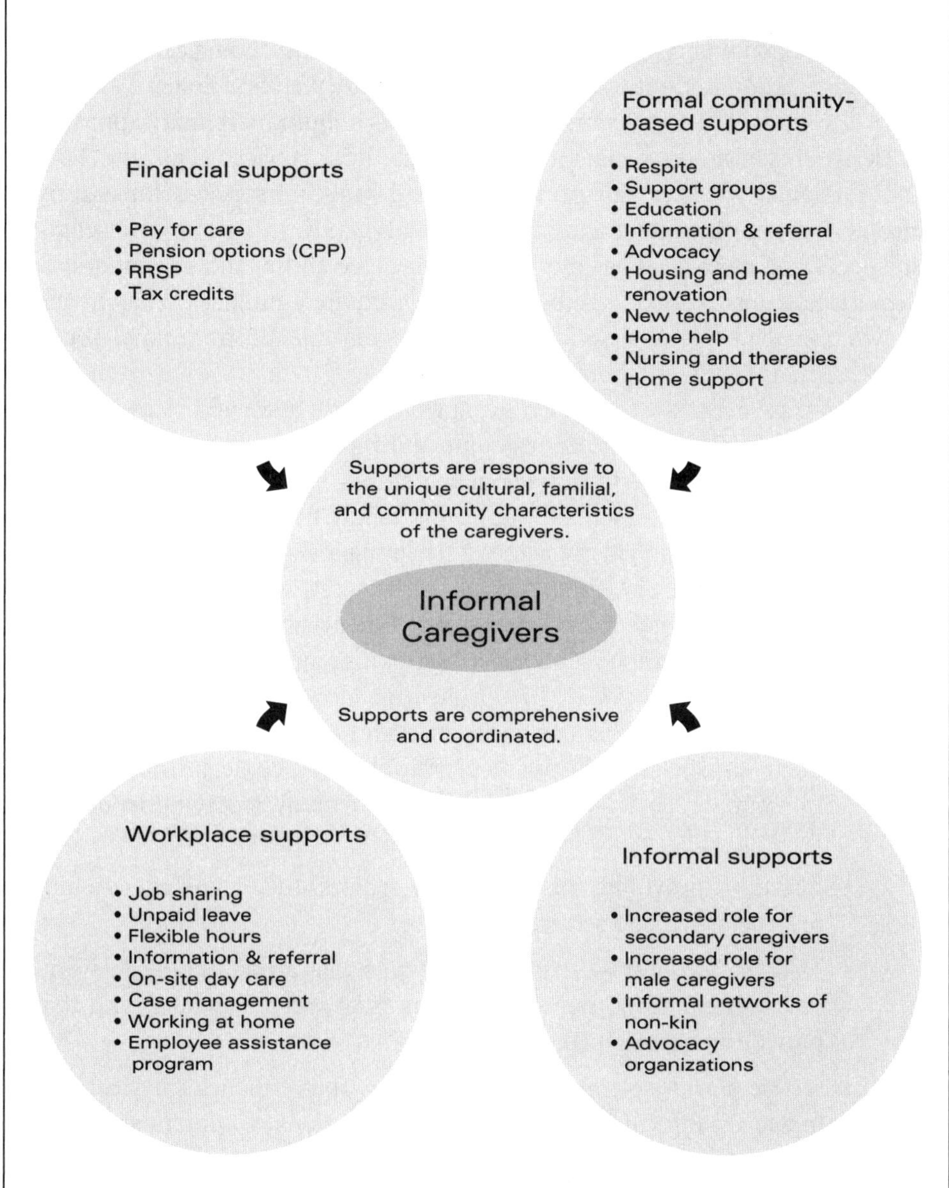

Source: *Volunteer Caregiving: Meeting the Challenges of the New Reality (Executive Summary)* (Toronto: Ontario Ministry of Citizenship, 1994), 6. Reproduced courtesy of the Ontario Ministry of Citizenship.

Gerontological social workers use a variety of methods to help individual elderly clients. During the assessment phase, workers must pay particular attention to biopsychosocial functioning. For example, they must find out how the biological changes associated with aging affect the individual's emotional well-being and social interaction. Determining the impact of the death of a spouse and/or peers on the elderly client's psychological and physical health is another important goal of assessment (Watt and Soifer, 1996).

Gerontological social work usually requires a multidisciplinary approach with an emphasis on social, health, and medical services (Feit and Feit, 1996). Social workers can provide a broad range of services for elderly people and their families, including individual, family, and group counselling in specialized areas such as elder abuse, substance abuse, and grief and loss. Gerontological social work in the future may require a multiskilled approach in which social workers perform tasks in areas outside traditional social work, such as health and home care.

There are many ways in which social workers can assist and be assisted by the families of elderly clients. For example, during assessment family members can provide valuable information about the client's needs and wants. In turn, social workers can give emotional support to family members who are having difficulty coping with an elderly relative's declining abilities, change in life situation, or institutional placement. Social workers can also provide hands-on assistance with caregiving tasks or help family caregivers connect with community resources such as respite services and support groups (Osterkamp, 1991).

MacLeod and Associates (1997) have developed a population health model (see Exhibit 11.8) that has implications for the roles and activities that may characterize social work practice with elderly people in the years to come. For example, social workers may find themselves serving in one or more of the following capacities:

- *educator*—providing information to seniors, their families, community members, and service providers;
- *program developer*—designing programs that are culturally relevant, that accommodate the needs of seniors of various abilities, and that provide an outreach component;
- *service provider*—emphasizing activities that enhance physical and mental health, that highlight the contributions of seniors and their informal caregivers, and that promote mutual aid, peer advocacy, and peer education;
- *volunteer coordinator*—training and supporting volunteers who provide services for elderly people and their families.

EXHIBIT 11.8

POPULATION HEALTH PROMOTION MODEL

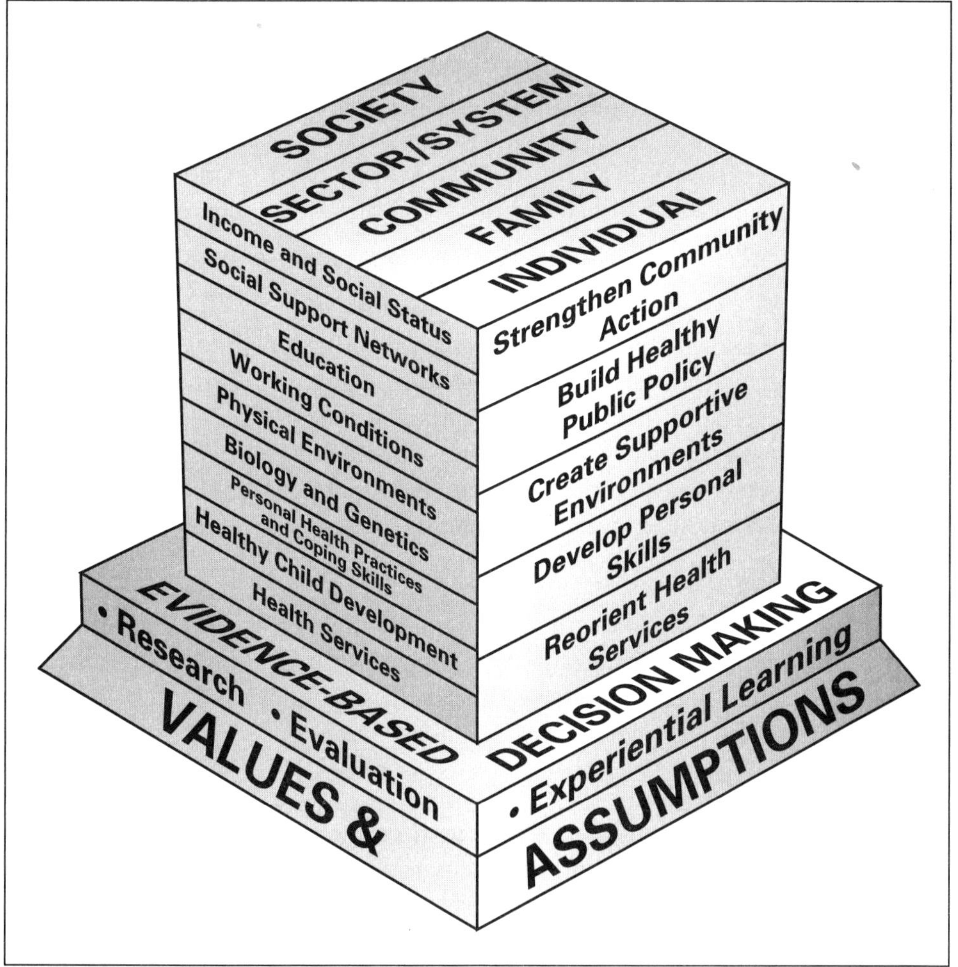

Source: N. Hamilton & T. Bhatti, *Taking the Next Step to Stop Woman Abuse: From Violence Prevention to Individual, Family, Community and Societal Health* (Ottawa: Health Promotion and Development Division, Health Canada, 1996), 13. Copyright © Minister of Public Works and Government Services Canada, 2000.

Gerontological social work, like other types of social work, promises both challenges and rewards. One of the greatest challenges is working with elderly people "in an age of belt-tightening and economic constraint" (Holosko, White, and Feit, 1996, 402). Among the many rewards is the opportunity to work with a population that is becoming healthier, more active, better educated, and more politically involved with each generation.

Introduction

Like other industrialized countries, Canada has an aging population. The International Year of Older Persons promoted awareness of aging and called attention to the contributions of seniors. The pressures that an aging population will put on programs and institutions will be offset to an extent by the cost savings associated with other demographic shifts, such as a reduced school-age population.

Responses to Canada's Aging Population

A variety of national initiatives have focused on improving conditions for Canada's seniors. The National Framework on Aging was introduced to help governments respond to the needs of an aging society. The New Horizons: Partners in Aging initiative assisted individuals and groups in developing seniors' programs across Canada. Many seniors organizations and councils are found in the public and voluntary sectors.

Creating Supportive Environments for Seniors

The majority of seniors live with a spouse or by themselves; for other seniors, there are a variety of living arrangements to choose from. In addition to supportive housing, there are programs that help seniors live independently in their own homes.

Components of Healthy Aging

Much of the research on seniors has focused on the concept of healthy aging. Canadians are living longer, and most seniors report being healthy and physically active. Innovative treatment methods are needed to address the problems of prescription drug abuse, dementia, and depression among seniors. Various programs are designed to enhance social support—a key factor in maintaining good health in the senior years. The problem of elder abuse is being addressed by adult protection legislation and a variety of community services. Although Canada's retirement income system has contributed to a drop in the poverty rate for seniors, it has been criticized for keeping the incomes of many seniors below the poverty line. Canadian seniors keep active through paid employment, volunteering, and political activism/consultation.

Caring for Seniors

Institutional programs are available for seniors who require a high level of care. A variety of community- and home-based programs aim to help seniors postpone or avoid being institutionalized. The provision of elder care by family members (especially adult daughters) is a growing trend in Canada, creating the need for a wider range of supports for informal caregivers.

Social Work Practice with Elderly Populations

Gerontological social work requires advanced assessment and intervention skills on the part of the social worker. Social workers can form mutually beneficial relationships with the families of elderly clients. Within the context of a population health approach, social workers can fulfil a variety of roles.

KEY TERMS

AGING POPULATION 245
AGE IN PLACE 246
HEALTHY AGING 247
LIVING ARRANGEMENT 249
SUPPORTIVE HOUSING 252
LIFE EXPECTANCY 253
DEMENTIA 255
SOCIAL SUPPORT 256
INTERGENERATIONAL PROGRAMS 257
ELDER ABUSE 258
ADULT PROTECTION LEGISLATION 258
RETIREMENT INCOME SYSTEM 259
CAREGIVER BURDEN 263
RESPITE SERVICES 264
GERONTOLOGICAL SOCIAL WORK 264

CHAPTER 12

ABORIGINAL CANADIANS AND THE SOCIAL WELFARE SYSTEM

• OBJECTIVES •

I. To review the government's evolving role in Aboriginal affairs, legislation governing Aboriginal activities, and the First Nations movement.

II. To examine partnerships between Aboriginal people and governments, and aspects of Aboriginal self-government.

III. To explore the concept of healing and wellness in Aboriginal communities as it relates to residential schools, family violence, mental-health issues, and substance abuse.

IV. To consider the needs of Aboriginal children and some of the initiatives and programs that aim to meet those needs.

V. To look at various issues related to social work education and practice in an Aboriginal context.

INTRODUCTION

Aboriginal people were the first inhabitants of Canada. The Aboriginal population comprised several separate nations—each with its own culture, language, and system of government—long before the arrival of European settlers (RCAP, 1996a). Canada's Aboriginal population is still far from homogeneous. Commenting on registered Indians living in First Nations communities across Canada, Armstrong (1999, 14) writes: "Separated by distance and differentiated by history, language and culture, individual communities often developed unique ways of life."

A large segment of the Aboriginal population lives outside First Nations communities. About one out of five Aboriginal people—mostly children and youth—live in large urban centres, and Aboriginal people are moving to the cities at a much faster rate than members of the general population. Although they reside in all parts of the country, most Aboriginal people live in the Yukon, the Northwest Territories, and Nunavut (Statistics Canada, 1998a; Lee, 1999).

There are approximately 800,000 Aboriginal people living in Canada (about 3 percent of the country's total population). The Aboriginal population is growing at nearly twice the rate of the non-Aboriginal population. Almost half of all Aboriginal people are under the age of 25; by 2006, the Aboriginal youth population is expected to increase by 26 percent (INAC, 1998a; Statistics Canada, 1998a). Exhibit 12.1 shows the distribution of the registered Indian population according to age.

EXHIBIT 12.1

REGISTERED INDIAN POPULATION BY AGE

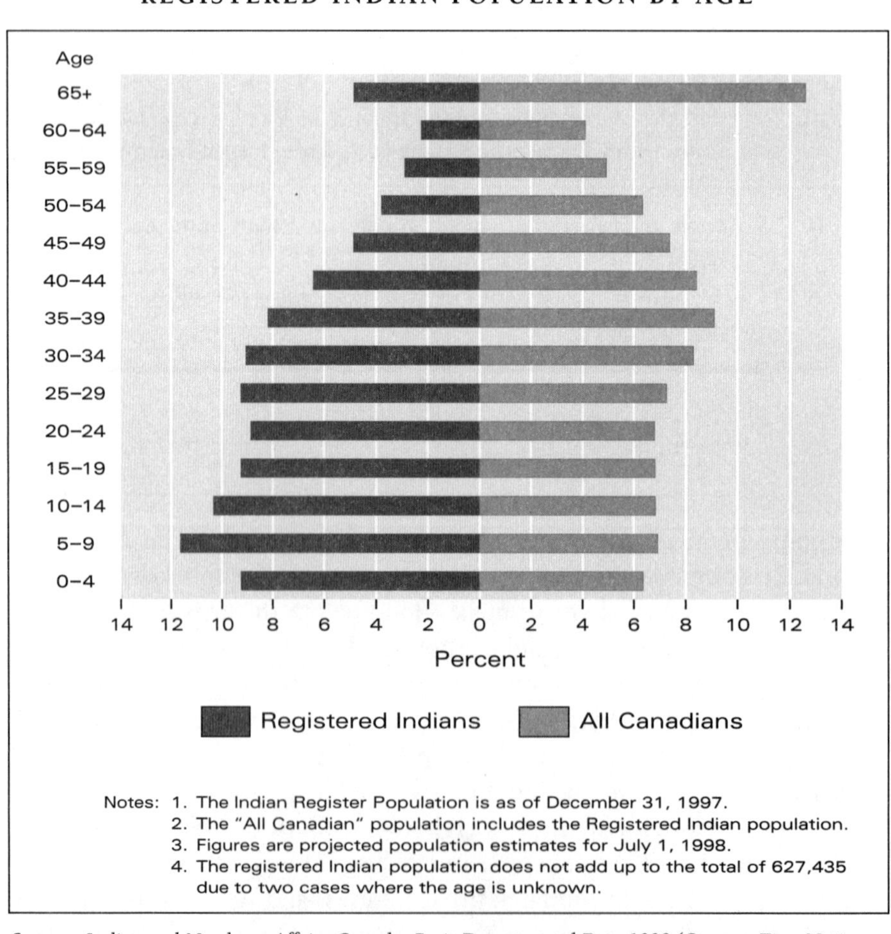

Source: Indian and Northern Affairs Canada, *Basic Departmental Data 1998* (Ottawa: First Nations and Northern Statistics Section, Information Management Branch, 1999), 17. Reproduced with the permission of the Minister of Public Works and Government Services Canada, 2000.

The United Nation's proclamation of 1993 as the International Year of the World's Indigenous People drew attention to the conditions in Aboriginal communities around the world. Toward the end of 1993, when the United Nations decided to extend the International Year of Indigenous People into an International Decade of the World's Indigenous People, countries from around the world responded with commitments "to solve the problems faced by Indigenous people in such areas as human rights, the environment, development, education and health" (INAC, 1998b, 2).

Over the last decade, Aboriginal communities have witnessed social, economic, legal, and political reforms. Aboriginal groups that have achieved self-government have or are in the process of developing their own social assistance, child welfare, substance abuse, family violence, and other social welfare programs. Many self-governed communities have also gained control over related human services such as health care, education, law enforcement, justice, taxation, and cultural programs (Simpson, 1995).

Despite the recent progress in many areas, Aboriginal Canadians continue to face a variety of social and economic problems. The federal government describes some of these problems:

> The unemployment rate on reserves is about 29 percent, nearly three times the Canadian rate, and the unemployment rate for registered Indians off reserves is about 26 percent. Furthermore, many Aboriginal communities continue to lack the appropriate resources and expertise needed to deal effectively with such serious problems as high rates of infant mortality, youth suicide, and dependence on social assistance which are higher than the national average. (INAC, 1998a)

A recent study of the socioeconomic status (i.e., education levels, employment rates, income, and housing conditions) of 500 First Nations communities found that not only do most First Nations communities have far lower standards of living than non-Aboriginal communities, but "First Nations communities with the best socioeconomic circumstances [meet] the standards of only the poorest regions of non-Aboriginal Canada" (Armstrong, 1999, 17) (see Exhibit 12.2). Some social analysts have attributed the social and economic problems experienced by Aboriginal groups to the decades of repressive government control over Aboriginal affairs, the failure of mainstream social welfare programs to resolve Native problems, and a gradual erosion of Native social and economic autonomy (Carniol, 1995).

Exhibit 12.2

DEMOGRAPHIC PROFILE OF POOREST NON-ABORIGINAL REGIONS AND BEST-OFF FIRST NATIONS COMMUNITIES

	BEST-OFF FIRST NATIONS COMMUNITIES	WORST-OFF NON-ABORIGINAL REGIONS
% with less than Grade 9[1]	12	20
% employed[1]	58	57
Number of persons per room	0.7	0.6
Average annual income	$18,200	$18,900
% speaking Aboriginal language at home	2	n.a.
% under 18 years	36	25

1. As percentage of population aged 20 to 64.

Source: R. Armstrong (1999, Winter), "Mapping the Conditions of First Nations Communities," *Canadian Social Trends* (Ottawa: Statistics Canada, Cat. No. 11-008), No. 55, p. 17.

I. ABORIGINAL–GOVERNMENT RELATIONS: A HISTORICAL REVIEW

RESPONSIBILITY FOR ABORIGINAL AFFAIRS

The Canadian government of the early 1800s assumed a paternal role in Aboriginal affairs. Duncan Campbell Scott, who served as deputy superintendent in the federal Department of Indian Affairs from 1913 to 1932, described this role:

> The apparent duty was to raise [the Indian] from the debased condition into which he had fallen due to the loose and pampering policy of former days. Protection from vices which were not his own, and instruction in peaceful occupations, foreign to his natural bent, were to be substituted for necessary generosity. (cited in Patterson, 1987, 178–179)

According to the Royal Commission on Aboriginal Peoples (RCAP, 1996a, 7), "protection" was actually a form of domination and "a code word implying encouragement to stop being Aboriginal and merge into the settler society." With the confederation of Canada in 1867, Prime Minister John A. Macdonald announced that the goal of his government would be to eliminate the tribal system and totally assimilate Aboriginal people into the new Dominion's Christian and non-Aboriginal way of life (RCAP, 1996a, 1996b).

At Confederation, responsibility for Aboriginal people was divided between the two levels of government: the federal government assumed responsibility for all status Indians, while the provinces became responsible for nonstatus Indians (for definitions of "status Indian" and other terms, see Exhibit 12.3). A central administration was formed to regulate status Indians, and in 1966 the Department of Indian Affairs and Northern Development (DIAND) was established (INAC, 1997a); this department is now called Indian and Northern Affairs Canada (INAC).

THE INDIAN ACT

The Indian Act of 1876 provided the federal government with both a framework for administering Aboriginal affairs and a mechanism for controlling the lives of Aboriginal people. The act allowed the government to introduce across the nation a system of Indian **reserves** on which only registered Indians were allowed to live. Certain provisions in the act were highly discriminatory. For example, an Aboriginal woman who married a non-Aboriginal man lost her status; in contrast, an Aboriginal man who married a non-Aboriginal woman was allowed to keep his status (INAC, 1990).

Indian agents were placed on each reserve to monitor the activities of the Aboriginal residents. Outsiders needed the permission of the agent to enter a reserve, and no Aboriginal resident could leave without a "pass" issued by the agent. The agent also exerted control over children's education, the administration of justice, and the extent to which Indian languages, ceremonies, and rituals could be used (Barnes, 1991).

A primary intent of the Indian Act was to increase **enfranchisement**—that is, to convince Aboriginal people to reject their status as Indians and become fully assimilated into non-Native culture. Few Aboriginal people chose to be enfranchised. This resistance was met with government laws and policies that were intended to force enfranchisement on Aboriginal people. Aboriginal land and resources were confiscated, Aboriginal people were denied the right to speak their own language or live according to traditional customs, and Aboriginal communities were severely disrupted by the relocation of adults to other communities and by the placement of children in distant residential schools (Patterson, 1987; INAC, 1990).

Exhibit 12.3

DEFINITION OF TERMS

ABORIGINAL PEOPLES

Aboriginal peoples are the descendants of the original inhabitants of North America. The Canadian Constitution recognizes three groups of Aboriginal people: Indians, Métis, and Inuit.

ABORIGINAL RIGHTS

Aboriginal rights are the rights that some Aboriginal peoples of Canada hold as a result of their ancestors' longstanding use and occupancy of the land.

ABORIGINAL SELF-GOVERNMENT

Aboriginal self-government refers to government that is designed, established, and administered by Aboriginal peoples.

BAND

A **band** is a group of First Nations people for whom lands have been set apart and whose money is held by the Crown. Many bands prefer to be known as First Nations.

FIRST NATIONS PEOPLES

First Nations peoples, a term that is often used in lieu of the word "Indian," refers to both status and nonstatus Indians living in Canada.

INDIAN

The term **Indian** refers to all the Aboriginal people in Canada who are not Inuit or Métis. Legal recognition has been extended to three groups of Indians living in Canada: status Indians, nonstatus Indians, and treaty Indians. A **status Indian** is someone who is registered under the Indian Act. A **nonstatus Indian** is not registered. A **treaty Indian** is a status Indian who belongs to a band that has signed a treaty with the Crown.

INUIT

The **Inuit** are Aboriginal people who inhabit the northern regions of Canada, primarily in the Northwest Territories, northern Quebec, and Labrador.

MÉTIS

The **Métis** are people of mixed Aboriginal and European ancestry who identify themselves as distinct from Inuit and First Nations people.

Source: Adapted from Department of Indian Affairs and Northern Development (1997), "Definitions 2000," *Information* [on-line], available: http://www.inac.gc.ca/pubs/information/info101.html [2000 May 19]. Reprinted with the permission of the Minister of Public Works and Government Services Canada, 2000.

REFORM OF THE INDIAN ACT

By World War II, the federal government controlled most aspects of life on reserves. However, efforts to colonize and enfranchise Aboriginal people had been largely unsuccessful. Instead of assimilating Aboriginal people into mainstream society, the Indian Act served only to deprive them of power and keep them in a state of dependency (INAC, 1990). As poverty, health problems, and social disorganization worsened, "Aboriginal people struggled for survival as individuals, their nationhood erased from the public mind and almost forgotten by themselves" (RCAP, 1996a, 10).

Increased public concern about Aboriginal Canadians, and the emergence of Aboriginal leaders who defended Native rights, led to Parliament's decision to reform the Indian Act. In particular, Aboriginal people wanted to change enfranchisement policies, the amount of power that government had over Aboriginal affairs, and the lack of attention paid by government to treaty rights. However, the new Indian Act of 1951 did little to change conditions for Aboriginal people (INAC, 1990).

In 1969 the federal government developed a strategy that would fully integrate Aboriginal people into the social, political, and economic life of mainstream society. The Statement of the Government of Canada on Indian Policy (commonly known as the White Paper) recommended that the federal government abolish the Indian Act, relinquish its responsibility for First Nations, and give Aboriginal people control over their land. In turn, Aboriginal people would lose their special status and be treated similarly to other Canadians. The majority of Aboriginal groups rejected the proposal on the basis that the loss of special status would jeopardize Aboriginal rights and land claims. However, the White Paper was not a complete failure; in response to its recommendations, all government-appointed Indian agents were removed from reserves (Patterson, 1987; INAC, 1990).

In 1985 the Indian Act was amended to bring it in line with the Canadian Charter of Rights and Freedoms. This amendment guaranteed equal treatment of Aboriginal men and women, restored status and membership rights to First Nations, allowed bands to determine their own membership, and abolished enfranchisement policies.

The Government of Canada and Aboriginal people continue to negotiate reforms to the Indian Act and other legislation affecting Aboriginal people. In 1999 the Minister of Indian and Northern Affairs announced that the 123-year-old Indian Act may soon be replaced with new legislation that emphasizes an administrative partnership between the federal government and First Nations (Ottawa will consider abolishing Indian Act, 1999).

THE FIRST NATIONS MOVEMENT

No single event sparked the **First Nations movement**. However, the issues raised by the 1969 White Paper made Aboriginal Canadians realize that their struggles were not unique: Aboriginal people around the world shared similar issues and collectively formed "a worldwide human rights movement of Indigenous peoples" (RCAP, 1996a, 10). In the early 1970s, Aboriginal people began to form groups that could represent the diverse cultures, needs, concerns, and goals of Native people across the country. These groups included the Assembly of First Nations (representing status Indians living on reserves); the Native Council of Canada (representing nonstatus Indians, newly registered Indians, nonband members who live off reserves, and Métis people living outside the Prairie provinces); the Métis National Council (representing Métis people living on the Prairies); and the Inuit Tapirisat of Canada (representing Inuit people living in northern Canada) (Dunn, 1992).

The central issues for the First Nations movement are justice for Aboriginal people, recognition of inherent rights (such as the right to self-government), settlement of land claims, respect for treaties, and opportunities to work alongside other Canadians (Gray, 1991). Demands for change in Aboriginal affairs have not been restricted to Aboriginal people. Public-opinion polls indicate that a growing number of non-Aboriginal Canadians want to see justice for First Nations (RCAP, 1996a).

II. RENEWAL AND RENEGOTIATION: A NEW AGENDA FOR THE 21ST CENTURY

Much of the recent literature on Native issues focuses on how Aboriginal communities are breaking free from their oppressive past and progressing toward a better future. Exhibit 12.4 illustrates how Aboriginal people see the past as a period of cultural disruption and dehumanizing lifestyle and look to the present and future as a time for restructuring their society. An important aspect of restructuring is the improvement of relationships with non-Aboriginal people and government. According to the Royal Commission on Aboriginal Peoples (RCAP, 1996a, 11), any "new partnership" will have to be "much more than a political or institutional one. It must be a heartfelt commitment among peoples to live together in peace, harmony and mutual support."

INITIATIVES IN THE 1990S

Canada's Native agenda was originally proposed by Prime Minister Brian Mulroney. In 1990 the federal government made a commitment to work with

EXHIBIT 12.4

ABORIGINAL PEOPLES: A HISTORICAL PERSPECTIVE

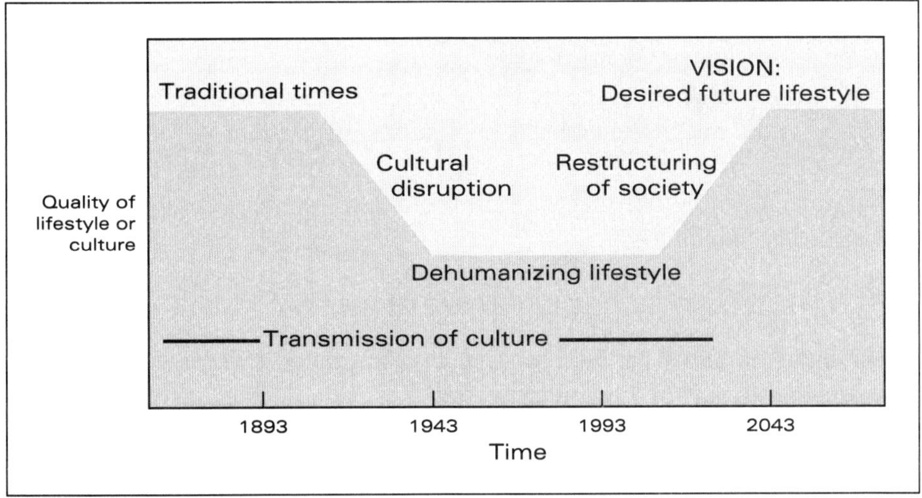

Source: *National Aboriginal Organizations in Canada 1998* (Ottawa: Indian and Northern Affairs Canada). Reprinted with the permission of the Minister of Public Works and Government Services Canada, 2000.

First Nations for the purpose of settling land claims, improving social and economic conditions on reserves, enhancing Aboriginal–government relationships, and addressing other issues of concern to Aboriginal people (INAC, 1993). Progress in these areas was hindered by the inability of the federal government and Aboriginal peoples to reach an agreement on several constitutional issues.

In 1991 the federal government appointed a Royal Commission on Aboriginal Peoples (RCAP) to look at a broad range of issues concerning Aboriginal people, including the troubled relationship between Aboriginal and non-Aboriginal Canadians. The RCAP's final report in 1996 contained 440 recommendations for resolving a wide range of Aboriginal issues (INAC, 1996).

In 1998 the federal government made a commitment to work with Aboriginal people, other levels of government, and the private sector to improve the living conditions of Aboriginal people. To formalize this commitment, the federal government launched Gathering Strength—Canada's Aboriginal Action Plan. This government-wide scheme sought to renew the partnership with Aboriginal people and to make improvements to the structure and implementation of government social and economic programs for Aboriginal people. An important first step in the reform process was the Government of Canada's recognition of past mistakes and injustices. In 1998 the federal government made a formal apology to Aboriginal people in the form of a Statement of Reconciliation. This statement, which is reproduced in Appendix C, set the tone for future policies, legislation, and programs concerning Aboriginal Canadians.

In late 1999 the Federal-Provincial-Territorial Council on Social Policy Renewal (see Chapter 3) met for the first time with the Ministers Responsible for Aboriginal Affairs and the leaders of five national Aboriginal organizations "to discuss the role of the national Aboriginal organizations in the implementation of the Social Union Framework Agreement" (Canada, 1999f). The Aboriginal organizations that are participating in the social union process are described in Exhibit 12.5.

ON THE ROAD TO SELF-GOVERNMENT

Although Aboriginal people had their own forms of government centuries before the arrival of European settlers in Canada, legal recognition of Aboriginal self-government was slow in coming. Section 35 of the Constitution Act of 1982 recognizes that Aboriginal people have an inherent right to self-government. Although self-government often implies total sovereignty (i.e., the formation of a separate country), in this context it means that Aboriginal people will remain citizens of Canada, have the same rights and freedoms as other Canadians, and work within the existing Canadian political and parliamentary structures.

An important aspect of self-government and self-determination is the authority of Aboriginal people to design, administer, and deliver their own programs and services. Areas and services that self-governed Aboriginal communities are likely to control include education, policing, health, housing, child welfare, adoption, and counselling. By the end of the 1990s, three self-government agreements had been struck, with the Kativik regional government in northern Quebec, with the Sechelt of British Columbia, and with Nunavut, an Inuit government in the eastern Arctic. Over 90 self-government agreements are in the process of negotiation (Frideres, 1999; INAC, 1998a; Privy Council Office, 1996).

Several federal departments, including Indian and Northern Affairs Canada, Human Resources Development Canada, and Health Canada, are working together with Aboriginal groups to prepare Aboriginal communities for managing and delivering local programs and services. While these communities are making the gradual transition to self-government, many of the responsibilities for Aboriginal programs will be shared. For example, alcohol and drug counselling programs may be fully funded by government but totally administered by Aboriginal groups (INAC, 1998a; Hudson and Taylor-Henley, 1993).

Exhibit 12.5

NATIONAL ABORIGINAL ORGANIZATIONS IN THE SOCIAL UNION

ASSEMBLY OF FIRST NATIONS (AFN)

AFN is the national organization of First Nations in Canada. It represents the views of its member First Nations in areas such as Aboriginal and treaty rights, environment, economic development, education, housing, health, social services and land claims.

THE CONGRESS OF ABORIGINAL PEOPLES (CAP)

CAP is the national advocacy organization designed to serve and protect the interests of Aboriginal people living off reserve. It represents the collective and individual interests of its constituents through member associations in all the provinces and territories.

INUIT TAPIRISAT OF CANADA (ITC)

ITC is the national organization representing more than 40,900 Inuit living in 53 communities in the Northwest Territories, Northern Quebec and Labrador. ITC deals with issues ranging from Inuit self-determination to the preservation of Inuit culture.

METIS NATIONAL COUNCIL (MNC)

MNC is the national organization representing the Metis people in Canada. It was established in 1983 after the recognition of the Metis as Aboriginal people in the Constitution Act, 1982.

NATIVE WOMEN'S ASSOCIATION OF CANADA (NWAC)

NWAC was incorporated in 1974 to promote the social, economic, cultural and political well-being of Status and Non-Status Indian and Metis women across Canada ...

Source: Excerpted from Department of Indian Affairs and Northern Development (1998), "National Aboriginal Organizations in Canada," *Information* [on-line], available: http://www.inac.gc.ca/pubs/information/info112.html [2000 June 1].

Since the federal government adopted its policy of devolution (see Chapter 4), there has been a steady transfer of responsibility from the federal level to Aboriginal groups, which currently manage over 75 percent of all funds for Aboriginal programs and 80 percent of INAC's programs. The federal government is also devolving many of its traditional responsibilities for

Aboriginal affairs to provincial and territorial governments. The perception that the provinces are less interested than the federal government in preserving Aboriginal rights, and more apt to cater to the needs of non-Aboriginal citizens, has made some Aboriginal groups reluctant to partner with provincial governments (Frideres, 1999; Privy Council Office, 1996).

ECONOMIC CONSIDERATIONS

If self-government is to succeed, it is important that the First Nations develop a strong economy. Whittington (2000, 111) writes:

> In a perfect world, the financing of aboriginal governments would be achieved totally by their own taxation regimes. The aboriginal government would finance its own programs and services and would bear the same burden of fiscal responsibility in its spending practices as any other government.

In reality, the conditions in many First Nations communities have been obstacles to economic self-sufficiency; thus, Aboriginal governments continue to be financially supported by the Government of Canada. At the same time, Aboriginal governments are working with the federal government "to increase their capacity to generate their own revenue through economic development and internal sources" (INAC, 1997b, 21). The Aboriginal Procurement Strategy, for example, provides funding for the startup of Aboriginal businesses and job creation.

Considerable amounts of government revenue have been spent on Aboriginal projects and programs in recent years. In its 1995 budget the federal government outlined a three-year projection for spending in each of its departments (see Exhibit 12.6); while Indian and Northern Affairs expected a budget increase, all other federal departments expected budget cuts. In 1996 alone, Aboriginal people received $56 billion from the federal government (more than twice the amount received by an equivalent number of non-Aboriginal Canadians); this figure is expected to rise to $60 billion by the year 2000 (Frideres, 1999). Coates and Morrisson (1993, 21) suggest that such large expenditures will do little to solve the underlying problems facing Aboriginal people. Rather, spending money on Aboriginal communities may simply be a way for liberal governments to "assuage their collective guilt" and cast themselves in a more favourable light than their less generous predecessors.

EXHIBIT 12.6

PROJECTED PERCENTAGE CHANGE IN FEDERAL DEPARTMENT BUDGETS, 1995–1998

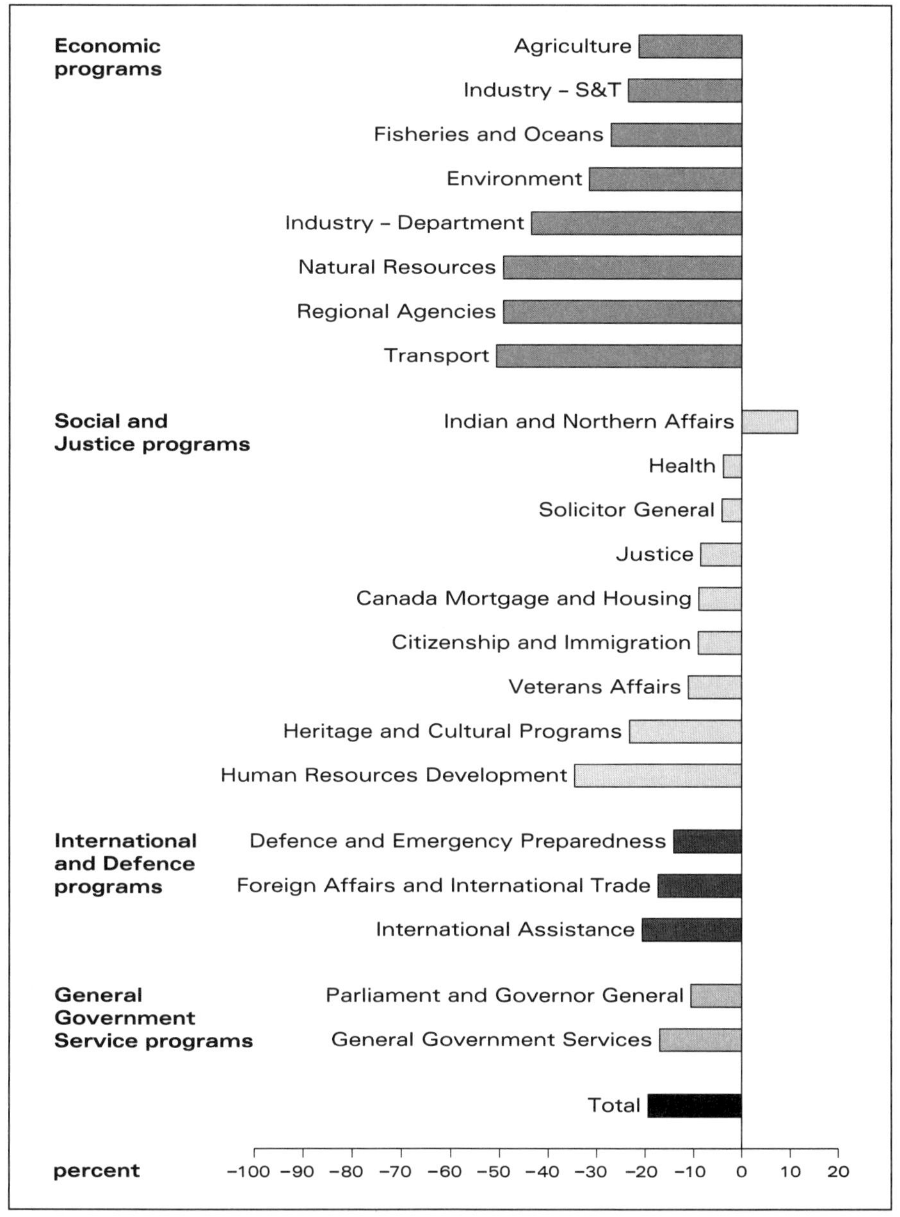

Source: Canada, *Budget in Brief* (Ottawa, 1995), 9. Reproduced with the permission of the Minister of Public Works and Government Services Canada, 2000.

III. HEALING AND WELLNESS IN ABORIGINAL COMMUNITIES

ADDRESSING THE EFFECTS OF RESIDENTIAL SCHOOLS

From 1883 until the 1950s, the federal government attempted to assimilate Natives into mainstream society by separating Aboriginal children from their parents and placing them in faraway schools where they would be taught European values and customs (Quantz, 1997; RCAP, 1996b). The Canadian government removed generation after generation of Aboriginal children from their families and sent them to **residential schools**. Lee (1992, 215) describes the effect of this practice:

> Countless numbers lost their language and were unable to reintegrate into the traditional community life. In turn, the communities from which they had been taken lost them as a resource ... Young men and women became alienated from the people and culture that could give their life meaning and strength.

Many Aboriginal children in residential schools also suffered sexual and physical abuse (often under the guise of "discipline") or died from disease and neglect.

To help Aboriginal people deal with the adverse effects of the residential school system, the Aboriginal Healing Strategy was established in 1997–98 as a collaborative effort between the First Nations and Inuit Health Program Directorate, Indian and Northern Affairs Canada, and Aboriginal Affairs of the Privy Council Office. This strategy supported the creation of the Aboriginal Healing Foundation, a nonprofit, Aboriginal-run corporation. The foundation funds community-based healing centres, which provide services that are based on a holistic model and address the physical, emotional, mental, and spiritual needs of individuals and families. Counselling and other services are used to address family violence, sexual abuse, alcohol and drug abuse, grief and loss, and other problems (Aboriginal Healing Foundation, 2000a, 2000b).

FAMILY VIOLENCE

In traditional Aboriginal societies, the family was regarded as the basic unit and building block of the community. Raising a child was a community effort involving the active participation of parents, grandparents, and other extended family members (Theilheimer, 1991).

The familial disruption that occurred as a result of the residential school system, colonization, and enfranchisement policies is closely linked to family violence (Quantz, 1997; Health Canada, 1996b). An estimated 8 out of 10 women and 4 out of 10 children in Aboriginal families experience violence in the home (RCAP, 1995; Health Canada, 1996b). The Ontario Native Women's Association attributes the pervasiveness of family violence to the fact that many Aboriginal families are isolated, stigmatized, and poverty-stricken: "With no outlet for societal pressure, the family has become the immediate place to release overwhelming frustration and to reassert power" (cited in Canadian Council on Social Development, 1992, 40).

A number of programs exist to help Aboriginal people prevent family violence and heal from the negative affects of abuse. One such program is profiled in Exhibit 12.7. In some cases, Aboriginal family violence programs are developed in partnership with mainstream social agencies. The involvement of non-Aboriginal professionals in Aboriginal-run programs is expected to decline as the programs become more established and Aboriginal people make progress in their own healing work (Mathews, 1995).

As with most Aboriginal programs, the approach to family violence is holistic, meaning that the individual is treated "in the context of the family; the family in the context of the community; [and] the community in the context of the larger society" (Health Canada, 1996b, 4). Reflecting their broad focus, Aboriginal family violence programs often involve the offender in the healing process—a practice in sharp contrast to the treatment strategies found in non-Aboriginal programs (Health Canada, 1996b).

MENTAL-HEALTH ISSUES

There is little evidence to suggest that Aboriginal people are more prone to psychiatric disorders (e.g., depression or schizophrenia) than other populations. However, studies indicate that depressed economic conditions, a general reluctance among Aboriginal people with problems to seek help, and a variety of other factors put many Aboriginal communities "at a significantly greater risk for mental health problems" (Quantz, 1997, 3).

Suicide

There is a strong correlation between mental-health problems—especially depression—and suicide; a study by Laurence J. Kirmayer found that between 81 and 95 percent of Aboriginal suicide victims had a mental disorder (cited in Quantz, 1997). Suicide is a persistent problem in First Nations communities, especially among the younger age groups. Health Canada (1998e) reports:

One of the largest disparities between First Nations and Canadian health indicators is in suicide rates. They remain high in First Nations communities and send a powerful signal about the devastating effects of poor living conditions and lack of economic opportunity. The gap is especially wide at age 15–24, where rates among First Nations people are from five to eight times the national average.

Exhibit 12.7

THE MOOKA'AM (NEW DAWN) TREATMENT PROGRAM

The Mooka'am program was created in 1990 to provide a combination of mainstream methods of healing with First Nations traditional teachings, values and practices for the Aboriginal community in Toronto. The reason the program was developed was because it was evident that Native people were not making use of the mainstream agencies for treatment because of cultural differences, insensitivity, the historical relationship with social workers and a lack of trust. Mooka'am provides healing services for women, men, children and teens who suffer unhealed trauma from sexual, physical, emotional and spiritual abuse. It further provides healing for women and children in violent homes and children living in alcohol and drug addicted families. Its aim is to break the cycle of violence and abuse by providing treatment that combines contemporary forms of therapy with traditional healing approaches.

AVAILABLE PROGRAMS

Individual Therapy—combines mainstream psychotherapy with traditional healing techniques

Healing Circles—are held for women and children twice a year; a more intensive Circle is led by an Elder once a month

Family Violence Initiative—provides support, counselling, and advocacy for victims of family violence

Children's Circle—is for children living in addicted families

Kognaasowin ("raising our children in a good way")—offers prenatal programs, parent–child support, and early childhood education

Source: Excerpted from "Mooka'am," *Programs* [on-line], available: http://www.nativechild.org/mookaam.html [2000 June 16]. Excerpt appears courtesy of the Native Child and Family Services of Toronto.

Suicide rates are believed to underestimate the extent of the problem since they are often based on reports from Indians who have status and/or live on reserves and do not include the general Aboriginal population (Quantz, 1997).

In 1994, Health Canada (1994a) introduced Building Healthy Communities, a health-care initiative for Indians and Inuit that supports a variety of crisis intervention programs, as well as training in suicide intervention for professional caregivers and community members. Health Canada (1999c) admits that such efforts have so far had little impact on the suicide rate.

Substance Abuse

Substance abuse is a common problem in some Aboriginal communities (Health Canada, 1999d; RCAP, 1995). Most at risk are Aboriginal youth, who are two to six times more likely to abuse alcohol than are non-Aboriginal youth. Abuse of marijuana, other illicit drugs, and solvents (e.g., gasoline or glue) is also higher among Aboriginal youth (Scott, 1997). Substance abuse is usually viewed as a symptom of more complex socioeconomic problems (such as persistent unemployment and poverty) facing Aboriginal people. "For young and old alike," Quantz (1997, 4) writes, "the outlook for the future appears bleak and the only escape is often in the form of drugs or alcohol."

The National Native Alcohol and Drug Abuse Program (NNADAP) was established in 1982 to set up prevention and treatment programs for First Nations and Inuit people living on-reserve. By 1998, NNADAP had coordinated 53 residential treatment centres and over 500 community-based alcohol and drug abuse prevention programs across Canada (Health Canada, 1999d). Although NNADAP is funded by the Medical Services Branch of Health Canada, responsibility for program administration and delivery was recently transferred to First Nations communities and organizations, in keeping with the federal government's devolution policy (Health Canada, 1999d).

Under the Building Healthy Communities initiative, the federal government launched the Solvent Abuse Program in 1994 to deal with solvent abuse among Aboriginal youth. Six Aboriginal-run solvent abuse treatment centres were subsequently established across Canada to combat the problem (Solvent abuse centres planned, 1995; INAC, 1997c).

IV. CARING FOR ABORIGINAL CHILDREN

NATIONAL CHILDREN'S AGENDA

In 1997 the federal government concluded that "Aboriginal children face greater disadvantages and risks in childhood than any other group of children in Canada" (Canada, 1997). More specifically, Aboriginal children are

- twice as likely to be born prematurely or underweight, or die within their first year of life;
- three or four times more likely to suffer sudden infant death syndrome;
- fifteen to thirty-eight times more likely to suffer from the effects of fetal alcohol syndrome;
- three times more likely to be physically disabled;
- six times more likely to die by injury, poisoning, or violence; and,
- five times more likely to take their own life. (Canada, 1999c, 19)

In addition, since over half of Aboriginal families live in poverty, Aboriginal children are at risk for physical and mental-health problems, poor achievement in school, and welfare dependency.

Five national Aboriginal organizations are actively involved in the development of a long-term action plan known as the National Children's Agenda. This plan will involve the creation of new programs for Aboriginal children, as well as an expansion of existing programs such as those operating under Health Canada's Brighter Futures initiative and Aboriginal Head Start (Canada, 1999c).

Brighter Futures

A variety of programs are provided in First Nations and Inuit communities as a result of the Aboriginal component of Health Canada's Brighter Futures initiative. While Aboriginal programs offered under this initiative vary in terms of their specific activities, all use a holistic approach, are culturally relevant, and focus on establishing and managing programs aimed at helping Aboriginal children get a positive start in life. This initiative supports prenatal care, infant development, parent education, and child-care programs (Health Canada, 1998b).

Aboriginal Head Start

In 1995, Health Canada introduced the Aboriginal Head Start initiative, an early intervention program targeted at Aboriginal children aged 0–6 and their families. The initiative is modelled after the Head Start programs in the United States. Its primary objectives are outlined below:

- Foster the spiritual, emotional, intellectual, and physical growth of the child.
- Foster a desire in the child for lifelong learning.

- Support parents and guardians as the prime teachers and caregivers of their children, making sure parents/caregivers play a key role in the planning, development, operation, and evaluation of the program.
- Recognize and support extended families in teaching and caring for children.
- Make sure the local Aboriginal community is involved in the planning, development, operation, and evaluation of the program.
- Make sure that the initiative works with and is supported by other community programs and services.
- Ensure that human and financial resources are used in the best way possible to produce positive outcomes and experiences for Aboriginal children, parents, families, and communities. (Health Canada, 2000b, 1)

To meet these objectives, the Aboriginal Head Start initiative supports projects that prepare children for school, promote health, improve nutrition, and encourage children to learn about their culture (Health Canada, 1998d). In some cases, projects operate out of Aboriginal child-care centres or Native Friendship Centres and are run by Aboriginal women's groups, parents, and other community members. There are over 90 Aboriginal Head Start project sites across Canada (Canada, 1997).

CHILD CARE

In 1995, Human Resources Development Canada (1999a) launched the First Nations and Inuit Child Care Initiative as part of a strategy to improve the economic situation for Aboriginal families. The creation of more affordable quality child-care spaces increases opportunities for parents of young children to attend work or school. Several new child-care facilities have opened across Canada as a result of this initiative.

While some child-care programs operate out of community centres, others are home-based. The Odawa Sweetgrass Home Child Care Agency in Ontario, for example, contracts with individual families in the community to provide child-care services in the home. Before placing a child in a caregiver's home, an Odawa supervisor/home visitor ensures that the home is in the child's neighbourhood, and that the caregiver's lifestyle and culture match those of the child. Odawa staff also supervise the caregiver and provide ongoing support for both the parent(s) and caregiver (Odawa, 2000).

CHILD WELFARE SERVICES

Aboriginal children have traditionally been overrepresented in Canada's child welfare system. During the 1950s and 1960s it was particularly common for Aboriginal children to be removed from their families by provincial child welfare workers (Lee, 1992). By 1991, 20 percent of all children in foster care or other substitute homes were Aboriginal, even though Aboriginal children made up only 2 percent of the Canadian child population (Clarke, 1991).

The common practice of placing Aboriginal children in non-Aboriginal foster homes created long-term problems for many children, their families, and communities. For example, on reaching adolescence many Aboriginal children suffered identity crises when they realized they did not belong fully to either Aboriginal or non-Aboriginal culture (Carniol, 1995). Family breakdown and a general lack of cohesion in Aboriginal communities are among the other negative effects of removing Aboriginal children from their homes. Mawhiney (1995, 226) observes that "the values and spiritual base have been seriously eroded in some First Nations because of the lack of continuity from one generation to the next."

Recognition that mainstream child welfare systems did not adequately meet the needs of Aboriginal children led to a joint effort by Indian bands and provincial child welfare departments to develop Aboriginal child welfare agencies. A First Nations–controlled child welfare program was established in Manitoba in 1982, and "by the early 1990s, most provinces were negotiating parallel arrangements to serve both Native communities and also Native families in towns and cities" (British Columbia, 1996a). Aboriginal-run child welfare programs incorporate traditional norms and practices but are required to operate in accordance with provincial child welfare legislation.

Wachtel (1997, 34) comments on the broader significance of Aboriginal-controlled child services: "The efforts of First nations and other Aboriginal peoples to take back prime responsibility for child welfare within their communities ... is itself an important element (along with governance and economic development) in the process of rebuilding these communities."

ABORIGINAL YOUTH AND NATIVE FRIENDSHIP CENTRES

The **Friendship Centre movement** began in the early 1950s in response to the migration of large numbers of Aboriginal people to Canada's urban centres. Native Friendship Centres provide a variety of services to Aboriginal people, whose needs are not adequately met by mainstream social agencies. These services include information and referral, alcohol and drug counselling, employment services, life-skills training, and programs for children and elders (National Association of Friendship Centres, 1993).

Native Friendship Centres have traditionally exhibited a strong commitment to meeting the needs of Aboriginal urban youth. Since 1997, many Friendship Centres have expanded to include Aboriginal youth centres. By providing career planning, employment opportunities, and recreational activities, these centres encourage Aboriginal teens living off-reserve to complete their high-school education and make a successful transition to the labour force. Among the centres' other objectives are "provid[ing] positive alternatives for those caught up in violent and anti-social lifestyles ... [and] strengthen[ing] positive ties of Aboriginal youth with others in the Aboriginal and non-Aboriginal community" (National Association of Friendship Centres, 1998).

V. THE ROLE OF SOCIAL WORK

Social workers and social welfare policies have been criticized for removing generations of Aboriginal children from their families and communities and for denying Aboriginal people "their language, history, identity, and ultimately, their dignity" (CASW, 1994c, 158). Not surprisingly, this past treatment from albeit well-intentioned professionals has contributed to considerable strain and alienation between social workers and Aboriginal people.

Mainstream social work schools have been attacked for emphasizing their "dominantly held middle-class, patriarchal and white values, traditions, assumptions and ways of thinking; ways that are limited in their application to First Nations" (Mawhiney, 1995, 226). To address this problem, many social work schools have added Aboriginal materials to their curricula. This has given social workers an opportunity to become more aware of past injustices and current problems endured by Aboriginal people (CASW, 1994c; Mawhiney, 1995).

There is a growing demand for trained Aboriginal social workers in self-governed communities and Aboriginal-run social services. In response to this demand, many postsecondary institutions in Canada have developed Aboriginal-controlled social work programs that are culturally appropriate and that prepare social workers for service in Aboriginal communities. The School of Indian Social Work in Saskatchewan, for example, aims "to provide social work knowledge and develop skills based on First Nations culture, values and philosophy"; elders and other First Nations people assist in the development of the curriculum to ensure that training reflects a First Nations approach (School of Indian Social Work, 2000). In a social work program offered at Grant MacEwan Community College in Alberta, Aboriginal instructors teach cultural awareness and include Aboriginal ceremonies in the classroom activities. Exhibit 12.8 provides a visual representation of this program's instructional model.

Developing a better understanding of Aboriginal cultures is a positive step for social workers, but it is not enough. New ways to assess and interpret personal problems are required. For instance, social problems (such as alco-

EXHIBIT 12.8

SOCIAL WORK INSTRUCTIONAL MODEL

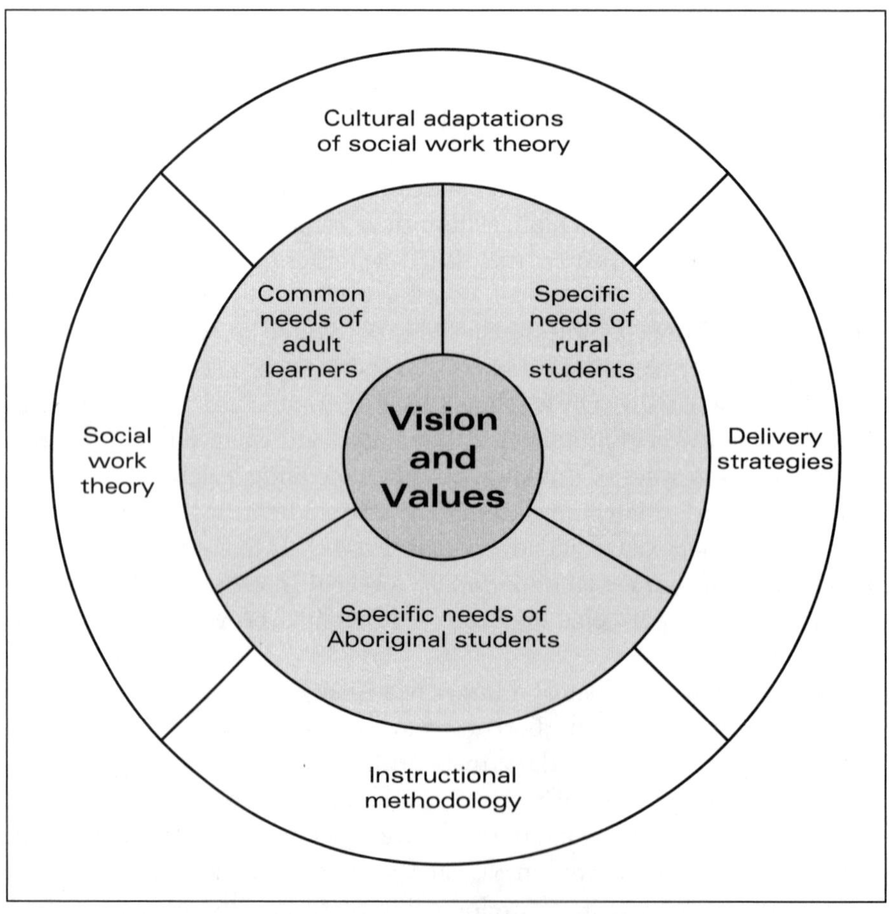

Source: K. Feehan, "Vision and Values," in K. Feehan and D. Hannis (Eds.), *From Strength to Strength: Social Work Education and Aboriginal People* (Edmonton: Grant MacEwan Community College, 1993), 15. Reproduced courtesy of Grant MacEwan Community College.

holism, family violence, and poverty) in many Aboriginal communities are still being framed in terms of dysfunctional individual and family processes; however, these problems may be more appropriately understood in terms of the continuing effects of abuse, colonialism, and racism (Carniol, 1995).

New practice models are also required. According to the Canadian Association of Social Workers (CASW, 1994c, 158), an "emphasis on the wisdom of elders and the strengths of community healers, the importance of the relationship of Aboriginal peoples to their environment, and values assigned to community and extended family rather than individuality, form some of the basis for a significantly different approach to addressing human needs."

Introduction

Aboriginal people account for about 3 percent of Canada's population and have a population growth rate nearly twice that of the non-Aboriginal population. An international recognition of Aboriginal peoples drew attention to the conditions in Aboriginal communities. Despite progress in some areas, Aboriginal people face ongoing social and economic problems.

Aboriginal–Government Relations: A Historical Review

At Confederation, responsibility for Aboriginal people was divided between the federal government and the provinces. The Indian Act and enfranchisement policies put the federal government in control of people living on reserves. Attempts to reform the Indian Act have not always been in the best interests of Aboriginal people. The First Nations movement began in the early 1970s, when Aboriginal people formed groups that have advocated Aboriginal needs and rights.

Renewal and Renegotiation: A New Agenda for the 21st Century

Aboriginal people are breaking free from their oppressive past and concentrating on restructuring their society. In the 1990s, the federal government introduced a variety of initiatives aimed at renewing its partnership with First Nations. Many Aboriginal communities are in the process of negotiating self-government agreements with the federal government. The means by which self-governed programs and services are to be financed is an important consideration for Aboriginal communities and Canadian governments.

Healing and Wellness in Aboriginal Communities

The Aboriginal Healing Strategy was established to help Aboriginal people deal with the negative effects of residential schools. Aboriginal programs use a holistic approach in addressing the problem of family violence. The problems of suicide and substance abuse in Aboriginal communities have been attributed to the feelings of hopelessness that accompany a life of economic disadvantage. A variety of federally funded and Aboriginal-run programs exist to address abuse and mental-health issues.

Caring for Aboriginal Children

Living in poverty puts Aboriginal children at risk for physical and mental-health problems, poor achievement in school, and welfare dependency. The needs of Aboriginal children are being addressed by programs under the Brighter Futures initiative and Aboriginal Head Start. The Child Care Initiative provides services for children whose parents are working or in school. Many Aboriginal communities are developing their own child welfare programs, while Native Friendship Centres are expanding services for urban youth.

The Role of Social Work

Mainstream social welfare programs and social work training programs have failed to meet the needs of Aboriginal people. To address the growing demand for trained Aboriginal social workers, many postsecondary institutions are developing social work programs that reflect a First Nations approach. Some social work programs are specifically training social workers to serve Aboriginal communities. To improve the relationship between Aboriginal people and mainstream social workers, new practice models and methods of assessment are required.

KEY TERMS

CHAPTER 13

SOCIAL WELFARE IN A MULTICULTURAL SOCIETY

• OBJECTIVES •

I. To review the benefits and history of Canadian immigration, and changes to Canada's immigration policy over the years.

II. To examine settlement programs and efforts by the federal government to devolve responsibility for them to the regional governments.

III. To explore issues related to adaptation and review strategies that are used to help newcomers adapt to life in Canada.

IV. To discuss the role of social work practice in a multicultural society.

INTRODUCTION

One of the most distinguishing features of Canada is its ethnic diversity. The term **ethnic** is derived from the Greek *ethnos*, which means "people" or "nation." Although all Canadians can be considered "ethnic" according to this interpretation, common usage applies the term only to nondominant or minority groups—that is, anyone who is not white, has a mother tongue other than English or French, or has an ancestry other than British or French (Stasiulis and Abu-Laban, 2000).

Canada is home to over 100 ethnic groups whose members share similar racial, political, religious, ancestral, or cultural backgrounds. According to the 1996 census, 19 percent of Canadians have a Canadian **ethnic origin**; 17 percent have a British Isles origin; 9 percent report a French origin; and 28 percent have a European, East or Southeast Asian, or South Asian origin. Sixty-four percent of Canadians report having a single ethnic origin, while 36 percent have a multiple ethnic origin (Statistics Canada, 1998b).

The term **multiculturalism** is applied to countries that exhibit ethnic or cultural diversity, as well as equality, mutual respect, and acceptance among various ethnic groups (Burnet, 1999). Canada has always been a multicultural society. Aboriginal groups, with their diverse cultures and languages, were the original inhabitants of what was to become Canada. Later came the European settlers, most of whom were from the United Kingdom and France. Others followed, including immigrants from Africa, Asia, and the Ukraine. These and other settlers contributed to Canada's ethnocultural diversity and development as a nation (Multiculturalism and Citizenship Canada, 1991).

EXHIBIT 13.1

ETHNIC ORIGIN

Source: Andy Donato, *Duds 'n' Scuds: Political Cartoons* (Toronto: Key Porter Books, 1991). Reprinted with permission from the Toronto Sun.

In the last few decades, Canadian governments have introduced legislation to promote multiculturalism and protect the rights and freedoms of all citizens equally. For example, the Canadian Charter of Rights and Freedoms guarantees equal protection under the law "without discrimination based on race, nationality or ethnic origin." The passage of the Canadian Multiculturalism Act in 1988 officially committed the Canadian government to a policy of multiculturalism designed to promote the multicultural heritage of Canadians and the equality of all citizens in the shaping of Canadian society (Canada, 1988). The provinces have adopted multicultural policies of their own.

Central to Canada's development as a nation have been efforts to create a **cultural mosaic** that welcomes and respects ethnocultural diversity. For the most part, Canadians have been "encouraged to maintain their heritage languages, customs and beliefs, and to project the multicultural reality of Canada in their activities at home and abroad" (Canadian Task Force, 1988, 11). Although many Canadians agree with the cultural mosaic ideal, an increasing number of people are voicing concerns about the economic and social costs of multicultural programs, including those designed for Canadian immigrants. Multicultural policies have also been criticized for calling attention to the differences between various ethnic groups and thereby preventing certain groups, such as visible minorities, from fully integrating into the mainstream society (Burnet, 1999; Stasiulis and Abu-Laban, 2000).

The extent to which multiculturalism is promoted in Canada has important implications for social welfare. For example, in a society that promotes multiculturalism, social policies, programs, and services aim to be inclusive rather than exclusive. To be inclusive, social agencies must continually transform their policies and methods of operation in accordance with the evolving makeup of the community. This strategy allows an agency to be more responsive to the diverse ethnocultural needs of the community and to attract or include a clientele that represents both mainstream and ethnic groups (Carter, 1997).

Public and political forums suggest that Canadians are generally more supportive of conservative multicultural and immigration policies than of the cultural mosaic ideal. Almost three-quarters of the respondents in a 1993 survey recommended "that the longstanding image of Canada as a nation of communities, each ethnic and racial group preserving its own identity with the help of government policy, must give way to the U.S. style of cultural absorption" (Kapica, 1993). The "U.S. style" is commonly referred to as a **melting pot**, which has been described as a process

> in which cultures are "melted" or "assimilated" to form one cultural identity ... The outcome of the melting model is the creation of an exclusive society in which: minority cultural groups must mimic the values and beliefs of the dominant group; minority cultures are not valued; differences are tolerated but not recognized as strengths; a unique culture is not created; members of minority cultural groups are encouraged to assimilate into the established dominant culture. Those who do not assimilate have less opportunity to participate fully in society. (British Columbia, 2000)

Stasiulis (1995, 210) suggests that the growing support for cultural assimilation reflects Canadians' frustration with the problems related to cultural diversity and a desire for "policies that 'melt away' troublesome differences." Exhibit 13.2 illustrates Canadians' diminishing support for the mosaic ideal.

I. CANADA'S IMMIGRATION POLICY

THE BENEFITS OF IMMIGRATION

Citizenship and Immigration Canada (CIC, 1994b) defines an **immigrant** as someone who was born in another country, is currently living in Canada, and is seeking permanent residency here. People move to a new country for a variety of reasons. For example, they may be motivated by a desire "to seek greater economic opportunities; to improve their standard of living; and to experience greater social, religious or political freedom and stability" (Christensen, 1995, 180). For those countries that open their doors to immigrants there are the following social, economic, and demographic benefits:

- *Social benefits*. In Canada, immigration provides "linguistic and cultural assets which strengthen our economic, social and cultural relations and foster friendly ties with nations around the world" (Employment and Immigration Canada, n.d.).
- *Economic benefits*. According to CIC (1998, 9), "in an environment where one in three Canadian jobs depends on trade, immigration plays a vital role in building bridges between Canada and other countries. Immigrants bring expertise, capital and initiative." Working adult immigrants also contribute to the economy through the purchase of domestic goods and services, while business owners

EXHIBIT 13.2

SUPPORT FOR MOSAIC VERSUS MELTING POT APPROACHES, 1985 AND 1995

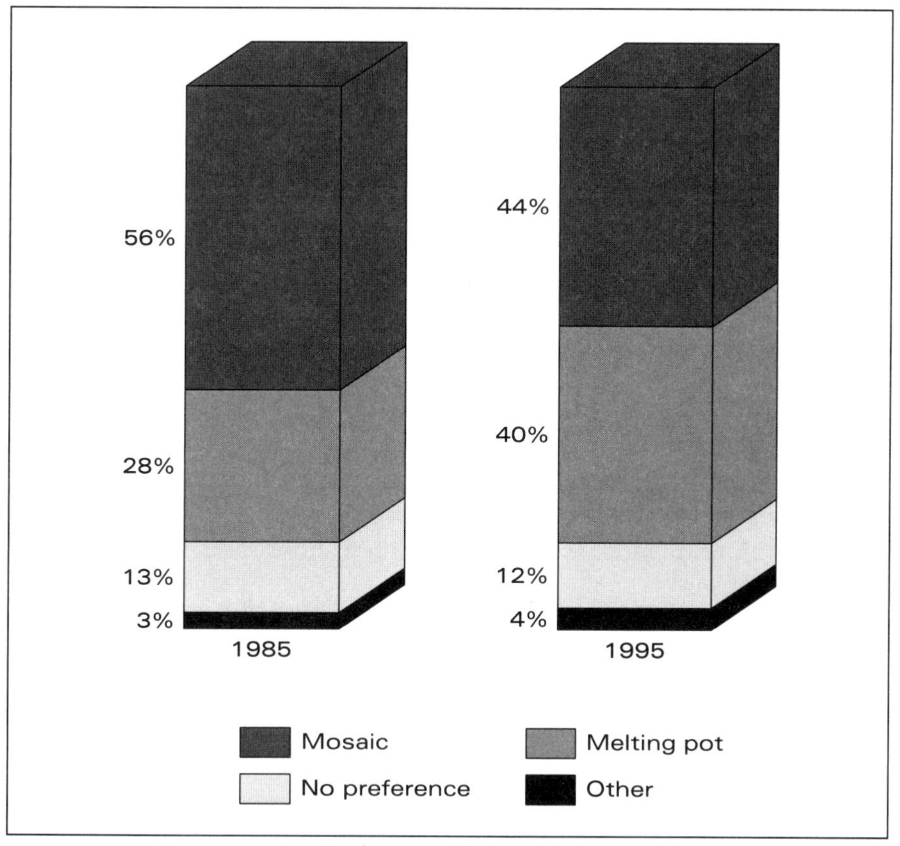

Source: R. Bibby, *The Bibby Report: Social Trends Canadian-Style* (Toronto: Stoddart, 1995), 95.

often create new jobs for Canadians (Employment and Immigration Canada, n.d.).

- *Demographic benefits*. Canada's declining birth rate and aging population have created the need to increase the country's population through immigration. Only with a larger workforce and expanded tax base will Canadian governments be able to provide health care and other services for a growing number of old people (Trempe, Davis, and Kunin, 1997).

Canada also has a humanitarian commitment to accept people who enter the country as refugees. The United Nations (1951) defines a **refugee** as any person who

> owing to well founded fear of being persecuted for reasons of race, religion, nationality, membership of a particular social group or political opinion, is outside the country of his nationality and is unable, or owing to such fear, is unwilling to avail himself of the protection of that country.

Under the UN Convention Relating to the Status of Refugees, Canada is obligated to protect refugees who are fleeing their homeland; Canada can also provide a temporary haven for refugees fleeing from civil war, famine, or other time-limited crises. In 1986 the United Nations awarded Canada the Nansen Medal in recognition of its humanitarian work done on behalf of refugees—Canada was the first country to ever receive this honour.

A BRIEF REVIEW OF IMMIGRATION POLICY

During the 18th and 19th centuries, Canada welcomed newcomers who would develop the vast and sparsely populated land and participate in the building of the national railways. Between 1901 and 1911, the number of immigrants to Canada was close to 30 percent of the country's population; immigration reached a peak in 1913, when more than 400,000 people moved to Canada.

Until 1906, Canada had an "open-door" immigration policy that allowed most white people to move to Canada. The Canadian Immigration Acts of 1906 and 1910 imposed restrictions on immigration that were intended to keep out poor, sick, or "immoral" applicants. Asian immigrants, in particular, were unwelcome in Canada; the Canadian government kept the entry of Asians into Canada to a minimum by imposing a head tax on Chinese immigrants and by being highly selective about Japanese and East Indian immigrants (CIC, 1995).

A serious labour shortage during the 1940s prompted the Canadian government to revise its immigration policies and accept a greater number of immigrants. Canada also introduced its first refugee policy after thousands of displaced Europeans sought refuge in Canada after World War II. The new Immigration Act of 1953 opened Canada's doors wider to those from Europe, the United States, and other "white" nations. At the same time, the Immigration Act made it more difficult for people from less-favoured nations to become citizens of Canada. Applicants from "undesirable" countries were admitted only if they were sponsored by a close relative (CIC, 1995).

The more restrictive aspects of Canada's immigration policy led to a growing problem of illegal immigration and eventually forced the Canadian government to amend the Immigration Act. From 1967 on, the acceptance of immigrants was no longer based on discriminatory criteria such as ethnic origin, race, colour, or religion. Instead, applicants were assessed according to a new points system and admitted on the basis of education, occupation, age, knowledge of English or French, employment opportunities in Canada, and other "objective" criteria (Anderson and Marr, 1987). Before 1967, more than 85 percent of immigrants were from Europe; by 1998, the majority of immigrants were coming from Asia and the Pacific Rim (see Exhibit 13.3) (CIC, 1995, 1999a).

A new Immigration Act passed in 1976 established the main objectives of Canada's immigration policy, including a commitment to help newcomers adapt to Canadian life, to reunite families, and to assist in the resettlement of refugees. The act also required the federal government to project desired

EXHIBIT 13.3

IMMIGRATION SUMMARY BY SOURCE AREA, 1996–1998

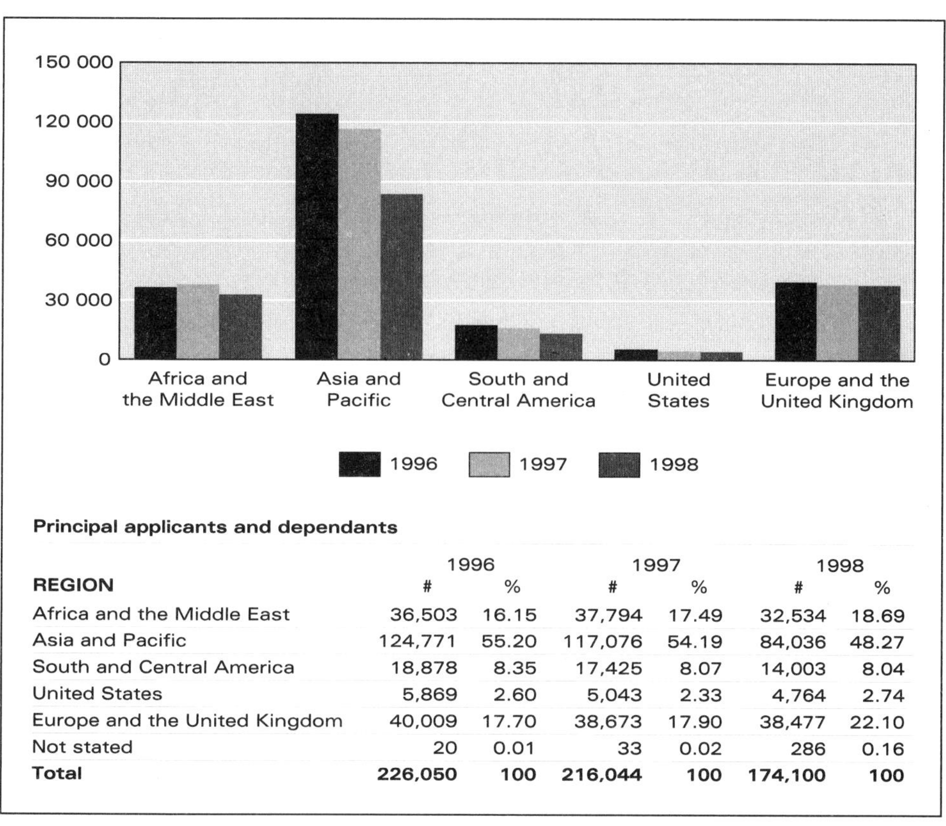

Principal applicants and dependants

REGION	1996 #	1996 %	1997 #	1997 %	1998 #	1998 %
Africa and the Middle East	36,503	16.15	37,794	17.49	32,534	18.69
Asia and Pacific	124,771	55.20	117,076	54.19	84,036	48.27
South and Central America	18,878	8.35	17,425	8.07	14,003	8.04
United States	5,869	2.60	5,043	2.33	4,764	2.74
Europe and the United Kingdom	40,009	17.70	38,673	17.90	38,477	22.10
Not stated	20	0.01	33	0.02	286	0.16
Total	**226,050**	**100**	**216,044**	**100**	**174,100**	**100**

Source: Citizenship and Immigration Canada, *Facts and Figures 1998: Immigration Overview* (Ottawa, 1999), 7. Reproduced with the permission of the Minister of Public Works and Government Services Canada, 2000.

immigration levels for one- to three-year periods. Since 1980—when the practice of projecting began—the actual number of immigrants admitted to Canada has typically fallen short of the projections and far below the numbers required to replace the loss of population due to death and emigration (Dirks, 1999). Exhibit 13.4 gives a historical perspective of the number of immigrants admitted to Canada.

EXHIBIT 13.4

CANADIAN IMMIGRATION, 1860–2000

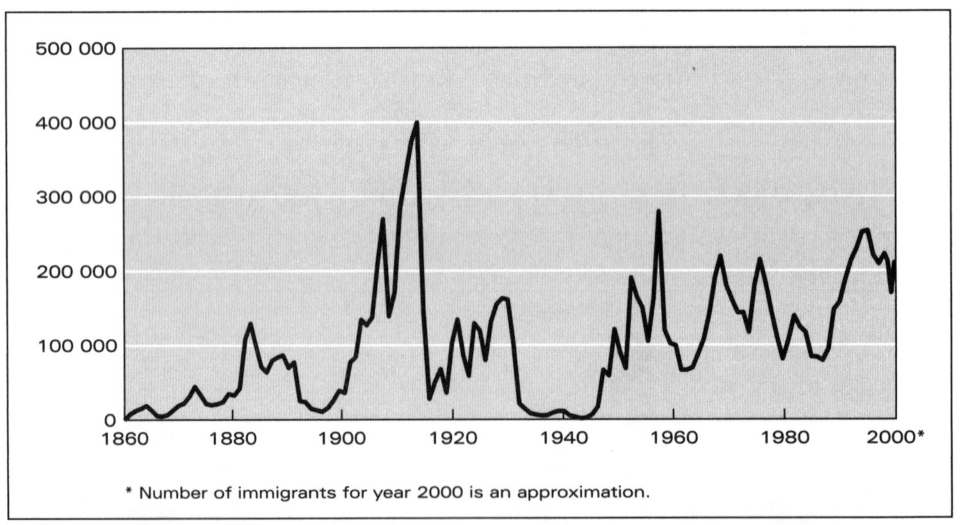

Source: Adapted from Citizenship and Immigration Canada, *Facts and Figures 1998: Immigration Overview* (Ottawa, 1999), 2. Reproduced with the permission of the Minister of Public Works and Government Services Canada, 2000.

NEW DIRECTIONS FOR IMMIGRATION POLICY

By the 1990s a number of problems with the Immigration Act had become apparent: immigration procedures were complicated and inconsistent in their application, globalization and changes in the labour market made the selection process outdated, and existing legislation was ill equipped to deal with the growing problem of illegal aliens entering Canada. Immigration was also becoming a burden on social programs: while new immigrants were expected to assume responsibility for the support of sponsored family members, too many sponsors reneged on their support agreements, costing taxpayers millions of dollars in welfare costs (CIC, 1995).

These problems prompted the federal government to undertake an extensive review of its immigration and refugee policies. Beginning in 1994, public consultations were held across the country to find out what

Canadians thought about various aspects of immigration. The federal government planned to use the information generated from the consultations "to forge a comprehensive, forward-looking and progressive immigration policy framework to take Canada into the next century" (CIC, 1994a, 1). In 1997, a federally appointed Legislative Review Advisory Group summarized the views of Canadians in *Not Just Numbers: A Canadian Framework for Future Immigration*; this report also included the advisory group's recommendations for revising Canada's immigration and refugee policies.

In response to the advisory group's recommendations, the federal government introduced a number of changes to Canada's immigration policy. Some of these changes are described below:

- The immigration categories were reorganized into three categories: (1) independent class (includes skilled workers and business immigrants such as entrepreneurs, investors, and self-employed individuals; (2) family class; and (3) refugees.
- The points system—which was virtually unchanged since its introduction in 1967—was revised to place a greater emphasis on selecting independent immigrants who would bring skills, education, experience, and other assets to Canada's labour force. (Exhibit 13.5 outlines the current selection criteria for independent immigrants.)
- For immigrants in the family class, a higher priority was placed on reuniting spouses and children with individuals who had already immigrated to Canada. While immigrants in the family class accounted for nearly 46 percent of all immigrants in 1996, this figure had dropped to 32 percent by 1999 (CIC, 1999a).
- Beginning in 1998, the federal government signed short-term agreements with many of the regional governments giving them more control over the selection of immigrants who were destined for their jurisdictions (CIC, 1998). (Quebec already had full control over its selection of immigrants and refugees as a result of the 1991 Canada–Quebec Accord.)

Reform efforts that began in 1997 culminated in 2000 with the Liberal government's proposal to replace the Immigration Act of 1976 with a new Immigration and Refugee Protection Act. If passed, the act is expected to "curb criminal abuse of the immigration and refugee systems" and expand "policies to attract the world's best and brightest to Canada." The new act includes measures to

- severely penalize "people smugglers";
- expedite decisions made about refugee claims;

- deny immigrant sponsorship for people (1) convicted of spousal abuse, or (2) receiving social assistance; and
- revise the selection criteria to attract more independent immigrants.

According to the federal government, the new act "[affirms] immigration as a key priority for the government over the years to come" (CIC, 2000c).

Exhibit 13.5

SELECTION CRITERIA FOR INDEPENDENT IMMIGRANTS

FACTOR	UNIT OF ASSESSMENT	NOTES
Education	16 points maximum	Must have a minimum of secondary school completion to qualify
Experience	8 points maximum	Must have a minimum of one year of experience to qualify
Education/training factor	18 points maximum	Refers to the level of training required for the applicant's occupation
Age	10 points maximum	Maximum points are given if the applicant is between 21 and 44 years old
Knowledge of English and/or French	15 points maximum	Maximum points are given to applicants who can speak, write, and read either language fluently
Personal suitability	10 points maximum	Refers to the applicant's ability to settle successfully in Canada
Demographic factor	8 points maximum	Points are based on the federal government's criteria at the time of application
Arranged employment or self-employed	10 points maximum	Refers to a job offer that is approved by Human Resources Development Canada
Occupation	10 points maximum	Must be found on the General Occupations List to qualify
Bonus points for relatives in Canada	5 points maximum	Points are awarded if the applicant has a sibling, parent, grandparent, aunt, uncle, niece, or nephew living in Canada as a permanent resident or citizen

Source: "Summary of Requirements—Self-Supporting Class and Family Class," from *Not Just Numbers*. Available: http://www.cic.gc.ca/english/immigr/iindepen-e.html [2000 September 10]. Copyright © 1997, page 46. Reproduced with the permission of the Minister of Public Works and Government Services Canada, 2000.

II. INTEGRATION AND SETTLEMENT STRATEGY

SETTLEMENT PROGRAMS

Since 1948, Canada has offered programs to help immigrants adapt to Canadian life "[and] become self-reliant, participating members of Canadian society as quickly as possible" (CIC, 1999b). **Settlement programs** are intended to facilitate the integration—as opposed to assimilation—of newcomers into Canadian life. These programs are delivered by a variety of service delivery systems, including voluntary organizations, businesses, and individuals. The Ottawa-Carleton Immigrant Services Organization (OCISO) is one example of an agency that focuses its activities on meeting the needs of immigrants, refugees, and people from culturally diverse backgrounds. In addition to helping newcomers settle in their new homeland, OCISO provides counselling, language instruction, cross-cultural education, multicultural liaison, and assistance in finding nonprofit housing. The agency relies on a mix of funding from the United Way, the Regional Municipality of Ottawa-Carleton, and the United Nations (OCISO, 1999).

While organizations such as OCISO concentrate on meeting the needs of new Canadians in specific communities, a number of national organizations address the long-term needs of newcomers. The Jewish Immigrant Aid Services of Canada (JIAS), for instance, works on behalf of Jewish immigrants and refugees to facilitate their settlement and integration in Canada. Through its partnerships with government, employers, voluntary and charitable organizations, and immigrants, JIAS also "champion[s] the cause of new immigrants and refugees by positively influencing Canadian immigration laws, policies and practices, and by ensuring that they are humane in nature and responsive to the needs of potential newcomers" (JIAS, 2000).

The federal government, through Citizenship and Immigration Canada, sponsors a variety of programs for new Canadians. Some programs, such as the Adjustment Assistance Program, provide financial assistance to help newcomers meet their basic needs during their first year in Canada. Other programs offer personal social services that help new citizens integrate into Canadian life; three of these programs are briefly described below.

Immigration Settlement and Adaptation Program

In 1974 the federal government established the Immigration Settlement and Adaptation Program (ISAP) to fund a wide range of direct services to immigrants. These services include the following:

- *Reception*—meeting newcomers when they arrive in Canada and ensuring that their basic needs (e.g., shelter, clothing, transportation) are met.
- *Referral*—linking newcomers to community resources and services such as stores, banks, health services, and cultural centres.
- *Information and orientation*—providing newcomers with basic information about their rights and responsibilities as Canadian citizens, assisting them with the tasks of daily living, and helping them learn about their community.
- *Interpretation and translation*—providing language interpretation as needed and translating documents and forms required to access health, legal, education, employment, and other services.
- *Counselling*—assessing needs and helping newcomers find specialized services (with the exception of in-depth psychological or social counselling) they might need to adjust to Canadian life.
- *Employment-related services*—helping newcomers find job search services, connect with potential employers, and apply for a review of their academic credentials (CIC, 2000a).

Businesses, educational institutions, individuals, nonprofit organizations, and other service providers that wish to deliver these bridging services to newcomers are eligible to apply for ISAP funding.

Host Program

The Host Program provides funding for individuals and organizations to recruit people who are familiar with Canada, train them to be volunteers, and then pair them with newcomers to Canada. The Host Program can benefit both newcomers and volunteers: newcomers learn about Canada and its customs, while volunteers have an opportunity to make new friends and learn about other cultures (CIC, 1999b).

Language Instruction for Newcomers to Canada

To be able to communicate effectively with others is essential to a newcomer's full integration into a country's social, economic, and cultural life. Through Language Instruction for Newcomers to Canada (LINC), adults who are new to Canada receive basic instruction in English or French. At the same time, the LINC curriculum gives newcomers an opportunity to learn about various aspects of Canadian life. Language instruction occurs in a classroom setting or through self-assisted or distance learning programs. When necessary, LINC helps participants cover the costs of child care and transportation (CIC, 1999b, 2000b).

SETTLEMENT RENEWAL

Soon after the 1993 election, the Liberal government began searching for ways to devolve certain responsibilities for settlement services to other levels of government and the private sector. In 1994 the government launched Settlement Renewal, an initiative that involves three phases: (1) consultations with Canadians, (2) the negotiation of new partnerships, and (3) the transfer of responsibilities (CIC, 1996).

During the first round of consultations in 1994, Canadians expressed a wide range of opinions about settlement programs and how they should be changed. Some people thought that too much money was being spent on settlement programs (especially given the downturn in the economy) and that funding should therefore be cut. Other Canadians argued that settlement programs were so important that *more* money should be spent on them. Still others thought that immigrants should assume more of the financial burden for maintaining settlement programs. A common complaint among social agencies who delivered or administered settlement programs was that the funding system was unnecessarily complex and inflexible; to obtain funds for these programs, agencies were required to apply to several levels of government and to more than one government department (CIC, 1996).

During the negotiation phase of Settlement Renewal, the federal government gave the regional governments the authority to redesign and administer their own settlement programs and to receive federal funding for that purpose (CIC, 1998). (Quebec was not involved in this process since it already controlled its own settlement programs—including language training—as a result of the 1991 Canada–Quebec Accord.) Despite the devolution of responsibility to the regional governments, the federal government continues to play a role in funding and setting standards for settlement programs (Trempe, Davis, and Kunin, 1997).

There have been few studies on the effectiveness of settlement programs. Research is likely to be emphasized in the future, with programs engaging in such activities as tracking the progress of immigrants from the point of arrival in Canada; identifying the factors that influence immigrants' integration (or lack thereof) into Canadian society; identifying and assessing the effects of settlement programs on the lives of immigrants; and applying a cost-benefit analysis to the programs. The findings from studies on immigration and integration (e.g., the Metropolis Project) that are being conducted in Canada's new Centres of Excellence are expected to serve as a guide for settlement programs in the future (Trempe, Davis, and Kunin, 1997).

III. ADAPTATION ISSUES AND STRATEGIES

FACTORS AFFECTING ADAPTATION

Adapting to a new culture can be a lengthy and highly complex process. According to Aycan and Berry (1996, 4), **adaptation** takes place on three interrelated levels:

1) *Psychological adaptation* includes a sense of well-being and satisfaction with regard to different aspects of one's life.
2) *Sociocultural adaptation* emphasizes immigrants' progress in becoming full participants in society and acquiring the skills required to manage everyday situations.
3) *Economic adaptation* is conceptualized as the sense of accomplishment and full participation in the economic life in Canada.

Several factors influence the extent to which newcomers are able to adapt psychologically, socially, and economically to the Canadian way of life. These factors include:

> who [the newcomers] are; where they came from; why they left; whether they came alone or with family; what qualifications they bring to the job market; what languages they speak; how long they've been in Canada; where they've settled; which services their community offers; and what reception they're given by other Canadians. (McCloskey 1998, 2)

In his study on immigration, Dr. Morton Weinfeld (Immigration facts, 1998) found that recent immigrants, refugees, visible minorities, and family-class immigrants tend to face the greatest integration challenges. People who move to a new country on their own are confronted with social isolation and other problems resulting from the limited opportunities to share customs and communicate with others in their native language.

IMMIGRANTS AND EMPLOYMENT

Employment plays an important role in a newcomer's adaptation and integration. As Aycan and Berry (1996, 11) point out:

> [Work] provides purpose to life, it defines status and identity, and enables individuals to establish relationships with

> others in the society. It is especially the latter function that becomes critical for immigrants, because adaptation is facilitated by social interactions. The more one interacts with the groups in the larger society, the faster one acquires skills to manage everyday life.

Immigrants who experience employment problems are likely to suffer economic hardships and be limited in their participation in Canadian society. Difficulties in finding work can also negatively affect a newcomer's psychological well-being.

The employment prospects for new immigrants appear to be worsening: the unemployment rate for this group increased from 19 percent in 1986 to 29 percent in 1996. Unemployment is especially high among non-European and female immigrants (Badets and Howatson-Leo, 1999). Among immigrants who do find work, almost one-third are concentrated in low-skill jobs that are "temporary, poorly paid, afford few health and safety protections ... and rarely offer pensions and other benefits" (Immigration facts, 1998).

Badets and Howatson-Leo (1999, 18) suggest that high unemployment among new immigrants

> may be the result of the economy's difficulties in absorbing new entrants. But a host of other issues, such as the types of skills immigrants bring with them, their cultural background and their personal characteristics, are likely at work as well.

For some immigrants, the problem is one of timing: the labour market demand that exists for their skills at the point of selection may no longer be there once they are actually admitted to Canada. Other immigrants cannot legally work until their educational or occupational credentials are assessed. As Aycan and Berry (1996) point out, this can be a lengthy, demanding, and expensive process, and one that does not offer any guarantee that the newcomer will be able to work without first undergoing further occupational tests or training.

Since 1994, the federal government has been engaged in efforts to

> - facilitate adaptation, so that recent immigrants who come to Canada with needed job skills and professional qualifications can more easily gain access to employment services, and succeed in the transition into the Canadian labour market; [and]

- work with the provinces, employers and unions, and voluntary groups to develop a Canada-wide system of credits recognition to assist immigrants to find and keep meaningful employment commensurate with their skills and knowledge. (CIC, 1994b, 21)

Work creation programs and employment services for new citizens are available through Human Resources Development Canada. In addition, formal credential assessment agencies that evaluate the educational credentials of foreign-trained individuals have been established across Canada; the majority of these agencies are run by provincial governments or universities (CIC, 1998).

ADDRESSING RACISM IN SOCIAL SERVICES

The Canadian Race Relations Foundation (cited in Roy, 2000, 1) identifies and describes three main forms of **racism**:

1) *Individual racism* manifests itself in individual's attitudes and behaviours, and is the easiest type to identify.
2) *Systemic racism* consists of the policies and practices of organizations, which directly or indirectly operate to sustain the advantages of peoples of certain "social races." This type of racism is more difficult to address because it is implicit in the policies of organizations and [is] often unconscious.
3) *Cultural racism* is the basis of both other forms of racism, as it is the value system that is embedded in society that supports and allows discriminatory actions based on perceptions of racial difference, cultural superiority, and inferiority.

These forms of racism can affect all aspects of life, including employment, access to services, education, and social connection (Tator, 1996).

Canadian governments promote antiracism through a variety of activities, including campaigns intended to raise public awareness of racism (see Exhibit 13.6). Discrimination on the basis of race is prohibited under the Charter of Rights and Freedoms, provincial human rights codes, and the Employment Equity Act; these pieces of legislation are nevertheless limited in their ability to fight racism, since they protect government workers but cannot control many discriminatory practices in the private sector (Stasiulis and Abu-Laban, 2000).

Social agencies may have policies and practices that are racist and that intentionally or unintentionally discourage members of minority groups from

EXHIBIT 13.6
ANTIRACISM POSTER

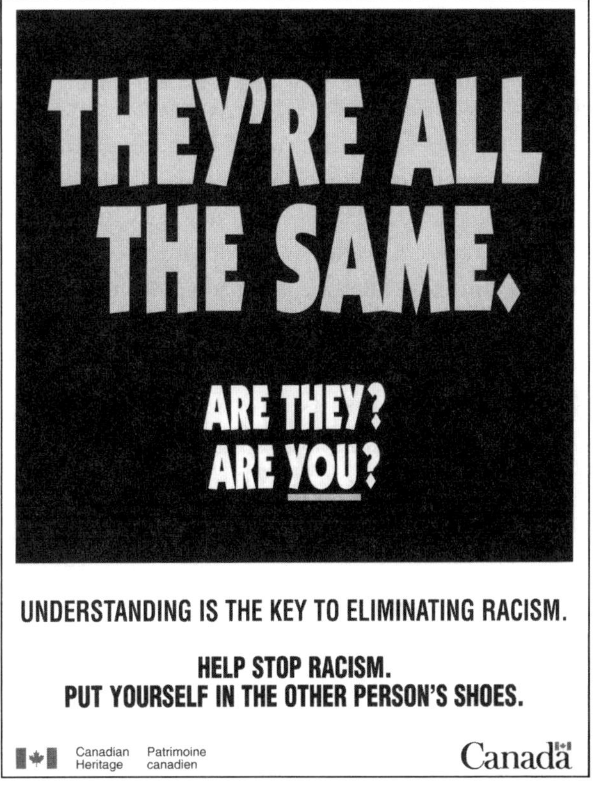

Source: "They're All the Same" [poster], Department of Canadian Heritage. Reproduced with the permission of the Minister of Canadian Heritage and the Minster of Public Works and Government Services, 1996.

accessing services. Language is often a barrier for newcomers seeking health care or social services. According to Weinfeld and Wilkinson (1999, 71), another barrier "might be subtle prejudice or stereotypes of the majority group professionals, and yet another is the simple lack of cultural knowledge that could enhance the interaction between immigrant clients and native-born professionals."

Weinfeld and Wilkinson (1999) suggest that the following steps be taken to make social and health services more culturally sensitive, and thus more accessible to minority groups:

1) the establishment of "ethnospecific institutions" to deliver services to minority groups;

2) the employment of service providers who belong to the same minority group as their clients; and
3) the transformation of mainstream services to better accommodate different cultural norms.

The third step may be the most challenging. According to Tator (1996), Canadian social and health institutions tend to prefer "sameness" among their clientele and a strategy of assimilation rather than integration.

Immigration service agencies (ISAs) are voluntary organizations that focus on culturally sensitive service delivery and are often established in communities with concentrated immigrant populations. According to Tator (1996, 157), ISAs "have traditionally filled the huge gap created by the failure of mainstream institutions to serve the needs of minority and immigrant populations." Beyene et al. (1996) identify four ways in which ISAs are culturally sensitive:

1) ISAs are governed by boards of directors who are representative of and accountable to the communities they serve. Their policies, procedures, and programs are developed with the aim of promoting equal participation.
2) ISAs are actively involved in community education and development activities such as publishing newsletters, holding public forums on immigrant and multicultural issues, and managing resource libraries that have materials in different languages.
3) ISAs advocate for changes in policies (mostly at the government level) that support discrimination and racism.
4) ISAs orient clients to mainstream organizations by providing cultural information and by ensuring that clients are able to access programs.

Although there have been efforts in recent years to strengthen the linkages between mainstream agencies and ISAs, the two service delivery systems usually operate as separate identities (Tator, 1996). Exhibit 13.7 profiles Immigrant and Visible Minority Women Against Abuse, an immigration service agency located in the Ottawa-Carleton area.

SPECIAL POPULATIONS AND THE ADAPTATION PROCESS

Families and Children

Recent studies suggest that young immigrants are for the most part adapting well to life in Canada. In his study on immigration, Dr. Morton Weinfeld (Immigration facts, 1998) found that immigrant children tend to catch up

Exhibit 13.7

IMMIGRANT AND VISIBLE MINORITY WOMEN AGAINST ABUSE

Immigrant and Visible Minority Women Against Abuse (IVMWAA) is a community-based agency in the Ottawa-Carleton area.

Mission

IVMWAA exists:

- to empower immigrant and visible minority women in the Ottawa-Carleton region to participate in the elimination of all forms of abuse against women;
- to provide a culturally responsive crisis intervention counselling service and a cultural interpretation service that will facilitate an abused woman's access to community and mainstream services.

History

IVMWAA was founded in March 1988 in response to the need for culturally appropriate services for abused women. The initial project, entitled Project to Help Assaulted Immigrant Women, focused on public education, research, networking, and organizational development. In 1989, an integrated model of Crisis Counselling and Support Service and Cultural Interpretation was developed. At about the same time, IVMWAA began the first cultural training program for interpreters in Ottawa-Carleton.

Financially supported by the Ministry of Community and Social Services, the crisis counselling support service was provided to Spanish- and Vietnamese-speaking women. The service was gradually expanded to include other linguistic groups.

The Cultural Interpretation Service (CIS), one of seven cultural interpreters' projects in Ontario funded by the Ministry of Citizenship, bridges communication between immigrant and visible minority women and mainstream service providers (e.g., Crown Attorney's office, Legal Aid, hospitals, shelters, and community agencies). This service is provided with the help of a pool of over 50 interpreters who together speak 54 languages and dialects.

Source: Adapted from Immigrant and Visible Minority Women Against Abuse (1999), "Welcome to IVMWAA" [on-line], available: http://www.ivmwaa.ottawa.on.ca [2000 May 25].

with their nonimmigrant peers in many aspects of school performance (the extent to which they do so depends on such factors as the family's country of origin, age at immigration, and parental characteristics). In addition, Beiser et al. (1998) found that new immigrant children are less likely than their nonimmigrant peers to experience mental-health problems in the form of hyperactivity and a variety of emotional and conduct disorders (see Exhibit 13.8).

Immigrant families would appear to be at high risk for mental-health problems, given (1) the correlation between poverty and poor mental health, and (2) the fact that over 30 percent of immigrant families are poor. However, many immigrant families interpret their poverty in positive ways that can lower their risk of developing mental-health problems. Beiser et al. (1998, iii) found that new immigrant families tend to accept poverty as a

EXHIBIT 13.8

PREVALENCE OF MENTAL-HEALTH PROBLEMS IN CHILDREN: NEW IMMIGRANT VERSUS NATIONAL POPULATIONS

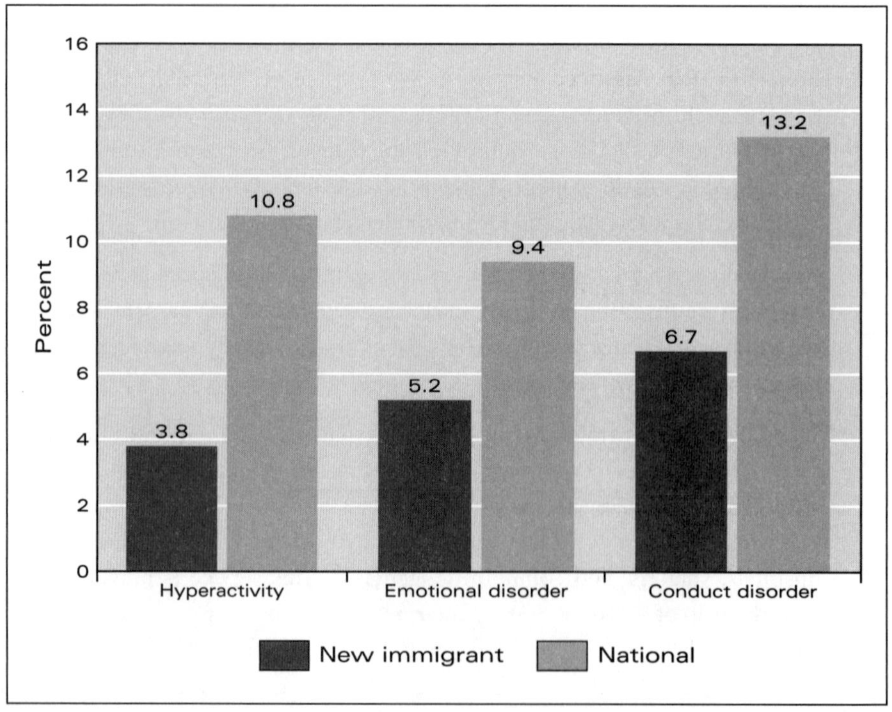

Source: M. Beiser, F. Hou, I. Hyman, and M. Tousignant, *Growing Up Canadian—A Study of New Immigrant Children* (Hull: Research Branch Strategic Policy, Human Resources Development Canada, 1998), 14.

temporary state, a natural part of the resettlement process, and something they can overcome; in contrast, families in nonimmigrant groups tend to interpret poverty as "the end stage of a cycle of disadvantage, despair, family dysfunction and alcohol abuse."

For immigrant children who are having difficulty adjusting to their new country, there are programs designed to enhance their emotional well-being and help them deal more effectively with change and cope with mental-health problems such as depression and anxiety. Many of these programs are funded through Health Canada's Children's Mental Health Strategies Program.

Immigrant Women

A number of barriers prevent immigrant and refugee women from successfully integrating into Canadian society. Women who cannot speak French or English can find themselves socially isolated and excluded from the many social, political, and economic opportunities that Canada can offer. Some of these women depend on their children to be interpreters and their link to the outside world. This responsibility can affect the child's functioning and keep the parent isolated and dependent for a long time (Kamateros, 1998).

There is evidence that immigrant women are less likely than nonimmigrant women to report wife abuse. This is particularly true of women who are from patriarchal cultures, are dependent on their husbands, are socially isolated, and do not speak French or English. Kamateros (1998) identifies some of the reasons an immigrant woman may fail to report wife abuse:

- a combination of fear and shame;
- a firmly held conviction that an individual's right to privacy is more important than the state's right to investigate the affairs of individuals;
- a fear that the abuse will prompt social workers or child protection officers to interfere in the family's business and perhaps even take the children away;
- an expectation that other family members will criticize her for going outside the family to resolve her problems; and
- a sense of fatalism—often stemming from religious conviction—that is associated with feelings of powerlessness and a belief that the abusive situation is her lot in life.

The programs in Canada that are specifically designed for abused immigrant women can be classified into four main groups:

- services provided by immigrant women's organizations;
- immigrant family counselling services;

- information and programs through settlement and ethno-specific organizations; and
- transition houses and transition services specifically for immigrant women. (Miedema and Wachholz, 1998, 6)

Many of these programs are funded through the Family Violence Initiative and are the result of partnerships between federal departments. For example, the Department of Canadian Heritage supports programs aimed at reducing family violence in communities where fluency in English or French is limited. In addition, the Department of Justice Canada is revising certain policies and procedures to "make the criminal justice system and justice-related services more accessible for abused immigrant women" (Health Canada, 1998c, 24). Despite these efforts, programs for abused immigrant women tend to lack sufficient funding; the result is long waiting lists and delays for people seeking help (Miedema and Wachholz, 1998).

IV. IMPLICATIONS FOR SOCIAL WORK PRACTICE

CROSS-CULTURAL TRAINING

During the 1970s, social workers were encouraged to be "colour-blind" when working with racial minority clients. Proctor and Davis (1994, 316) explain:

> **Colour-blind practice** was assumed to control client–worker racial differences, to foster the conveyance of "true regard" for minority clients, and to ensure that all clients were treated equally. The acknowledgment of racial difference was seen as akin to racism.

The main problem with colour-blind practice was that it ignored obvious and important parts of a client's identity and social reality; this allowed practitioners to avoid the issue of racial injustice and its impact on the client.

Whereas colour-blind practice ignored racial differences, the cross-cultural practice models that have emerged in recent years tend to view racial, cultural, social, and other differences as enriching for both personal relationships and general society. Today's social workers use cross-cultural practice models to guide their practice with minority group clients. Tsang and George (1998) have developed a model that

1) recognizes the reality of cultural differences;
2) encourages change not only in individuals but also within organizations and other social institutions;
3) emphasizes justice and equity and the elimination of discrimination and oppression;
4) stresses the importance of respect for differences between service providers and clients; and
5) encourages research to ensure that services are effective and of high quality.

This model can be applied in many different contexts and to many different ethnic groups.

Social workers can raise their level of cultural sensitivity by engaging in **cross-cultural training**. This type of training often involves a form of cultural immersion: social workers are transported into ethnocultural communities, where they become sensitized to the cultural values of others and at the same time arrive at a better understanding of their own cultural values. The ultimate goal of this exercise is to learn how not to impose one's values on others (Herberg and Herberg, 1995).

Although it is widely used in Canada, cross-cultural training is limited in some respects. Tator (1996, 158) points out that "while [cross-cultural] courses are well intended, the study of the history, values, and norms of minorities often leads to stereotyping and to erroneous generalizations." In order to be effective, cross-cultural training must challenge participants "to become aware of the existence of their prejudices, stereotypes, and racist behaviours, and of the potential impact of these factors on clients" (Christensen, 1996, 148).

Cross-cultural training also requires on the part of social workers a willingness to adapt their traditional knowledge frameworks and practice methods to their work with minority clients. For example, a social worker may choose to focus less on individual counselling approaches (which tend to view the individual as needing to change) and to concentrate on advocacy and community development (which encourage change in external systems). Without these types of adaptations, nonminority social workers may find it difficult to establish rapport with minority group clients and help them stay engaged in the change process (Christensen, 1996).

MINORITY SOCIAL WORKERS

Instead of training mainstream professionals to work with minority group clients, some social agencies hire minority workers. Weinfeld (1999, 118) describes an **ethnic match** between minority workers and same-origin clients as "a short cut that automatically guarantees the provision of culturally sensitive services."

Social agencies that employ professionals from diverse cultures may attract a more culturally diverse clientele. Tator (1996, 160) explains:

> Minority clients are more likely to use the service if they can communicate and interact with someone of the same or similar cultural background. In the case of racial-minority clients, it is quite likely they will feel more comfortable with a worker of colour, who understands the experience of racism.

Despite these potential benefits, there is little evidence to date that matching minority professionals with clients improves services or prevents workers from having racist attitudes and stereotypes (Weinfeld, 1999).

Although an increasing number of minority professionals are working in Canadian social services, minority workers—like their minority clients—face barriers to employment. A study of black graduates from a Nova Scotian social work program found that these minority social workers were hired for less prestigious positions and, once employed, were paid less and had fewer opportunities for advancement than their nonminority peers (Bambrough, Bowden, and Wien, 1992). According to Tator (1996), it is common for minority social workers to feel isolated, marginalized, and powerless in their places of work. Social agencies may have to modify their recruiting, hiring, and supervision practices to make them more compatible with the principle of cultural diversity. Educational institutions also have an important role to play in training students to become more culturally sensitive to and supportive of one another.

Introduction

One of Canada's most distinguishing characteristics is its ethnic diversity. Over 100 ethnic groups live in Canada, and a large percentage of Canadians have a multiple ethnic origin. Although Canada officially promotes multiculturalism and a cultural mosaic ideal, support among Canadians for a melting pot approach has been increasing in recent years.

Canada's Immigration Policy

Canada admits immigrants because of the many social, economic, and demographic benefits of doing so; Canada also has an international obligation to accept refugees. Canada's immigration policy has continued to evolve over the years. The number of immigrants admitted to Canada is typically below projected levels. A review of Canada's immigration process led to changes in immigration categories, selection criteria, priorities for family-class immigrants, and the way in which governments control the selection process. A new Immigration Act was tabled in the House of Commons in 2000.

Integration and Settlement Strategy

The federal government sponsors a wide range of settlement programs that aim to help newcomers adjust to Canadian society. The launching of the Settlement Renewal initiative in 1994 was the first step in the federal government's plan to transfer responsibility for settlement programs to the regional governments. Some regional governments are now designing and delivering their own settlement programs, but the federal government continues to fund and set standards for these programs.

Adaptation Issues and Strategies

Adaptation to a new culture takes place on the psychological, sociocultural, and economic levels. Employment plays an important role in the adaptation process; the federal and provincial governments are working to break down the barriers that prevent immigrants from gaining access to meaningful employment. Racism in its various forms is a major barrier to successful adaptation. Social and health agencies need to make their services more culturally sensitive in order to attract a culturally diverse clientele. Immigration service agencies (ISAs) meet the needs of immigration populations that are not being addressed by mainstream organizations. Immigrant children generally adapt well to Canadian life; however, language and cultural barriers may prevent immigrant women from doing the same.

Implications for Social Work Practice

Today's cross-cultural practice models tend to view cultural difference as something that enriches relationships and society. Social workers sometimes take cross-cultural training to raise their level of cultural awareness and sensitivity. One way for social agencies to provide culturally sensitive services is to hire minority social workers. Unfortunately, minority social workers—like their minority clients—are subject to various forms of discrimination.

KEY TERMS

ETHNIC 295
ETHNIC ORIGIN 295
MULTICULTURALISM 295
CULTURAL MOSAIC 297
MELTING POT 297
IMMIGRANT 298
REFUGEE 299
SETTLEMENT PROGRAMS 305
ADAPTATION 308
RACISM 310
IMMIGRATION SERVICE AGENCIES (ISAs) 312
COLOUR-BLIND PRACTICE 316
CROSS-CULTURAL TRAINING 317
ETHNIC MATCH 318

CHAPTER 14

SOCIAL WELFARE AND PEOPLE WITH DISABILITIES

• OBJECTIVES •

I. To provide a profile of Canadians with disabilities in terms of definitions and disability types; prevalence, severity, and causes of disabilities; and at-risk populations.

II. To review government efforts to meet the income, employment, and housing needs of people with disabilities.

III. To examine government initiatives in the 1980s and 1990s to promote the full inclusion of people with disabilities in Canadian society.

IV. To look at various types of voluntary organizations that serve the disability community.

V. To consider social work practice with clients who have disabilities.

INTRODUCTION

Although people with physical or mental disabilities have always been part of Canadian society, they have not always had access to the opportunities that nondisabled people have enjoyed. Social attitudes have largely determined the extent to which people with disabilities have been included in society. These attitudes have had a major impact on disability-related policies, programs, and services throughout Canada's history.

During Canada's colonial era, people with disabilities were seen as "deviant," "defective," and generally inferior to nondisabled people. They were also considered "deserving of charity" and placed in overcrowded and unsanitary poorhouses (Roeher Institute, 1996). By the mid-1800s, a more compassionate view of people with disabilities in general resulted in the establishment of large institutions to educate, train, and otherwise "cure" people with mental disabilities. When these people later made efforts to re-enter society, however, communities were unwelcoming; people with disabilities came to be seen as individuals who should be pitied and, more important, institutionalized for the purpose of protecting them from mainstream society (Roeher Institute, 1996).

The popularity of eugenics at the turn of the 20th century was accompanied by the view that people with mental disabilities were a danger not only to themselves but to others. Institutional programs were redesigned for the purpose of protecting mainstream society from people with mental disabilities. Sterilization became a widely used method for controlling the "menace of the feeble-minded" (MacMurchy, 1932, 36) and preventing mentally "defective" people from "poisoning" the race (Roeher Institute, 1996, 4).

From the 1920s to the 1960s, people with disabilities were considered incompetent, with little or nothing to contribute to society or the labour force (Status of Disabled Persons Secretariat, 1994). Most services for this group were provided in institutions where disability was viewed as an illness or disease. Treatment was guided by "rehabilitation teams" consisting of physicians, psychiatrists, medical social workers, and related professionals.

A growing awareness of human rights in the 1960s and 1970s fostered the **disability rights movement**, which aimed to eliminate socially imposed restrictions on people with disabilities and give them equal access to the resources available to the nondisabled population (New Brunswick, 1992). This led to new methods of rehabilitation and to the establishment of sheltered workshops and community-based group homes.

More recent approaches to disability have been guided by the principle of **normalization**, which is distinguished by the view that people with disabilities should "enjoy patterns and conditions of everyday life which resemble, as closely as possible, the norms and patterns of mainstream society" (Nova Scotia, 1995, 2). Accompanying this philosophy are more progressive theories about what "causes" disability. The narrow view of disability as a problem stemming from the individual has given way to a more inclusive view in which disability is seen as the product of external as well as internal factors (Roeher Institute, 1996). Exhibit 14.1 illustrates how risk, environmental, and other factors converge to create a "handicap situation."

People with disabilities are becoming increasingly visible members of society. Vargo (1999, 667) observes:

> As barriers to mobility are removed it is no longer unusual to see people in wheelchairs in public places; deaf people using sign language have appeared in television programs and advertising; famous actors and entertainers discuss their blindness or mental illness in the media.

EXHIBIT 14.1

THE HANDICAPS CREATION PROCESS

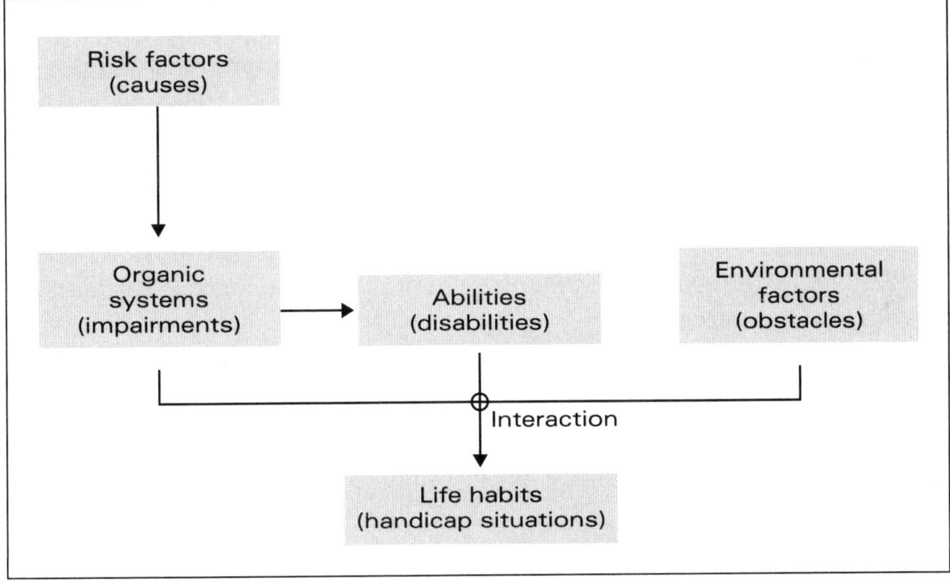

Source: G. Fawcett, *Living with a Disability in Canada: An Economic Portrait* (Hull: Office for Disability Issues, Human Resources Development Canada, 1996), 5.

This new visibility has been accompanied by greater public acceptance of people with disabilities. Public acceptance, in turn, is reflected in more inclusive government policies. The practice of administering programs for people with disabilities separately from mainstream programs is coming to an end. People with disabilities will increasingly meet their needs through generic or mainstream employment, training, and other programs. At the same time, mainstream programs will be modified to accommodate people with disabilities, and government support will continue for "those individuals whose needs cannot be met through generic programs and services" (Canada, 1999j).

I. A PROFILE OF PERSONS WITH DISABILITIES

DEFINITIONS

Various terms are used to describe people who are physically, mentally, socially, or otherwise limited in their capabilities. Four terms that are commonly used are "disorder," "impairment," "disability," and "handicap." The International Classification of Impairments, Disabilities, and Handicaps

(ICIDH), a system developed by the World Health Organization in 1980, has defined these terms as follows:

- **Disorder** refers to the cause of the limited condition, which may be present at birth or developed later on. Cerebral palsy, spina bifida, and stroke, for example, all have the potential to cause a disorder.
- **Impairment** is seen as an abnormality or loss of physical functioning. A person may be born with an impairment or acquire it later in life; impairments can be either temporary or permanent. Examples of physical impairments include hearing loss, blindness, and disfigurement; mental impairments include intellectual impairment, brain damage (usually the result of physical trauma), and mental illness (e.g., schizophrenia).
- **Disability** refers to a restriction or lack of ability to do what is within the range of "normal" human activity. Some disabilities are characterized by a temporary or permanent loss of certain abilities (e.g., an inability to read due to a loss of vision). An excess of ability may also be disabling (e.g., hyperactivity or stuttering). In general, disabilities result from some type of impairment.
- **Handicap** is the result of an impairment or disability that limits or prevents an individual from successfully fulfilling culturally accepted social roles (e.g., worker, spouse, parent). People with handicaps tend to be at a disadvantage in their ability to maintain employment, be economically independent, and/or form relationships.

Exhibit 14.2 illustrates the relationships among these four conditions. This chapter refers primarily to people with *disabilities*—that is, people who are limited in their ability to carry out activities due to a physical or mental impairment.

EXHIBIT 14.2

INTERNATIONAL CLASSIFICATION OF DISORDER, IMPAIRMENT, DISABILITY, AND HANDICAP

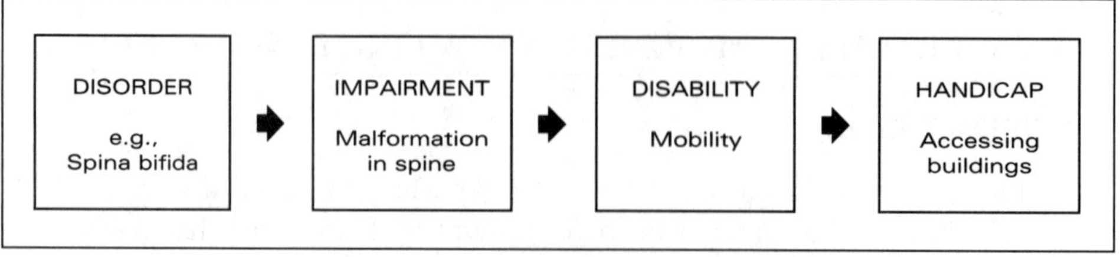

Source: Modified from Statistics Canada, *The User's Guide to the 1991 Health and Activity Limitation Survey (HALS)*, Cat. No. 82F0011GPD, 1992.

TYPES OF DISABILITIES

Although the term *disability* is often used generically to refer to a broad range of limiting conditions, there are many specific forms of disability (see Exhibit 14.3). Three types of disability are briefly described below.

Physical Disability

Physical disabilities account for about two-thirds of all disabilities among Canadians. Most people with a **physical disability** have limited mobility (e.g., difficulty walking or standing for long periods) and/or problems with agility (e.g., difficulty dressing or getting in and out of bed). Other physical disabilities are the result of impaired hearing, sight, or speech.

Mental Illness

Mental disability may be the result of a psychiatric or mental illness. The International Classification of Disease is a diagnostic tool that is used in many countries to classify the various mental disorders. According to this

EXHIBIT 14.3

NATURE OF DISABILITY AMONG PERSONS WITH DISABILITIES, 1991

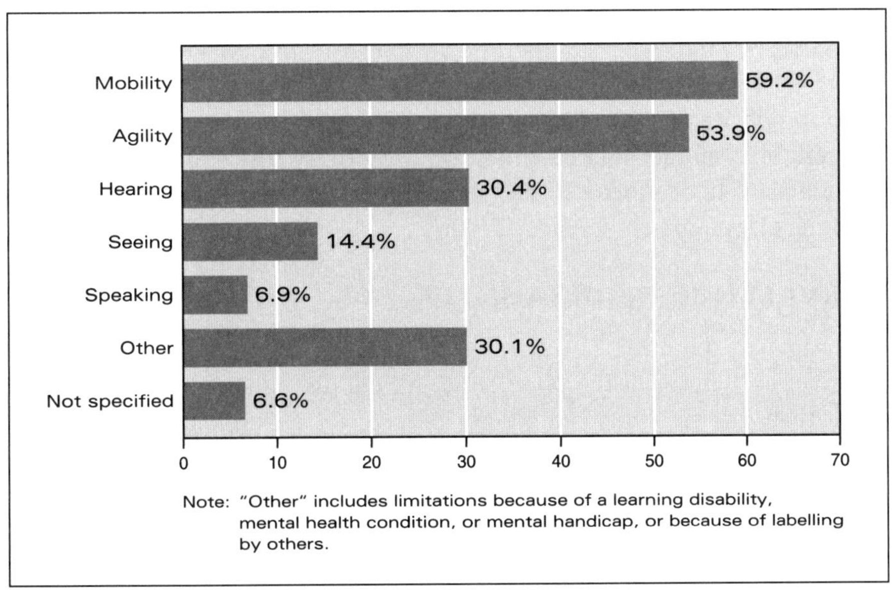

Note: "Other" includes limitations because of a learning disability, mental health condition, or mental handicap, or because of labelling by others.

Source: Statistics Canada, *A Portrait of Persons with Disabilities*, Cat. No. 89-542 (Ottawa: Minister of Industry, Science and Technology, 1995), 11.

system, a **mental illness** includes psychotic disorders (e.g., schizophrenia and paranoia), affective disorders (e.g., mania and depression), neuroses (e.g., anxiety and hypochondriasis), and personality disorders. Some mental disorders, such as dementia and Alzheimer's disease, result from a physical deterioration of brain tissue. Mental illness is one of Canada's most pervasive health problems, affecting one in five Canadian adults (Canadian Psychiatric Research Foundation, 1999).

Intellectual Disability

People with a developmental or **intellectual disability** have a perceptual or cognitive impairment that originates from birth and usually manifests in the first 20 years of a person's life. In the past, this type of disability was referred to as "mental retardation." Intellectual disabilities can interfere with developmental processes and usually hamper a person's ability to learn, conceptualize, and master social skills. In many cases, people with an intellectual disability will also have a physical disability such as cerebral palsy (CACL, n.d.; Roeher Institute, 1996).

HEALTH AND ACTIVITY LIMITATION SURVEY

Much of what we know about Canadians with disabilities—that is, the type of disabilities they have, their needs, and the limitations they face—comes from the Health and Activity Limitation Survey (HALS), which was undertaken shortly after the Canada census in 1986 and again in 1991. The fact that HALS was not repeated after the 1996 census has undermined Canada's ability to create a current profile of people with disabilities and their needs, develop policies and programs to meet those needs, and evaluate the effectiveness of disability-related programs. To rectify this problem, Statistics Canada plans to conduct a HALS following the next census in 2001 (Human Resources Development Canada, 1999b).

PREVALENCE OF DISABILITY

According to the 1991 HALS, about 4.2 million Canadians, or approximately 15.5 percent of the population, have a disability. Some people have more than one disability; an elderly person, for example, may have difficulty walking (a physical disability) and also suffer from dementia (a mental disability).

Disability rates vary across the country. Nova Scotia's disability rate is 6 percent higher than the national average, with over one-fifth of that province's population reporting a disability. Newfoundland and Quebec, two

EXHIBIT 14.4

PERCENTAGE OF THE POPULATION WITH DISABILITIES, 1986 AND 1991

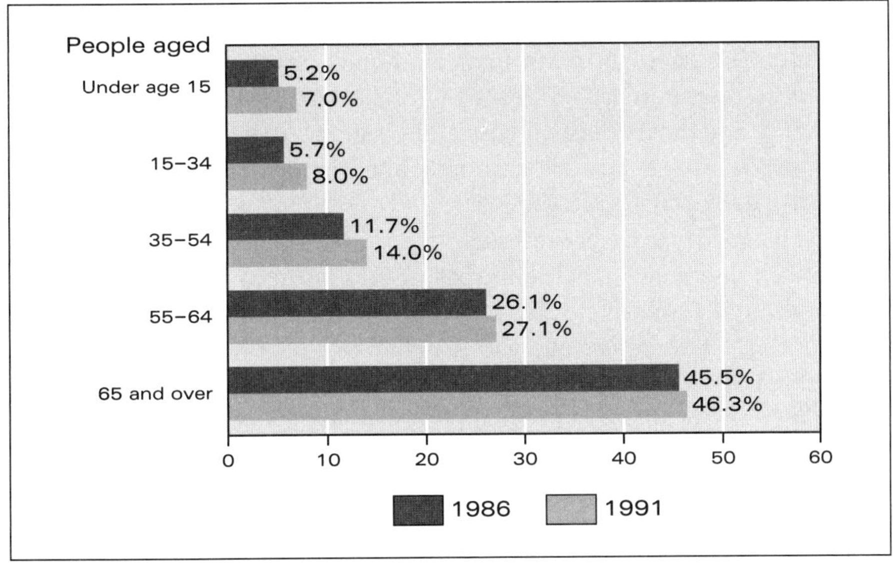

Source: Statistics Canada, *A Portrait of Persons with Disabilities*, Cat. No. 89-542 (Ottawa: Minister of Industry, Science and Technology, 1995), 10.

provinces with relatively low senior populations, have the lowest disability rates (10 percent and 12 percent respectively) (Nova Scotia, 1999b; Statistics Canada, 1995). As Exhibit 14.4 shows, the incidence of disability increases with age.

CAUSES AND SEVERITY OF DISABILITY

There are many potential causes of disability; the majority of disabilities are believed to result from aging, disease, or illness. In some cases, the cause or causes of a disability are well known. Fetal alcohol syndrome (FAS), for example, "is the largest cause of mental disability with 3–5 per 1000 births and up to 10 per 1000 in high-risk populations" (CCD, 2000b). A variety of health and social service programs in Canada are working to prevent FAS and other substance-related disabilities.

Only a small proportion (3 percent) of children with disabilities have severe disabilities. While most adults with disabilities report being only mildly disabled, about one-third of seniors are severely disabled (Statistics Canada, 1995).

Because the causes of disability are so numerous, the severity of a disability among the people who have it can vary widely. For example, one person with an intellectual disability may have no difficulty performing daily tasks of living, while another person who has been identified as having the same disability may experience serious functional limitations. The wide differences in performance among people with the same disability presents politicians and other decision-makers with the challenge of planning and developing policies and programs that will meet the needs of a group whose needs are anything but homogeneous (Vargo, 1999; Torjman, 1996).

On a broader scale, government must foster public acceptance of all people with disabilities. The public has not always been willing to acknowledge that certain conditions are, in fact, disabilities. For example, according to the B.C. Coalition of People with Disabilities, some members of the general public, as well as people in the AIDS and disability communities, are reluctant to accept AIDS as a disability-related condition. Much of this resistance can be attributed to homophobia in both the general society and disability community, and "disability phobia" in the AIDS community. However, the view of AIDS as a disability-related condition is gradually gaining acceptance as people in the disability and AIDS communities recognize the challenges, such as discrimination in the workplace, that are confronting both groups (B.C. Coalition of People with Disabilities, 1994).

POPULATIONS AT RISK

Some Canadians with a physical and/or mental disability are more likely than other Canadians to experience social and economic problems. The Roeher Institute (1995, vii) attributes these problems not so much to the particular disability as to the "accompanying marginalization, discrimination, disregard and neglect of the appalling social and economic conditions" that people with disabilities face in our society. This section considers two at-risk groups: Aboriginal people and women.

Aboriginal People

Studies show that Aboriginal people on and off reserves have a higher disability rate than any other group in Canada. Almost one-third of all Aboriginal people have a disability, a rate that is twice the national average. The incidence of disability among Aboriginal people aged 15 to 34 is three times the national rate (Canada, 1999j).

The high rate of disability among Aboriginal people is related to broader issues facing many Native communities, such as poor housing, geographic isolation, inadequate transportation, lack of access to health care and culturally sensitive services, poverty, and unemployment (Bridges, 1994; Alberta, 1993). In addition, there are few disability-related programs and services available on-reserve; Aboriginal people are often forced to "abandon their communities in search of these supports [in mainstream communities]" (Canada, 1999j).

Women

Women with disabilities face employment and economic barriers. According to Doe and Kimpson (1999, vi), these women "tend to be more prone to cyclical and fluctuating illness that creates difficulty in sustaining employment and basic life activities." Autoimmune conditions, chronic fatigue syndrome, and depression, together with other illnesses to which women with disabilities are prone, are not always easily detected but can severely affect one's ability to work.

Women with disabilities are more likely to live in poverty than their male counterparts: 35 percent of disabled women compared with 16 percent of disabled men have annual incomes of $5000 or less. In addition, disabled women are more likely than disabled men to live alone, be socially isolated, and be perceived more negatively by others. Women with disabilities also have difficulty accessing rehabilitation and sexual health-care services (Alberta Committee of Citizens with Disabilities, n.d.).

Violence against women with disabilities is another problem. According to a report by Health Canada (1992, 2), women with disabilities who live in institutions

> are most vulnerable to abuse because they are more dependent upon even larger numbers of people, and less able to get away. It is estimated that women with disabilities are 1.5 to 10 times as likely to be abused as non-disabled women, depending on whether they live in the community or in institutions.

Negative stereotypes of people with disabilities may contribute to the victimization of institutionalized disabled women. These stereotypes include a belief that people with disabilities are "stupid," "easily taken advantage of," "more controllable," and "less [valuable] as human beings—as objects or as children" (Roeher Institute, 1995, 16).

II. MEETING INCOME, EMPLOYMENT, AND HOUSING NEEDS

THE DISABILITY INCOME SYSTEM

The income-security system for people with disabilities has evolved over several decades, resulting in a mix of largely uncoordinated programs (Torjman, 1996). Despite this lack of coordination, the system may be generally understood in terms of the four categories described below:

1) *Earnings replacement* aims to replace income that has been lost due to an injury, illness, disability-related condition (e.g., AIDS), or accident. Included in this category are the Canada and Quebec Pension Plans, workers' compensation, Employment Insurance, and private disability insurance.
2) *Income support programs* are aimed at people with no or little income. These programs are usually provided through provincial welfare departments.
3) *Compensation for loss* is paid to those who have suffered pain and loss as a result of a disabling injury or accident. These programs include workers' compensation and some private insurance programs.
4) *Compensation for disability-related costs* includes special benefits that offset the costs of having a disability (e.g., purchase of a wheelchair or medication). These benefits are usually provided through provincial social assistance or disability income programs (Torjman, 1996).

Each type of program has its own systems of funding and administering benefits. Depending on the jurisdiction, eligibility for benefits may be determined on the basis of a person's condition or disease, assessed needs, employability, ability to perform basic and/or job-related tasks, and place of residence or status (in the case of Aboriginal people). This diversity across programs has contributed to the excessive complexity of the overall disability income system (Canada, 1999j).

Many people with disabilities are capable of working if the workplace provides certain accommodations such as adapted workplaces and technical aids. However, some disability income programs have been criticized for having built-in disincentives to work. In provinces and territories where disability income programs are part of general welfare programs, people receiving disability income are usually classified as "long-term cases" or as "permanently unemployable." These individuals are given benefits that exceed those provided by welfare, offered a variety of additional supports, and not required to show proof that they are looking for work. All of this gives recipients little incentive to take work that pays less than their benefits (Canada, 1999j; Torjman, 1996).

Systems are in place to reduce disincentives to work. At the federal level, reforms to the Canada Pension Plan Disability Program make it more difficult for people to collect disability benefits; once on the system, recipients are more carefully monitored (Human Resources Development Canada, 1998a). At the provincial and territorial levels, governments have made a commitment to "rapid reinstatement"; under this policy, if an individual leaves assistance for a job and the job does not pan out, the assistance is reinstated immediately (National Council of Welfare, 1997).

Since 1996, governments have implemented changes to improve the disability income system. For instance, provincial governments are making a greater effort to enhance **portability** so that "disability supports are attached to the individual; they go with that person regardless of the region or setting in which they are required." Portability of income is enhanced through **individualized funding**. In contrast to the traditional government practice of giving professionals funding to purchase services for clients with disabilities, individualized funding allows money to go directly to the person with a disability. In addition, the amount the person receives can be adjusted as his or her needs change over time (Canada, 1999j).

EMPLOYMENT SERVICES AND VOCATIONAL REHABILITATION

The inclusion of people with disabilities in mainstream employment opportunities is a relatively new phenomenon in Canada. Until recently, people with disabilities worked primarily in "sheltered" or "supported" employment situations. Today there is more emphasis placed on opening doors to employment in mainstream settings and making accommodations so that people with disabilities can successfully do the job. People with disabilities are also creating their own jobs through community economic development opportunities and self-employment. Abel Enterprises in Simcoe, Ontario, for example, is a business run by psychiatric survivors that specializes in carpentry and custom-made furniture production (Abel Enterprises, 2000).

Government has played an important role in the employment of people with disabilities. During the first half of the 20th century, governments provided vocational rehabilitation to injured war veterans and industrial workers through the Veterans' Rehabilitation Act and the Workmen's Compensation Act. In 1961, vocational rehabilitation programs were expanded with the passage of the Vocational Rehabilitation of Disabled Persons Act (VRDP). This cost-shared program provided a wide range of employment-related services and benefits for Canadians with mental and physical disabilities. Services included assessment, rehabilitation counselling, training, and employment placement, while financial assistance covered training allowances and the cost of technical aids, books, and specialized equipment.

A review of Canada's rehabilitation legislation and programs was launched in 1996 as part of the social union process. Representatives from the federal, provincial, and territorial governments formed a working group to, among other things, reform the VRDP. In 1997 the working group proposed that the VRDP be replaced by the Employability Assistance for People with Disabilities (EAPD), an initiative that aims to increase the labour force participation rate for people with disabilities (see Exhibit 14.5) by helping them prepare for, find, and keep jobs. Under the EAPD, the federal and regional governments share the costs of programs and make separate agreements as to the types of programs and services that will be offered in each

EXHIBIT 14.5

LABOUR FORCE STATUS OF ADULTS WITH DISABILITIES (15–64) COMPARED TO ADULTS WITHOUT DISABILITY

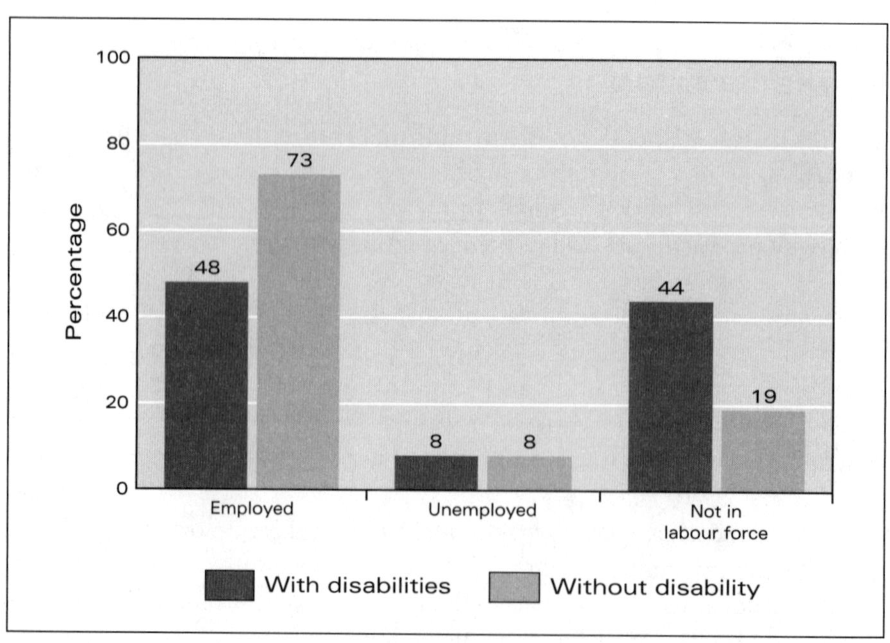

Source: Canada (1999), *In Unison: A Canadian Approach to Disability Issues*, Appendix B [on-line], available: http://socialunion.gc.ca/pwd/unison/appendixb_e.html.

province and territory. Although each agreement is unique, all programs across the country have the following elements:

- a focus on individual need, community participation, and flexibility in the design and delivery of services;
- an emphasis on service outcomes and accountability;
- measures to reduce program overlap and duplications; and
- a maximum of 15 percent of funding spent on administration (Human Resources Development Canada, 1998b).

The federal government has entered into several bilateral agreements under the EAPD, including those with Quebec, Manitoba, Alberta, Saskatchewan, Nova Scotia, Newfoundland, and Prince Edward Island.

HOUSING AND LIVING ARRANGEMENTS

The **deinstitutionalization movement** that began in the 1960s and continued into the 1990s resulted in the closure of mental institutions across Canada and the return of residents to their communities. Today only 7 percent of people with disabilities live in institutional settings; the majority of these individuals are adults with severe disabilities and seniors who require health-related institutional care (Statistics Canada, 1995).

This dramatic movement of people from large institutions to community-based settings created a need for alternative housing for people with disabilities. Community residences or **group homes** became the preferred housing choice during the first 20 years of the deinstitutionalization movement. These facilities looked like other houses, were located in residential neighbourhoods, and housed an average of 14 people. In many cases, residential care included supports such as homemaker services, respite care, and life-skills training (Roeher Institute, 1996).

A growing dissatisfaction with the group home system resulted in the development of a broader range of housing options for people living with disabilities. Some of these options are described below:

- *Health-related institutions* are institutions of varying sizes for people who require nursing or medical care and support services such as life-skills training.
- *Care facilities and group homes* are nonmedical residences that provide 24-hour support.
- *Room and board* is an arrangement whereby room, meals, laundry, and other services are provided in private residences to those who require minimal support.

- *Supported housing* refers to individual apartments or housing units for people who are generally independent but may require assistance with meal preparation, housework, or activities of daily living.
- *Parental care* is provided by a foster family to a person with a disability (usually a child) outside of the family home.
- *Independent living* is an arrangement whereby a person with a disability lives (either alone or with a spouse or roommate) in a single-detached home or apartment (Roeher, 1996).

The development of additional housing designs and programs has helped make independent living a reality for many people with disabilities. For example, the Canada Mortgage and Housing Corporation subsidizes the modification of residences to make them more accessible, adaptable to the changing functional needs of residents, or safer and healthier. According to the 1991 HALS, about 75 percent of people with disabilities live in single-detached homes, apartments, or other independent housing.

III. THE ROLE OF GOVERNMENT IN DISABILITY ISSUES

INITIATIVES IN THE 1980S

The United Nations' declaration of 1981 as the International Year of Disabled Persons, and its designation of 1983 to 1993 as the International Decade of Disabled Persons, sparked efforts on the part of the Canadian government to make the full inclusion of people with disabilities a reality. In the 1980s, a number of committees and government departments with a disability focus were established. For example, the federal Status of Disabled Persons Secretariat was set up to raise public awareness of disability issues and support the inclusion of people with disabilities in Canadian society. The federal government also established the Standing Committee on Human Rights and the Status of Disabled Persons to consult with people in the disability community and make recommendations to Parliament.

A historic step was taken when the federal government established the Special Committee on the Disabled and the Handicapped to study the needs of people and existing supports. The committee's 1981 report, titled *Obstacles*, called attention to the various types of **barriers** facing people with disabilities; among the barriers identified in the report were *physical* barriers that prevented people with disabilities from accessing public buildings, and *attitudinal* barriers that limited access to certain health and social services (Roeher Institute, 1996).

A whole new set of legal rights and freedoms for people with disabilities came with the 1982 Canadian Charter of Rights and Freedoms and the 1985 Canadian Human Rights Act. The Charter prohibited physical and mental disability as a basis for discrimination and "marked the first time that any national Constitution in the world referred specifically to persons with disabilities" (Human Resources Development Canada, 1998a, 1).

Eliminating Barriers to Access

Human rights legislation prompted a flurry of reforms aimed at eliminating the barriers to access faced by people with disabilities. For example, communication systems were modified so that people with speech or hearing impairments can now use teletypewriter (TTY), voice carry over (VCO), and hearing carry over (HCO) telephone systems. Voice-activated computers, "talking books," videotapes, and other alternatives to written communication were made available in educational, government, and other public institutions. More recently, Canada's major television broadcasters have been required to provide closed-captioning in their local news programming.

Changes to the National Building Code of Canada make it mandatory for newly constructed public buildings—such as office buildings, restaurants, stores, and schools—to be **barrier-free**. In addition, all existing government buildings have been renovated to improve accessibility. New, barrier-free buildings are being designed and built to allow entrance and use by persons with physical or sensory disabilities; included in these buildings are Braille elevator controls, motion-sensitive electric doors, and wheelchair-accessible washrooms.

The ability to move from place to place within and outside the community is important to persons with disabilities. To promote barrier-free access within their transportation and related systems, provincial and local governments have made public transit wheelchair-accessible and introduced visual and auditory traffic control signals, wider sidewalks with curb cuts, and designated handicapped parking stalls.

INITIATIVES IN THE 1990S

Following the Conference of Federal, Provincial, and Territorial Ministers of Social Services in 1992, Mainstream 1992 was launched for the purpose of developing a framework that would guide the full integration of Canadians with disabilities into the mainstream of society. Mainstream 1992 was the catalyst for a variety of actions that were taken in the 1990s to improve conditions for people with disabilities. These actions included the passage of federal legislation to improve disabled people's access to electoral, communication, and legal systems and a commitment of federal funds to support further research on disability issues (Human Resources Development Canada, 1998a). Between 1991 and 1996, several hundred projects to improve access to transportation, education, housing, employment, and communications were funded through Canada's National Strategy for the Integration of Persons with Disabilities.

By 1996 the federal government had realized that far more action on disability issues was needed. It was decided that future efforts would be focused on reducing the following three types of barriers facing Canadians with disabilities:

1) personal day-to-day challenges of living with a disability;
2) attitudinal barriers presented by people who focus on a person's disability rather than what he or she can contribute to society; and
3) systemic challenges—the result of confusing and uncoordinated government policies and programs—that prevent a transition from dependence to independence (Human Resources Development Canada, 1999c).

In 1996 a Task Force on Disability Issues was appointed to consult with Canadians across the country and make recommendations that would "bring persons with disabilities closer to full participation in society and the economy" (Human Resources Development Canada, 1998a). Many of the task force's recommendations have already been acted on. For example, the federal government has:

- expanded tax credits to cover disability-related medical expenses;
- given additional funding to organizations that serve the disability community;
- amended the Canadian Human Rights Act to ensure that federal government employers and service providers accommodate employees with disabilities;
- revised the Canada Evidence Act to improve access to the justice system; and
- established the Opportunities Fund to help people with disabilities find and keep jobs (Human Resources Development Canada, 1998a, 1999c).

In Unison: A Canadian Approach to Disability Issues

Cooperation among the various levels of government is essential to the advancement of policies and programs for people with disabilities. The social union paved the way for governments to focus on a number of common concerns. By mid-1996, the ministers responsible for social services had identified Canadians with disabilities as a national priority. A policy framework titled *In Unison: A Canadian Approach to Disability Issues* was developed to guide future efforts in this area. In preparing the following vision statement for the *In Unison* initiative, the first ministers drew upon some of the statements Canadians with disabilities had made during the consultations with the Task Force on Disability Issues:

> Persons with disabilities participate as full citizens in all aspects of Canadian society. The full participation of persons with disabilities requires the commitment of all segments of society. The realization of the vision will allow persons with disabilities to maximize their independence and enhance their well-being through access to required supports and the elimination of barriers that prevent their full participation. (Canada, 1999j)

Exhibit 14.6 outlines the various components of the *In Unison* vision.

EXHIBIT 14.6

THE *IN UNISON* VISION

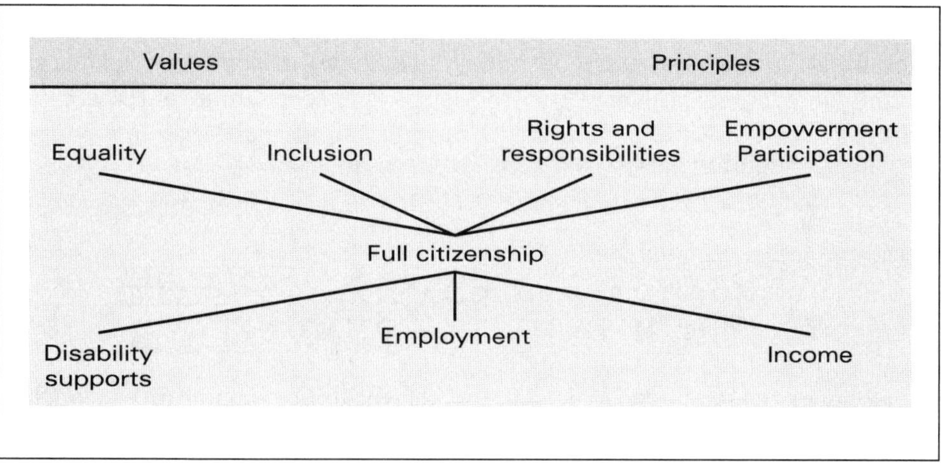

Source: Canada (1999), *In Unison: A Canadian Approach to Disability Issues* [on-line], available: http://socialunion.gc.ca/pwd/unison/unison_e.html [2000 May 11].

Full citizenship for persons with disabilities—the overriding theme of *In Unison*—is to be achieved by means of the three "building blocks" described below:

1) *Disability supports.* A variety of goods, services, and supports—including technical aids, special equipment, life-skills training, and interpreter services—will be made available to help people with disabilities perform the tasks of daily living and maximize personal and financial independence.
2) *Employment.* Greater access to education, increased flexibility in training programs, and other supports that enhance employability and encourage people with disabilities to enter (or re-enter) the workforce will be provided.
3) *Income.* Although independence achieved through employment will be rewarded, income-security programs will be available to people with disabilities who are unemployed.

In Unison also requires government to report on a regular basis its progress in lifting barriers and promoting inclusion (Canada, 1999j).

The *In Unison* initiative is said to reflect the social attitudes and changing needs of people with disabilities in Canada. To match those attitudes and needs, the framework calls for a new approach to disability-related programs and services (see Exhibit 14.7). In addition, *In Unison* focuses attention on those populations—such as women, Aboriginal Canadians, and young people—that face particular social and economic challenges because of a disability. For example, the development of disability-related policies and programs for Aboriginal people is being guided by input from a wide range of groups, including the Aboriginal Technical Committee on Social Policy, the Aboriginal Reference Group on Disability Issues, and the National Clearing House on Aboriginal Disability Issues (Canada, 1999j).

IV. VOLUNTARY ORGANIZATIONS AND THE DISABILITY COMMUNITY

In Unison recognizes the importance of the **disability community**—which includes individuals, groups, and voluntary organizations—in identifying disability issues and contributing to policy and program development. To ensure the continued participation of the disability community, governments provide funding and other supports for voluntary organizations that serve people with disabilities. This section looks briefly at the goals and activities of some of those organizations.

EXHIBIT 14.7

A NEW APPROACH TO DISABILITY ISSUES

OLD . . .	NEW . . .
Recipients →	Participants
Passive income support →	Active measures to promote employment in addition to providing necessary income support
Dependence →	Independence
Government responsibility →	Shared Responsibility
Labelled as "unemployable" →	Identification of work skills
Disincentives to leave income support →	Incentives to seek employment and volunteer opportunities
Insufficient employment supports →	Opportunities to develop skills and experience
Program-centred approach →	Person-centred approach
Insufficient portability of benefits and services →	Portable benefits and services
Multiple access requirements →	Integrated access requirements

Source: Canada (1999), *In Unison: A Canadian Approach to Disability Issues* [on-line], available: http://socialunion.gc.ca/pwd/unison/unison_e.html [2000 May 11].

CANADIAN ASSOCIATION FOR COMMUNITY LIVING

The Canadian Association for Community Living (CACL) is a private, non-profit national federation of over 400 local associations across Canada. Since its inception in 1958, CACL has worked on behalf of persons with an intellectual disability.

CACL is engaged in a variety of efforts aimed at promoting the full inclusion of people with intellectual disabilities in Canadian society. These efforts include the following:

- Building and supporting personal networks for people with intellectual disabilities and their families.

- Developing and advocating for programs, services, supports and policy to ensure that people with intellectual disabilities have opportunities for meaningful family life.
- Supporting individuals with intellectual disabilities to find meaningful jobs in regular workplaces.
- Continuing the fight for integrated and inclusive education for children with intellectual disabilities.
- Demonstrating, advocating, and establishing programs for people with intellectual disabilities who are aging or who are without family support.
- Advocating for the closing of all institutions in Canada and abroad.
- Supporting the overall meaningful inclusion of people with intellectual disabilities in the community (CACL, 2000, 1).

CACL has been a driving force behind government decisions to deinstitutionalize people with intellectual disabilities and to assist in integrating former institutionalized residents into the community. In addition to these efforts, CACL has worked closely with the federal government to develop community-based supports to take the place of institutional programs, and to demonstrate that people with disabilities can function in noninstitutional settings.

INDEPENDENT LIVING CENTRES

By the 1980s the rehabilitation model was losing ground to new approaches to disability that were more compatible with the principles underlying the human rights movements of the 1960s and 1970s. The **independent living (IL) model** was one approach that rapidly gained popularity in Canada. Whereas old models operated on the premise that people with disabilities were dependent and in need of medical treatment, the IL approach "enables persons with disabilities to have access to resources which ensure that individuals have the right to examine options, make choices, take ... risks[,] and ... make mistakes" (CAILC, n.d.). Exhibit 14.8 presents a comparison of the rehabilitation and independent living models.

The IL philosophy is based on the following four principles:

1) *Consumer control*. The people who use a particular service participate in the development and administration of that service.
2) *Cross-disability*. Programs and services under the IL umbrella are developed for people with any type of disability.
3) *Community-based centres*. Facilities are established in communities to meet community needs and complement existing community services.

Exhibit 14.8

A COMPARISON OF THE REHABILITATION AND INDEPENDENT LIVING MODELS

	REHABILITATION MODEL	INDEPENDENT LIVING MODEL
Focus of attention	Disability, illness	Ability, wellness
Perceived problem	Insufficient vocational skills	Dependence on professionals
Where problem resides	In the individual	In the environment, society
Proposed intervention	Medical care, vocational rehabilitation	Removal of barriers, self-help, advocacy, peer support
Preferred setting for intervention	Segregation (e.g., sheltered workshops, special schools, custodial institutions)	Integration (e.g., full participation in mainstream workplaces, schools, independent living units)
Social role	Professional/client, physician/patient	Consumer
One in control	Professional	Consumer
Rights and responsibilities	State is paternalistic; individual is relieved of personal responsibility	Individual is self-determined and responsible for own decisions and actions
Likely outcomes	Individual is marginalized and disenfranchised; dependent; takes passively	Individual is empowered; a full participant in society; self-sufficient; gives actively

Sources: Adapted from Gerben DeJong (1979, October), "Independent Living: From Social Movement to Analytic Paradigm," *Archives of Physical Medicine and Rehabilitation, 60*(10); Canadian Association of Independent Living Centres, *A Guide to Independent Living Centres* (Ottawa, 1990); and Canadian Association of Independent Living Centres, *A Time for Change, The Time for Choices: A Proposal for Improving Social Security Arrangements for Canadians with Disabilities* (Ottawa, 1994). Courtesy of the Canadian Association of Independent Living Centres.

4) *Integration and full participation.* The inclusion of people with disabilities is promoted through centre programs.

In many ways, the IL philosophy has shaped the way in which social welfare and related programs have responded to people with disabilities in the last two decades. For example, the IL approach encourages the development of organizations *of* people with disabilities, not just *for* people with disabilities. This means that people who use an agency's services also work for the agency as paid staff or participate on the agency's board of directors (CAILC, 1997).

A direct result of Canada's independent living movement has been the establishment of **independent living centres** (ILCs). All ILCs are private, nonprofit organizations that are controlled by people with disabilities. While many social welfare programs concentrate on helping individuals adapt to their environment, ILC programs focus on adapting the environment so that it meets the individual's needs. This approach encourages people "to focus on the barriers in society, rather than being told that the individual's disability is the barrier." ILCs provide four core programs to help people with disabilities live more independently: (1) information and referral; (2) peer support counselling; (3) independent living/empowerment skills development; and (4) research and demonstration (CAILC, 1997).

COUNCIL OF CANADIANS WITH DISABILITIES

The Council of Canadians with Disabilities (CCD) was set up by people with disabilities "to create a voice for Canadians with disabilities and to promote the full participation and equal opportunity of people with disabilities in Canadian society" (Roeher Institute, 1996, 166). The CCD consists of 14 member organizations across the country, including the Prince Edward Island Council of the Disabled, the Manitoba League of People with Disabilities, the Alberta Committee of Citizens with Disabilities, and the DisAbled Women's Network Canada.

The CCD, which speaks on behalf of many Canadians with disabilities, bases its activities on four main principles:

1) *Citizenship*—barriers to the full participation in Canadian society must be eliminated.
2) *Self-determination*—people with disabilities assert the right to live their own lives and make their own decisions.
3) *Consumer control*—people with disabilities seek involvement in decision-making processes that affect them.
4) *Equality*—any piece of legislation that is discriminatory must be revised and brought into line with the Charter of Rights and Freedoms (CCD, 2000a).

The CCD has been a powerful influence in the gradual breakdown of barriers that prevent people with disabilities from fully participating in society. For example, CCD's lobbying efforts have helped make transportation systems and voting practices more accessible (CCD, 2000a). At present, the CCD is assessing the feasibility of enacting a Canadians with Disabilities Act, which has been described as "comprehensive barrier-removal legislation" (Kerzner and Baker, 1999, 2).

COMMUNITY CLUBHOUSES

The **clubhouse model** originated in 1948 with the opening of Fountain House in New York City; today there are approximately 400 clubhouses in operation around the world. Clubhouses are community-based programs that give people with mental-health problems an opportunity to socialize and work toward common goals.

Clubhouse staff and members share the work required to keep the clubhouse running smoothly. For example, work units may be struck to publish a newsletter, provide food services, raise funds, orient new members, advocate on behalf of members, and maintain the building and grounds. It is believed that through clubhouse events and mutual support, members "can achieve or regain the confidence and skills necessary to live, learn, work, and socialize as independently as possible in the setting of their choice" (Abby Clubhouse, n.d.).

V. IMPLICATIONS FOR SOCIAL WORK PRACTICE

THE OPEN HOUSE APPROACH

Over the years, social workers, like other helping professionals, have gradually modified their approach to working with people with disabilities. The evolution of social work practice with the disability community in many respects parallels the transition from segregation to mainstreaming (see Exhibit 14.9). The **open house concept** emphasizes the full participation of people with disabilities in school, work, social, and other activities and their enjoyment of the same rights and privileges as nondisabled Canadians. Each component of the open house approach as it relates to social work practice is reviewed below.

Accommodation

Accommodation involves modifying the environment so that a person with a disability is able to participate in activities that take place in that environment. Social workers can promote accommodation in a variety of ways. For

Exhibit 14.9

FROM SEGREGATION TO MAINSTREAMING: A CONCEPTUAL MODEL

WAREHOUSE →	GREENHOUSE →	OPEN HOUSE
Caring for	Enabling	Accomodating
Protection	Support	Autonomy/empowerment
Labelled permanently incapacitated	Adaptation of individual	Adaptation of social and physical environment
Deemed incompetent	Recognition of capacity	Rights/responsibilites

Sources: Canada (1999), *In Unison: A Canadian Approach to Disability Issues*, Appendix D [on-line], available: http://socialunion.gc.ca/pwd/unison/appendixd_e.html [2000 June 5].

instance, a worker may help someone obtain wheelchair access or special computer equipment that is needed for training or employment. Similarly, social workers can help people with disabilities advocate for change in a public transportation system so that they can access work, school, and community activities.

Autonomy and Empowerment

Although social workers do not directly empower others, they can help people gain the knowledge and skills that enhance independence and a sense of personal empowerment. Social workers facilitate many activities that are personally empowering, including assertiveness training, life-skills training, problem-solving skill building, and peer leadership training. In order for clients with disabilities to become empowered, social workers may need to challenge attitudes, values, or techniques that are ultimately disempowering. The Roeher Institute (1996, 177) suggests four areas of practice that may need to change:

1) *The "best-interests approach."* Rather than doing what seems to be in the person's best interests, workers can provide adequate information about possible options so that people can make their own informed choices and decisions.
2) *Paternalistic attitudes*. Instead of protecting individuals from the consequences of their choices, workers can encourage people to express their wishes and exercise their right to self-determination; they can also acknowledge the capabilities that people have to manage their own lives.

3) *Professional control.* Instead of supporting rules, diagnoses, assessments, and other mechanisms that classify and control individuals, workers can help others advocate for themselves, challenge oppressing labels, and regain control in their lives.

4) *Cost-effectiveness agendas.* Rather than withholding resources because it is "fiscally responsible" to do so, workers can demonstrate how the consumption of resources can meet individual needs and contribute to "output effectiveness."

Adaptation of the Social and Physical Environment

Social workers help staff in social agencies, educational institutions, and other organizations focus on the problems that reside in their own systems rather than on the person with the disability. In addition, social workers participate in reviews of agency policies, programs, and practices, as well as in modifications of agency systems to make them more inclusive (i.e., barrier-free). Many social workers who serve the disability community find that a community development approach is more effective than traditional counselling approaches: "By promoting community development, the focus is shifted away from individuals and placed on strengthening the capacity of communities to be inclusive" (Panitch, 1998, 10).

Rights and Responsibilities

Traditionally, social workers have called attention to, and demanded changes in, policies and programs that inhibit independent living for people with disabilities. In recent years, however, social workers have shifted much of their attention to helping people with disabilities speak out and assert their rights on their own behalf. One of the underlying themes of the disability movement is the demand for "rights, not charity"; social workers can play an important role in helping people with disabilities gain both control of resources and the right to make decisions that affect their lives.

Introduction

For much of Canada's history, social attitudes have kept people with disabilities excluded—often through institutionalization—from mainstream society. The disability rights movement sought to remove the barriers to opportunity faced by people with disabilities. That movement and other efforts have led to a greater public acceptance and government accommodation of people with disabilities.

A Profile of Persons with Disabilities

Various terms are used to refer to a person's limited capability. About 4.2 million Canadians have a disability, the majority of whom have a physical disability. Much of what we know about Canadians with disabilities comes from the Health and Activity Limitation Survey. The likelihood that a person will have a disability increases with age. Disability has many potential causes; some disabilities whose causes are known are preventable. Certain groups, such as Aboriginal people and women, are at high risk for social and economic problems as a result of their disability.

Meeting Income, Employment, and Housing Needs

The disability income system includes programs aimed at providing earnings replacement, income support, and compensation. Recent reforms to provincial and territorial disability income programs have included the introduction of individualized funding and attempts to increase work incentives. Employment and rehabilitation programs for people with disabilities are becoming more inclusive. Under the Employability Assistance for People with Disabilities initiative, regional governments are developing programs that help people with disabilities prepare for, find, and keep jobs. The deinstitutionalization movement resulted in an increased demand for alternative housing among people with disabilities.

The Role of Government in Disability Issues

An international recognition of people with disabilities motivated Canada to develop more inclusive disability policies. To address the needs of people with disabilities, communication systems have been modified, legislation mandating barrier-free buildings has been introduced, and provincial and local governments have promoted barrier-free access within their transportation systems. A national policy framework entitled *In Unison* was developed to guide the future development of policies and programs for people with disabilities. Disability-related supports, employment, and income are the building blocks of full citizenship.

Voluntary Organizations and the Disability Community

The "disability community" is made up of people with disabilities and voluntary organizations that provide disability-related programs and services. These organizations include the Canadian Association for Community Living, independent living centres, the Council of Canadians with Disabilities, and community clubhouses.

Implications for Social Work Practice

Social workers can use the open house approach to help people with disabilities participate fully in society. This approach emphasizes accommodation, autonomy, and empowerment, adaptation of the social and physical environment, and rights and responsibilities.

KEY TERMS

DISABILITY RIGHTS MOVEMENT 322
NORMALIZATION 322
DISORDER 324
IMPAIRMENT 324
DISABILITY 324
HANDICAP 324
PHYSICAL DISABILITY 325
MENTAL ILLNESS 326
INTELLECTUAL DISABILITY 326
PORTABILITY 331
INDIVIDUALIZED FUNDING 331
DEINSTITUTIONALIZATION MOVEMENT 333
GROUP HOMES 333
BARRIERS 334
BARRIER-FREE 335
DISABILITY COMMUNITY 338
INDEPENDENT LIVING MODEL 340
INDEPENDENT LIVING CENTRES (ILCs) 342
CLUBHOUSE MODEL 343
OPEN HOUSE CONCEPT 343
ACCOMMODATION 343

APPENDIX A

A CENTURY OF RESPONSE:
Historical Highlights in Social Welfare and Related Systems

1900–1910

1900 The majority of female property owners gain the right to vote in municipal elections.

1908 The Juvenile Delinquents Act is passed.

The Annuities Act—precursor of the Old Age Pension Act—is passed.

1910–1920

1914 Ontario becomes the first province to enact workers' compensation legislation when it passes the Workmen's Compensation Act.

1916 Manitoba becomes the first province to give women the right to vote.

Canada's first mothers' allowances are implemented in Manitoba.

1918 Women gain the right to vote in federal elections.

The Canadian Mental Health Association is founded.

The Canadian National Institute for the Blind opens.

1919 The Soldier Settlement Act is passed.

1920–1929

1920 The Returned Soldiers' Insurance Act is passed.

1921 The first woman is elected to the House of Commons.

1927 The Old Age Pension Act is passed.

1928 The Canadian Association of Social Workers is founded.

1929 The Juvenile Delinquents Act is amended.

Women become eligible for appointment to the Canadian Senate after they are declared "persons" by the Judicial Committee of the British Privy Council.

1930–1939

1930 The federal government provides municipalities with unemployment relief.

The War Veterans Allowance Act is passed.

1935 The On to Ottawa Trek takes place.

The Employment and Social Insurance Act is passed (and repealed in 1937).

1937 The Royal Commission on Dominion–Provincial Relations (Rowell-Sirois Commission) is appointed by the federal government.

1938 The Canadian Association of Social Workers develops a code of ethics.

1939 The Youth Training Act is passed.

1940–1949

1940 The Unemployment Insurance Act is passed.

1943 The Marsh Report on Social Security is released by the House of Commons Advisory Committee on Post-War Reconstruction.

1944 The Family Allowances Act is passed (program is implemented in 1945).

The National Housing Act is passed.

The Department of National Health and Welfare is established.

The Department of Veterans Affairs is established.

1945 The Veterans Rehabilitation Act is passed.

1946 The Central Mortgage and Housing Corporation (later renamed Canada Mortgage and Housing Corporation) is established.

The War Veterans Allowance Act is passed (replaces War Veterans Allowance Act of 1930).

1947 Canada's first health insurance program begins in Saskatchewan.

1948 The federal government implements settlement and integration programs for immigrants.

1950–1959

1951 The Indian Act is amended.

The Old Age Assistance Act is passed.

The Old Age Security Act is passed.

The Blind Persons Act is passed.

Canada's first social work doctorate program is established at the University of Toronto.

1952 Ontario becomes the first province to enact equal pay legislation.

1953 The Immigration Act is amended.

1954 The Disabled Persons Act is passed.

1956 The Unemployment Assistance Act is passed (federal government begins sharing cost of provincial social assistance).

The Hospital Insurance Act is passed.

1957 The Hospital Insurance and Diagnostic Services Act is passed.

1958 The Canadian Association for Community Living is founded.

1960–1969

1960 Aboriginal people gain the right to vote in federal elections.

1961 The Vocational Rehabilitation Act is passed.

The Canadian Bill of Rights is passed.

1964 The Youth Allowances Act is passed.

1965 The Canada and Quebec Pension Plans are introduced.

1966 The Canada Assistance Plan is initiated.

The Guaranteed Income Supplement is introduced.

The Medical Care Act is passed.

Canada's first Bachelor of Social Work program is established.

1967 The Canadian Association of Schools of Social Work is established.

1968 The Senate Committee on Poverty (the Croll Committee) is appointed by the federal government.

The Divorce Act is amended (makes divorce easier to obtain).

1969 Statement of the Government of Canada on Indian Policy (White Paper) is released.

Women gain legal access to information on birth control and the use of contraceptives.

Homosexual acts between consenting adults are decriminalized.

1970–1979

1971 The Unemployment Insurance Act is amended.

The Senate Committee on Poverty releases its final report.

The Office of Status of Women (federal) is established.

The Canada Labour Code is amended (gives maternity leave to female federal government employees).

The National Council of Welfare is founded.

1973 Newfoundland's Neglected Adults Welfare Act—the first legislation in Canada to protect adults from neglect—is passed.

A Social Security Review is launched by the Trudeau government.

The Canadian Council on the Status of Women is established.

1974 Canada's first large-scale guaranteed annual income experiment, MINCOME, is launched in Manitoba.

1975 International Women's Year (followed by Decade for Women) is declared.

The Spouse's Allowance is introduced.

1976 A new Immigration Act is passed (implemented in 1978).

1977 Established Programs Financing—which puts funding for hospital, medicare, and postsecondary education under one funding formula—is initiated.

The Canadian Human Rights Act is passed.

Quebec becomes the first province to forbid discrimination on basis of sexual orientation.

1978 The federal government establishes a Non-Profit Housing Program.

The Refundable Child Tax Credit is introduced (first time the Canadian income tax system is used to deliver benefits to families who do not pay income tax).

1980–1989

1980 The International Classification of Impairments, Disabilities, and Handicaps (ICIDH) is released by the World Health Organization.

The Special Committee on the Disabled and the Handicapped is established.

1981 The International Year of Disabled Persons (followed by the International Decade of Disabled Persons, 1983-93) is declared.

The Special Committee on the Disabled and the Handicapped releases *Obstacles* report.

1982 The Canadian Charter of Rights and Freedoms is entrenched in the Canadian Constitution.

The National Native Alcohol and Drug Abuse Program is established.

The National Clearinghouse on Family Violence is established.

1984 The federal election is won by the Progressive Conservative Party under Brian Mulroney.

The Canada Health Act is passed.

1985 The Royal Commission on the Economic Union and Development Prospects for Canada (Macdonald Commission) releases its final report.

The Indian Act is amended (restores status and property rights of Aboriginal women).

1986 The first Health and Activity Limitation Survey (HALS) is completed.

The Child Sexual Abuse Initiative is launched.

The Employment Equity Act is passed (ensures equitable participation of women and other minority groups in the workforce).

1987 The Meech Lake Accord to amend the Constitution is agreed to by the federal and provincial governments. (It fails in 1990 when two provinces refuse to ratify it.)

The Parliamentary Committee on Human Rights and the Status of Disabled Persons is established.

1988 Prince Edward Island's Adult Protection Act—the first legislation in Canada to protect adults from both neglect and abuse—is passed.

The Refundable Child Tax Credit is converted to the Non-Refundable Child Tax Credit.

Phase I of the federal Family Violence Initiative is announced.

The Canada–U.S. Free Trade Agreement is ratified.

The Seniors Independence Program is launched.

The Canadian Multiculturalism Act is passed.

1989 The House of Commons resolves to end child poverty by the year 2000.

Clawbacks are introduced into family allowances and Old Age Security.

1990–2000

1990 Toronto becomes the first municipality in Canada to extend same-sex benefits to municipal workers.

The Unemployment Insurance Act is amended (responsibility for funding shifts to employers and employees).

1991 The Canada–Quebec Accord is signed.

Phase II of the federal Family Violence Initiative is announced.

The Royal Commission on Aboriginal Peoples is appointed by the federal government.

A "cap" is imposed on the Canada Assistance Plan.

Canada ratifies the United Nations Convention on the Rights of the Child.

The Goods and Services Tax (GST) is introduced.

The second HALS is completed.

1992 Mainstream 1992 is launched to develop a framework for guiding the full integration of people with disabilities into society.

The Charlottetown Accord to amend the Constitution is agreed to by Canada's first ministers. (It is subsequently defeated in a national referendum.)

1993 The Liberal Party under Jean Chrétien defeats the Progressive Conservatives in the federal election.

The International Year of the World's Indigenous People (followed by International Decade of the World's Indigenous People) is declared.

The findings of the Violence Against Women Survey—Canada's first national survey of violence against women—are released.

The Brighter Futures initiative is launched.

Stalking becomes a criminal offence.

Family allowances are replaced by the Canada Child Tax Benefit.

The Ventures in Independence program for seniors is initiated.

The Unemployment Insurance Act is amended (reduces benefits).

The North American Free Trade Agreement (NAFTA) is ratified.

The Conservatives under Ralph Klein win a victory over the Liberals in Alberta's provincial election.

1994 A Social Security Review is launched by the Chrétien government.

Public consultations on immigration begin.

The International Year of the Family is declared.

The National Longitudinal Survey of Children and Youth is launched.

The National Framework on Aging is released.

The federal government's Program Review is completed.

1995 The New Horizons: Partners in Aging initiative is launched. (It is terminated in 1997.)

Aboriginal Head Start is introduced.

The First Nations and Inuit Child Care Initiative is launched.

The Voluntary Sector Roundtable is established.

Ontario's provincial election is won by the Conservatives under Mike Harris.

Federal Plan for Gender Equity is released.

The federal budget announces plan to cut transfers to the regional governments.

Intoxication in crimes of violence (including sexual assault) is removed as a basis of legal defence.

1996 The Task Force on Disability Issues is established and releases its final report that same year.

The Royal Commission on Aboriginal Peoples releases its final report.

The Canada Assistance Plan is replaced by the Canada Health and Social Transfer (CHST).

Unemployment Insurance (UI) is converted to Employment Insurance (EI).

The child poverty rate rises to almost 21 percent.

The Federal-Provincial-Territorial Council on Social Policy Renewal is established to develop the social union.

1997 Phase III of the Family Violence Initiative begins.

The Employability Assistance for People with Disabilities (EAPD) replaces the Vocational Rehabilitation of Disabled Persons Act.

The Canadian Framework for Future Immigration is released.

The Canada Child Tax Benefit (CCTB) is introduced.

Canada's National Survey of Giving, Volunteering and Participating is launched.

The implementation of welfare-to-work programs in Ontario is made possible by the creation of Ontario Works, the province's new social assistance program.

Canada's first comprehensive family/child policy is introduced in Quebec.

The National Transition Home Survey is launched.

The federal government makes a formal apology to Aboriginal people in the form of a Statement of Reconciliation.

The Aboriginal Healing Strategy is launched.

1998 Canada is found to have the tenth-largest income gap between rich and poor in a United Nations survey of 17 countries.

Gathering Strength—Canada's Aboriginal Action Plan is released.

The Aboriginal Healing Foundation is established.

The National Child Benefit is introduced.

The federal government achieves a balanced budget for the first time in nearly 20 years.

Ontario's Social Work and Social Service Work Act is passed.

Human Resources Strategic Analysis of Social Work in Canada is launched.

1999 The International Year of the Older Person is declared.

Ontario becomes the first province to extend to same-sex couples the same rights as those extended to heterosexual common-law couples.

A Framework to Improve the Social Union for Canadians is released.

The National Children's Agenda is launched.

In Unison: A Canadian Approach to Disability Issues is launched.

The Equalization Program is renewed for another five years.

CHST transfers are increased for a five-year period.

The Supporting Communities Partnership Initiative begins (aims to eliminate and prevent homelessness).

2000 Canada's unemployment rate falls to its lowest level in 25 years (6.8 percent).

The Immigration and Refugee Protection Act is tabled in the House of Commons.

APPENDIX B

A FRAMEWORK TO IMPROVE THE SOCIAL UNION FOR CANADIANS

An Agreement between the Government of Canada and the Governments of the Provinces and Territories February 4, 1999

The following agreement is based upon a mutual respect between orders of government and a willingness to work more closely together to meet the needs of Canadians.

1. PRINCIPLES

Canada's social union should reflect and give expression to the fundamental values of Canadians—equality, respect for diversity, fairness, individual dignity and responsibility, and mutual aid and our responsibilities for one another.

Within their respective constitutional jurisdictions and powers, governments commit to the following principals:

ALL CANADIANS ARE EQUAL

- Treat all Canadians with fairness and equity
- Promote equality of opportunity for all Canadians
- Respect the equality, rights and dignity of all Canadian women and men and their diverse needs

MEETING THE NEEDS OF CANADIANS

- Ensure access for all Canadians, wherever they live or move in Canada, to essential social programs and services of reasonably comparable quality
- Provide appropriate assistance to those in need
- Respect the principals of medicare: comprehensiveness, universality, portability, public administration and accessibility
- Promote the full and active participation of all Canadians in Canada's social and economic life
- Work in partnership with individuals, families, communities, voluntary organizations, business and labour, and ensure appropriate opportunities for Canadians to have meaningful input into social policies and programs

SUSTAINING SOCIAL PROGRAMS AND SERVICES

- Ensure adequate, affordable, stable and sustaining funding for social programs

ABORIGINAL PEOPLES OF CANADA

- For greater certainty, nothing in this agreement abrogates or derogates from any Aboriginal, treaty or other rights of Aboriginal peoples including self-government

2. MOBILITY WITHIN CANADA

All governments believe that the freedom of movement of Canadians to pursue opportunities anywhere in Canada is an essential element of Canadian citizenship.

Governments will ensure that no new barriers to mobility are created in new social policy initiatives.

Governments will eliminate, within three years, any residency-based policies or practices which constrain access to postsecondary education, training, health and social services and social assistance unless they can be demonstrated to be reasonable and consistent with the principles of the Social Union Framework.

Accordingly, sector Ministers will submit annual reports to the Ministerial Council identifying residency-based barriers to access and providing action plans to eliminate them.

Governments are also committed to ensure, by July 1, 2001, full compliance with the mobility provisions of the Agreement on Internal Trade by all entities subject to these provisions, including the requirements for mutual recognition of occupational qualifications and for eliminating residency requirements for access to employment opportunities.

3. INFORMING CANADIANS — PUBLIC ACCOUNTABILITY AND TRANSPARENCY

Canada's social union can be strengthened by enhancing each government's transparency and accountability to its constituents. Each government therefore agrees to:

ACHIEVING AND MEASURING RESULTS

- Monitor and measure outcomes of its social programs and report regularly to its constituents on the performance of these programs
- Share information and best practices to support the development of outcome measures, and work with other governments to develop, over time, comparable indicators to measure progress on agreed objectives
- Publicly recognize and explain the respective roles and contributions of governments
- Use funds transferred from another order of government for the purposes agreed and pass on increases to its residents
- Use third parties, as appropriate, to assist in assessing progress on social priorities

INVOLVEMENT OF CANADIANS

- Ensure effective mechanisms for Canadians to participate in developing social priorities and reviewing outcomes

ENSURING FAIR AND TRANSPARENT PRACTICES

- Make eligibility criteria and service commitments for social programs publicly available
- Have in place appropriate mechanisms for citizens to appeal unfair administrative practices and bring complaints about access and service
- Report publicly on citizens' appeals and complaints, ensuring that confidentiality requirements are met

4. WORKING IN PARTNERSHIP FOR CANADIANS

JOINT PLANNING AND COLLABORATION

The Ministerial Council has demonstrated the benefits of joint planning and mutual help through which governments share knowledge and learn from each other.

Governments therefore agree to

- Undertake joint planning to share information on social trends, problems and priorities and to work together to identify priorities for collaborative action

- Collaborate on implementation of joint priorities when this would result in more effective and efficient service to Canadians, including as appropriate joint development of objectives and principles, clarification of roles and responsibilities, and flexible implementation to respect diverse needs and circumstances, complement existing measures and avoid duplication

RECIPROCAL NOTICE AND COLLABORATION

The actions of one government or order of government often have significant effects on other governments. In a manner consistent with the principles of our system of parliamentary government and the budget-making process, governments therefore agree to:

- Give one another advance notice prior to implementation of a major change in a social policy or program which will likely substantially affect another government
- Offer to consult prior to implementing new social policies and programs that are likely to substantially affect other governments or the social union more generally. Governments participating in these consultations will have the opportunity to identify potential duplication and to propose alternative approaches to achieve flexible and effective implementation

EQUITABLE TREATMENT

For any new Canada-wide social initiatives, arrangements made with one province/territory will be made available to all provinces/territories in a manner consistent with their diverse circumstances.

ABORIGINAL PEOPLES

Governments will work with Aboriginal peoples in Canada to find practical solutions to address their pressing needs.

5. THE FEDERAL SPENDING POWER—IMPROVING SOCIAL PROGRAMS FOR CANADIANS

SOCIAL TRANSFERS TO PROVINCES AND TERRITORIES

The use of the federal spending power under the Constitution has been essential to the development of Canada's social union. An important use of the spending power by the Government of Canada has been to transfer money to the provincial and territorial governments. These transfers support the delivery of social programs and services by provinces and territories in order to promote equality of opportunity and mobility for all Canadians and to pursue Canada-wide objectives.

Conditional social transfers have enabled governments to introduce new and innovative social programs, such as Medicare, and to ensure that they are available to all Canadians. When the federal government uses such conditional transfers, whether cost-shared or block-funded, it should proceed in a cooperative manner that is respectful of the provincial and territorial governments and their priorities.

FUNDING PREDICTABILITY

The Government of Canada will consult with provincial and territorial governments at least one year prior to renewal or significant funding changes in existing social transfers to provinces/territories, unless otherwise agreed, and will build due notice provisions into any new social transfers to provincial/territorial governments.

NEW CANADA-WIDE INITIATIVES SUPPORTED BY TRANSFERS TO PROVINCES AND TERRITORIES

With respect to any new Canada-wide initiatives in health care, postsecondary education, social assistance and social services that are funded through intergovernmental transfers, whether block-funded or cost-shared, the Government of Canada will:

- Work collaboratively with all provincial and territorial governments to identify Canada-wide priorities and objectives
- Not introduce such new initiatives without the agreement of a majority of provincial governments

Each provincial and territorial government will determine the detailed program design and mix best suited to its own needs and circumstances to meet the agreed objectives.

A provincial/territorial government which, because of its existing programming, does not require the total transfer to fulfil the agreed objectives would be able to reinvest any funds not required for those objectives in the same or a related priority area.

The Government of Canada and the provincial/territorial governments will agree on an accountability framework for such new social initiatives and investments.

All provincial and territorial governments that meet or commit to meet the agreed Canada-wide objectives and agree to respect the accountability framework will receive their share of available funding.

DIRECT FEDERAL SPENDING

Another use of the federal spending power is making transfers to individuals and to organizations in order to promote equality of opportunity, mobility, and other Canada-wide objectives.

When the federal government introduces new Canada-wide initiatives funded through direct transfers to individuals or organizations for health care, post-secondary education, social assistance and social services, it will, prior to implementation, give at least three months' notice and offer to consult. Governments participating in these consultations will have the opportunity to identify potential duplication and to propose alternative approaches to achieve flexible and effective implementation.

6. DISPUTE AVOIDANCE AND RESOLUTION

Governments are committed to working collaboratively to avoid and resolve intergovernmental disputes. Respecting existing legislative provisions, mechanisms to avoid and resolve disputes should:

- Be simple, timely, efficient, effective and transparent
- Allow maximum flexibility for governments to resolve disputes in a non-adversarial way
- Ensure that sectors design processes appropriate to their needs
- Provide for appropriate use of third parties for expert assistance and advice while assuring democratic accountability by elected officials

Dispute avoidance and resolution will apply to commitments on mobility, intergovernmental transfers, interpretation of the Canada Health Act principles, and, as appropriate, on any new joint initiative.

Sector Ministers should be guided by the following process, as appropriate:

Dispute avoidance

- Governments are committed to working together and avoiding disputes through information-sharing, joint planning, collaboration, advance notice and early consultation, and flexibility in implementation.

Sector negotiations

- Sector negotiations to resolve disputes will be based on joint fact-finding
- A written joint fact-finding report will be submitted to governments involved, who will have the opportunity to comment on the report before its completion
- Governments involved may seek assistance of a third party for fact-finding, advice, or mediation
- At the request of either party in a dispute, fact-finding or mediation reports will be made public

Review provisions

- Any government can require a review of a decision or action one year after it enters into effect or when changing circumstances justify

Each government involved in a dispute may consult and seek advice from third parties, including interested or knowledgeable persons or groups at all stages of the process.

Governments will report publicly on an annual basis on the nature of intergovernmental disputes and their resolution.

ROLE OF THE MINISTERIAL COUNCIL

The Ministerial Council will support sector Ministers by collecting information on effective ways of implementing the agreement and avoiding disputes and receiving reports from jurisdictions on progress on commitments under the Social Union Framework Agreement.

7. REVIEW OF THE SOCIAL UNION FRAMEWORK AGREEMENT

By the end of the third year of the Framework Agreement, governments will jointly undertake a full review of the Agreement and its implementation and make appropriate adjustments to the framework as required. This review will ensure significant opportunities for input and feed-back from Canadians and all interested parties, including social policy experts, private sector and voluntary organizations.

Canadian Intergovernmental Conference Secretariat—Agreement Ref: 800-37/01 [On-line]. Available: http://www.scics.gc.ca/cinfo99/80003701_e.html [2000 September 6].

APPENDIX C

STATEMENT OF RECONCILIATION

LEARNING FROM THE PAST

As Aboriginal and non-Aboriginal Canadians seek to move forward together in a process of renewal, it is essential that we deal with the legacies of the past affecting the Aboriginal peoples of Canada, including the First Nations, Inuit and Métis. Our purpose is not to rewrite history but, rather, to learn from our past and to find ways to deal with the negative impacts that certain historical decisions continue to have in our society today.

The ancestors of First Nations, Inuit and Métis peoples lived on this continent long before explorers from other continents first came to North America. For thousands of years before this country was founded, they enjoyed their own forms of government. Diverse, vibrant Aboriginal nations had ways of life rooted in fundamental values concerning their relationships to the Creator, the environment, and each other, in the role of Elders as the living memory of their ancestors, and in their responsibilities as custodians of the lands, waters and resources of their homelands.

The assistance and spiritual values of the Aboriginal peoples who welcomed the newcomers to this continent too often have been forgotten. The contributions made by all Aboriginal peoples to Canada's development, and the contributions that they continue to make to our society today, have not been properly acknowledged. The Government of Canada today, on behalf of all Canadians, acknowledges those contributions.

Sadly, our history with respect to the treatment of Aboriginal people is not something in which we can take pride. Attitudes of racial and cultural superiority led to a suppression of Aboriginal culture and values. As a country, we are burdened by past actions that resulted in weakening the identity of Aboriginal peoples, their languages and cultures, and outlawing spiritual practices. We must recognize the impact of these actions on the once self-sustaining nations that were disaggregated, disrupted, limited or even destroyed by the dispossession of traditional territory, by the relocation of Aboriginal people, and by some provisions of the Indian Act. We must acknowledge that the result of these actions was the erosion of the political, economic and social systems of Aboriginal people and nations.

Against the backdrop of these historical legacies, it is a remarkable tribute to the strength and endurance of Aboriginal people that they have maintained their historic diversity and identity. The Government of Canada today formally expresses to all Aboriginal people in Canada our profound regret for the past actions of the federal government which have contributed to these difficult pages in the history of our relationship together.

One aspect of our relationship with Aboriginal people over this period that requires particular attention is the Residential School system. This system separated many children from their families and communities and prevented them from speaking their own languages and from learning about their heritage and cultures. In the worst cases, it left legacies of personal pain and distress that continue to reverberate in Aboriginal communities to this day. Tragically some children were the victims of physical and sexual abuse.

The Government of Canada acknowledges the role it played in the development and administration of these schools. Particularly to those individuals who experienced the tragedy of physical and sexual abuse at residential schools, and have carried this burden believing that in some way they must be responsible, we wish to emphasize that what you experienced was not your fault and should never have happened. To those of you who suffered this tragedy at Residential Schools, we are deeply sorry.

In dealing with the legacies of the Residential School system, the Government of Canada proposes to work with First Nations, Inuit and Métis people, the Churches and other interested parties to resolve the long standing issues that must be addressed. We need to work together on a healing strategy to assist individuals and communities in dealing with the consequences of this sad era of our history.

No attempt at reconciliation with Aboriginal people can be complete without reference to the sad events culminating in the death of Métis leader Louis Riel. These events cannot be undone; however, we can and will continue to look for ways of affirming the contributions of Métis people in Canada and of reflecting Louis Riel's proper place in Canada's history.

Reconciliation is an ongoing process. In renewing our partnership, we must ensure that the mistakes which marked our past relationship are not repeated. The Government of Canada recognizes that policies that sought to assimilate Aboriginal people, women and men, were not the way to build a strong country. We must instead continue to find ways in which Aboriginal people can participate fully in the economic, political, cultural and social life of Canada in a manner which preserves and enhances the collective identities of Aboriginal communities, and allows them to evolve and flourish in the future. Working together to achieve our shared goals will benefit all Canadians, Aboriginal and non-Aboriginal alike.

On behalf of the Government of Canada
The Honourable Jane Stewart, P.C., M.P.
Minister of Indian Affairs and Northern Development

The Honourable Ralph Goodale, P.C., M.P.
Federal Interlocutor for Métis and Non-Status Indians

[On-line]. Available: http://www.inac.gc.ca/gs/rec_e.html [2000 September 17]. Excerpted from Indian and Northern Affairs Canada (1997), *Gathering Strength—Canada's Aboriginal Action Plan* (Ottawa: Minister of Public Works and Government Services Canada).

REFERENCES

Abby Clubhouse/Cheamview Clubhouse. (n.d.). *Mental Illness: You Are Not Alone.* Pamphlet. Abbotsford and Chilliwack, B.C.: Author.

Abele, F., Graham, K., Ker, A., Maioni, A., and Phillips, S. (1998). *Talking with Canadians: Citizen Engagement and the Social Union.* Ottawa: Canadian Council on Social Development.

Abel Enterprises. (2000). *Home Page* [On-line]. Available: http://www.hnmentalhealth.com/abel.htm [2000 June 7].

Aboriginal Healing Foundation. (2000a, March 13). *About Us: Mission, Vision, Values* [On-line]. Available: http://www/ahf.ca/english/mission.html [2000 May 23].

———. (2000b, March 13). *Aboriginal Healing Foundation Announces Healing Centre Calls for Proposals* [On-line]. Available: http://www/ahf.ca/english/mission.html [2000 May 23].

Adoption Council of Canada. (2000). *Adoption Trends and a Political Agenda for Ontario* [On-line]. Available: http://www.adoption.ca/sobol.htm [2000 April 27].

Agriculture and Agri-Food Canada. (1998, October 16). *Notes for an Address by Lyle Vanclief, P.C., M.P., Minister of Agriculture and Agri-Food, at the Launch of Canada's Action Plan for Food Security—Canada's Response to the World Food Summit, Toronto, October 16, 1998.* [On-line]. Available: http://www.agr.ca/cb/speeches/s981016e.html [2000 June 28].

Albert, J., and Kirwin, B. (1999). Social and welfare services. In J.A. Marsh (Ed.), *The Canadian Encyclopedia, Year 2000 Edition* (pp. 2191–2192). Toronto: McClelland & Stewart.

Alberta. (1993, September). Premier's Council on the Status of Persons with Disabilities. *Removing Barriers: An Action Plan for Aboriginal People with Disabilities.* Pamphlet. Edmonton: Author.

Alberta Alcohol and Drug Abuse Commission. (1992, May). Poverty and addictions. *Developments, 12*(4).

Alberta Committee of Citizens with Disabilities. (n.d.). *Women with Disabilities: Fact Sheet.* Edmonton: Author.

Alberta eliminates net debt. (1999, June). *Canadian News Facts* (p. 5889). Toronto: MPL Communications.

Alberta struggles with gay issues. (1999, March 16–31). *Canadian News Facts* (p. 5844). Toronto: MPL Communications.

Anderson, G., and Marr, W. (1987). Immigration and social policy. In Shankar A. Yelaja (Ed.), *Canadian Social Policy* (rev. ed., pp. 88–114). Waterloo: Wilfrid Laurier University Press.

Armit, A., and Bourgault, J. (1996). *Hard Choices or No Choices: Assessing Program Review.* Toronto: Institute of Public Administration of Canada.

Armitage, A. (1996). *Social Welfare in Canada Revisited: Facing Up to the Future* (3rd ed.). Don Mills: Oxford University Press.

Armstrong, R. (1999, Winter). Mapping the conditions of First Nations communities. *Canadian Social Trends*, 14–18.

Aycan, Z., and Berry, J.W. (1996). *Impact of Employment-Related Experiences on Immigrants' Psychological Well-Being and Adaptation to Canada* [On-line]. Available: http://www.cpa.ca/cjbsnew/1996/ful_aycan.html [2000 June 8].

Ayed, N. (2000, March 2). Reform MP raises ire of justice minister. *The Canadian Press* [On-line]. Available: http://www.slam.ca/CNEWSPolitics0003/03_reform_CP.html [2000 May 26].

Badets, J., and Howatson-Leo, L. (1999, Spring). Recent immigrants in the workforce. *Canadian Social Trends*, 16–22.

Baker, M. (1997). Women, family policies and the moral right. *Canadian Review of Social Policy*, *40*, 47–64.

Bakvis, H. (1997). Getting the giant to kneel: A new human resources delivery network for Canada. In R. Ford and D. Zussman (Eds.), *Alternative Service Delivery: Sharing Governance in Canada* (p. 154). Toronto: Institute of Public Administration of Canada.

Bala, N.M.C., Bertrand, L.D., Paetsch, J.J., Knoppers, B.M., Hornick, J.P., Noel, J.F., Boudreau, L., and Miklas, S.W. (1998, March). *Spousal Violence in Custody and Access Disputes: Recommendations for Reform*. Ottawa: Status of Women Canada.

Balthazar, H. (1991). *Caring Communities: Proceedings of the Symposium on Social Supports*, Cat. No. 89-514E. Ottawa: Statistics Canada.

Bambrough, J., Bowden, W., and Wien, F. (1992). *Preliminary Results from the Survey of Graduates from the Maritime School of Social Work*. Halifax: Maritime School of Social Work, Dalhousie University.

Banting, K.G. (1985). Institutional conservatism: Federalism and pension reform. In J.S. Ismael (Ed.), *Canadian Social Welfare Policy: Federal and Provincial Dimensions* (pp. 48–74). Kingston and Montreal: McGill-Queen's University Press.

———. (1987a). Visions of the welfare state. In S.B. Seward (Ed.), *The Future of Social Welfare Systems in Canada and the United Kingdom* (pp. 147–163). Proceedings of a Canada/UK Colloquium, October 17–18, 1986, Ottawa/Meech Lake. Halifax: Institute for Research on Public Policy.

———. (1987b). *The Welfare State and Canadian Federalism* (2nd ed.). Kingston and Montreal: McGill-Queen's University Press.

Barber, K. (Ed.). (1998). *Canadian Oxford Dictionary*. Don Mills: Oxford University Press.

Barker, R.L. (1991). *The Social Work Dictionary* (2nd ed.). Silver Spring: National Association of Social Workers.

Barnes, J. (1991, February). Taking charge. *Canada and the World*, 29–31.

Barnsley, J., and Ellis, D. (1992). *Research for Change: Participatory Action Research for Community Groups*. Vancouver: Women's Research Centre.

Battle, K. (1997, December). *Persistent Poverty*. Ottawa: Caledon Institute of Social Policy.

Battle, K., and Mendelson, M. (1997). *Child Benefit Reform in Canada: An Evaluation Framework and Future Directions*. Ottawa: Caledon Institute of Social Policy.

Battle, K., and Torjman, S. (1993). *Opening the Books on Social Spending*. Ottawa: Caledon Institute of Social Policy.

B.C. Coalition of People with Disabilities. (1994). *HIV/AIDS & Disability: Building Partnerships*. Vancouver: AIDS & Disability Action Program.

Bedard, M. (1996, June). *The Economic and Social Costs of Unemployment*. Hull: Applied Research Branch, Strategic Policy, Human Resources Development Canada.

Beiser, M., Hou, F., Hyman, I., and Tousignant, M. (1998, October). *Growing Up Canadian—A Study of New Immigrant Children*. Hull: Applied Research Branch, Strategic Policy, Human Resources Development Canada.

Bell, D.V.J. (1995). Political culture in Canada. In Michael S. Whittington and Glen Williams (Eds.), *Canadian Politics in the 1990s* (pp. 105–108). Scarborough: Nelson Canada.

Bellamy, D. (1965). Social welfare in Canada. *Encyclopedia of Social Work* (15th ed., pp. 36–48). New York: National Association of Social Workers.

Bellefeuille, G. (1997). *Breaking the Rules: Transforming Governance in Social Services*. Thompson: Awasis Agency of Northern Manitoba.

Bellemare, D. (1993). The history of economic insecurity. In *Family Security in Insecure Times* (pp. 57–86). Ottawa: National Forum on Family Security.

Bergob, M. (1994, Summer). Drug use among senior Canadians. *Canadian Social Trends*, 25–29.

Beyene, D., Butcher, C., Joe, B., and Richmond, T. (1996). Immigrant service agencies: A fundamental component of anti-racist social services. In C.E. James (Ed.), *Perspectives on Racism and the Human Services Sector* (pp. 172–182). Toronto: University of Toronto Press.

Big Brothers and Sisters of Canada. (2000). *About Our Organization* [On-line]. Available: http://www.bbsc.ca [2000 February 10].

Block, W. (1983). Social welfare in Canada: The case for selectivity. *Canadian Social Work Review'83*, 25–33.

Boadway, R. (1995). *The Canada Health and Social Transfer: Address to the Liberal Caucus*. Ottawa: House of Commons.

Boessenkool, K.J. (1997, April). *Back to Work: Learning from the Alberta Welfare Experiment*. Toronto: C.D. Howe Institute.

Boothroyd, P. (1991). Community development: The missing link in welfare policy. In Bill Kirwin (Ed.), *Ideology, Development and Social Welfare: Canadian Perspectives* (2nd ed., pp. 101–136). Toronto: Canadian Scholars' Press.

Boothroyd, P., and Davis C. (1991). *The Meaning of Community Economic Development.* UBC Planning Papers, Canadian Planning Issues No 25. Vancouver: School of Community and Regional Planning.

Bracken, D., and Walmsley C. (1992, Spring). The Canadian welfare state. *The Social Worker*, *60*(1), 21–24.

Bridges, C. (1994, November). Aboriginal disability issues: Are they still on the agenda? *Status Report* (pp. 6–7). Edmonton: Alberta Premier's Council on the Status of Persons with Disabilities.

British Columbia. (1996a). Ministry of Human Resources. *Ministry of Social Services Annual Report, 1995/96* [On-line]. Available: http://www/ mhr.gov.bc.ca/publicat/reports/ar9596.htm [1998 July 28].

———. (1996b). Ministry of the Attorney General, Policy on the Criminal Justice System Response to Violence Against Women and Children. *Violence Against Women in Relationships Policy*. Victoria: Author.

———. (1999a, December). Ministry of Community Development, Cooperatives, and Volunteers. *Building Our Communities: Celebrating and Strengthening the Voluntary Sector and Volunteering in British Columbia.* Victoria: Author.

———. (1999b). Ministry of Social Development and Economic Security. *Building a Better Future for British Columbia's Kids.* Discussion paper. Victoria: Author.

———. (2000). Ministry Responsible for Multiculturalism and Immigration. *What Is Multiculturalism? The Myths and Facts* [On-line]. Available: http://www/mrmi.gov.bc.ca/publications/index3.html [2000 May 11].

Browne, P.L. (1996). *Love in a Cold World? The Voluntary Sector in an Age of Cuts.* Ottawa: Canadian Centre for Policy Alternatives.

Bruce, M. (1966). *The Coming of the Welfare State.* New York: Schocken Books.

Burghardt, S. (1987). Community-based social action. In A. Minahan (Ed.), *Encyclopedia of Social Work*, (18th ed., vol. 1, pp. 292–299) Washington: National Association of Social Workers.

Burke, M.A., Lindsay, J., McDowell, I., and Hill, G. (1997, Summer). Dementia among seniors, *Canadian Social Trends*, 24–27.

Burnet, J. (1999). Multiculturalism. In J.A. Marsh (Ed.), *The Canadian Encyclopedia, Year 2000 Edition* (p. 1535). Toronto: McClelland & Stewart.

CACL (Canadian Association for Community Living). (n.d.). *Creating Supportive Communities.* Pamphlet. North York: Author.

———. (2000). *Goals* [On-line]. Available: http://www.cacl.ca/english/goals/ html [2000 June 1].

CAILC (Canadian Association of Independent Living Centres). (n.d.). *An Introduction.* Ottawa: Author.

———. (1997). *What Is Independent Living?* [On-line]. Available: http:// www.cailc.ca/ [2000 February 10].

Canada. (1988, July). *Canadian Multiculturalism Act*. Ottawa: Minister of Supply and Services Canada.

———. (1992a). *Brighter Futures: Canada's Action Plan for Children*. Ottawa: Minister of Supply and Services Canada.

———. (1992b, August 28). *Consensus Report on the Constitution*. Final text. Charlottetown: Government of Canada.

———. (1994a). *Creating a Healthy Fiscal Climate: The Economic and Fiscal Update*. Ottawa: Department of Finance.

———. (1994b). *Improving Social Security in Canada—The Context of Reform: A Supplementary Paper*. Hull-Ottawa: Minister of Human Resources Development.

———. (1994c). *Improving Social Security in Canada: A Discussion Paper*. Hull-Ottawa: Minister of Supply and Services Canada.

———. (1994d). *Improving Social Security in Canada—Guaranteed Annual Income: A Supplementary Paper*. Hull-Ottawa: Minister of Supply and Services Canada.

———. (1994e). *Improving Social Security in Canada—Reforming the Canada Assistance Plan: A Supplementary Paper*. Hull-Ottawa: Minister of Supply and Services Canada.

———. (1994f). *Social Security in Canada: Background Facts*. Hull-Ottawa: Ministry of Supply and Services Canada, Human Resources Development Canada.

———. (1994g). *Improving Social Security in Canada—From Unemployment Insurance to Employment Insurance: A Supplementary Paper.* Hull-Ottawa: Ministry of Supply and Services Canada, Human Resources Development Canada.

———. (1995a). *Budget in Brief*. Ottawa: Department of Finance, Her Majesty the Queen in Right of Canada.

———. (1995b). *Budget Speech*. Ottawa: Department of Finance.

———. (1996). *Social Workers, Job Futures: Occupational Outlooks* (vol. I, pp. 170–171). Ottawa: Minister of Supply and Services Canada.

———. (1997). *Expanding Aboriginal Head Start to On-Reserve Children* [On-line]. Available: http://socialunion.gc.ca/nca_e.html [2000 February 10].

———. (1998). *Annual Report of the Canada Pension Plan, 1997–1998*. Hull: Human Resources Development Canada's Income Security Programs Communications Unit.

———. (1999a) *The Fiscal Balance in Canada, August 1999*. Ottawa: Department of Finance.

———. (1999b). *Federal Transfers to Provinces and Territories*. Fact sheet. Ottawa: Federal Provincial Relations Division, Department of Finance.

———. (1999c). *A National Children's Agenda: Developing a Shared Vision*. Ottawa: Government of Canada.

———. (1999d). *Budget 1999—Providing Tax Relief and Improving Tax Fairness*. Ottawa: Department of Finance.

———. (1999e, October 6). *Stats on Seniors: Facts on Seniors* [On-line]. Available: http://iyop-aipa.ic.gc.ca/english/stats.htm [2000 April 4].

———. (1999f, December 16). *Meeting of the Federal-Provincial-Territorial Ministerial Council on Social Policy Renewal.* News releases. [On-line]. Available: http://socialunion.gc.ca/news/161299_e.html [2000 January 27].

———. (1999g). *Annual Report of the Canada Pension Plan Fiscal Year 1998–1999.* Hull: Human Resources Development Canada's Income Security Programs Communications Unit.

———. (1999h, July). *The National Child Benefit: What It Means for Canadian Families* [On-line]. Available: http://socialunion.gc.ca/ncb/ncb_e19.html [2000 June 23].

———. (1999i). *The National Child Benefit: Progress Report 1999—Executive Summary* [On-line]. Available: http://socialunion.gc.ca/NBC-99/toceng.html [2000 January 27].

———. (1999j, December 6). Federal-Provincial-Territorial Ministers Responsible for Social Services. *In Unison: A Canadian Approach to Disability Issues* [On-line]. Available: http://socialunion.gc.ca/pwd/unison/unison_e.html [2000 May 11].

———. (2000a). *Budget 2000: Improving the Quality of Life of Canadians and Their Children.* Ottawa: Department of Finance.

———. (2000b). *The Budget Speech 2000.* Ottawa: Department of Finance.

———. (2000c). *The Budget in Brief 2000.* Ottawa: Department of Finance.

———. (2000d). *Canada's Participation in the International Year of Older Persons (IYOP)—1999* [On-line]. Available: http://iyop-aipa.ic.gc.ca/english/raising.htm [2000 April 4].

———. (2000e, February 11). *Government of Canada to Amend Legislation to Modernize Benefits and Obligations* [On-line]. Available: http://canada.justice.gc.ca/en/news/nr/2000/doc_25019.html [2000 June 19].

———. (2000f, April). *National Child Benefit: Summary of Provincial/Territorial/First Nations Initiatives Under the National Child Benefit 1999–2000* [On-line]. Available: http://socialunion.gc.ca/NCB-2000/summary-reinvest2000.html [2000 June 23].

———. (2000g, February 28). *Backgrounder—National Child Benefit (NCB)* [On-line]. Available: http://socialunion.gc.ca/ncb/sp-155-02-2000.html [2000 June 23].

Canada Mortgage and Housing Corporation. (1999). *Working Group on Senior's Housing* [On-line]. Available: http://www.cmhc-schl.gc.ca/rd-dr/en/nhrc-cnrl/wgsh/index.html [2000 May 8].

Canada/National Advisory Council on Aging. (1992). *Housing an Aging Population: Guidelines for Development and Design* (2nd ed.). Ottawa: Author.

Canada/Seniors Secretariat. (1992). *A Shared Concern: An Overview of Canadian Programs Addressing the Abuse of Seniors.* Ottawa: Minister of Supply and Services Canada.

Canadian Council on Social Development. (1969). *Social Policies for Canada, Part 1.* Ottawa: Author.

———. (1990). *Canada's Social Programs Are in Trouble*. Ottawa: Author.

———. (1992, Fall/Winter). Breaking free. *Perception, 15*(4)/*16*(1), 40–43.

———. (1996). *Maintaining a National Social Safety Net: Recommendations on the Canada Health and Social Transfer* [On-line]. Available: http://www.ccsd.ca/pos_chst.html [2000 February 21].

———. (1999a). *Crime Prevention Through Social Development* [On-line]. Available: www.ccsd.ca/cp/bulletin/1e.pdf [2000 April 27].

———. (1999b, March 3). *CCSD Response to Recent Development of Welfare-to-Work Programs* [On-line]. Available: http://www.ccsd.ca/pr/w2wpos.htm [2000 February 21].

———. (2000a). *Urban Poverty in Canada: A Statistical Profile* [On-line]. Available: http://www.ccsd.ca/pubd/2000/up/hl.htm [2000 April 29].

———. (2000b, April 26). *Personal Security Index 2000—Money, Health, Safety: How Do Canadians Feel?* [On-line]. Available: http://www.ccsd.ca/pubs/2000/psi/hl.htm [2000 April 29].

Canadian Intergovernmental Conference Secretariat. (2000). 41st Annual Premiers' Conference. News release. [On-line]. Available: http://www.scics.gc.ca/cinfo../850080013_.html [2000 September 6].

Canadian Paediatric Society. (2000, June 13). *Support Your Kids by Getting Along* [On-line]. Available: http://www.cps.ca/english/about/Separating%20parents.htm [2000 June 16].

Canadian Psychiatric Research Foundation. (1999). *Mental Health Facts* [On-line]. Available: http://www.cprf.ca/Resource/facts.htm [2000 June 1].

Canadian Task Force on Mental Health Issues Affecting Immigrants and Refugees. (1988). *After the Door Has Been Opened: Mental Health Issues Affecting Immigrants and Refugees in Canada*. Ottawa: Government of Canada.

Canadians to work longer. (1995 July 16–31). *Canadian News Facts* (p. 5161). Toronto: MPL Communications.

Cardozo, A. (1996). Lion taming: Downsizing the opponents of downsizing. In G. Swimmer (Ed.), *How Ottawa Spends, 1996–97: Life Under the Knife* (pp. 303–336). Ottawa: Carleton University Press.

Carniol, B. (1990). Social work and the labour movement. In B. Wharf (Ed.), *Social Work and Social Change in Canada* (pp. 114–143). Toronto: McClelland & Stewart.

———. (1995). *Case Critical: Challenging Social Services in Canada* (3rd ed.). Toronto: Between the Lines.

Carter, S. (1997, September). Building diversity considerations into social planning. *Perception, 21*(2), 7–8.

Cassidy, H.M. (1943). *Social Security and Reconstruction in Canada*. Toronto: Ryerson Press.

CASW (Canadian Association of Social Workers). (1983). *Canadian Association of Social Work Code of Ethics*. Ottawa: Author.

———. (1994a). *Annual Report 1993–94*. Ottawa: Author.

———. (1994b). *Social Work Code of Ethics*, Ottawa: Author.

———. (1994c). The social work profession and the Aboriginal peoples. *The Social Worker*, *62*(4), 158.

———. (1997, January). *The Social Work Profession*. Ottawa: Author.

———. (1998, November). *CASW Position on Multiskilling*. Ottawa: Author.

———. (2000, February 21). Letter from H. Bourguignon to R. Chappell. Ottawa: Author.

CASSW (Canadian Association of Schools of Social Work). (2000). *Human Resources Strategic Analysis of Social Work in Canada* [On-line]. Available: http://www.cassw-acess.ca/!Projects/!Sector%20STudy/Eng/SW-TOC.htm [2000 March 21].

CCD (Council of Canadians with Disabilities). (2000a). *Council of Canadians with Disabilities* [On-line]. Available: http://www.pcs.mb.ca/~ccd/ [2000 May 30].

———. (2000b, January). *A Voice of Our Own, 18*(1) [On-line]. Available: http://www.pcs.mb.ca/vojan00.html [2000 June 1].

Celebrating seniors' contributions. (1998, Winter). *Expression*, *12*(2).

Changes in living arrangements and housing needs over the life course. (1996 June 15). *Info-Age*.

Chisholm, P. (2000, January 17). All in the family. *Maclean's*, 16–21.

Chisholm, S. (1995, Winter). Holding our own: Threats to social housing in Canada. *Perception*, *19*(2), 18–20.

Christensen, C.P. (1995). Immigrant minorities in Canada. In Joanne C. Turner and Francis J. Turner (Eds.), *Canadian Social Welfare* (3rd ed., pp. 179–212). Scarborough: Allyn & Bacon.

———. (1996). The impact of racism on the education of social service workers. In C.E. James (Ed.), *Perspectives on Racism and the Human Services Sector* (pp. 140–151). Toronto: University of Toronto Press.

Chung Yan, M. (1998). Towards a complete view of the social policy process: An integration of policy formulation and implementation. *Canadian Review of Social Policy*, *42*, 37–53.

CIC (Citizenship and Immigration Canada). (1994a). *Immigration Consultations Report*. Ottawa-Hull: Minister of Supply and Services Canada.

———. (1994b). *Into the 21st Century: A Strategy for Immigration and Citizenship*. Ottawa-Hull: Minister of Supply and Services Canada.

———. (1995, December). *Growing Together—A Backgrounder on Immigration and Citizenship: The History of Immigration* [On-line]. Available: http://www.cic.gc.ca/english/pub/grow/grow_00e.html [2000 February 3].

———. (1996). *Round II—Consultations on Settlement Renewal: Finding a New Direction for Newcomer Integration*. Ottawa: Minister of Public Works and Government Services Canada.

———. (1998). *Building on a Strong Foundation for the 21st Century: New Directions for Immigration and Refugee Policy and Legislation*. Ottawa: Minister of Public Works and Government Services Canada.

———. (1999a). *Canada ... The Place to Be: Annual Immigration Plan for the Year 2000*. Ottawa: Minister of Public Works and Government Services Canada.

———. (1999b). *You Asked About ... Immigration and Citizenship*. Ottawa: Minister of Public Works and Government Services Canada.

———. (2000a). *Immigrant Settlement and Adaptation Program (ISAP): Guide for Applicants*. Ottawa: Minister of Public Works and Government Services Canada.

———. (2000b). *Language Instruction for Newcomers to Canada (LINC): Guide for Applicants*. Ottawa: Minister of Public Works and Government Services Canada.

———. (2000c). *Caplan Tables New Immigration and Refugee Protection Act*. News release. [On-line]. Available: http://www.cic.gc.ca/english/press/../...9_re.html [2000 September 10].

Clark, C. (1995a). *Work and Welfare: Looking at Both Sides of the Equation* [On-line]. Available: http://www.ccsd.ca/perchris.html [2000 February 21].

———. (1995b, Winter). UI Becomes EI: From unemployment insurance to employment insurance. *Perception*, *19*(2), 14–15.

Clarke, M. (1991). *Fighting Poverty Through Programs: Social and Health Programs for Canada's Poor Children and Youth*. Ottawa: Children*Enfants*Jeunesse*Youth.

Clarke, T. (1992, December). North America's new corporate constitution. *Action Dossier* (Action Canada Network), No. 38, 12–13.

Coalition of National Voluntary Organizations. (1994, August). *NVO Bulletin*, *13*(2). Ottawa: Author.

Coates, K.S., and Morrisson, W.R. (1993). In whose best interest?: The federal government and the Native people of Yukon, 1946–1991. In A. Mawhiney (Ed.), *Rebirth: Political, Economic and Social Development in First Nations* (pp. 19–33). Toronto: Dundurn Press.

Collins, K. (1976, January/February). Three decades of social security in Canada. *Canadian Welfare*, *51*(7), 5–9.

Collins, S.B. (1998). The challenge of equity in Canadian social welfare policy. *Canadian Review of Social Policy*, 42, 1–14.

Compton, B. (1980). *Introduction to Social Welfare and Social Work: Structure, Function, and Process*. Homewood: Dorsey Press.

Compton, B., and Galaway, B. (1994). *Social Work Processes* (5th ed.). Pacific Grove: Brooks/Cole.

Connaway, R.S. and Gentry, M.E. (1988). *Social Work Practice*. Englewood Cliffs: Prentice-Hall.

Courchene, T.J. (1987). *Social Policy in the 1990s: Agenda for Reform*. Policy Study No. 3. C.D. Howe Institute. Scarborough: Prentice-Hall.

Coyle, G.L. (1959). Some basic assumptions about social group work. In M. Murphy (Ed.), *The Social Group Work Method in Social Work Education* (Curriculum Study XI, pp. 91–100). New York: Council on Social Work Education.

Cranswick, K. (1997, Winter). Canada's caregivers. *Canadian Social Trends*, 2–6.

Crompton, S., and Kemeny, A. (1999, Winter). In sickness and in health: The well-being of married seniors. *Canadian Social Trends*, 22–27.

Cross, S. (1985, Spring). Professionalism: The occupational hazard of social work, 1920–1960. *The Social Worker*, *53*(1), 29–33.

CS/RESORS Consulting, Ltd. (1998). *Final Report on a Literature Review and Gap Analysis of the Social Worker Occupation* [On-line]. Available: http://www.cassw-acess.ca/!Projects/!Sector%20STudy/CSR%20Report/report.html [2000 June 26].

Davis, B., and Tarasuk, V. (1994). Hunger in Canada. *Agriculture and Human Values*, *11*, 50–57.

Day, S., and Brodsky, G. (1998). *Women and the Equality Deficit: The Impact of Restructuring Canada's Social Programs*. Ottawa: Status of Women Canada.

Dillon, J. (1996). *Challenging Free Trade in Canada: The Real Story.* Ottawa: Canadian Centre for Policy Alternatives.

Dingledine, G. (1981). *A Chronology of Response: The Evolution of Unemployment Insurance from 1940 to 1980*. Ottawa: Employment and Immigration Canada.

Dirks, G.E. (1999). Immigration policy. In J.A. Marsh (Ed.), *The Canadian Encyclopedia, Year 2000 Edition* (pp. 1141–1143). Toronto: McClelland & Stewart.

Djao, A.W. (1983). *Inequality and Social Policy*. Toronto: John Wiley and Sons.

Dobell, A.R., and Mansbridge, S.H. (1986). *The Social Policy Process in Canada*. Montreal: Institute for Research on Public Policy.

Dobelstein, A.W. (1978). Introduction: Social resources, human need, and the field of social work. In Arthur Fink (Ed.), *The Field of Social Work* (7th ed., pp. 3–21). New York: Holt, Rinehart and Winston.

Doe, T., and Kimpson, S. (1999, March). *Enabling Income: CPP Disability Benefits and Women with Disabilities*. Ottawa: Status of Women Canada.

Doherty, G., Friendly, M., and Oloman, M. (1998, March). *Women's Support, Women's Work: Child Care in an Era of Deficit Reduction, Devolution, Downsizing and Deregulation*. Ottawa: Status of Women Canada.

Drover, G. (1992, December). The harmonization of a "sacred trust." *Action Dossier* (Action Canada Network), No. 38, 16–17.

Dunn, M. (1992, Fall/Winter). One heart—many voices: Canada's national Native organization. *Perception, 15*(4)/*16*(1), 24–27.

Economic Council of Canada. (1968). *Fifth Annual Review.* Ottawa: Author.

EI changes evaluated. (1999, March 16–31). *Canadian News Facts* (p. 5946). Toronto: MPL Communications.

EI surplus said excessive. (1999, October). *Canadian News Facts* (p. 5951). Toronto: MPL Communications.

Eichler, M. (1987). Social policy concerning women. In Shankar A. Yelaja (Ed.), *Canadian Social Policy* (rev. ed., pp. 139–156). Waterloo: Wilfrid Laurier University Press.

Eichler, M., and Lavigne, M. (1999). Women's movement. In J.A. Marsh (Ed.), *The Canadian Encyclopedia, Year 2000 Edition* (pp. 2532–2534). Toronto: McClelland & Stewart.

Emmerij, L. (1999). Paradoxes of globalization and what nation states can do to address them. In S.A. Rosell (Ed.), *Renewing Governance: Governing by Learning in the Information Age* (pp. 252–263). Don Mills: Oxford University Press.

Employment and Immigration Canada. (n.d.). *Facts at a Glance: Immigration (Canada/B.C.).* Hull: Author.

Epstein, L. (1980). *Helping People: The Task-Centered Approach.* St. Louis: C.V. Mosby.

———. (1988). *Helping People: The Task-Centered Approach* (2nd ed.). Columbus: Merrill Publishing.

Fabiano, L., and Martyn, R. (1992). Social work practice with institutionalized frail elderly. In M.J. Holosko and P.A. Taylor (Eds.), *Social Work Practice in Health Care Settings* (2nd ed., pp. 323–351). Toronto: Canadian Scholars' Press.

Farrell, M. (1997). Rebuilding our social supports. *Canadian Review of Social Policy,* No. 40, 76–78.

Fawcett, G., and Shillington, R. (1996). Income support and tax relief for people with disabilities. *Perception, 20*(2), 5–7.

Feit, M.D., and Feit, N.C. (1996). An overview of social work practice with the elderly. In M.J. Holosko and M.D. Feit (Eds.), *Social Work Practice with the Elderly* (2nd ed, pp. 3–20). Toronto: Canadian Scholars' Press.

Finance Canada. (2000a). *The Fiscal Balance in Canada* [On-line]. Available: http://www.fin.gc.ca/fiscbal_e.pdf [2000 February 16].

———. (2000b). *The Canada Health and Social Transfer* [On-line]. Available: www.fin.gc.ca/fedprove/chse.html [2000 May 30].

Findlay, P. (1983). Social welfare in Canada: The case for universality. *Canadian Social Work Review '83*, 17–24.

First Nations/Medical Services Branch, Community Action Initiative Working Group. (1992, September 29). *Brighter Futures: Program Framework for the Child Development Initiative: First Nations and Inuit Component.* Ottawa: Author.

Fischer, J. (1978). *Effective Casework Practice: An Eclectic Approach*. New York: McGraw-Hill.

Fitzgerald, R. (1999, June). *Family Violence in Canada: A Statistical Profile 1999*. Ottawa: Statistics Canada.

Food bank use on rise. (1999, September 16–30). *Canadian News Facts* (p. 5934). Toronto: MPL Communications.

Ford, R., and Zussman, D. (1997). Conclusion. In R. Ford and D. Zussman (Eds.), *Alternative Service Delivery: Sharing Governance in Canada* (pp. 273–278). Toronto: Institute of Public Administration of Canada.

Forsey, E. (1974). The Canadian Labour Movement, 1812–1902. *Historical Booklet*, No. 27. Ottawa: Canadian Historical Association.

Foucault, M. (1965). *Madness and Civilization*. London: Random House.

Frederick, J.A., and Fast, J.E. (1999, Autumn). Eldercare in Canada: Who does how much? *Canadian Social Trends*, 26–31.

Free trade evaluated. (1999, January 1–15). *Canadian News Facts* (p. 5804). Toronto: MPL Communications.

Frenzel, A. (1987). Unemployment. In S.A. Yelaja (Ed.), *Canadian Social Policy* (rev. ed., pp. 115–138). Waterloo: Wilfrid Laurier University Press.

Frideres, J. (1999). Altered states: Federal policy and Aboriginal peoples. In P.S. Li (Ed.), *Race and Ethnic Relations in Canada* (2nd ed., pp. 116–147). Don Mills: Oxford University Press.

Friedlander, W.A., and Apte, R.Z. (1980). *Introduction to Social Welfare* (5th ed.). Englewood Cliffs: Prentice-Hall.

Galper, J.H. (1975). *The Politics of Social Services*. Englewood Cliffs: Prentice-Hall.

Gays win landmark ruling. (1999, May 16-31). *Canadian News Facts* (p. 5876). Toronto: MPL Communications.

Gender and need for technical aids for mobility among seniors. (1999, April 21). *Info-Age*.

George, V., and Wilding, P. (1985). *Ideology and Social Welfare*. London and New York: Routledge.

Germain, C.B., and Gitterman, A. (1980). *The Life Model of Social Work Practice*. New York: Columbia University Press.

Ginsler, E. (1988, September). Social planning councils. *Perception*, 2(2), 52–53.

Gorey, K.M., Hansen, F.C., and Chacko, J. (1997, Winter). The effectiveness of social services in Ontario. *Canadian Social Work Review*, *14*(1), 43–53.

Gorlick, C., and Brethour, G. (1999). *Welfare-to-Work Programs in Canada: A Discussion Paper* [On-line]. Available: www.ccsd.ca/pr/w2wbg.htm [2000 February 21].

Gottlieb, B.H. (1983). *Social Support Strategies*. Beverly Hills: Sage Publications.

Grady, P., Howse, R., and Maxwell, J. (1995). *Redefining Social Security*. Kingston: School of Policy Studies, Queen's University.

Gray, G. (1990, March). Social policy by stealth. *Policy Options*, 17–29.

———. (1991, September). A new deal for Aboriginals. *Policy Options*, 3–5.

Grinnell, R.M., Rothery, M., and Thomlison, R.J. (1995). Research in social work. In J.C. Turner and F.J. Turner (Eds.), *Canadian Social Welfare* (3rd ed., pp. 525–543). Scarborough: Allyn & Bacon.

Guest, D. (1980). *The Emergence of Social Security in Canada*. Vancouver: University of British Columbia Press.

———. (1988). Social security. *The Canadian Encyclopedia* (2nd ed., vol. 3, pp. 2032–2034). Edmonton: Hurtig Publishers.

———. (1999). Social security. In J.A. Marsh (Ed.), *The Canadian Encyclopedia, Year 2000 Edition* (pp. 2200–2204). Toronto: McClelland & Stewart.

Hale, I. (1999, June). Does anyone know this is the IYOP? *Perception*, 23(1), 3–5.

Hall, M., Knighton, T., Reed, P., Bussiere, P., McRae, D., and Bowen, P. (1998, August). *Caring Canadians, Involved Canadians: Highlights from the 1997 National Survey of Giving, Volunteering and Participating*. Ottawa: Statistics Canada.

Handel, G. (1982). *Social Welfare in Western Society*. New York: Random House.

Hareven, T.K. (1969, April). An ambiguous alliance: Some aspects of American influences on Canadian social welfare. *Social History: A Canadian Review*, 3, 82–98.

Harrison, W.D. (1995). Community development. In R.L. Edwards (Ed.), *Encyclopedia of Social Work* (19th ed, vol. 1, pp. 555–562). Washington, DC: National Association of Social Workers.

Hartman, A., and Laird, J. (1983). *Family-Centered Social Work Practice*. New York: Free Press.

Head, W. (1984). Human rights and social welfare: An uneasy relationship. In M.D. Nair, R.C. Hain, and J.A. Draper (Eds.), *Issues in Canadian Human Services* (pp. 186–208). Toronto: OISE Press.

Health and Welfare Canada. (1988). *Guidelines for Comprehensive Services to Elderly Persons with Psychiatric Disorders*. Ottawa: Author.

———. (1990). *Geriatric Services in Acute-Care Hospitals: (A) Geriatric Assessment and Treatment Units; (B) Geriatric Hospitals—Guidelines*. Ottawa: Author.

Health Canada. (1992, November). *Family Violence Against Women with Disabilities* [On-line]. Available: http://www.hc.sc.gc.ca./hppb/familyviolence/html/womendiseng.html [2000 May 6].

———. (1993). *Adult Survivors of Child Sexual Abuse*. Ottawa: National Clearinghouse on Family Violence.

———. (1994a, September 26). *National Strategy to Deal with Urgent Health Priorities of First Nations and Inuit: Backgrounder—Solvent Abuse Program*. News release. Ottawa.

———. (1994b). *Suicide in Canada: Update of the Report of the Task Force on Suicide in Canada*. Ottawa: Author.

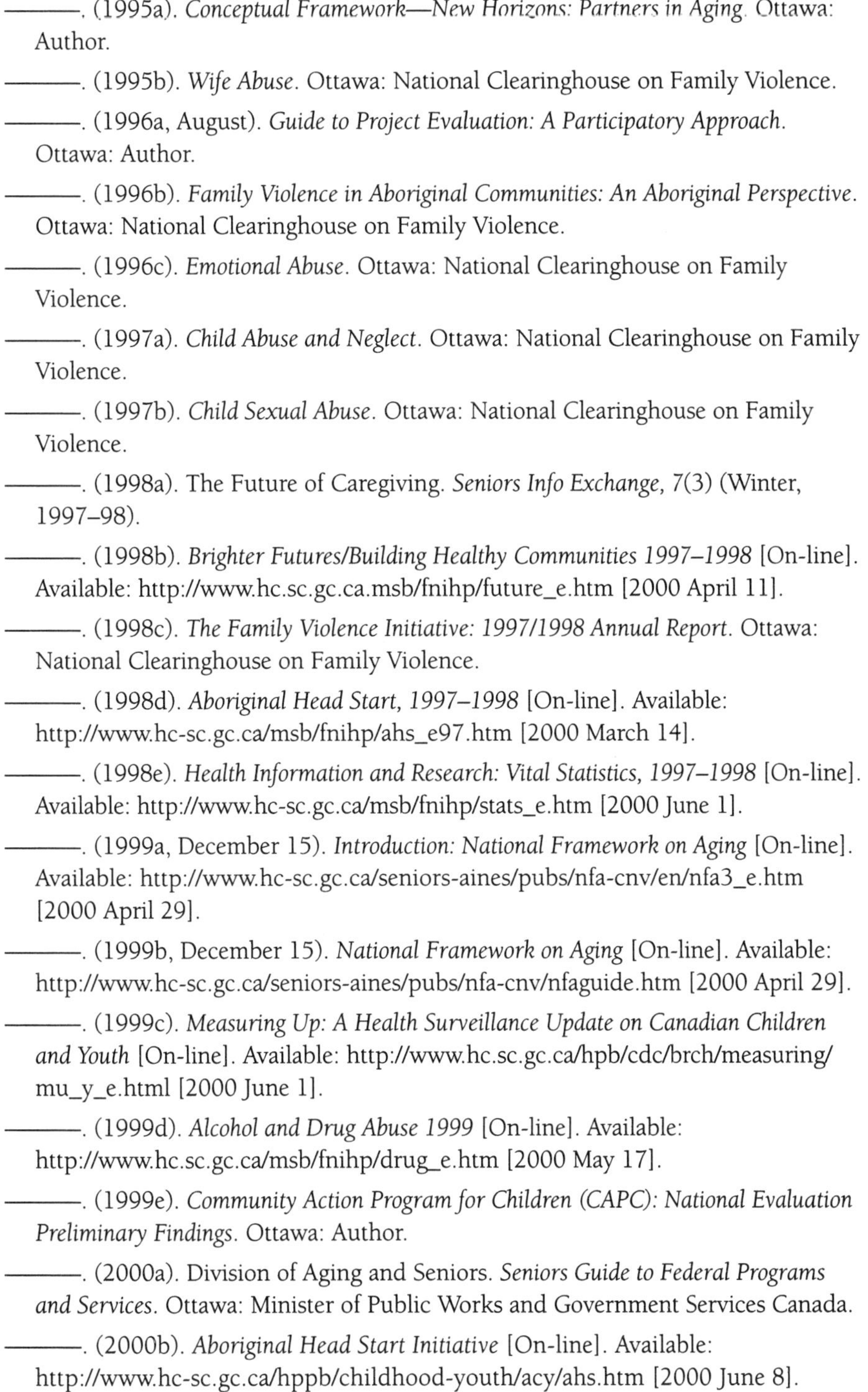

———. (1995a). *Conceptual Framework—New Horizons: Partners in Aging*. Ottawa: Author.

———. (1995b). *Wife Abuse*. Ottawa: National Clearinghouse on Family Violence.

———. (1996a, August). *Guide to Project Evaluation: A Participatory Approach*. Ottawa: Author.

———. (1996b). *Family Violence in Aboriginal Communities: An Aboriginal Perspective*. Ottawa: National Clearinghouse on Family Violence.

———. (1996c). *Emotional Abuse*. Ottawa: National Clearinghouse on Family Violence.

———. (1997a). *Child Abuse and Neglect*. Ottawa: National Clearinghouse on Family Violence.

———. (1997b). *Child Sexual Abuse*. Ottawa: National Clearinghouse on Family Violence.

———. (1998a). The Future of Caregiving. *Seniors Info Exchange*, *7*(3) (Winter, 1997–98).

———. (1998b). *Brighter Futures/Building Healthy Communities 1997–1998* [On-line]. Available: http://www.hc.sc.gc.ca.msb/fnihp/future_e.htm [2000 April 11].

———. (1998c). *The Family Violence Initiative: 1997/1998 Annual Report*. Ottawa: National Clearinghouse on Family Violence.

———. (1998d). *Aboriginal Head Start, 1997–1998* [On-line]. Available: http://www.hc-sc.gc.ca/msb/fnihp/ahs_e97.htm [2000 March 14].

———. (1998e). *Health Information and Research: Vital Statistics, 1997–1998* [On-line]. Available: http://www.hc-sc.gc.ca/msb/fnihp/stats_e.htm [2000 June 1].

———. (1999a, December 15). *Introduction: National Framework on Aging* [On-line]. Available: http://www.hc-sc.gc.ca/seniors-aines/pubs/nfa-cnv/en/nfa3_e.htm [2000 April 29].

———. (1999b, December 15). *National Framework on Aging* [On-line]. Available: http://www.hc-sc.gc.ca/seniors-aines/pubs/nfa-cnv/nfaguide.htm [2000 April 29].

———. (1999c). *Measuring Up: A Health Surveillance Update on Canadian Children and Youth* [On-line]. Available: http://www.hc.sc.gc.ca/hpb/cdc/brch/measuring/mu_y_e.html [2000 June 1].

———. (1999d). *Alcohol and Drug Abuse 1999* [On-line]. Available: http://www.hc.sc.gc.ca/msb/fnihp/drug_e.htm [2000 May 17].

———. (1999e). *Community Action Program for Children (CAPC): National Evaluation Preliminary Findings*. Ottawa: Author.

———. (2000a). Division of Aging and Seniors. *Seniors Guide to Federal Programs and Services*. Ottawa: Minister of Public Works and Government Services Canada.

———. (2000b). *Aboriginal Head Start Initiative* [On-line]. Available: http://www.hc-sc.gc.ca/hppb/childhood-youth/acy/ahs.htm [2000 June 8].

Healthy lifestyles and aging. (n.d.). *Expression, 10*(2). Ottawa: National Advisory Council on Aging.

Heclo, H. (1981). Toward a new welfare state? In P. Flora and A.J. Heidenheimer (Eds.), *The Development of Welfare States in Europe and America* (pp. 383–406). New Brunswick (USA) and London (UK): Transaction Books.

Herberg, D.C., and Herberg, E.N. (1995). Canada's ethno-racial diversity: Policies and programs for Canadian social welfare. In J.C. Turner and F.J. Turner (Eds.), *Canadian Social Welfare* (3rd ed., pp. 165–178). Scarborough: Allyn & Bacon.

Hess, M. (1993). *An Overview of Canadian Social Policy*. Ottawa: Canadian Council on Social Development.

Hikel, R. (1997). Alternative service delivery and the prospects for success: Political leadership and performance measurement. In R. Ford and D. Zussman (Eds.), *Alternative Service Delivery: Sharing Governance in Canada* (pp. 74–84). Toronto: Institute of Public Administration of Canada.

Hillmer, N. (1999). Harris, Michael Deane. In J.A. Marsh (Ed.), *The Canadian Encyclopedia, Year 2000 Edition* (p. 1047). Toronto: McClelland & Stewart.

Holosko, M.J., White, L., and Feit, M.D. (1996). Gerontological social work practice in the 1990s and beyond. In M.J. Holosko and M.D. Feit (Eds.), *Social Work Practice with the Elderly* (2nd ed., pp. 395–402). Toronto: Canadian Scholars' Press.

Horn, M. (1984). The Great Depression of the 1930s in Canada. *Historical Booklet*, No. 39. Ottawa: Canadian Historical Association.

Hourston, S. (2000). Wellness and Disability Initiative. *Health and Homelessness*. [On-line]. Available: http://www.bccpd.bc.ca/trmarapou/health/html [2000 June 1].

Howlett, D. (1992, May/June). The arithmetic, chemistry, and art of coalition projects. *Action Canada Dossier* (Action Canada Network), No. 37, 7–9.

Hudson, P., and Taylor-Henley, S. (1993). Linking social and political developments in First Nations communities. In A. Mawhiney (Ed.), *Rebirth: Political, Economic and Social Development in First Nations* (pp. 45–61). Toronto: Dundurn Press.

Hum, D. (1985). Social security reform during the 1970s. In J.S. Ismael (Ed.), *Canadian Social Welfare Policy* (pp. 29–47). Kingston and Montreal: McGill-Queen's University Press.

Hum, D., and Simpson, W. (1993, Fall). What ever happened to Canada's guaranteed income project? *Canadian Public Administration, 36*(3), 442–450.

Human Resources Development Canada. (1994a). *Adults and Jobs: Background Facts*. Prepared by Strategic Communications. Ottawa-Hull: Author.

———. (1994b). *Annual Report, 1993–1994*. Ottawa: Author.

———. (1995a). *A 21st Century Employment System for Canada* [On-line]. Available: http://www.hrdc-drhc.gc.ca/hrdc/initiatv/eilaunch/sc11411e.html [2000 June 28].

———. (1995b). *The Need for Change* [On-line]. Available: http://www.hrdc-drhc.gc.ca/hrdc/initiatv/eilaunch/newsrele/9579b2e.html [2000 June 7].

———. (1996, September 19). *Getting Canadians Back to Work: A Proposal to Provinces and Territories for a New Partnership in the Labour Market.* [On-line]. Available: http://www.hrdc-drhc.gc.ca/hrdc/initiatv/eilaunch/prop96_e.html [2000 June 28].

———. (1998a). *The Government of Canada's Record on Disability Issues* [On-line]. Available: http://www.hrdc-drhc.gc.ca/common/news/9821b4.html [2000 June 28].

———. (1998b). *Canada and New Brunswick Sign New Agreement to Assist People with Disabilities* [On-line]. Available: http://www.hrdc-drhc.gc.ca/common/news/dept9851.shtml [2000 June 28].

———. (1999a, October 15). *First Nations and Inuit Child Care Initiative* [On-line]. Available: http://www.hrdc-drhc.gc.ca/hrib/aro/child/child.shtml [2000 June 8].

———. (1999b, July). Office for Disability Issues. *Future Directions: The Policy Directions to Guide Future Action* [On-line]. Available: http://www.hrdc-drhc.gc.ca/socpol/reports/disability/sect6e.shtml [2000 June 8].

———. (1999c, July). Office for Disability Issues. *Future Directions: The Challenges Facing Persons with Disabilities* [On-line]. Available: http://www.hrdc-drhc.gc.ca/socpol/reports/disability/sect3e.shtml [2000 June 8].

———. (1999d, December 17). Office of the Minister of Labour. *Building Partnerships to Help Canada's Homeless Persons.* News release [On-line]. Available: http://www.hrdc-drhc.gc.ca/common/news/labour/99-88.shtml [2000 March 2].

Immigration facts. (1998, September). *Transition*, 28(3), 8–9.

INAC (Indian and Northern Affairs Canada). (1990). *The Canadian Indian.* Hull-Ottawa: Minister of Supply and Services Canada.

———. (1993, May). *The International Year of the World's Indigenous People.* Information Sheet No. 58. Ottawa: Author.

———. (1996, November 21). *Final Report of the Royal Commission on Aboriginal Peoples Issued.* News release. [On-line]. Available: http://www.inac.gc.ca/news/sept96/1-9648.html [2000 May 15].

———. (1997a, December). *The Department of Indian Affairs and Northern Development* [On-line]. Available: http://www.inac.gc.ca/pubs/information/info108.html [2000 May 30].

———. (1997b). *Gathering Strength—Canada's Aboriginal Action Plan.* Booklet. Ottawa: Minister of Indian Affairs and Northern Development.

———. (1997c). *Aboriginal Agenda: Renewing the Partnership.* Ottawa: Minister of Indian Affairs and Northern Development.

———. (1998a). *Gathering Strength—Canada's Aboriginal Action Plan: A Progress Report, Year 1.* Poster. Ottawa: Minister of Indian Affairs and Northern Development.

———. (1998b, November). *The International Decade of the World's Indigenous People* [On-line]. Available: http://www.inac.gc.ca/pubs/information/info123.html [2000 June 1].

Institute for the Prevention of Child Abuse. (1994). *Stop the Hurt*. Toronto: Rotary Club of Toronto (Don Valley).

Irving, A. (1987). Federal–provincial issues in social policy. In S.A. Yelaja (Ed.), *Canadian Social Policy* (rev. ed., pp. 326–349). Waterloo: Wilfrid Laurier University Press.

Ismael, J. (1988). Privatization of social services: A heuristic approach. In J. Ismael and Y. Vaillancourt (Eds.), *Privatization and Provincial Social Services in Canada* (pp. 1–11). Edmonton: University of Alberta Press.

Jaco, R.M. (1995). Social agencies and human service organizations. In J.C. Turner and F.J. Turner (Eds.), *Canadian Social Welfare* (3rd ed., pp. 392–423). Scarborough: Allyn & Bacon.

Jacobs, L.A. (1995). What are the normative foundations of workfare? In A. Sayeed (Ed.), *Workfare: Does It Work? Is It Fair?* (pp. 13–37). Montreal: Institute for Research on Public Policy.

Janzen, C., and Harris, O. (1986). *Family Treatment in Social Work Practice* (2nd ed.). Itasca: F.E. Peacock.

Jewish Immigrant Aid Services of Canada. (2000). *Home Page* [On-line]. Available: http://www.jias.ca [2000 May 11].

Johnson, A.W. (1987). Social policy in Canada: The past as it conditions the present. In S.B. Seward (Ed.), *The Future of Social Welfare Systems in Canada and the United Kingdom* (pp. 29–70). Proceedings of a Canada/UK Colloquium, October 17–18, 1986, Ottawa/Meech Lake. Halifax: Institute for Research on Public Policy.

Johnson, L.C. (1998). *Social Work Practice: A Generalist Approach* (6th ed.). Needham Heights: Allyn & Bacon.

Johnson, L.C., Schwartz, C.L., and Tate, D.S. (1997). *Social Welfare: A Response to Human Need* (4th ed.). Needham Heights: Allyn & Bacon.

Johnston, J.R. (1994). High conflict divorce. *The Future of Children*, *4*(1), 165–182.

Juggling the demands of children and work: Family challenges in the 1990s. (1997). *Perception*, *21*(3), 6–7.

Kahn, A. (1979). *Social Policy and Social Services* (2nd ed.). New York: Random House.

Kahn, S. (1995). Community organization. In R.L. Edwards (Ed.), *Encyclopedia of Social Work* (19th ed., vol. 1, pp. 569–576). Washington, DC: National Association of Social Workers.

Kalina, L. (1995, Winter). Food security for Canadian families. *Perception*, *19*(2), 21–22.

Kamateros, M. (1998, September). The isolated immigrant family. *Transition, 28*(3), 13–14.

Kapica, J. (1993, December 14). Canadians want mosaic to melt, survey finds. *The Globe and Mail*, A1–A2.

Kerzner, L., and Baker, D. (1999, May 14). *A Canadians with Disabilities Act?* [On-line]. Available: http://www.pcs.mb.ca/~ccd/cda.html [2000 May 26].

Khan, R.A., McNiven, J.D., and MacKown, S.A. (1977). *An Introduction to Political Science* (rev. ed.). Georgetown: Irwin-Dorsey.

Kramer, R. (1981). *Voluntary Agencies in the Welfare State*. Berkeley: University of California Press.

Kroeger, A. (1996). Changing course: The federal government's program review of 1994–95. In A. Armit and J. Bourgault (Eds.), *Hard Choices or No Choices: Assessing Program Review* (pp. 21–28). Toronto: Institute of Public Administration of Canada.

Laliberte, P. (1998, December). Setting new priorities for Canada's employment insurance program. *Perception*, *22*(3), 8–9.

Lawton, V. (2000, February 8). Same-sex legislation is expected this week. *The Toronto Star* [On-line]. Available: http://www.egale.ca/archives/press/000208ts.htm [2000 March 30].

Lecomte, R. (1995). Trends and issues in education for social work practice. In J.C. Turner and F.J. Turner (Eds.), *Canadian Social Welfare* (3rd ed., pp. 554–562). Scarborough: Allyn & Bacon.

Lee, B. (1992, July). Colonization and community: Implications for First Nations development. *Community Development Journal*, *27*(3), 211–219.

Lee, K. (1999, September). Measuring poverty among Canada's Aboriginal people. *Perception*, *23*(2), 9–12.

Lindsay, C. (1999, Spring). Seniors: A diverse group aging well. *Canadian Social Trends*, 24–27.

Lipman, E.L., Boyle, M.H., Dooley, M.D., and Offerd, D.R. (1998, October). *Children and Lone Mother Families: An Investigation of Factors Influencing Child Well-Being*. Ottawa: Applied Research Branch, Strategic Policy, Human Resources Development Canada.

Little, M.H. (1999). The limits of Canadian democracy. *Canadian Review of Social Policy*, *43*, 59–76.

Lochhead, C. (1998). Who benefits from Canada's income security programs? *Perception*, *21*(4), 9–12.

Loizides, S. (1994). *The Role of the Private Sector in Community Economic Development*, Report No. 126-94. Ottawa: Conference Board of Canada.

Lukawiecki, T. (1993). *Community Awareness and Response: Abuse and Neglect of Older Adults*. Ottawa: Health and Welfare Canada.

Macarov, D. (1978). *The Design of Social Welfare*. New York: Holt, Rinehart and Winston.

McCarthy, S. (1995, March 1). Cuts keep programs alive: Martin. *The Toronto Star*, A10.

McClosky, D. (1998). Newcomers: Immigrant families adapting to life in Canada. *Transition*, *28*(3), 2.

McCready, D. (1986). Privatized social service systems: Are there any justifications? *Canadian Public Policy*, *12*(1), 253–257.

McDaniel, S. (1993, Spring). Emotional support and family contacts of older Canadians, *Canadian Social Trends*, 30–33.

McDonald, G. (1995). Evaluating social welfare. In J.C. Turner and F.J. Turner (Eds.), *Canadian Social Welfare* (3rd ed., pp. 554–553). Scarborough: Allyn & Bacon.

McDonald, M. (1995, July 31). Ontario cuts back. *Maclean's*, 20–21.

McGill University, School of Social Work, Greater Victoria Survey Committee. (1931). *Problems in Family Welfare, Relief and Child Development*. Montreal: Author.

McGilly, F. (1990). *An Introduction to Canada's Public Social Services*. Toronto: McClelland & Stewart.

McIntyre, L., Connor, S., and Warren, J. (1998, October). *A Glimpse of Child Hunger in Canada*. Hull: Applied Research Branch, Strategic Policy, Human Resources Development Canada.

MacLeod, L. (1996). *Counselling for Change: Evolutionary Trends in Counselling Services for Women Who Are Abused and for Their Children in Canada*. Ottawa: National Clearinghouse on Family Violence.

MacLeod, L., and Associates (1997). Division of Aging and Seniors, Health Canada. *Toward Healthy-Aging Communities: A Population Health Approach* [On-line]. Available: http://www.hc-sc.gc.ca/seniors-aines/pubs/toward_healthy_aging_com/toward.htm [2000 May 26].

MacLeod, L., and Kinnon, D. (1996). *Taking the Next Step to Stop Woman Abuse: From Violence Prevention to Individual, Family, Community and Societal Health*. Ottawa: National Clearinghouse on Family Violence.

McMahon, M.O. (1994). *Advanced Generalist Practice with an International Perspective*. Englewood Cliffs: Prentice Hall.

MacMurchy, H. (1932). *Sterilization? Birth Control?* Toronto: Macmillan.

McQuaig, L. (1995). *Shooting the Hippo: Death by Deficit and Other Canadian Myths*. Toronto: Penguin.

MADD Canada. (2000). *About MADD Canada* [On-line]. Available: http://madd.ca/about/index.htm [2000 June 6].

Manion, I.G., and Wilson, S.K. (1995). *An Examination of the Association Between Histories of Maltreatment and Adolescent Risk Behaviours*. Ottawa: National Clearinghouse on Family Violence.

Manitoba Adolescent Treatment Centre. (1999). *Community and Hospital Services: Annual Report, 1998–1999*. Winnipeg: Author.

Marsh, L. (1943). Report on social security for Canada. In M. Bliss (Ed.), *The Social History of Canada* (1975 reprint). Toronto: University of Toronto Press.

———. (1950). *The Welfare State: Is It a Threat to Canada?* Proceedings on the Canadian Conference on Social Work, 1950. Ottawa: Canadian Conference on Social Work.

Mathews, F. (1995). *Combining Voices: Supporting Paths of Healing in Adult Female and Male Survivors of Sexual Abuse*. Ottawa: National Clearinghouse on Family Violence.

Mawhiney, A. (1994). *Towards Aboriginal Self-Government: Relations Between Status Indian Peoples and the Government of Canada, 1969–1984*. New York: Garland Publishing.

Mawhiney, A.M. (1995). The First Nations in Canada. In J.C. Turner and F.J. Turner (Eds.), *Canadian Social Welfare* (3rd ed., pp. 213–230). Scarborough: Allyn & Bacon.

Melchers, R. (1999). Local governance of social welfare: Local reform in Ontario in the nineties. *Canadian Review of Social Policy*, *43*, 29–57.

Melichercik, J. (1995). Canadian approaches to income security. In J.C. Turner and F.J. Turner (Eds.), *Canadian Social Welfare* (3rd ed., pp. 474–494). Scarborough: Allyn & Bacon Canada.

Mendelson, M. (1993). *Social Policy in Real Time*. Ottawa: Caledon Institute of Social Policy.

———. (1999). *Aboriginal People in Canada's Labour Market*. Ottawa: Caledon Institute of Social Policy.

Menzies, H. (1997, September). Whose brave new world? *Perception*, *3*(6), 3–6.

Meston, J. (1993). *Child Abuse and Neglect Prevention Programs*. Ottawa: Vanier Institute of the Family.

Miedema, B., and Wachholz, S. (1998, March). *A Complex Web: Access to Justice for Abused Immigrant Women in New Brunswick*. Ottawa: Status of Women Canada.

Milan, A. (2000, Spring). One hundred years of families. *Canadian Social Trends*, 2–12.

Minnesota Department of Human Services. (1996, March). *Focus on Client Outcomes: A Guidebook for Results-Oriented Human Services*. St. Paul: Author.

Mishra, R. (1981). *Society and Social Policy: Theories and Practice of Welfare* (2nd ed.). London and Basingstoke: Macmillan Press.

———. (1995). The political bases of Canadian social welfare. In J.C. Turner and F.J. Turner (Eds.), *Canadian Social Welfare* (3rd ed., pp. 59–74). Scarborough: Allyn & Bacon.

———. (1999). After globalization: Social policy in an open economy. *Canadian Review of Social Policy*, *43*, 13–28.

Mitchinson, W. (1987). Early women's organizations and social reform: Prelude to the welfare state. In A. Moscovitch and J. Albert (Eds.), *The Benevolent State: The Growth of Welfare in Canada* (pp. 77–92). Toronto: Garamond Press.

Montgomery, J.E. (1977). The housing patterns of older people. In R.A. Kalish (Ed.), *The Later Years* (pp. 253–261). Belmont: Wadsworth Publishing.

Morgan, J.S. (1961). Social welfare services in Canada. In M. Oliver (Ed.), *Social Purpose for Canada* (pp. 130–167). Toronto: University of Toronto Press.

Moroney, R., and Grub, C.T. (1981). Research and evaluation: Contribution to social work practice. In N. Gilbert and H. Specht (Eds.), *Handbook of the Social Services* (pp. 589–619). Englewood Cliffs: Prentice-Hall.

Moscovitch, A., and Drover, G. (1987). Social expenditures and the welfare state: The Canadian experience in historical perspective. In A. Moscovitch and J. Albert (Eds.), *The Benevolent State: The Growth of Welfare in Canada* (pp. 13–43). Toronto: Garamond Press.

Mullaly, B. (1997). *Structural Social Work*. Toronto: Oxford University Press.

Multiculturalism and Citizenship Canada. (1991). *Multiculturalism: What Is It Really About?* Ottawa: Minister of Supply and Services Canada.

Muszynski, L. (1994, December). *Passive to Active! Rhetoric or Action*. Ottawa: Caledon Institute of Social Policy.

NAPO (National Anti-Poverty Organization). (n.d.). *Fact Sheet on Homelessness*. Ottawa: Author.

———. (1999, April). *NAPO Facts—Poverty in Canada: Some Facts and Figures* [On-line]. Available: http://www.napo-onap.ca/nf.figur2.html [2000 June 7].

———. (2000). *About Us* [On-line]. Available: http://www.napo-onap.ca/about/index/html [2000 Apr 20].

National Advisory Council on Aging. (1989, Summer). Volunteering: The essential gift. *Expression*, 6.

———. (1993a). *The NACA Position on Canada's Oldest Seniors: Maintaining the Quality of Their Lives*, Document No. 13. Ottawa: Author.

———. (1993b, Spring). Freedom and responsibility. *Expression*, 9(2), 2–8.

———. (1996, March). Health consequences of inadequate incomes. *Info-Age*, No. 14.

National Association of Friendship Centres. (1993). *Final Report to the Royal Commission on Aboriginal Peoples*. Intervenor Participation Project. Ottawa: Author.

———. (1998). *Urban Multipurpose Aboriginal Youth Centres Program Guidelines for Fiscal Year 1999–2000*. Ottawa: Author.

National Council of Welfare. (1990). *Pension Reform*. Ottawa: Author.

———. (1992). *The 1992 Budget and Child Benefits*. Ottawa: Author.

———. (1995). *The 1995 Budget and Block Funding*. Ottawa: Author.

———. (1997, Autumn). *Another Look at Welfare Reform*. Ottawa: Author.

———. (1998, Autumn). *Child Benefits: Kids Are Still Hungry*. Ottawa: Author.

———. (1999a, Autumn). *Poverty Profile, 1997*. Ottawa: Author.

———. (1999b, Summer). *A Pension Primer*. Ottawa: Author.

———. (1999c, Spring). *Preschool Children: Promises to Keep*. Ottawa: Author.

———. (2000). *Welfare Incomes, 1997 and 1998*. Ottawa: Author.

National Union of Public and General Employees. (1996, April). *No More! CAP-in-Hand: Social Services in a Post-CAP Era* [On-line]. Available: http://members.xcom.com/_XMCM/gilseg/nupgeap.htm [2000 September 6].

NCA (National Children's Agenda). (1999a). *Backgrounder: A National Children's Agenda—Measuring Child Well-Being and Monitoring Progress* [On-line]. Available: http://socialunion.gc.ca/nca/may7-measure_e.html [2000 February 10].

———. (1999b). *Backgrounder—A National Children's Agenda: Developing a Shared Vision* [On-line]. Available: http://socialunion.gc.ca/news/99may7e.html [2000 February 10].

New Brunswick Association for Community Living (1992). *A Social Policy Framework for People with a Mental Handicap in New Brunswick*. Fredericton: Author.

Newfoundland and Labrador. (1999, September 14). Department of Health and Community Services. *Federal/Provincial/Territorial Ministers Examine Issues Facing an Aging Society* [On-line]. Available: http://www.gov.nf.ca/releases/1999/health/0914n05.htm [2000 March 1].

Nova Scotia. (1995, February). Department of Community Services. *Appendix D—Moving Towards Deinstitutionalization: A Discussion Paper* [On-line]. Available: http://www.gov.ns.ca/coms/small4.htm [2000 June 7].

———. (1999a, June 17). Department of Community Services. *Enhanced Mental Health Services for Children* [On-line]. Available: http://www.gov.ns.ca/health/media/1999/jun18.htm [2000 May 11].

———. (1999b, June 3). Department of Housing and Municipal Affairs. *Improving Access for Disabled Persons, Department of Housing and Municipal Affairs* [On-line]. Available: http://www.gov.ns.ca/news/details.asp?id=19990603002 [2000 June 7].

———. (2000, March 6). Department of Health. *Mental Health Service Review Begins Today* [On-line]. Available: http://www.gov.ns.ca/news/details.asp?id=20000306002 [2000 June 19].

Novak, M. (1997). *Aging and Society: A Canadian Perspective* (3rd ed.). Scarborough: ITP Nelson.

OCISO (Ottawa-Carleton Immigrant Services Organization). (1999). *Our Services* [On-line]. Available: http://www.web.net.~ociso/OurServices/zserv.htm [2000 May 26].

Odawa Native Friendship Centre. (2000). *Sweetgrass Child Care* [On-line]. Available: http://www.odawa.on.ca/sweetgrass.htm [2000 May 23].

Oderkirk, J. (1996, Spring). Canada and Quebec Pension Plans. *Canadian Social Trends*, 8–15.

Ontario College of Certified Social Workers. (2000). *Fact Sheet for People Working in Social Services* [On-line]. Available: http://www.occsw.org/occsw.htm [2000 Mar 21].

Ontario Ministry of Community and Social Services. (2000a, February 7). *24 Straight Months of People Moving Off Welfare* [On-line]. Available: http://www.gov.on.ca/CSS/page/news/feb700.html [2000 June 6].

———. (2000b). *Welfare Reform: Making Welfare Work* [On-line]. Available: http:/www.gov.on.ca/CSS/ [2000 June 7].

Ontario Non-Profit Housing Association (1997). *Supportive Housing Reform* [On-line]. Available: http://www.onpha.on.ca/pubaff/suphr.html [2000 May 26].

Ontario passes gay-rights bill. (1999, October 16–31). *Canadian News Facts* (p. 5950). Toronto: MPL Communications.

Ontario Social Safety Network. (1998). *Welfare Reform in Ontario* [On-line]. Available: http://www.wefarewatch.toronto.on.ca/wrkfrw/bill142.html [2000 February 17].

Ontario Tories plan more cuts. (1999, August 1–31). *Canadian News Facts* (p. 5912). Toronto: MPL Communications.

Osterkamp, L. (1991). Family caregivers: America's primary long-term care resource. In H. Cox (Ed.), *Aging* (7th ed., pp. 180–183). Guilford: Dushkin Publishing Group.

Ottawa will consider abolishing Indian Act. (1999, September 25). *The Vancouver Sun*, A15.

Overton, J. (1991, Winter). Dissenting opinions. *Perception*, *15*(1), 17–21.

Pal, L.A. (Ed.). (1998). *How Ottawa Spends, 1998–99—Balancing Act: The Post-Deficit Mandate* (pp. 1–30). Toronto: Oxford University Press.

Panitch, M. (1998). Forty years on! Lessons from our history. *Entourage*, *11*(4), 9–16.

Pape, B. (1990, December). Canadian Mental Health Association, Social Action Series. *Self-Help/Mutual Aid*. [On-line]. Available: http://www.cmha.ca/english/sas/selfhelp.htm [2000 June 8].

Paquet, G. (1997) Alternative service delivery: Transforming the practices of governance. In R. Ford and D. Zussman (Eds.), *Alternative Service Delivery: Sharing Governance in Canada* (pp. 331–352). Toronto: Institute of Public Administration of Canada.

Paquet, G., and Shepherd, R. (1996). The program review process: A reconstruction. In G. Swimmer (Ed.), *How Ottawa Spends, 1996–97: Life Under the Knife* (pp. 39–72). Ottawa: Carleton University Press.

Parsons, T. (1960). *Structure and Process in Modern Societies*. New York: Free Press of Glencoe.

Patterson, E.P. II. (1987). Native peoples and social policy. In S.A. Yelaja (Ed.), *Canadian Social Policy* (rev. ed., pp. 175–194). Waterloo: Wilfrid Laurier University Press.

Patterson, S.L., Memmott, J.L., Brennan, E.M., and Germain, C.B. (1992, September). Patterns of natural helping in rural areas: Implications for social work research. *Social Work Research and Abstracts*, *28*(3), 22–28.

Perry, S.E. (1993). The community as a base for regional development (Paper 1: An assessment of the U.S. experience for purposes of Canadian development policy). In *Regional Development from the Bottom Up* (pp. 1–14). Vancouver: Westcoast Development Group, Centre for Community Enterprise.

Picard, A. (1997). *A Call to Alms: The New Face of Charities in Canada—A Special Report*. Toronto: Atkinson Charitable Foundation.

PM favours staying the course. (1999, June). *Canadian News Facts* (p. 5889). Toronto: MPL Communications.

Podnieks, E., Pillemer, K., Nicholson, J.P., Shillington, T., and Frizzel, A. (1990). *National Survey on Abuse of the Elderly in Canada*. Toronto: Ryerson Polytechnical Institute.

Pomeroy, S. (1996, April). Housing as social policy. In *The Role of Housing in Social Policy* (pp. 2–14). Ottawa: Caledon Institute of Social Policy.

Powell, T.J. (1995). Self-help groups. In R.L. Powell (Ed.), *Encyclopedia of Social Work* (19th ed., vol. 3, pp. 2116–2123). Washington: National Association of Social Workers.

Prasil, S. (1993, Autumn). Seniors 75+: Lifestyles. *Canadian Social Trends*, 26–29.

Priest, G.E. (1993, Autumn). Seniors 75+: Living arrangements and lifestyles. *Canadian Social Trends*, 23–25.

Prince, M.J. (1987). How Ottawa decides social policy: Recent changes in philosophy, structure, and process. In J.S. Ismael (Ed.), *The Canadian Welfare State: Evolution and Transition* (pp. 247–273). Edmonton: University of Alberta Press.

———. (1991, Spring). What's left of conservatism? *Perception, 15*(2), 41–45.

Prince Edward Island. (1998). Health and social services. *Continuing Care Programs and Services Overview*. Charlottetown: Author.

Prince Edward Island Self-Help Clearinghouse. (2000). *Home Page* [On-line]. Available: http://www3.pei.sympatico.ca/~cmha/programs2.html [2000 June 8].

Principal recommendations of the Voluntary Sector Roundtable. (1999, March). *Perception*, *22*(4), 9.

Privy Council Office. (1996). *Growth, Human Development, Social Cohesion.* Policy Research Committee. Ottawa: Author.

———. (1999a). *Cabinet Directive on Lawmaking* [On-line]. Available: http://www.pco-bcp.gc.ca/legislation/directive_e.htm [2000 February 17].

———. (1999b, June 15). *The Voluntary Sector—Society's Vital Third Pillar* [On-line]. Available: http://www.pco-bcp.gc.ca/volunteer/backgrounder3_e.htm [2000 February 17].

———. (1999c, June 15). *Joint Work: Federal Government and Voluntary Sector* [On-line]. Available: http://www.pco-bcp.gc.ca/volunteer/backgrounder4_e.htm [2000 February 17].

Proctor, E.K., and Davis, L.E. (1994 May). The challenge of racial difference: Skills for clinical practice. *Social Work*, *39*(3), 314–323.

Profile of Canada's seniors, A. (1999). *Perception*, *23*(1), 6–7.

Pross, P. (1996). Pressure groups and lobbying. In M.S. Whittington and G. Williams (Eds.), *Canadian Politics: Critical Approaches* (2nd ed., pp. 425–453). Scarborough: Nelson Thomson Learning.

Quantz, D.H. (1997). *Cultural and Self Disruption: Suicide Among First Nations Adolescents* [On-line]. Available: http://www compusmart.ab.ca/supnet/cultural.htm [2000 June 1].

Quarter, J. (1992). *Canada's Social Economy: Co-operatives, Non-Profits, and Other Community Enterprises*. Toronto: James Lorimer and Co.

Quebec. (1967). *Report of the Commission of Inquiry on Health and Social Welfare, Vol. 1—Health Insurance*. Quebec: Author.

Quebec rejects social union deal. (1999, February 1–15). *Canadian News Facts* (p. 5815). Toronto: MPL Communications.

Rainey, H.G., Backoff, R.W., and Levine, C.H. (1976, March/April). Comparing public and private organizations. *Public Administration Review*, 233–244.

RCAP (Royal Commission on Aboriginal Peoples). (1995). *Choosing Life: A special Report on Suicide Among Aboriginal People*. Ottawa: Minister of Supply and Services Canada.

———. (1996a). *Looking Forward, Looking Back* [On-line]. Available: http://www.inac.gc.ca/rcap/report/look.html [2000 March 30].

———. (1996b). *Final Report*. Vol. 1, chap. 10 (Residential Schools). [On-line]. Available: http://www.indigenous.bc.ca/v1/Vol1Ch10s1tos1.1.asp [2000 May 15].

Reid, T. (1992, Fall). NAFTA is an opportunity for Canada. *Perception, 16*(4), 9.

Rethinking child poverty. (1999, June). *Perception, 23*(1), 10–12.

Rice, J.J., and Prince, M.J. (1993). Life of Brian: A social policy legacy. *Perception, 17*(2), 6,8, 30–33.

Richards, J. (1997). *Retooling the Welfare State: What's Right, What's Wrong, What Needs to Be Done?* Policy Study No. 31. Ottawa: C.D. Howe Institute.

Richmond Connections (1999, May 7). *Richmond Caregivers Support Program* [On-line]. Available: http://www.vcn.bc.ca/rcs/care-net.html [2000 May 5].

Roeher Institute. (1995). *Harm's Way: The Many Faces of Violence and Abuse Against Persons with Disabilities*. North York: Author.

———. (1996). *Disability, Community, and Society: Exploring the Links*. North York: Author.

Romeder, J.M. (1990). *The Self-Help Way: Mutual Aid and Health*. Ottawa: Canadian Council on Social Development.

Rosell, S.A. (1999). The learning organization. In S.A. Rosell (Ed.), *Renewing Governance: Governing by Learning in the Information Age* (pp. 60–85). Don Mills: Oxford University Press.

Ross, D. (1995, Winter). Who will speak for Canada's children? *Perception, 19*(2), 2–3.

———. (1999, November 2). *Child Poverty in Canada: The Time to Act Is Now* [On-line]. Available: www.ccsd.ca/pr/oped99.htm [2000 February 21].

Ross, D.P. (1987). Income security. In S.A. Yelaja (Ed.), *Canadian Social Policy* (rev. ed., pp. 27–46). Waterloo: Wilfrid Laurier University Press.

Ross, D.P., Scott, K., and Kelly, M.A. (1996, November). *Overview: Children in Canada in the 1990s*. Hull: Human Resources Development Canada.

Ross, M. (1967). *Community Organization: Theory, Principles, and Practice* (2nd ed.). New York: Harper and Row.

Rothman, J. (1979). Three models of community organization practice, their mixing and phasing. In F.M. Cox, J.L. Erlich, J. Rothman, and J.E. Tropman (Eds.), *Strategies of Community Organization: A Book of Readings* (3rd ed., pp. 25–45). Itasca: F.E. Peacock.

———. (1987). Community theory and research. In A. Minahan (Ed), *Encyclopedia of Social Work* (18th ed., vol. 1, pp. 308–316). Washington: National Association of Social Workers.

Roy, J. (2000). *Acknowledging Racism* [On-line]. Available: http://www.crr.ca/crr/MediaCentre/Fact%20Sheets/Acknowledging%20Racism.html [2000 February 17].

Royal Canadian Mounted Police. (1991). External Review Committee. *Employee Assistance Programs: Philosophy, Theory, and Practice.* Discussion Paper No. 5. Ottawa: Author.

Royal Commission on the Economic Union and Development Prospects for Canada. (1985). *Report: Vols. 1, 2, and 3.* Ottawa: Ministry of Supply and Services Canada.

Rubington, E., and Weinberg, M.S. (1989). *The Study of Social Problems: Six Perspectives* (4th ed.). New York and Oxford: Oxford University Press.

Sainsbury, E. (1977). *The Personal Social Services.* London: Pitman Publishing.

Same-sex bill passes second reading. (2000, February 22). *The Vancouver Sun*, A8.

Sanger, M. (1992, December). A tool to dismantle the public sector. *Action Dossier* (Action Canada Network), No. 38, 30–31.

Sarri, R.C. (1977). Administration in social welfare. In J.B. Turner (Ed.), *Encyclopedia of Social Work* (17th ed., vol. 1, pp. 42–51). Washington: National Association of Social Workers.

Sauber, R. (1983). *The Human Services Delivery System.* New York: Columbia University.

Sayeed, A. (Ed.). (1995). *Workfare: Does It Work? Is It Fair?* Montreal: Institute for Research on Public Policy.

Schellenberg, G. (1997, September). The changing nature of part-time work. *Perception*, *21*(2), 9–12.

School of Indian Social Work. (2000). *Department of Social Work* [On-line]. Available: http://www/sifc.edu/Indian%20Social%20Work/ [2000 May 11].

Scott, K. (1997). Indigenous Canadians. In D. McKenzie, R. Williams, and R. Single (Eds.), *Canadian Profile: Alcohol, Tobacco and Other Drugs, 1997* (pp. 133–164). Ottawa: Canadian Centre on Substance Abuse.

Self-help groups. (1999, Summer). *Expression*, *12*(4). Ottawa: National Advisory Council on Aging.

Senge, P. (1990). *The Fifth Discipline: The Art and Practice of the Learning Organization.* New York: Double Day Currency.

Senior Citizens' Secretariat—Nova Scotia. (n.d.). *Aging: Independent Living—Planning with Seniors for the 21st Century*. Halifax: Author.

Seniors and disabilities. (n.d.). *Expression*, *11*(1). Ottawa: National Advisory Council on Aging.

Seniors Well Aware Program and Fertile Ideas. (1999, April 3). *SWAP Home Pages* [On-line]. Available http://www.bluecrow.com/swap/home.htm [2000 Apr 27].

Shade, L.R. (1996, August). *Report on the Use of the Internet in Canadian Women's Organizations*. Ottawa: Status of Women Canada.

Shipman, G. (1971, March/April). The evaluation of social innovation. *Public Administration Review*, *31*, 198–200.

Simpson, S. (1995, August 11). New powers for Indians won't avert crisis, leader says. *The Vancouver Sun*, A1–A2.

Smith, M. (2000). Interest groups and social movements. In M.S. Whittington and G. Williams (Eds.), *Canadian Politics in the 21st Century* (pp. 173–191). Scarborough: Nelson Thomson Learning.

Social Planning Council of Metropolitan Toronto. (1984). *Caring for Profit: The Commercialization of Human Services in Ontario*. Toronto: Author.

———. (1997). *Policy Statement on Provincial Devolution of Responsibilities to Municipalities and Communities* [On-line]. Available: http://www.worldchat.com/public/tab/polstmnt.htm [2000 March 16].

Social Planning Council of Winnipeg. (1987, June). *Community Needs Assessment*. Community Infokit. Winnipeg: Author.

Social Planning Network of Ontario. (2000, February 11). *Independent Community-Based Social Planning in the Voluntary Sector* [On-line]. Available: http://www.worldchat.com/public/hspc/sp/ingrtpln.htm [2000 June 8].

Solvent-abuse centres planned. (1995, May 1–15). *Canadian News Facts* (p. 5122). Toronto: MPL Communications.

Spergel, I.A. (1987). Community development. In A. Minahan (Ed.), *Encyclopedia of Social Work* (18th ed., vol. 1, pp. 299–308). Washington: National Association of Social Workers.

Spicker, P. (1984). *Stigma and Social Welfare*. New York: St. Martin's Press.

Splane, R. (1987). Further reflections: 1975–1986. In S.A. Yelaja (Ed.), *Canadian Social Policy* (rev. ed., pp. 245–265). Waterloo: Wilfrid Laurier University Press.

Spratt, S. (1992, Fall). The selfishness of "free" trade. *Perception, 16*(4), 8.

Standing Committee on Human Resources Development and the Status of Persons with Disabilities. (2000). *Interim Report* [On-line]. Available: www.parl.gc.ca/InfoComDoc/36/1/SC/R/studies/reports [2000 April 27].

Stasiulis, D. (1995). Deep diversity: Race and ethnicity in Canadian politics. In M.S. Whittington and G. Williams (Eds.), *Canadian Politics in the 1990s* (4th ed., pp. 191–217). Scarborough: Nelson Canada.

Stasiulis, D., and Abu-Laban, Y. (2000). Unequal relations and the struggle for equality: Race and ethnicity in Canadian politics. In M.S. Whittington and G. Williams (Eds.), *Canadian Politics in the 21st Century* (pp. 327–353). Scarborough: Nelson Thomson Learning.

Statistics Canada. (1995). *A Portrait of Persons with Disabilities*. Cat. No. 89-542E. Ottawa: Minister of Industry, Science and Technology.

———. (1997a, October 14). 1996 census: Marital status, common-law unions and families. *The Daily* [On-line]. Available: http://www.statcan.ca/Daily/English/971014/d71014.htm [2000 June 16].

———. (1997b, Spring). Canadian children in the 1990s: Selected findings of the National Longitudinal Survey of Children and Youth. *Canadian Social Trends*, 2-9.

———. (1998a). 1996 census: Aboriginal data. *The Daily* [On-line]. Available: http://www.statcan.ca/Daily/English/980113/d980113.htm [2000 June 16].

———. (1998b). 1996 census: Ethnic origin, visible minorities. *The Daily* [On-line]. Available: http://www.statcan.ca/Daily/English/980217/ d980217.htm [2000 February 17].

———. (1999a, October 8). A portrait of seniors in Canada. *Infomat—a Weekly Review.*

———. (1999b, October 15). Lowest unemployment rate in nine years. *Infomat—a Weekly Review.*

———. (1999c). *Labour Force, Employed and Unemployed, Numbers and Rates* [On-line]. Available: http://www.statcan.ca/english/Pgdb/People/Labour/labor17a.htm [2000 June 28].

Status of Disabled Persons Secretariat. (1994). *Disability Policy and Programs in Canada: A Brief Overview*. Ottawa: Human Resources Development Canada.

Steel, K. (1999). Klein, Ralph. In J.A. Marsh (Ed.), *The Canadian Encyclopedia, Year 2000 Edition* (pp. 1253–1254). Toronto: McClelland & Stewart.

Steinhauer, P. (1995). *The Canada Health and Social Transfer: A Threat to the Health, Development and Future Productivity of Canada's Children and Youth*. Ottawa: Caledon Institute of Social Policy.

———. (1996, April). *The Primary Needs of Children: A Blueprint for Effective Health Promotion at the Community Level*. Ottawa: Caledon Institute of Social Policy.

Stevenson, K. (1999, Winter). Family characteristics of problem kids. *Canadian Social Trends*, 2–6.

Stevenson, K, Tufts, J., Hendrick, D., and Kowalski, M. (1999, Summer). Youth and crime. *Canadian Social Trends*, 17–21.

Strike, C. (1989, Autumn). Residential care. *Canadian Social Trends*, 25–29.

Strong-Boag, V. (1979, Spring). Wages for housework: Mothers' allowances and the beginnings of social security in Canada. *Journal of Canadian Studies*, *14*(1), 24–34.

Struthers, J. (1983). *No Fault of Their Own: Unemployment and the Canadian Welfare State, 1914–1941*. Toronto: University of Toronto Press.

Stutt, T., and Adelberg, E. (1998, March). Can Ottawa eliminate Canada's social deficit? *Perception*, *21*(4), 5–7.

Swimmer, G. (Ed.). (1996). An Introduction to life under the knife. *How Ottawa Spends, 1996–97: Life Under the Knife* (pp. 1–37). Ottawa: Carleton University Press.

Tator, C. (1996). Anti-racism and the human-service delivery system. In C.E. James (Ed.), *Perspectives on Racism and the Human Services Sector* (pp. 152–170). Toronto: University of Toronto Press.

Taylor, G. (1969). *The Problem of Poverty, 1660—1834*. Seminar Studies in History, Kings College School. Wimbledon, England: Longmans, Green, and Company Ltd.

Taylor, R.J. (1991, February). Catalogue of failure. *Canada and The World*, 14–19.

Theilheimer, I. (1991, December). Aboriginal communities: Familial societies, familiar pressures. Interview with J. Berthelette. *Transition*, *21*(4), 4–6.

Thomas, P., and Wilkins, J. (1997). Special operating agencies: A culture change in the Manitoba government. In R. Ford and D. Zussman (Eds.), *Alternative Service Delivery: Sharing Governance in Canada* (pp. 109–122). Toronto: Institute of Public Administration of Canada.

Thurston, W.E., and O'Connor, M. (1996). *Health Promotion for Women* [On-line]. Available: http://www.hc-sc.gc.ca/canusa/papers/canada/english/promote/htm [2000 April 20].

Thursz, D. (1977). Social action. In J.B. Turner (Ed.), *Encyclopedia of Social Work* (17th ed., vol. 2, pp. 1274–1280). Washington, DC: National Association of Social Workers.

Time to grieve, A. (1998, Autumn). *Expression, 12*(1).

Torjman, S. (1995). *Milestone or Millstone: The Legacy of the Social Service Review.* Ottawa: Caledon Institute of Social Policy.

———. (1996, October). *The Disability Income System in Canada.* Ottawa: Caledon Institute of Social Policy.

———. (1997, November). *Welfare Warfare.* Ottawa: Caledon Institute of Social Policy.

———. (1998, February). *There's No Love in "Tough Love."* Ottawa: Caledon Institute of Social Policy.

Townson, M. (1999). *How Social and Economic Factors Affect Our Well-Being.* Ottawa: Canadian Centre for Policy Alternatives.

Trattner, W.I. (1989). *From Poor Law to Welfare State* (4th ed.). New York: Free Press.

Trempe, R., Davis, S., and Kunin, R. (1997). Advisory Group, Citizenship and Immigration Canada. *Not Just Numbers: A Canadian Framework for Future Immigration.* Ottawa: Minister of Public Works and Government Services Canada.

Tropp, E. (1977). Social group work: The developmental approach. In J.B. Turner (Ed.), *Encyclopedia of Social Work* (17th ed., vol. 2, pp. 1321–1328). Washington, DC: National Association of Social Workers.

Trudeau, P.E. (1961). The practice and theory of federalism. In M. Oliver (Ed.), *Social Purpose for Canada* (pp. 371–393). Toronto: University of Toronto Press.

Tsang, A.K.T., and George, U. (1998). Towards an integrated framework for cross-cultural social work practice. *Canadian Social Work Review, 15*(1), pp. 73–93.

Turner, D. (1998a, September). Getting Canadians talking about their common future. *Perception*, 22(2), 8.

———. (1998b, December). Child hunger in Canada. *Perception*, 22(3), 5, 7.

Turner, J.C. (1995). The historical base. In J.C. Turner and F.J. Turner (Eds.), *Canadian Social Welfare* (3rd ed., pp. 75–88). Scarborough: Allyn & Bacon.

Tutty, L. (1999). *Husband Abuse: An Overview of Research and Perspectives.* Ottawa: National Clearinghouse on Family Violence.

United Church of Canada. (2000). *The Church and the Public Arena* [On-line}. Available: http://www.uccan.org/cansocialissues.htm [2000 September 6].

United Nations. (1951). *United Nations Convention Relating to the Status of Refugees.* Article 1. New York: Author.

United Way of Canada. (2000). *The Board's Role* [On-line]. Available: http://www.boarddevelopment.org/english/role.cfm [2000 March 2].

University of Toronto, Child Care Resource and Research Unit. (2000). *Statistics Summary: Canadian Early Childhood Care and Education in the 1990's, Financing Child Care* [On-line]. Available: http://www.childcare-canada.org/resources/CRRUpubs/factsheets/statsum3.html [2000 April 27].

Vancouver Public Library. (1999). *Parents Together Program* [On-line]. Available: http://www2.vpl.vancouver.bc.ca/DBs/RedBook/orgPgs/1/189820.html [2000 April 20].

Vanier Institute of the Family. (1992). *Canadian Families in Transition: The Implications and Challenges of Change*. Ottawa: Author.

Vargo, F. (1999). Disability. In J.A. Marsh (Ed.), *The Canadian Encyclopedia, Year 2000 Edition* (pp. 666–668). Toronto: McClelland & Stewart.

Voluntary sector pulls together. (1996, Fall). *Perception, 20*(2), 4.

Voluntary Sector Roundtable. (2000). *VSR Up-Date—February 2000* [On-line]. Available: http://www.web.net/vsr-trsb/newsletters/news-feb00.html [2000 February 17].

Wachtel, A. (1994). *Child Abuse and Neglect: A Discussion Paper and Overview of Topically Related Projects*. Ottawa: National Clearinghouse on Family Violence.

———. (1997). *The "State of the Art" in Child Abuse Prevention, 1997*. Ottawa: National Clearinghouse on Family Violence.

Wallace, E. (1950). The origin of the social welfare state in Canada: 1867–1900. *The Canadian Journal of Economics and Political Science, 16*(3), 383–393.

Watson, K. (1983, Summer). Efficiency versus process. *Public Welfare, 41*(3), 19–23.

Watt, S., and Soifer, A. (1996). Conducting psycho-social assessments with the elderly. In M.J. Holosko and M.D. Feit (Eds.), *Social Work Practice with the Elderly* (2nd ed., pp. 37–53). Toronto: Canadian Scholars' Press.

Weinfeld, M. (1999). The challenge of ethnic match: Minority origin professionals in health and social services. In H. Troper and M. Weinfeld (Eds.), *Ethnicity, Politics, and Public Policy: Case Studies in Canadian Diversity* (pp. 117–141). Toronto: University of Toronto Press.

Weinfeld, M., and Wilkinson, A. (1999). Immigration, diversity, and minority communities. In P.S. Li (Ed.), *Race and Ethnic Relations in Canada* (pp. 55–87). Don Mills: Oxford University Press.

Wharf, B. (1986). Social welfare and the political system. In J.C. Turner and F.J. Turner (Eds.), *Canadian Social Welfare* (2nd ed., pp. 103–118). Don Mills: Collier Macmillan Canada.

———. (1992, Spring/Summer). From coordination to social reform. *Perception, 16*(2-3), 41–46, 54.

Whitaker, R. (2000). Politics versus administration: Politicians and bureaucrats. In M. Whittington and G. Williams (Eds.), *Canadian Politics in the 21st Century* (pp. 55–78). Scarborough: Nelson Thomson Learning.

Whittington, M.S. (2000). Aboriginal self-government in Canada. In M. Whittington and G. Williams (Eds.), *Canadian Politics in the 21st Century* (pp. 105–125). Scarborough: Nelson Thomson Learning.

Wigdor, B.T., and Plouffe, L. (1991). Introductory chapter, Mental health and aging. In *National Advisory Council on Aging, Mental Health and Aging, Writings in Gerontology No. 10* (pp. 1–9). Ottawa: NACA.

Wilensky, H., and Lebeaux, C. (1965). *Industrial Society and Social Welfare*. New York: Free Press.

Wilson, B. (1999). *Hunger Count 1999: A Growing Hunger for Change*. Toronto: Canadian Association of Food Banks.

Wirick, R.G. (1999). Keynesian economics. In J.A. Marsh (Ed.), *The Canadian Encyclopedia, Year 2000 Edition* (p. 1242). Toronto: McClelland & Stewart.

Woodside, M., and McClam, T. (1994). *An Introduction to Human Services* (2nd ed.). Pacific Grove: Brooks/Cole Publishing Co.

World Summit for Social Development. (2000, February 10). *Overall Review and Appraisal of the Implementation of the Outcome of the World Summit for Social Development: Draft Agreed Conclusions* [On-line]. Available: http://www.icsw.org/copenhagen_implementation/csd38rev1.htm [2000 September 10].

Yalnizyan, A. (1994). Securing society: Creating Canadian social policy. In A. Yalnizyan, T.R. Ide, and A.J. Cordell (Eds.), *Shifting Time: Social Policy and the Future of Work* (pp. 17–71). Toronto: Between the Lines.

Yelaja, S.A. (1985). Introduction to the social work profession. In S.A. Yelaja (Ed.), *An Introduction to Social Work Practice in Canada* (pp. 2–23). Scarborough: Prentice-Hall.

———. (1987). Canadian social policy: Perspectives. In S.A. Yelaja (Ed.), *Canadian Social Policy* (rev. ed., pp. 1–26). Waterloo: Wilfrid Laurier University Press.

Zapotochny, J. (Ed.). (1999). *Scott's Canadian Sourcebook 2000*. Don Mills: Southam Information Products Group.

Zastrow, C. (1995). *The Practice of Social Work* (5th ed.). Pacific Grove: Brooks/Cole.

———. (1996). *Introduction to Social Work and Social Welfare* (6th ed.). Pacific Grove: Brooks/Cole Publishing Company.

Zyblock, M. (1996, December). *Why Is Family Market Income Inequality Increasing in Canada? Examining the Effects of Aging, Family Formation, Globalization and Technology*. Hull: Applied Research Branch, Human Resources Development Canada.

INDEX

To the owner of this book

We hope that you have enjoyed *Social Welfare in Canadian Society,* Second Edition (ISBN 0-17-616833-8), by Rosalie Chappell, and we would like to know as much about your experiences with this text as you would care to offer. Only through your comments and those of others can we learn how to make this a better text for future readers.

School ________________ Your instructor's name ______________________

Course ___________ Was the text required? _______ Recommended? _____

1. What did you like the most about *Social Welfare in Canadian Society*?

____

____

____

2. How useful was this text for your course?

____

____

____

3. Do you have any recommendations for ways to improve the next edition of this text?

____

____

____

4. In the space below or in a separate letter, please write any other comments you have about the book. (For example, please feel free to comment on reading level, writing style, terminology, design features, and learning aids.)

____

____

____

____

Optional

Your name ______________________________ Date _________________

May Nelson Thomson Learning quote you, either in promotion for *Social Welfare in Canadian Society,* or in future publishing ventures?

Yes _______ No _______

Thanks!

You can also send your comments to us via e-mail at **college@nelson.com**

PLEASE TAPE SHUT. DO NOT STAPLE.

TAPE SHUT

TAPE SHUT

FOLD HERE

NELSON

THOMSON LEARNING™

MAIL POSTE

Canada Post Corporation
Société canadienne des postes
Postage paid if mailed in Canada — Port payé si posté au Canada
Business Reply — Réponse d'affaires

0066102399 01

0066102399-M1K5G4-BR01

NELSON THOMSON LEARNING
HIGHER EDUCATION
PO BOX 60225 STN BRM B
TORONTO ON M7Y 2H1

TAPE SHUT

TAPE SHUT